THE STORY OF
DESIGN

THE STORY OF
DESIGN

From the Paleolithic to the Present

Charlotte & Peter Fiell

THE MONACELLI PRESS

Contents

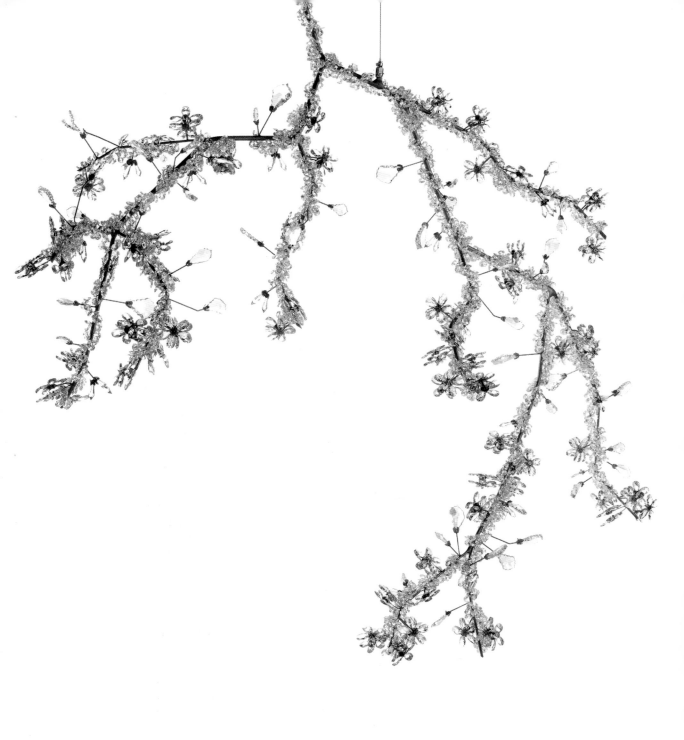

Blossom chandelier designed by Tord Boontje
for Prearo Collezione Luce and Swarovski, 2002.

Preface

This book is intended as an accessible guide to design history rather than an academic tome. For the sake of clarity, we have opted for a straightforward chronological, rather than thematic, approach that traces the story of design by introducing the different inventions, styles, movements, and schools that have shaped its practice, as well as the work of individual pioneering designers. Because design does not happen in a cultural vacuum, we have contextualized the various periods of design practice with reference to relevant social history and world events. The history of design is as long as the history of humanity, being essentially the story of how all man-made things came into being, so we have therefore aimed for objectivity in our account, while selecting events and designs that are widely acknowledged to be the most historically revealing. This volume does not discuss fashion design, which has its own history, but does concern itself with, among other fields, architecture, graphic design, product design, and interior design. In order to provide an overview, we have for the most part told this story with broad brushstrokes, although at times we have homed in on particular designs in order to illustrate specific themes; in most cases images of these accompany the text so the reader can see clearly what we are referring to. We have used primary research materials wherever possible, and have strived to give a more international and overarching assessment of the topic than has previously been attempted. Nevertheless, the story of design naturally has a European, American, and Japanese bias, because modern design is most often linked to mechanized production and, therefore, to a nation's industrial development. These regions were the earliest to industrialize and so the first to offer manufacturers the means to commercialize design ideas; these sorts of tradable or saleable products have driven the development of design throughout most of its history.

The constant change of approaches to design, each one essentially a rejection of the one before, is among the most pronounced narrative threads running through this story. Others include the search for new applications of state-of-the-art materials and technologies, and the moral conviction and entrepreneurial zeal that compels designers to find better ways of doing things for the wider social good or for personal betterment. Each chapter of this book covers a specific timeframe, determined not by the arbitrary datelines of centuries or decades but rather by the stylistic themes or world events that bookend periods of design endeavor. This story is, of course, open to a variety of interpretations, but we hope that this book, which is the culmination of many years of research, shows clearly what we want it to: the unique relationship between design and society, and the ways in which this reflects the human condition.

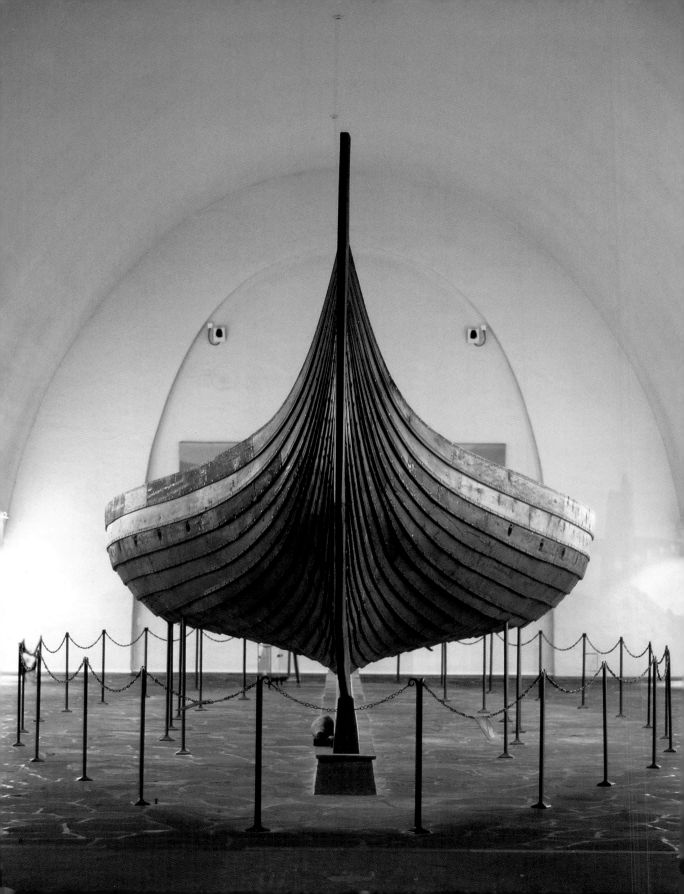

Introduction

Design is integral to human existence; it has shaped our material culture and influenced human history since its earliest origins. It has been and remains an omnipresent feature of daily life, simply because every man-made object is a designed object, and because it is through the use of such objects that we experience the world around us. Defined as the conception and planning of all man-made things, design is also the physical outcome of this creative process. Its remit is vast and encompasses consumer products, industrial goods, military hardware, graphic design, branding, transportation, telecommunications, production systems, urban planning, interaction design, games design, and a host of other disciplines. Design has transformed society by giving us the key inventions of civilization: the brick, the plow, the coin, the printing press, the car, and the computer, to name a few. As such, the power of design has allowed us to construct houses, to grow food, to build cities, to transmit knowledge, to travel across the globe, and to enrich human existence in countless other ways, large and small. The quality of the designs with which we surround ourselves unquestionably bears on the quality of our lives.

Since the earliest times, people have sought better solutions to particular problems—a better stone axe, a better cooking pot, a better weapon, a better spinning wheel—and have used some degree of forethought in the creation of these objects. Prior to the Industrial Revolution, most designs were individually handcrafted or produced serially in craft workshops in relatively small numbers. There were, though, certain factory-produced objects that used models of standardization and interchangeability to enable systemized multiple reproduction. By facilitating mass manufacturing through mechanization, the Industrial Revolution changed the role of design; with its introduction of the division of labor, designers were now largely separated from the act of making, and thus were placed in the position of having to decide whether to create for the benefit of the many in an industrialized system or to continue to pursue individual creative expression, using craft methods to create objects that were of necessity not for mass consumption. This tension between universalism and individualism is one of the main themes running through the story of design, particularly over the last two hundred years. The universal approach by its nature implies volume manufacture, and so standardized factory production, whereas individualism is prompted by designers' desires to express their personal creativity, or in evidence in bespoke solutions that do not need to be produced in any sizable quantity—solutions of which exclusivity is in fact one of the most appealing attributes.

And yet, though different in many ways, these approaches are driven by a shared desire: to fulfill a perceived need. They are also similarly subject to the availability of materials and technology; to the cultural, social, political, and commercial contexts of the time; and, of course, to the skills of the designer. Whether a design is successful in fulfilling the need identified is determined by the value of the forethought that went into it and the quality of its execution: any designed object, after all, is the realization of an idea, and throughout history when design thinking has been applied intelligently, through either a revolutionary or an evolutionary approach to problem-solving, the result has been life-enhancing.

Once the Industrial Revolution had provided the means to readily mass-manufacture objects, the morality of these objects was called into question, giving rise to the design-reform movement and its vision of design used as a democratic tool for social change. In advocating utility, simplicity, and appropriateness, the design reformers of the nineteenth century anticipated the Modern Movement that emerged in the early twentieth century, which applied these theories in the context of mechanized production. Through this link between design practice and ethics, the story of design becomes a tale of morality—one that reveals how at different times and in various contexts design has been used as a conduit for social reform, and how this sense of moral purpose has altered over time, changing with it the goals of design itself.

In general, designers are optimists who believe that a better design solution to a given problem can be found,

The Gokstad ship, built c. 890 AD, in the Viking Ship Museum, Oslo, Norway.

and that they are equipped to find it. Designers do not work in a cultural vacuum but are barometers of social, political, cultural, and economic change, and while they might take inspiration from the past or the future they, perhaps more than most other creative individuals, are bound to the present moment, using the technologies and materials of their own era and so capturing the spirit of their times. Underlying the design process, whichever approach the designer chooses to follow, is the spark of creative inspiration. And it has been these flashes of inventive design thinking that have given us the tools with which civilization has been built. Purposeful design thinking is actually hardwired into the human brain as a mechanism to enhance survival, and over the millennia that is exactly what it has done.

"Design" is a slippery word, being both a verb and a noun—an action and its result. Its scope also spans the whole spectrum of human creative problem-solving, from pure, process-driven engineering to more creative craft-based approaches that can be artistic, poetic, symbolic, or polemical. Design activities might include an engineer using technical procedures to create new mechanisms, a games designer developing new immersive environments, a graphic designer laying out a poster, a textile designer creating fabric patterns, or a ceramicist molding clay into studio pottery. So where does this tricky word come from? It can be traced to the Latin verb *designare*, which means "to mark out, to devise, to choose," and by the seventeenth century it was being used to refer to the making of an artistic pattern or the devising of a plan of construction. Since then it has more or less retained this all-embracing quality, although in most cases a designed object constitutes a careful balance of technical and aesthetic aspects—a delicate equilibrium of form and function, science and art. As the eminent historian of art and design Herbert Read noted in 1951, "Aesthetics is no longer an isolated science of beauty; science can no longer neglect aesthetic factors."[1] Very few designs are produced with no concern for appearance; among them are those that are "unseen," such as the internal workings of a machine, or that must be determined entirely by function, such as a mining drill bit. The reason for this is more complex than might at first be suspected: it is true that beauty invariably makes objects more pleasurable to use, but beyond that, beauty can be the result of an object's good functionality: the design maxim "If it looks right, it probably is right" still holds true. Even in the eighteenth century, at the very birth of the Industrial Revolution, beauty was being linked to function. As the Scottish philosopher and economist Adam Smith noted:

> That utility is one of the principal sources of beauty has been observed by every body, who has considered with any attention what constitutes the nature of beauty [. . .] That the fitness of any system or machine to produce the end for which it was intended, bestows a certain propriety and beauty upon the whole, and renders the very thought and contemplation of it agreeable, is so very obvious that nobody has overlooked it.[2]

It could even be argued that beauty derived from function is a law of design—an argument supported by the wonders of the natural world, which have themselves been honed for functionality by the processes of evolution.

Today, we see the beauty of an artifact—its "art," as it was referred to in the nineteenth century—as an integral part of its design. In the nineteenth century, though, "art" was seen as something to be applied as an accessory to a design, and the terms "applied arts" and "art manufactures" were given to objects that were professionally designed and deemed to have an artistic quality. During the early to mid-twentieth century this application of art was termed "styling" and again referred to the aesthetic aspect of an object. The belief that an object's appearance was somehow detached from its overall design helped to create the rather confusing term "industrial stylists," which was used until the late 1950s to describe designers who created products for mass manufacture. In automotive design at that time the terminology was even more perplexing, as the car designer Roy Axe explained: "Styling [. . .] had the connotation of something superficial and applied, as indeed it was in the early days. When styling became integrated into the process and took a role at the very beginning of a project, 'Design' became the term used for function."[3] This is revealing in showing that until that point, a design's styling was commonly seen as an afterthought rather than an integral part of its development.

And while styling might well only explicitly be concerned with appearances, it can also enhance designs' performances, as so brilliantly demonstrated by some of the streamlined designs created by the first generation of American industrial-design consultants during the 1930s. Today, the word "styling" used with reference to a designed object usually implies both technical and aesthetic aspects. As the celebrated Italian designer Vico Magistretti noted, the difference between design and styling is that "design does not need drawing, but styling does"—by which he meant that design could be described through spoken or written words, while styling has to be, as he put it, "expressed by the most exact drawings, not because it disregards function but simply because it wraps that function in a cloak that essentially [expresses] qualities that are called 'style' and that are decisive in making the quality of the object recognizable."[4]

The architect and designer Ludwig Mies van der Rohe described the drive to find better solutions to specific problems within given constraints as the urge to "create form out of the nature of our tasks, with the methods of our time."[5] For example, the Vikings built wooden longships with symmetrical shallow-draft hulls that were lightweight, very seaworthy, and easy to beach, which enabled them to attack without warning and then beat a hasty retreat before their foes could muster their forces—in other words, the form of their ships allowed the Vikings to sail wherever they wanted to go, and to indulge in their legendary occupation: plundering. As mankind ages, the nature of our tasks changes, as do the methods of our time, and this is why studying the designs of the past is so fascinating: it allows us to explore the material cultures of our ancestors and relate them to our own experience of what it is to be human. We might, for example, compare the longships of those Vikings with the design of a modern racing yacht. And within the history of design, there are successful and less successful outcomes. The British design reformer William Lethaby noted that good design is "the well-doing of what needs doing"—"not a special sauce applied to cooking, it is the cooking itself [. . .] design] is thoughtful workmanship."[6] For all that aesthetics have become an integral part of design, an object's ultimate success still depends on its functionality: it doesn't matter how attractive a teapot is if it doesn't pour tea properly it is a functional failure (unless, of course, it is

a postmodern teapot, in which case its primary function might have nothing to do with pouring tea at all).

Design has also been a vehicle for discussing ideas, beliefs, and values, and as such it is possible to talk about a language of design, ranging from the highly rational to the poetic. The whole discipline is in some ways a discourse communicated nonverbally—through form and function an object provides a particular insight into the character and thinking of the designer, as well as his or her attitude to the relationship between object and user, and the role of design in society. A designed object also conveys the social, economic, political, and technological contexts that gave rise to its conception and realization—for instance, an Art Nouveau lamp designed by Louis Majorelle looks very different from a table light designed by Marianne Brandt at the Bauhaus or a lighting solution by Joe Colombo from the 1960s. In the modern era, business has created an impetus for competitive products, driving an incessant evolution and diversification of design as well as the development of individual designers' careers. Designers today might choose to work at corporations in specialized in-house design teams, or at multidisciplinary design consultancies, or independently—many of this last group opting out of the industrial process because they find it too creatively restricting. Ultimately, though, whether a designer works for a large company or as an individual designer-maker, he or she uses design as a means of communication, and the work produced embodies the individual's ideologies, philosophies, and methodologies.

It is this unique ability of designed artifacts to tell both individual and shared stories that prompted us to write this book, for studying the development of design from its stone-tool origins is a way of making sense of human history—its motivations, its triumphs, its failures, its contradictions. This is also a study of avant-garde pioneers—of visionary practitioners, risk-taking design entrepreneurs, enlightened design-led manufacturers, revolutionary design schools, and forward-thinking stylistic movements, all striving to find better design solutions, which they believed would shape a better future—even if their instincts were sometimes misguided. The story of design is quite simply the story of how human civilization came into being, and how man-made objects have shaped existence.

1

THE EARLY ORIGINS OF DESIGN

The prehistoric tools
of the Three Ages

Design is the process by which humans from their earliest origins have turned raw materials into useful things, for ultimately design is a means of problem-solving. There is rich archeological evidence that people have conceived and made objects that have enhanced and embellished their daily lives since prehistoric times. This type of design activity, especially in relation to toolmaking, has shaped human existence since its very beginning and is ultimately a key feature of what it is to be human. As the pioneering Irish archaeologist Hodder Westropp stated in 1866, "Man, in all ages and in all stages of his development, is a tool-making animal, and his instincts and necessities lead him to fashion instruments and tools suited to his requirements."[1]

Some of the very earliest "man-made" tools to have been found are those discovered in the 1930s by the Kenya-born British archaeologist Louis Leakey in the Olduvai Gorge in Tanzania. Known as Oldowan tools, they were fashioned out of stone by our primate ancestor *Homo habilis*, which rather amusingly means "handy man"—and indeed that is exactly what he proved himself to be when he fashioned his relatively crude hand tools. The oldest Oldowan tools unearthed so far, sometimes referred to as pebble tools, come from Gona in Ethiopia and are dated to around 2.6 million years ago. These earliest of tools—and also the very first designed objects—were fashioned by roughly chipping away bits of stone from a pebble to create primitive chopping, scraping, and pounding tools. Our distant hominid forefathers must have discovered through trial and error the best way of making such tools, thereby demonstrating a degree of forethought, conception, and planning in their creation—in other words, of design. What was the best type of stone to use? Where was the

↖
Paleolithic stone tools found in Melka Kunture, Ethiopia, around 1.7 million years old.

←
Previous page: Paleolithic arrowheads, spearheads, and scrapers from excavations at Lisen and Ondranice, in the Czech Republic.

↑
Hand axes and bolas stones lie exposed in a demonstration dig at Olorgesailie, Kenya, 1965, conducted by Louis and Mary Leakey. These were stone tools similar to those they had earlier uncovered in the Olduvai Gorge in Tanzania.

real needs, these earliest of primitive design solutions can be seen as the first tentative steps on the path toward what we now think of as civilization.

Throughout the Paleolithic period or Old Stone Age—from 500,000 to 10,000 BC—*Homo erectus* continued to develop better performing stone tools, not only the aforementioned hand axes but also spearheads and arrowheads. These early designs got progressively sharper and more precisely shaped as, over generations, humanoids perfected the art of chipping away flint flakes from larger pieces of stone. It was also during the Stone Age that our direct ancestors known as *Homo sapiens* (wise man) emerged, roughly 200,000 years ago. Thanks to the larger frontal cortices and temporal lobes of their brains, *Homo sapiens* were equipped with enhanced reasoning capabilities, the exact mental facility needed to design better tools for living. Although *Homo erectus* had previously learned how to make fire—which was first used to keep warm

best place to strike the stone to get it to shear into the required form? Once made, presumably satisfaction was found in a job well done and in comparing the functionality of the tools; the better-performing design was undoubtedly perceived as more beautiful.

Later, around 1.5 million years ago, another early hominid, *Homo erectus* (upright man), began to fabricate more advanced hand axes from flaked stone, evidence of which has been found in Africa. By 700,000 years ago, these practical tools with two-sided cutting faces were being produced as far afield as West Asia, South Asia, and Europe, demonstrating a very early example of primitive technology being transferred from one region of the world to another. During the Stone Age, a period of around 2.5 million years, our hominid ancestors also began producing simple harpoons and hooks made of bone, or sometimes shell, which allowed them to fish far more effectively. They fashioned needles out of sharpened bone, which enabled them to make the first fitted garments out of animal skins. Wearing designed clothes rather than just pinned-together fur pelts enabled them to perform tasks with more freedom of movement and to keep themselves warmer. In demonstrating practical and well-reasoned responses to

↑
Mesolithic Acheulian hand axe, found in Saint Acheul, near Ams, France made by hammering flakes off a piece of flint using a tool made from bone, antler or wood, until the desired shape was obtained.

→
Prehistoric bone kitchen utensils, c. 4,000 BC, excavated at Çatalhöyük, Turkey.

The early origins of design

and protect against wild animals, then to cook—it would appear from archeological finds that it was *Homo sapiens* who actually fathomed how to use it to bake clay and thereby create simple ceramic wares. Researchers at Boston University recently discovered in China fragments of the earliest known human-crafted pots, which date from the last Ice Age some 20,000 years ago. As noted in the research team's paper, published in the journal *Science*, this discovery "demonstrates that hunter-gatherers in East Asia used pottery for some 10,000 years before they became sedentary or began cultivating plants."[2] It was only when our ancestors made the transition from hunter-gatherers to farmers during the Neolithic period, or New Stone Age (spanning roughly 12,000–2,000 BC, depending on which part of the world one is considering) that they began to design and make more sophisticated homeware, as the 6,000-year-old bone kitchen utensils excavated at Çatalhöyük in Turkey attest.

It was during the late Neolithic period that stone tools became more refined, with flakes of flint being painstakingly chipped into shape to produce sharp cutting edges or piercing arrowheads. Also during this era, the potter's wheel was invented in Mesopotamia, the region that corresponds to modern-day Iraq and Syria as well as small parts of Turkey and Iran, widely considered the cradle of civilization. This invention dates from between 6,000 and 4,000 BC, and went on to revolutionize the production of pottery. The humble potter's wheel was the very first machine to have been designed to enable the more efficient serial production of designed goods—making pot-throwing the earliest mechanized manufacturing process. Interestingly, this is also thought to be the first application of the wheel, and it was not until some three centuries later that someone put two and two together to create the first wheeled cart. This is believed to have resulted in a type of wheelbarrow, which led, step by step, to more advanced forms of wheeled vehicle, aiding the increased transportation of people, goods, and ideas.

The most beautiful prehistoric ceramics come from the Ban Chiang area in northeastern Thailand, and were not thrown on a wheel but handmade using a paddle-and-anvil method of production. These designs—

exquisitely formed and surprisingly modern-looking black-bodied and red-painted earthenware vessels—are markedly more sophisticated than crude pots pinched and coiled from clay. The earliest black-bodied vessels found at Ban Chiang date from 2,100 BC, but the earliest red-painted vessels are believed to date from 1,000 BC. The Ban Chiang hoards as a whole date from between 2,100 BC and AD 200 and were discovered by chance in 1966 by a young anthropology student from Harvard University. These early Southeast Asian ceramic wares —spanning the New Stone Age, the Bronze Age, and beyond—show a sophistication of firing techniques as well as an advanced understanding of proportion and pattern-making that is remarkably progressive.

Following the Stone Age, the Bronze Age, which spans the period of roughly 3,750–600 BC,[3] saw an enormous leap forward in design technology, with bronze and copper replacing stone for the manufacture of implements and weapons. Such objects were cast

↑
An example of the ancient pottery of Ban Chiang,
Late period 300 BC–200 AD.

using simple ingot molds, their forms being carved into blocks of stone. The use of molds meant that for the first time designs could be replicated more or less exactly, thereby making them easier and less time-consuming to manufacture. At this early stage in human development, we are still talking about relatively basic designs such as spearheads and axe heads. However, molding technology improved throughout the Bronze Age and into the Iron Age, which in Europe stretched from roughly 1,200 BC to AD 600. The third age saw the advent of iron smelting; now that they were able to extract purer iron from iron ore, blacksmiths could hammer the red-hot metal into more sophisticated weapons and other implements. This malleable material allowed the artisan-designer to experiment with form and function to create tools that performed even better, whether it was farm implements such as sickles and pruning hooks or weapons that were lighter, cheaper, and stronger than their bronze equivalents. The advent of the superior iron-headed axes accelerated land clearance, thereby providing more farmland to support a growing agrarian population. The design of such tools was necessarily determined by functional requirements and the availability of raw materials, often resulting in a visually satisfying purity of form. As the Canadian philosopher of communication theory Marshall McLuhan famously stated, "We shape our tools and then our tools shape us"—or to put it another way, design maketh man.

←
Iron Age spearheads from the Necropolis of San Marco dei Cavoti, Benevento, Italy, seventh century BC.

↑
Nineteenth century engraving showing the casting of Iron Age weapons. Left background: heating metal in furnace. Right: pouring molten metal into mold. Center: mold opened and cast object removed.

The ancient world and the birth of mass production

The relatively slow technological progress of the three ages—the Stone Age, the Bronze Age, and the Iron Age—was drawn out over tens of millennia. By comparison, the ancient world—beginning in Egypt some five thousand years ago—saw a rapid acceleration of technological progress. This in turn brought about a slew of new and innovative designs: in ancient Egypt ramps and levers were developed to aid the construction of buildings, while in ancient China the iron plow, crossbow, propeller, and magnetic compass were invented. It was in ancient Greece, however, that new technological discoveries occurred at the most remarkable rate, though often these discoveries were not properly developed into practical designs. The reason for this lack of widespread design application is thought to lie with the perceived lowly status of laborers, which was effectively a disincentive to anyone from the educated classes to apply these new developments or technologies, because it might endanger their social standing in a community that prided itself on thought rather than practical action. There were, of course, some notable exceptions, such as the giant catapult designed by Archimedes and used on Hieron II's ship the *Syracusa*, which could hurl boulders weighing up to 173 pounds some 200 yards into the hulls of enemy vessels—a feat of remarkable design ingenuity and engineering know-how.[4] The Romans had no such social hang-ups, and of all the ancient cultures theirs was the most adept at originating innovative design concepts and translating them into practical design solutions.

One ancient technology that was to have an enormous impact on human development was brick-making. It could be said that it was the brick more than anything else that created civilization, building by

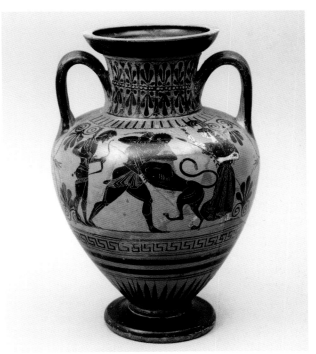

building, brick course by brick course. Although the humble brick is not often thought of as a designed artifact, that is exactly what it is, for through trial and error humans planned its exact form and size, determined the best materials to make it with, then developed the optimum production method to bring it into reality, working within the given constraints. Perhaps even more important in the overall story of design is the fact that the brick is a designed item that can be easily replicated and standardized, and was thus one of the earliest objects to be mass-produced. The first bricks, made of sun-dried mud, were used to build the famously structurally unsound walls of Jericho, as well as being used by the ancient Egyptians. Stronger fired bricks baked in kilns, which were used extensively by the Romans to construct their empire, soon succeeded these earlier sun-dried bricks. To this end, the Romans set up ceramics factories to produce fired bricks and tiles in high volumes, including one such facility recently excavated in Santa Venera al Pozzo, in Sicily.

Like their predecessors the Etruscans, who had used clay or plaster molds to serially produce funerary urns,

the Romans used molding technology to mass-produce high volumes of fired ceramic wares, most notably oil lamps. By pressing soft clay into plaster or fired clay molds, Roman manufacturers could mass-produce high-quality, standardized lamps easily and efficiently. Between the first and third centuries AD, these types of pottery lamps were manufactured in factories initially set up in Northern Italy and Southern Gaul and then exported widely across the Roman provinces. These *firmalampen* (factory lamps) often carried their manufacturers' stamps on their bases and were stylistically highly varied, ranging from plain utilitarian

↖
Sun-dried, partly fired brick from Ubaid (Iraq), early Dynastic period. The first kiln-fired bricks were made in Mesopotamia (now part of Iraq) in about 3,200–2,800 BC.

↑
Roman bakery oven built from Roman fired bricks, Pompeii, c. 79 AD.

→
Roman factory-made ceramic oil lamp depicting the goddess Fortuna, excavated near Este, Italy.

The early origins of design

The ancient world and the birth of mass production

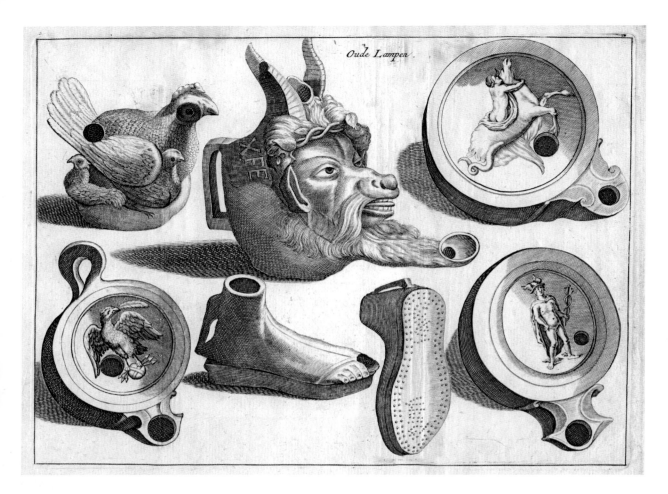

models to extremely elaborate ones. These latter examples were often embellished with an extraordinary and imaginative diversity of subject matter: intricate decoration, scenes of everyday life, depictions of gladiatorial battles, and even pornographic imagery.

Another type of ceramic ware that was manufactured by the Romans in huge numbers was the amphora; these distinctive storage vessels were wheel-thrown rather than molded, which meant that, unlike oil lamps, they were not standardized or so highly replicable. Nonetheless, amphorae can be seen as utilitarian artifacts that were functionally close to perfection. The amphorae's carefully considered generic form allowed for safe transportation on ships, enabling them to be stacked securely into specially designed racks. The classic amphora shape also facilitated easy carrying and pouring, thanks to its looping handles and long, narrow neck. Functionally honed over centuries, amphorae were absolutely essential to the development of vital trading links,

permitting olive oil, wine, *garum* (a popular fish sauce), and the like to be sent efficiently to all corners of the Roman Empire and beyond.

The production of coinage similarly had an enormous impact on the expansion of trade, and consequently on human development, allowing the shift from a direct-trading barter system to a currency system that enabled a more quantifiable understanding of value, which in turn further promoted trade. The coin, too, was (and still is), by its very nature, a mass-produced and standardized designed artifact, though because its circulation has such prevalence in our daily lives we often overlook its status as a designed object. In Western history the invention of minted coins took place in ancient Greece around 700 BC, though the adoption of cast monetary tokens in China goes back even further, to around 1,100 BC, during the Shang Dynasty. The introduction of a coinage system by the Roman Republic around 300 BC was, by southern European standards, relatively delayed.

The early origins of design

As the recognized coinage authority Andrew Burnett has noted, its introduction "did not result from any economic or military necessity [but] arose, arguably, from the cultural influence of Greece. . . the Romans wanted their city to have the civilization of Greek cities, and saw the production of their own coinage as one important aspect of this process."[5] Although the practice of featuring portraits on coins originated in 400 BC in Asia Minor, it was during the rule of Julius Caesar that the Roman Republic pioneered the practice of featuring a faithful likeness on coins. The image of Caesar was an authoritative iconographic symbol, not only of the emperor's domination but also of his empire's mighty power. These coins could be viewed as an early example of design being used as metaphor, for over and above their monetary worth they had a definite propaganda value.

Systems of mass production were also used by the Romans to equip their vast armies with weaponry in order to expand and defend their enormous empire, which at its height stretched from northern Britain to the deserts of North Africa. If the Romans were to mass-produce weapons in any significant volume, their designs needed to be highly standardized. To this end, Roman military equipment was produced using standard patterns that were carefully and rationally considered from both a functional standpoint and from a design-manufacturing perspective. For instance, the famous *gladius*, the thrusting sword with perfectly balanced handling used by foot soldiers in the Roman army from which the word "gladiator" was coined, was a decisive weapon not only because of its superior performance but also because it could be mass-produced efficiently. The Roman soldier's standard issue kit, which included body armor, helmet, sword, and javelin, was innovatively mass-produced in mobile arms factories sited along army supply routes. The production of this matériel was so crucial to the success of Roman military campaigns that the Roman authorities viewed their factory workers' skills as being of exceptional importance to the state: according to the military historian John Keegan, "a decree was issued for them [factory workers] to be branded, as a deterrent against desertion."[6] The standardization of Roman arms and armor was significant in separating the act of designing from the act of making, instigating an early form of the division of labor.

Engraving of various Roman oil lamps showing variations in pattern (a hen, a satyr, a foot, Mercury-Hermes, a sea horse, and an eagle) by Hans Kasper Arkstee, 1733.

Roman amphorae found in excavated storehouses at Saint-Romain-en-Gal, France.

Roman gold coin bearing the lifelike portrait of Julius Caesar, minted in Cisalpine Gaul, c. 43 BC.

The early origins of design

The success of the Roman Empire came from harnessing the power of purposeful design and applying it to the mass manufacture of weapons and domestic goods, as well as to the creation of buildings, towns, and cities—civilization's built environment. Perhaps the best summation of the Romans' thoughtful approach to life was given by the Greek philosopher and Roman citizen Plutarch, who stated, "Let us carefully observe those good qualities wherein our enemies excel us; and endeavor to excel them, by avoiding what is faulty, and imitating what is excellent in them."[7] It was this pragmatic type of thinking, particularly in relation to the purposeful application of design, that enabled the Romans to successfully translate ideas into factory-made objects, whether weapons, oil lamps, or roof tiles. It was these early mass-produced designs that allowed them to build, through conquest and trade, the largest and most sophisticated empire the world had ever seen.

↑
Roman *gladius* sword inside its bronze, wood, and bone scabbard from Pannerden, Netherlands. This weapon was in use from the fourth century BC to the third century AD.

←
Nineteenth-century print of a Roman legionary showing helmet, breastplate, and other standardized items of kit that would have been mass-produced in factories.

↓
Roman relief commemorating victorious gladiators, found on Via Appia, Rome, first century BC.

China's first emperor and the power of mass production

China's first emperor, Qin Shi Huang, who is sometimes tellingly referred to as the Chinese Caesar, also harnessed the power of design and mass production in the name of conquest. He is remembered for unifying by force the Seven Warring States into China, the most powerful country the world had ever seen, in 221 BC. He was also responsible for building the Great Wall of China to protect his new nation's borders from the raiding Mongolian hordes coming down from the steppes. He is even better known, certainly in archeological circles, for the Terracotta Army that was made to honor him and to protect him in the afterlife. This collection of ceramic funerary sculptures depicting the emperor's army is estimated to have included 8,000 life-sized statues of soldiers and 670 horses, as well as depictions of other members of his vast retinue, from officials and servants to musicians, singers, and acrobats. Although the army should probably be considered statuary rather than design, the figures were essentially factory-produced, using systemized methods of production similar to those used to make serially manufactured functional artifacts. The figures were also buried with weapons, and around forty thousand bronze spears, swords, crossbows, halberds, and staffs have been recovered by archeologists so far.

As with the manufacture of the terracotta warriors themselves, the production of their accompanying weapons reveals that the Qin workforce was organized into highly efficient production cells that used standardization measures and quality-control procedures. The technical knowledge of these Chinese weapon-makers, however, was not confined to equipping the Terracotta Army—far from it. Recent research has revealed that some of the burial matériel was actually used in battle and bears the scars to prove it. Emperor Qin's craftsmen perfected the art of bronze-making to such an extent that they were able to produce swords that are now considered some of the finest bronze weapons ever made. Because their raw material was of such a high grade, they could manufacture swords that were significantly longer than any that had gone before, which gave Qin's soldiers the benefit of 30 percent greater reach and cutting power. Thus the development of better quality materials enabled the production of better performing designs, which gave the first Chinese emperor's forces a decisive advantage. This is a recurring theme throughout the story of design: as more advanced materials are invented or discovered, their unique benefits are employed by designers to improve existing designs, thereby creating superior products.

Another reason that Qin was able to achieve his epic conquest of the Warring States was that his workers produced weaponry to such precise specifications that their parts were completely interchangeable. If,

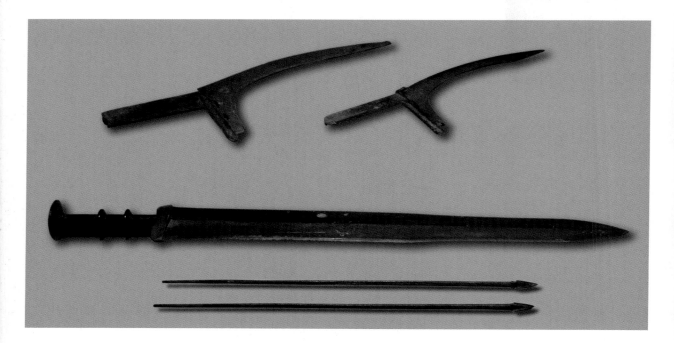

for example, a section of a crossbow broke in battle, it could be replaced easily with an exactly replicated piece. Similarly, the arrows used by his soldiers had interchangeable shafts so that their arrowheads could be reused even if the shaft had broken. This high degree of manufacturing efficiency and standardization was bolstered by a culture of manufacturing accountability, with workers' output overseen by supervisors to ensure that no defective workmanship was ever allowed to creep into the production system—and if it did, the consequences were severe. Precision-manufacturing and an exacting quality-control system were used not only for weaponry but also for weights and measures during Qin's reign, and this system of standardized production formed the basis upon which Chinese design and manufacturing would flourish over the succeeding centuries.

Over the next thousand years, the Chinese used methods similar to these to design and manufacture ceramics and bronze wares that were technically far superior to their European equivalents. The delicate blue-and-white porcelain crockery imported from China into Europe in increasing quantities during the 1700s must have seemed the epitome of refinement and modernity when compared to the heavy and rather rustic earthenware pottery produced closer to home.

A capacity for the precise replication of designs is still a defining characteristic of Chinese production, and it can surely be traced back to the first emperor's innovative implementation of rigorous design standards, which became inculcated into the nation's manufacturing culture.

Thus the relatively slow but vital design progress in the Stone Age, the Bronze Age, and the Iron Age gave way to the much more rapid innovations in, progressively, ancient Egypt, ancient Greece, ancient Rome, and ancient China. While each of these rich material cultures had its own creative highpoints, it was advances in design during the Roman Republic—which coincided with the reign of the first Chinese emperor—that provided the strongest roots of European design.

↑
Dagger-axe heads, swords, and crossbow bolts excavated at Guchengcun, China, dating from the Warring States Period, pre-221 BC.

→
Terracotta Army warriors at the tomb of Emperor Qin Shi Huang, Lingtong District, Xi'an, China.

The early origins of design

2

DESIGN AND CRAFTSMANSHIP FROM THE MIDDLE AGES TO THE EIGHTEENTH CENTURY

Medieval inventions and the guild system

Design and craftsmanship from the Middle Ages to the eighteenth century

In Europe, the decline of the Roman Empire, which occurred over a drawn-out time span of four centuries, marked the end of the Classical period and the beginning of a new chapter in Western history: the Middle Ages. This was a period of cultural retrenchment spanning the fifth to the fifteenth centuries, when the humanist philosophy of the Classical world was replaced by early Christian God-fearing religiosity. Also known as the Dark Ages or medieval period, it was a time that saw depopulation, de-urbanization, and the rise of the feudal system. Despite these factors, which slowed technological progress, a number of landmark inventions were designed or refined in Europe during this period that irrevocably changed the course of human history.

Among these groundbreaking developments were: in the seventh century, the improved water wheel, which allowed water power to be harnessed into energy to mill flour, saw wood, and cleanse woolen cloth of impurities; in the eighth century, the hourglass, the first dependable and reusable measurer of time; in the ninth century, the heavy moldboard plow, which increased food production;

in the twelfth century, the blast furnace, which allowed iron ore to be smelted at higher temperatures, reducing impurities and producing stronger iron for the manufacture of higher-quality goods; in the thirteenth century, the mechanical clock, which enabled for the first time the reliable and constant measurement of time; and finally, also in the thirteenth century, the spinning wheel, which mechanized the process of twisting wool or cotton into usable threads. All of these innovations were not just plucked out of thin air, but were the results of their creators' conception and planning within a rational approach to problem-solving. In other words, they were *designed*.

There is a common misunderstanding that invention and design are somehow different from one another, yet an invention can only be the result of design-led thinking and some form of developmental process, such as drawing, trial-and-error experimentation, or model-making. Design is ultimately about believing that there can be a better solution to a specific problem and then undertaking to realize that superior solution, and this practice is indiscernible from that of invention. Undoubtedly, these inventions of the Middle Ages were largely developed using a process that was

←
Previous page: Wineglass (Roemer), Dutch, 1600–30.

←
German- or Swiss-made silver ewers showing a high level of craftsmanship, fourteenth century.

↑
Detail from an Anglo-Saxon manuscript showing plow in use. This type of plow was widely used in Europe from the ninth to the fourteenth century.

↗
Early water wheel shown in a woodcut from *Hortus Sanitatis* (Garden of Health) printed by Johann Pruss in Strasbourg, 1497.

↑
Engraving showing a medieval English
goldsmith shop, fourteenth century.

based on trial-and-error together with a high level of forethought—an approach that in each case led to the optimum designed solution.

Like their Greek and Roman predecessors, European craftsmen of the Middle Ages used a significant degree of standardization in order to manufacture items ranging from weapons to floor tiles serially. For example, they used standard molds to mass-produce ceramic wares with simple forms, such as wine flagons, which could then be decorated with incised or stamped motifs or with differently colored glazes. They also mass-produced seals using molds, which were then widely used to verify documents, as the majority of people were illiterate—an example of design fundamentally influencing social and economic development.

During the Middle Ages there was also exponential growth in trade, and this led to the expansion of certain cities, such as Florence, Venice, Nuremberg, Cologne, Ghent, and Bruges. In these important trading and cultural centers, large workshops produced high-quality designed goods to cater to the increasingly sophisticated tastes of their wealthy patrons, which included royal courts, churches, and prosperous merchants. Although they often used traditional methods of production, the workshops became increasingly specialized and often, as the industrial design historian John Heskett notes, "Many objects of the same type were made, though the process of production was essentially the repetitive duplication of existing models by craft methods."[1] Craftsmen based in urban centers often possessed a considerable degree of artistic creativity as well as a high level of technical skill; because of this there was a frequent blurring of boundaries between the roles of the artist and the artisan. These figures were frequently involved in very similar projects; often the only distinction between artist and craftsman was their level of training and technical accomplishment. The expansion of trade and its ensuing commercial opportunities created an increasingly competitive marketplace in which technological advancement was necessary in order to keep up with growing demand. Innovation in design helped workshops to distinguish their products from those of others, and so helped them to gain a vital competitive edge.

Another way in which medieval craftsmen protected their interests was through the formation of craft guilds. These professional bodies were hugely important for a number of reasons. The most significant benefit was that they provided artisans of the same occupation with a mutually beneficial association, creating what was effectively a monopoly, in which no one who was not a member of the town or city's guild was allowed to practice their craft. The craft guilds protected not only their members' interests but also the consumer's, by putting in place codes of conduct and regulations so as to prevent poor quality workmanship from tarnishing the guild's reputation. This often meant that the work of guild members had to be examined by a board of individuals and then given a stamped approval before being sold.

The craft guilds, like the related merchant guilds that were formed even earlier, became an important aspect of medieval civic life and helped to empower the artisan by their collective nature: this early form of labor organization effectively helped raise the status

of the designer-craftsman. By the thirteenth century there were three distinct stages that a guildsman had to go through to reach the highest level of his chosen craft: as a young man he would be an apprentice (a student whose family or benefactor had paid for his teaching on the job); once he had become proficient in his craft, he became a journeyman (a salaried day worker); and finally, once he had perfected his craft, he became a master—the highest level of craftsman, whose "masterpiece" had to be approved by the guild as having met the quality criteria. Even after the Middle Ages gave way to the blossoming of the Renaissance in the late fourteenth and early fifteenth centuries, the craft guilds continued to play an increasingly important sociopolitical role, and consequently enhanced the livelihood of the individual designer while also ensuring a certain standard of execution.

↑
Nuremberg brass alms dish decorated with a representation of Adam and Eve flanking the Tree of Life, Germany, sixteenth century.

↘
Overleaf: engraving showing various household objects produced during the fifteenth, sixteenth, and seventeenth centuries.

Ferdinand Seré, pinx et lith.

Design and craftsmanship from the Middle Ages to the eighteenth century

Imprimé par Hangard Mauge, à Paris.

Renaissance men: the design thinker, the printer, and the goldsmith

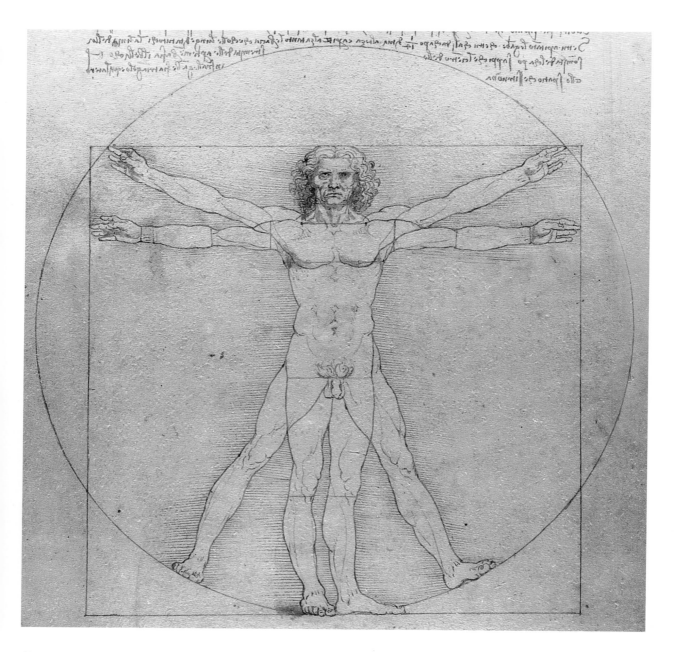

Design and craftsmanship from the Middle Ages to the eighteenth century

Immediately after the Middle Ages came the Renaissance, a cultural movement that transformed society between the fourteenth and the seventeenth centuries. It was a period of classical philosophical renewal and heightened creative endeavor within the realms of art, science, and, of course, design. The Renaissance—which takes its name from the word for "rebirth"—was a time of reawakening as designers and artists shrugged off the pious religiosity and Gothic mantle of the Middle Ages and rediscovered the humanist ideals and sensual refinement of the Classical period. One of the greatest designers of this period was the artist Leonardo da Vinci, a true Renaissance man who during his lifetime was admired as much for his inventive designs as for his art. His understanding of the natural world and its mechanisms often inspired his design work; for example, his carefully drawn studies of birds directly informed his designs of conceptual flying machines, including a hang glider and a

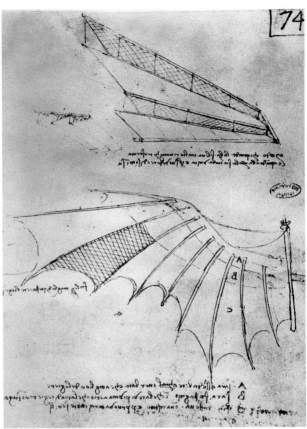

helicopter-like machine. Although the vast majority of da Vinci's designs remained concepts on paper in his beautifully drawn and curiously annotated sketchbooks, it was his personal embodiment of the Renaissance man as an innovative design thinker that would, more than anything else, focus attention on the practice of design and distinguish it from vocational craft.

Leonardo was one of the great polymaths of his day, courted by popes and kings alike, and his ability

←
Vitruvian Man drawing by Leonardo da Vinci, 1485–90, a study of Classical proportion, based on the ideal man.

↑
An armored tank designed by Leonardo da Vinci, c. 1486, later constructed at the Château d'Amboise, France, based on original drawings.

↑
Designs by Leonardo da Vinci for the wings of a flying machine, fifteenth century.

to conceptualize revolutionary designs helped to raise the status of design practice. In 1482 he sent a letter to his prospective client Ludovico Sforza, the Duke of Milan, outlining not only his artistic talents but also his design-engineering skills—showing that for him creativity did not respect any distinctions between art and design. As a visionary design thinker, Leonardo drew on his experiences as an artist, engineer, and natural scientist to create designs that looked into the future. Yet because they were so far ahead of their time, they almost exclusively remained theoretical, only pointing potential ways forward rather than having any practical application.

The most significant invention to be designed during the Renaissance was Johannes Gutenberg's printing press of 1440. Developed and constructed in the German city of Strasbourg, the mechanical press arguably changed the course of human history more than any other designed object. The construction of this groundbreaking hand-operated printing press employed technology adapted from screw-type presses already being used for winemaking in the Rhine Valley. Heralding the advent of mechanized printing, Gutenberg's design led to the mass production of books, enabling thoughts and ideas to be disseminated widely for the first time in history. This was to have an enormous impact on the development of design, as designers subsequently began to publish pattern books for the first time. These books were filled with engravings showing innovative high-style furniture designs, metalwork designs, embroidery patterns, or just general decorative motifs, which could then be copied by other craftsmen who bought the publications of creative inspiration. The designs in these pattern books were, of course, intended to be replicated by someone other than the original designer, which meant that the creator was now completely removed from the production of his own designs and had no say in the quality standards employed in their execution. This divorce of the act of designing from the act of making was a highly significant departure within the history of design, and raised the status of the designer from that of a humble artisan to that of a skilled artist. A considerable amount of work executed outside of the larger urban workshops during this period did not copy designs from a pattern book but still relied on craft production, whereby the design—conception

↑
Woodcut by Jost Amman showing a printing press being used in a printer's workshop, 1568—a "puller" removes a printed sheet from the press, while a "beater" inks the forme and compositors are setting type in the background.

↑
Photograph of a printer's workshop with a Gutenberg-type printing press.

Design and craftsmanship from the Middle Ages to the eighteenth century

and planning—and the making of an object was undertaken by a single person.

One of the most celebrated designers of the sixteenth century was the goldsmith Benvenuto Cellini, whose work reached its exquisite jewel-encrusted zenith in his famous Mannerist-style saltcellar created for King Francis I of France. This lavishly ornamented work was a confection of enameled gold that was primarily intended to express the culture, wealth, and power of its royal owner—it was high-style design used to convey status rather than to create a particularly functional object. Cellini also wrote a fascinating—though somewhat embellished—autobiography that gives a rare insight into the training and life of a Renaissance designer and the elevated social position that such master craftsmen could enjoy. In addition to this, Cellini wrote two

treatises on goldsmithing and sculpture that were essentially how-to guides to these two related fields; they were translated into English by the Arts and Crafts designer Charles Robert Ashbee in 1898. The fact that Cellini chose to group these two disciplines together is telling, revealing that at the time there was little distinction between fine art and design, both being essentially the domain of the craftsman.

↑
Enamelend gold saltcellar designed and executed by Benvenuto Cellini, 1540–43.

Functional wares and basic tools

Design and craftsmanship from the Middle Ages to the eighteenth century

While Cellini's high-style designs were intended for the top stratum of society, the majority of designs from the Renaissance period were altogether more utilitarian. The famous Great Bed of Ware, which now resides in London's Victoria and Albert Museum, might have been larger than the average merchant's bed, being intended for an inn and the accommodation of up to fifteen people, but is still an excellent example of European design during the Renaissance period, with its solid, no-nonsense oak-plank construction enlivened with heavy carving. Among the other designs from this period that reveal a similar kind of functional honesty are the many kitchen items illustrated in a six-volume treatise on cooking, *Opera di Bartolomeo Scappi* (The Work of Bartolomeo Scappi), written by the celebrated papal chef and published in 1570. However, the study of even more mundane everyday wares found in a Renaissance house during this period might better reflect the design and manufacturing practices of the era—from simple cast-iron firebacks and earthenware bowls to jointed stools and basketry.

During the Renaissance, many people relied on the skills of their local blacksmith, carpenter, mason, potter, and weaver to furnish their homes with everything they needed, and this remained the case right up until the advent of the Industrial Revolution in the mid 1700s. Similarly, the tools needed for agriculture were most often locally produced and frequently reveal a fitness for purpose attuned to local climatic conditions, availability of local materials, and regional customs and practices. The pots and pans of everyday life and the common tools of husbandry often possess the most purposeful and, therefore, the purest and most beautiful forms—a fact that was recognized by the Renaissance author

Baldassare Castiglione when he noted in *The Book of the Courtier* (1528) that "no matter what things you study, you will find that those which are good and useful are also graced with beauty."[2]

The classicism of the Renaissance was eventually replaced in the late sixteenth century by the short-lived Mannerist style, before the theatrical Baroque style took root in the early 1600s. During the seventeenth and early eighteenth centuries various decorative styles came and went, often according to the succession of monarchs and the influences at their courts. Yet while high-style designs were the preserve of the elite, there was a trickle-down effect rather like haute couture's influence on high-street fashion today. Stylistically speaking, provincial designs made outside the main cultural centers frequently lagged behind those produced in the cities by several years, and sometimes even by decades, which makes the precise dating of such designs especially difficult. There was also a vernacular design tradition that was often

Great Bed of Ware, 1590–1600, carved-oak bed with panels of marquetry by Hans Vredeman de Vries.

←

↑

Plates from *Opera de Bartolomeo Scappi* showing various Renaissance kitchenware designs, 1570.

Design and craftsmanship from the Middle Ages to the eighteenth century

used to hone certain regional design typologies to formal and functional perfection over decades or even centuries. Similarly, some design replication took place within workshops, when craftsmen would repeat the manufacture of a successful object over and over again. As the design historian Edward Lucie-Smith wrote:

> Medieval attitudes towards design were still very much present in the workshops of the seventeenth and eighteenth centuries. It is a temptation, for example, to think of a rushlight holder as a typically "craft" object, especially when one is confronted with a whole series of slightly differing examples. . . However, if one looks at the holder itself . . . one sees immediately that it is in fact very well designed for its purpose, which is to hold a burning rush dipped in tallow in a safe and stable fashion. A modern industrial designer, handed the same problem, would be hard put to find a better basic solution.[3]

This notion of finding, developing, and evolving optimum solutions—designs that have an exacting "rightness"—is at the very heart of design practice. And it doesn't matter whether an object is craft-produced or machine-made. The underlying objective remains the same: to realize, given the constraints presented, the most appropriate way of addressing a specific need.

←
Typical rushlight holder. This type of lighting device was used right up to the 1830s–40s.

↑
Pair of brass candlesticks, Belgian, late fifteenth century.

↖
Armchair made from turned oak and ash, English, late fifteenth century.

The high styles of the eighteenth century: from Chippendale to Adam

The fundamental design of basic tools and functional home wares—the cooking pot, the wooden spoon, the rushlight holder—changed almost imperceptibly over decades and even centuries. This was not the case when it came to more elaborate and costly household furnishings, especially those intended for the upper echelons of society. From the early seventeenth to the mid-eighteenth centuries there was a discernible lightening of mass within the decorative and applied arts, with the heavy chunkiness and overblown floridity of the Baroque style giving way to the overtly feminine, sumptuously opulent Rococo style.

Rococo—which took its name from the French word *rocaille*, meaning the encrusted shell work or pebble work used during the eighteenth century to decorate grottos and fountains—had an altogether lighter air than Baroque and frequently referenced Chinese patterns and motifs, or chinoiserie. One of the greatest proponents of the Rococo style within the decorative arts was the British cabinetmaker and furniture designer Thomas Chippendale, who plied his trade in London's fashionable Saint Martin's Lane. In 1754, Chippendale

published a book entitled *The Gentleman and Cabinet-Maker's Director*, which was lavishly illustrated with 161 engraved plates showing "elegant and useful designs of household furniture in the Gothic, Chinese and modern taste"—with "Chinese" referring to Rococo chinoiserie and "modern" in this context meaning pared-down Georgian Neoclassicism. There was certainly a rather eclectic attitude to styles in design around this period, as Chippendale's pattern book attests. The *Director* was, as the Chippendale Society notes, "the first attempt in England to publish a book of designs for furniture as means of self-promotion. The result was that his business immediately became known to a wide circle of potential clients and for ever afterwards his name became a by-word for a distinctive rococo style." Not only did the *Director* act like a catalogue to help potential clients choose what they wanted to commission from Chippendale himself, but it also functioned as an inspirational pattern book for other cabinetmakers in Britain and even further afield in

↑
French Rococo serpentine commode with Japanese lacquer and ormolu mounts designed by the Parisian *ébéniste*, Bernard II van Risamburgh, c. 1755-65.

←
Interior of Peterskirche (St. Peter's Church) in Vienna, Austria, designed by Johann Lukas von Hildebrandt, constructed 1701–20. A glorious example of the overblown and theatrical Baroque style.

↑
Mirrored room (cabinet) at the Episcopal Residence, Würzburg, Germany. A Rococo interior showing the use of asymmetrical rocaille forms.

France, Russia, and the United States, thereby helping to disseminate his designs far further than could ever have been achieved otherwise.

In France there was a similar progression of styles, with Baroque being succeeded by Rococo in the late 1720s then completely usurped by Neoclassicism in the mid-1750s. The refinement of early French Neoclassicism was perhaps best exemplified by the work of the *ébénistes* (wood-carvers), most notably Jean-Henri Riesener, Adam Weisweiler, and Jean-François Leleu. Their designs combined architectural forms with classical motifs to create elegant furniture typified by its incorporation of exquisitely detailed marquetry and gilt-bronze mounts. After the French Revolution, the Directoire style, which emerged in the mid 1790s, adopted a plainer and more rational interpretation of Neoclassical forms that was more suited to the republican sentiment of the period. As the art historian Hugh Honour noted of this short-lived yet influential

style: "The stoic virtues of Republican Rome were upheld as standards not merely for the arts but also for political behavior and private morality. . . Even the chairs in which the committee of Salut Publique sat were made on antique models devised by David."[4] The Directoire style anticipated the bold and imperialistic Empire style, which emerged after Napoleon Bonaparte had established the First French Empire in 1804 and dominated design in France for most of the nineteenth century. The Neoclassical style in all its guises and iterations had an inherent pared-down rationalism that reflected a new and emerging empirical mindset that would ultimately be responsible for the birth of the Industrial Revolution.

Across the channel in Britain, Neoclassical architecture and design also became the height of fashion during the latter half of the eighteenth century and the first decades of the nineteenth. Following the success of Chippendale's *Director*, the two other most prominent British furniture designers of the eighteenth century, George Hepplewhite and Thomas

↑
Jacques-Louis David, *Portrait of Madame Récamier*, 1800, showing furnishings in the fashionable post-revolutionary Directoire style.

←
Carved mahogany chair designed by Thomas Chippendale, 1754–80. This design was published in the first edition of *The Gentleman and Cabinet-Maker's Director* (1754) and in subsequent editions.

→
Golden cabinet/study of Queen Marie-Antoinette at the Château de Versailles designed by Jean-Henri Riesener, 1783, in the elegant pre-revolutionary Neoclassical style.

The high styles of the eighteenth century: from Chippendale to Adam

Sheraton, had their design compendiums published in 1788 and 1791 respectively. Although he was apprenticed as a cabinetmaker, Sheraton did not actually have a workshop at the time of publication of his four-volume *The Cabinet-Maker and Upholsterer's Drawing-Book,* and, therefore, no piece of furniture has ever been attributed to him personally. His Grecian-inspired designs were widely made by other cabinetmakers, and the term "Sheraton style" was used to describe such work. Thomas Sheraton became famous for his designs rather than for his execution of them, a notable distinction as it was one of the first instances of a designer becoming renowned as a tastemaker and trendsetter based purely on his design concepts.

Also well known during the eighteenth century was the Scottish architect Robert Adam, who developed his own distinct approach to Neoclassicism. Rejecting the robust neo-Palladianism that had been advocated earlier by Lord Burlington, Adam and his brother James promoted a more delicate style that was based on their studies of surviving examples of actual Greek architecture, instead of the secondhand interpretation of them by the Renaissance architect Andrea Palladio. There were some critics of their tracery-style stucco work, with its icing-like delicacy contrasting against pastel shades of paintwork:

Horace Walpole damned it as "gingerbread and sippets of embroidery."[5] But the graceful and feminine "Adam style" quickly became highly fashionable in Britain and remained so from the 1760s up to the 1780s. At the time it must have seemed the height of refined taste and modernity, introducing a much lighter look, as revealed in the dazzling interiors Robert Adam designed for the Child family at Osterley Park—or indeed in any of his other interior design commissions. As Ralph Harrington, an expert on Georgian plasterwork, wrote: "The Adam style, as it developed over the course of the eighteenth century, made sophisticated use of motifs and patterns from a wide range of sources, combining the fruits of recent archeological investigations with decoration from Renaissance, Baroque, and contemporary styles."[6] The discovery during this period of virtually intact domestic architecture at Pompeii and Herculaneum was especially influential to the Adam brothers, as it gave them a new insight into the decoration and artifacts used in Roman villas. It also inspired their development of highly integrated interior design schemes that were both stylistically complex and functionally adaptable. Robert Adam essentially pioneered the "total design look," his commissions often encompassing not only the design of the building but also its interior architectural fittings, such as fireplaces and door furniture, as well as all of its stylistically unified furnishings, from bookcases, commodes, and armchairs to mirrors, pedestals, and candelabra. But while Adam's work was all about the decorative motifs and design typologies of ancient Greece and Rome being reinterpreted into a prettified "modern" Georgian idiom, there was another side to eighteenth-century Neoclassical design that had a far more functional aspect, and would in due course have a larger bearing on the development of modern design. The plainer version of the Neoclassical style was widely adopted in the design of less expensive furnishings made for the merchant and professional classes during the reign of King George III and the succeeding Regency period, and was notable for its elegant practicality and use of stripped-down Classical forms.

George III mahogany Hepplewhite-style dining chairs, c. 1790.

Entrance hall of Osterley Park in Middlesex, England, designed by Robert Adam, 1767, with stucco decoration by the firm Joseph Rose and grisaille paintings by Giovanni Battista Cipriani.

The high styles of the eighteenth century: from Chippendale to Adam

↑
The long gallery at Strawberry Hill,
Twickenham, Middlesex, designed 1760–62 in
the eighteenth-century "Gothick" style.

↗
Royal Pavilion in Brighton, remodeled by John
Nash, 1815–22.

Design and craftsmanship from the Middle Ages to the eighteenth century

An alternative to Neoclassicism that was popular during the eighteenth century—and that was also used by Thomas Chippendale and referenced by Robert Adam—was Gothic Revivalism. However, the interpretation of medievalism in the mid- to late 1700s was markedly different from that in the following century. One of the finest examples of this early neo-Gothic style, which is often referred to as "Gothick"[7] to distinguish it from the nineteenth-century Gothic Revival, was Strawberry Hill, a villa built in Twickenham on the outskirts of London by the politician Horace Walpole. The building of this vast confection of towers, turrets, faux ramparts, and Elizabethan-style chimneys began in 1749 and lasted for decades, resulting in a suitably fashionable yet eccentric fairytale building with matching interiors, accommodating Walpole's extensive collection of antiques. Lord Burlington, a similarly wealthy patron of the arts, had earlier constructed a comparable villa, the elegant Chiswick House (completed 1729), a sort of "ultimate party house," but which had been built in a neo-Palladian style and revealed the influence of the Grand Tour.

Like Chiswick House and Strawberry Hill, the Royal Pavilion in Brighton (commenced in 1787), was an extraordinary and extravagant pleasure palace that reflected the whimsical pick-and-mix stylistic attitude of wealthy Georgian patrons. The original architect, Henry Holland, designed this magnificent royal palace starting in 1787, and it was later redesigned and extended by the architect John Nash between 1815 and 1822. This later refurbishment included the pavilion's distinctively exotic exterior, with its onion-shaped domes built in the fanciful Indo-Saracenic style. Used by the Prince Regent as a seaside residence, the pavilion became the epicenter of fashionable society, and its theatrical interiors—executed by the prominent London decorator John C. Crace—were something to behold.

Despite the rather over-the-top high-style design foibles of the eighteenth century found in Britain and in continental Europe, for the most part designs, especially those intended for the middle-to-upper classes rather than the aristocracy, had a purposeful functionality that was at times almost proto-modern, and that reflected a new intellectualized rationality within design. The rational thinking that emerged in the eighteenth century, stylistically embodied by Neoclassicism, ultimately led to the Industrial Revolution. This saw the division of labor being implemented on a previously unimaginable scale, and with it came the birth of a new vocation: industrial design.

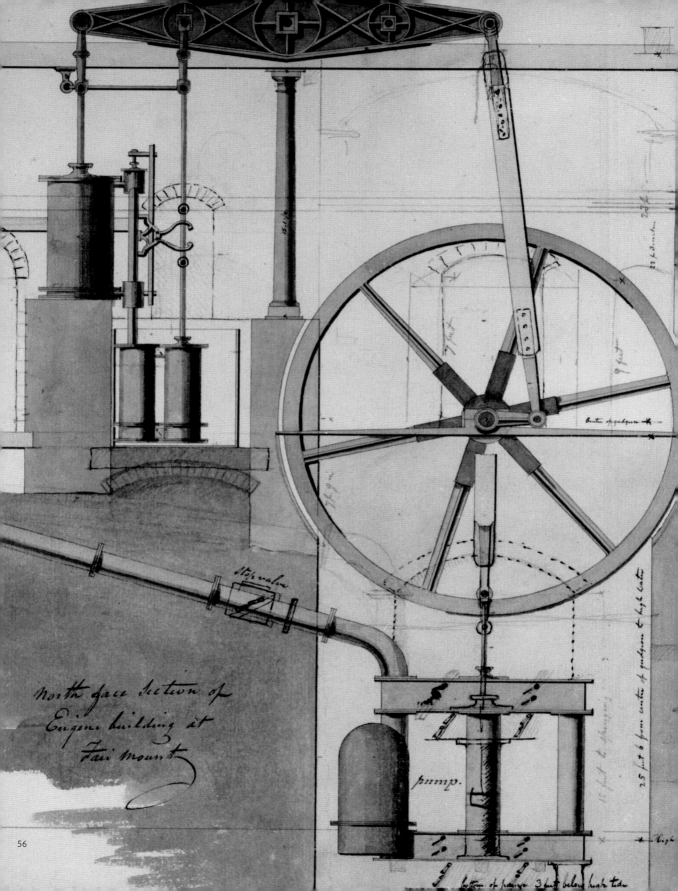

North face section of
Engine building at
Fair Mount

stop valve

pump.

bottom of passage 3 feet below high tide

56

3

THE AGE
OF REASON
AND THE
INDUSTRIAL
REVOLUTION

The Enlightenment and Neoclassicism

During the seventeenth and eighteenth centuries an intellectually led secularism arose, bringing about a new forward-looking cultural movement. Known as the Enlightenment, it not only challenged age-old religious dogma but also promoted scientific knowledge and, accordingly, industrial progress. The movement's first controversial shoots emerged around 1650–1700 in the work of the Dutch Jewish rationalist philosopher Baruch Spinoza; in the writings of John Locke, the English philosopher known as the "father of classical liberalism"; in the humanist ideas of the French writer Voltaire; and in the scientific principles of the English physicist Isaac Newton. It was a freethinking cultural groundswell based on a liberalized sense of morality and a scientific interpretation of the world, and it laid the philosophical foundation for not only the French Revolution but also the American Revolution. Not surprisingly, its adherents looked to ancient Greece— the cradle of democracy—for a sociopolitical and cultural blueprint, and this in turn influenced the taste of the day toward Neoclassicism.

By the eighteenth century, the classical past of the ancient Greeks and Romans had become so venerated that the Grand Tour had become a de rigueur rite of passage for many young gentlemen. And although the Grand Tour functioned as a sort of Georgian "gap year" to take in some classical studies at first hand, it had a hugely formative influence on the young, well-to-do men who undertook it, whether they subsequently became artists, architects, or designers, or became the wealthy patrons of such men. For most who undertook it, the Grand Tour was an edifying immersion in the culture of the ancient past, and it helped to promote the belief that a fundamental understanding of design— both past and present—was a necessary aspect of a young gentleman's fully rounded education. This new awareness of design was reflected in, among other things, the classically inspired yet functional proportions of contemporary Georgian furniture. And although different foreign influences—Dutch and French, Chinese and Indian—became fashionable within the decorative arts during this period, they only ever had a short-lived modishness and were never permitted to overly disrupt the graceful proportions or purposeful function of a design.

For a period of roughly eighty years of seismic social and political change—from around 1750 to 1830—Neoclassicism was the dominant style in art, architecture, and design. While in England it is most commonly referred to as Georgian or Regency, in France Neoclassicism was initially associated with the reign of Louis XVI and was a decorative style of design that was notable for its elegance and airy lightness. Later, however, it was more robustly interpreted in France during the reign of Napoleon. This second phase of French Neoclassicism became known as Empire style, and as the name suggests, it had definite imperialistic overtones.

In America, Neoclassicism was to become known as the Federal style, also thanks to its political connotations—with two of the American Founding Fathers, the architect Thomas Jefferson and the silversmith Paul Revere, both working within the Neoclassical style themselves. The ripples of Neoclassicism were also felt in Scandinavia, where in Sweden it was called the "Gustavian style" in homage to King Gustav III, who promoted through patronage a less ornate, Scandinavian version of the Louis XVI style. In Denmark, which was experiencing its so-called "Golden Age," there was a similar adoption of Neoclassicism, most notably in the work of Nicolai Abraham Abildgaard, whose klismos chairs, though

carefully based on ancient Greek precedents, had an outstanding, almost modern structural simplicity.

While Neoclassicism looked back to a classical past, it was essentially a forward-looking style that sought to reinterpret the classical rules of proportion into a graceful modern form. In comparison with the decorative styles that had gone before it, Neoclassicism had an inherent pared-down functionality that at times almost verged on modern. It was a style of design based on reason and was therefore perfectly attuned to the cultural and political sentiments of the era, which would itself eventually be defined as the Age of Reason by the English-American political theorist and revolutionary Thomas Paine.

←
Previous page: section of the engine house at the Fairmount Waterworks, Philadelphia, showing a Boulton and Watt engine, c. 1815.

↑
Klismos chair designed by Nicolai Abraham Abildgaard, 1790–95.

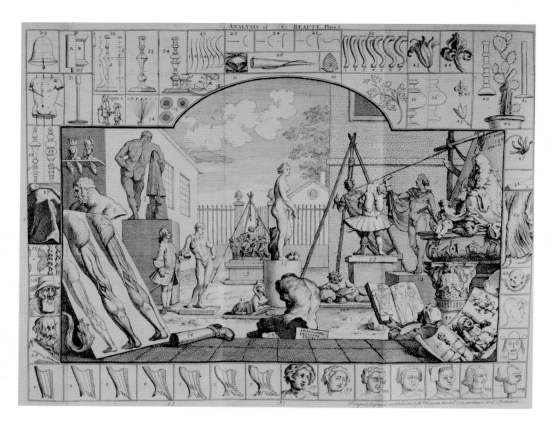

The Age of Reason and the Industrial Revolution

William Hogarth and
The Analysis of Beauty

The eighteenth-century fashion for Neoclassicism and its ideals of beauty were rejected by the British artist William Hogarth in his book *The Analysis of Beauty*, published in 1753. Instead, Hogarth championed grace and purpose in the practice of contemporary design, and sought to explain that it was functional rationale rather than applied decoration that was more likely to endow an object with aesthetic beauty. This illustrated tome, today mainly remembered for its espousal of the elegant serpentine line, was essentially an early treatise on aesthetic theory "written with a view of fixing the fluctuating ideas of taste." In this influential book, one of the first to consider the emergence of consumer products, Hogarth laid down immutable principles for the attainment of timeless beauty. These included, in relation to design practice, the notions of fitness, which he described as "the first fundamental law in nature with regard to beauty"; of simplicity, which "serves to prevent perplexity in forms of elegance"; and of proportion, which he defined as "a just symmetry and harmony of parts with respect to the whole."

It was Hogarth's overriding call for appropriateness of form within both art and industry that was to have a lasting influence on later designers and manufacturers. Although they were playfully satirical, Hogarth's popular series of engravings, such as *Marriage à-la-Mode* and *Industry and Idleness*, had a very strong underlying moral message, and this ethical dimension was also expressed in his belief that designed products should be suited to purpose. Using tongue-in-cheek engravings to illustrate *The Analysis of Beauty*, Hogarth was able for the first time to convey through memorable and engaging imagery a direct correlation between form and function, and as such had an immeasurable impact on the wider understanding of design in the eighteenth century. During the latter half of the century in England, there was a growing questioning within intellectual circles of the widespread taste for Neoclassicism as well as the validity of the values it embraced—simplicity, harmony, symmetry, and proportion—which were all too often doggedly pursued for the sake of fashion at the expense of design rationality. Thanks to Hogarth's book on beauty, there was now an increasing understanding of the fundamental relationship between the purpose of an object and the way it looks, and how this knowledge should be applied to so-called "art manufactures."

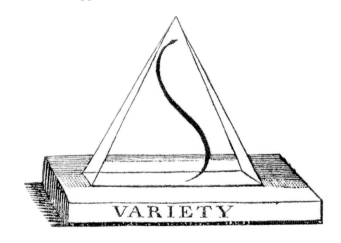

←
Plates I and II from *The Analysis of Beauty* by William Hogarth, 1753, showing the serpentine line of graceful beauty.

↑
Detail of frontispiece from *The Analysis of Beauty* by William Hogarth, 1753.

Steam power and the engines of change

While Hogarth was musing on the interrelationship of form and function, the logical, systematic mindset of the Enlightenment had spurred the appliance of science toward the goal of industrialized manufacturing, and the first stirrings of the Industrial Revolution were taking place. Although some might argue that the very first shoots of the Industrial Revolution sprouted as early as the late seventeenth century, it was not until the mid-eighteenth century that the momentum of industrial progress really started to pick up, particularly with the arrival of what many consider its first real design: the spinning jenny, designed by James Hargreaves around 1764. This first practical spinning machine used a single wheel to power eight spindles, thereby increasing productivity eightfold in comparison to traditional hand-spinning methods. Not everyone embraced this new labor-saving design. Fearful of the impact that Hargreaves's ingenious machine would have on livelihoods, a number of Lancashire hand-spinners marched on his house and destroyed his machinery. This first desperate act of machine wrecking, however, could not stem the tide of progress, and by the time of Hargreaves's death in 1778 more than 20,000 spinning jennies were in operation in mills across Great Britain. Hargreaves's design was eventually replaced by Richard Arkwright's water-powered spinning machine of 1769, which was itself usurped by even more efficient power looms invented by Samuel Crompton, Edmund Cartwright, and Joseph Marie Jacquard in 1779, 1785, and 1801, respectively—such was, and still is, the nature of industrial design's progress. One of the most profound effects that these early mechanized looms had was a decisive change in working patterns, with workers, instead of individually laboring at home, now having to work collectively in mills, where they were often bullied by mill owners and subjected to appalling working conditions, and in some cases literally worked to death for the sake of commercial gain.[1] These stark social and economic disparities would in due course galvanize the design reformers of the nineteenth century into action and lay the moral and philosophical foundations of design practice.

It was the transforming power of steam that would really drive the engines of industrialization and thereby fundamentally alter the goals of design, with the conception and planning of a design becoming increasingly divorced from its physical realization. Or to put it more simply, the act of designing an object was no longer the sole preserve of the designer–maker but was increasingly becoming the remit of a professional "designer for industry." The first successful steam engine was designed as early as 1698 by Thomas Savery, then Thomas Newcomen developed an improved "fire engine" to pump water out of mines in 1712; but neither of these engines was sufficiently powerful nor efficient enough for wider manufacturing applications. It was not until the Scottish engineer James Watt developed a significantly improved engine that steam became a really viable source of power to drive the machinery that would produce the new designed goods. With his refined engine, designed over a period of many years, Watt entered into a partnership in 1775 with Matthew Boulton, who owned the Soho manufactory in Birmingham. By the following year, two Boulton and Watt steam-driven beam engines were in full commercial operation—one being used to pump water at the Bloomfield Colliery in Staffordshire and the

←
Engraving showing a rotative steam engine by Boulton and Watt, 1788.

other to blow air into the furnaces of John Wilkinson's ironworks in Willey, Shropshire. That same year, the famous diarist James Boswell visited the Boulton–Watt factory, and it was during that tour that Boulton uttered his famously ambiguous quote, "I sell here, Sir, what all the world desires to have – POWER."[2] As the industrial historian John Lienhard rightly notes, this declaration "says a great deal about English thinking on the eve of the Industrial Revolution. For power, in both senses, was becoming the great English obsession."[3]

By the end of the eighteenth century, Watt's design had been improved by the addition, around 1780, of a rotative engine with a reciprocating action. Together with other makes of steam engines, it was being used to perform a variety of specialized tasks that were vital for the acceleration of industrialization and the birth of modern industrial design. While some of these engines were being employed to pump out mines, to extract more coal that would stoke yet more engines, others were being used to power heavy machinery that enabled the increasingly efficient production of goods. At the time, these advances were simply thought of as inevitable progress, and it was not until 1848 that the term "Industrial Revolution" was used by John Stuart Mill to define this period of rapid growth.[4]

→
Engraving of a spinning jenny designed by James Hargreaves, 1764. This was the first machine to allow the spinning of multiple spools of yarn or thread at the same time.

HARGREAVES'S

Engraved by T.E. Nicholson.

Steam power and the engines of change

Improved materials and precision tooling

The two great materials of the Industrial Revolution were iron and steel. While the former had been used for millennia, it was actually a relatively soft metal. It wasn't until Abraham Darby began successfully smelting it at higher temperatures, using coke rather than charcoal, that it became a viable metal for the production of a whole host of cast wares. Because Darby was able to achieve higher smelting temperatures, his iron had fewer impurities and, therefore, greater tensile strength. Darby's invention revolutionized the production of iron and, with it, design-manufacturing applications. In 1707 he patented a method of casting thin-walled cooking pots that employed reusable patterns to make the molds—constructed from sand—into which the molten red-hot iron was poured. The resulting simple cast-iron cooking pots were not only the earliest and most successful products manufactured by Darby's Coalbrookdale foundry in Shropshire, England, but they are generally regarded to be the earliest commercial designs to have been industrially produced on any meaningful scale. As such, they are hugely important artifacts within the overall story of design. Coalbrookdale was also where the world's first steam railway locomotive was built to Richard Trevithick's design, in 1803. This event heralded the arrival of a new mode of modern transport that, after being improved by George Stephenson with his famous Rocket locomotive of 1829, would accelerate the pace of the Industrial Revolution.

←
Rocket locomotive designed by George Stephenson, 1829. This image shows the incomplete remains of the original Rocket without its tender.

↑
Coalbrookdale by Night by Philip James de Loutherbourg, 1801, depicting the Madeley Wood Furnaces (Bedlam Furnaces) belonging to the Coalbrookdale foundry.

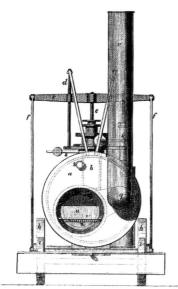

The other transformative material of the Industrial Revolution was steel. The metal had been used since ancient times but, like iron, its production and quality were improved greatly during the eighteenth century. Steel is actually an alloy containing a mixture of metallic elements. In the eighteenth century steel usually contained a high proportion of iron and, depending on the manufacturing requirements, other elements might have been added to enhance its material properties.[5] Although its chemical composition might have varied, it contained (as it still does today) between 0.2 and 1.5 percent carbon, and as such was a much harder material than wrought iron, while being less brittle than cast iron.

Steel did have the major drawback of being much more difficult to manufacture successfully than iron. In fact, it was not until the early 1740s, when the English clockmaker Benjamin Huntsman began resmelting bars of blistered steel in closed crucibles, that a satisfactory "crucible steel" could be produced. Huntsman initially used his improved steel for clock springs and later approached the cutlers of Sheffield with a view to them using it—however, rather bizarrely, they refused to work with it. Despite this initial setback, Huntsman's invention was the crucial first step toward the production of low-cost, high-volume, high-quality steel. This type of improved steel was eventually used to manufacture items including cutlery, fire tools, swords, and chisels during the eighteenth century, and rifle barrels in the early 1800s. It was not until the mid-nineteenth century, with the introduction of the Bessemer process (patented in 1856), that steel began to be produced on a truly industrial

scale. The increasing use of iron and steel during the Industrial Revolution was not just due to the significant quality improvements that had been introduced by Abraham Darby and Benjamin Huntsman. A new manufacturing technique developed and patented by the English ironmaster Henry Cort in 1783–84 enabled the rolling or "milling" of iron and steel and so made way for a whole host of new materials applications, such as the design and building of iron ships.

Apart from the availability of improved materials and access to steam power and milling technology, it was also the design of specialized machine tools that enabled the eventual mass production of designed goods. Widely considered to be the founding father of machine-tool technology, Henry Maudslay first came to manufacturing as a child worker who by the age of twelve was working as a "powder monkey," filling cartridges with gunpowder at the Royal Arsenal in Woolwich. Later he gained valuable experience of casting processes and boring techniques while working at the Royal Arsenal's foundry. He also trained as a blacksmith and specialized in the execution of highly refined and complex forged metalwork. His reputation for high-quality metalworking was such that when Joseph Bramah set out to find a production method that would enable him to inexpensively manufacture his new "Challenge Lock" (patented in 1784), he called on Maudslay to design and make the machinery to mass-produce the unpickable tumbler locks. As a skilled machine builder, Maudslay later also helped Bramah successfully realize another of his inventions, the hydraulic press (patented in 1795), which was subsequently employed to mass-produce all kinds of goods using a stamping process.

Another specially designed machine that would help to increase manufacturers' production capabilities was the steam hammer, which was invented by James Nasmyth in 1839. Also contributing greatly to manufacturing capability were various other types of early machine tools that were designed and developed during this period of industrial progress, including lathes, milling machines, and planers—all of which were in use

↖
Cast-iron cooking pot design by Abraham Darby for Coalbrookdale Company, c. 1710.

←
Richard Trevithick's first passenger-carrying steam-powered road locomotive, 1801, known as the "Puffing Devil," and the predessor of his Coalbrookdale locomotive.

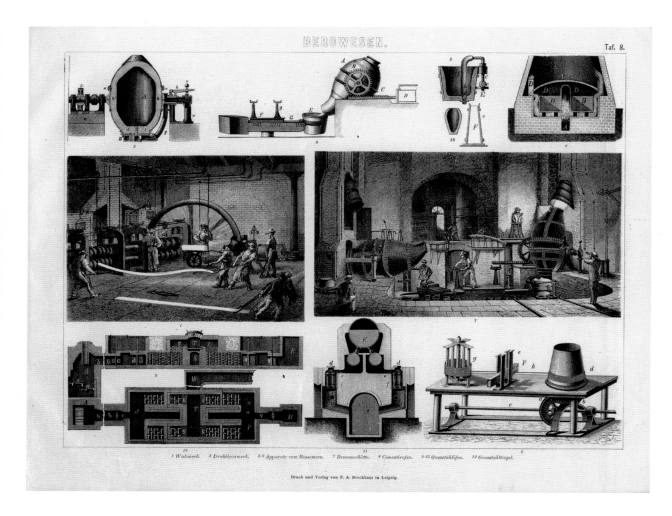

1 Walzwerk. 2 Drahtzieherwerk. 3–6 Apparate zum Bessemern. 7 Bessemerhütte. 8 Cementirofen. 9–11 Gussstahlöfen. 12 Gussstahltiegel.

Druck und Verlag von F. A. Brockhaus in Leipzig.

before 1840. The implementation of such precision machine tools eventually allowed industrialists to achieve a high degree of standardization in the production of their designs. And with this unprecedented level of consistency, the long-held manufacturing goal of interchangeability could finally be realized.

One of the greatest pioneers of accuracy and standardization in precision manufacturing was Joseph Whitworth, who honed his skills early in his career as a machinist working for Maudslay. A gifted mechanical engineer and designer, Whitworth became known as "the world's best mechanician" and was responsible for introducing an internationally recognized universal standard for screw threads in 1841.[6] He also designed various micrometers, some of which could measure to one millionth of an inch, which was a truly impressive feat considering that prior to this a skilled mechanic's work could only be expected to have an accuracy of one sixteenth of an inch. Having attained previously unimagined levels of measuring accuracy Whitworth went on to commercialize his technology by selling a wide range of measuring devices for workshops, and in so doing he aided the adoption of high-precision engineering techniques within the manufacturing industries.

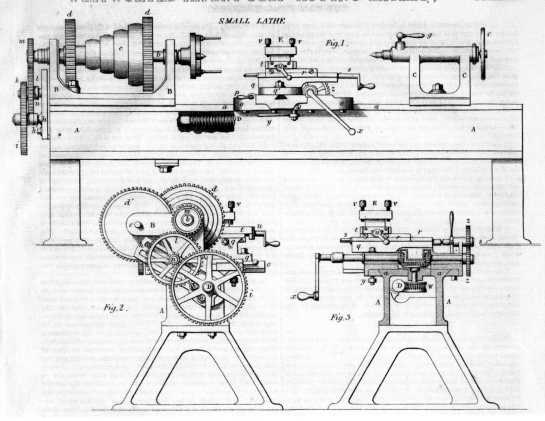

Engraving showing the Bessemer process for
steel milling, 1870s.

Self-acting lathes designed by Joseph
Whitworth, patented 1835.

Section showing the internal workings of an
unpickable tumbler lock designed by Joseph
Bramah, patented 1784.

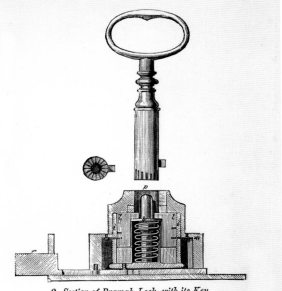

2. *Section of Bramah Lock, with its Key.*

The Portsmouth Block Mills

One of the very first instances of standardization being applied to the design of a mass-manufactured object occurred in the early 1800s. At that time, because of the Napoleonic Wars, the Royal Navy needed around 100,000 pulley blocks a year, and it sourced them from a variety of contractors who made them by hand. Because they were coming from numerous different suppliers, the quality of the blocks was often not as high as it should have been, and the reliability of the supply chain was hugely problematic. They were time-consuming to make individually, which meant the blocks were also relatively expensive to buy, especially given that at the time a typical ship needed around a thousand blocks of different sizes. While tasked with overseeing the redevelopment of Portsmouth Dockyard, the Inspector General of Naval Works, Brigadier-General Sir Samuel Bentham, introduced steam power and mechanized production techniques to shipbuilding. In 1802 he also implemented a patented system for block-making that employed a series of machines laid out in a production line. This addition to the dockyards' modernization program was devised by the British engineer Marc Isambard Brunel, father of the more famous engineer Isambard Kingdom Brunel.

At the newly built Portsmouth Block Mills—the first large-scale plant to employ machine tools for mass production—four separate machines were used to make the shell that formed the body of the pulley block. These were the boring machine, the mortising machine, the shaping engine, and the scoring machine. A further three specially engineered machines—the lignum vitae saw, the rounding saw, and the coaking machine—were used to make the sheave, which was the indented wheel around which the ropes ran smoothly. The first set of machinery was installed in January 1803

and was used to make medium-sized blocks. Following this, two more sets of machinery were introduced at the Portsmouth Block Mills for the manufacture of smaller and larger blocks, in January 1803 and March 1805, respectively. Although the standardized pulley blocks were essentially batch-produced rather than mass-produced because of the numerous different sizes of blocks that were required by the Royal Navy, the Block Mills were one of the earliest "manufactories" to initiate a revolutionary system of mechanized production that employed a production line. This innovative manufacturing structure meant that not only was productivity radically enhanced—with the mill able to produce up to 130,000 pulley blocks per annum in 1808—but also, for the first time, unskilled laborers rather than trained craftsmen could be employed to make the pulley blocks, thereby lowering employment costs significantly. Of outstanding interest in terms of industrial heritage, especially with regard to the development of design, the Portsmouth Block Mills demonstrated for the first time that machinery and its logical implementation could unequivocally make designs that were not only better in quality but also capable of being produced on a much larger scale and much more cheaply—a winning outcome not only for the Royal Navy but indeed for any canny manufacturer of goods interested in turning a larger profit.

↑
Engraving showing a scoring engine and rounding saw, which were part of the block-making machinery installed at the Portsmouth Block Mills between 1803 and 1805. The tools were manufactured by Henry Maudslay to the design of Marc Isambard Brunel.

↑
Standardized and machine-made ship's pulley blocks at the Portsmouth Block Mills.

↑
Image showing pulley blocks in use on an old ship.

Coalbrookdale and Wedgwood

Among the first manufacturers to pioneer the mass production of consumer goods, as opposed to designs for military use, was the Coalbrookdale foundry located near Telford. As one of the birthplaces of the Industrial Revolution, the foundry not only manufactured the first iron capable of being cast into cooking pots but also went on to produce a number of other industrial firsts. These included the first iron rails for railways, the first iron boat, and the first iron bridge, which, as any enthusiast of industrial heritage knows, was the nearby Iron Bridge designed by Thomas Pritchard to span the River Severn, erected between 1777 and 1779. By the early nineteenth century, the Coalbrookdale foundry had progressed from manufacturing utilitarian domestic wares to the mass production of much more ornate designs, such as finely detailed Neoclassical-style fireplace grates. Slightly later, during the Victorian period, facing increasingly stiff commercial competition, the factory began to specialize in the production of highly detailed decorative ironwork, most notably specially commissioned gates and statues. It even made the colossal entrance gates to the 1851 Great Exhibition, which brought the foundry greater international fame. During this period of rapid industrialization and consequent urbanization, the middle classes burgeoned and enjoyed newfound prosperity. In order to profit from this social change, Coalbrookdale significantly widened its product line to include more commercial and affordable designs, such as doorstops, firedogs, umbrella stands, tables, garden seats, planters, glasshouse frames, lampposts, fountains, flower stands, boot scrapers, and the like—all of which had a fashionable aesthetic that raised these objects from the functionally mundane. These were designs that

←
Queen's Ware (creamware) designed by Josiah Wedgwood and manufactured by Josiah Wedgwood & Sons, 1765.

↑
The Iron Bridge in Coalbrookdale, designed by Thomas Pritchard and erected between 1777 and 1779.

↑
George III Neoclassical cast-iron hob grate attributed to Coalbrookdale, c. 1790s.

could be mass-produced relatively cheaply and then sold throughout the country to the newly affluent homemaking middle classes.

Like Coalbrookdale, Wedgwood was another firm that would become inextricably linked to the Industrial Revolution and to the development of modern design. Acclaimed as the "father of English potters" and one of the great pioneers of industrialized manufacturing, Josiah Wedgwood established his first ceramics factory in Burslem (today Stoke-on-Trent) in 1759. It was there that he began to produce a new type of cream-glazed earthenware using simple Neoclassical forms. Less expensive and physically more robust than porcelain, Wedgwood's creamware could withstand sudden changes of temperature, which made it ideally suited to the new fashion for tea drinking. Perhaps even more important for its success, this practical yet attractive ceramic range was relatively easy to manufacture thanks to Wedgwood's adoption of clean lines and elegant shapes, which made it perfect for the molding

↑
Engraving of Etruria published by William MacKenzie, showing the expanded main Wedgwood factory opened in Stoke-on-Trent in 1769.

The Age of Reason and the Industrial Revolution

process. After Queen Charlotte, the wife of George III, ordered a creamware tea and coffee service, Josiah Wedgwood cleverly rebranded it as "Queen's Ware," and so many orders flowed in thanks to this royal patronage that Wedgwood was hard pressed to fulfill them. He found an especially ready market for his wares in the growing industrial towns, where tastes were more cosmopolitan and fashion-conscious. It was in these centers of trade and commerce that members of both the upper classes and the aspiring middle classes were especially keen "to distinguish themselves by exclusive and fashionable tastes of their own."[7]

To accommodate the growing demand for Queen's Ware and his other high-quality ceramic series, Wedgwood moved his potteries in 1764 to the larger Brick House Works in Burslem, whose canal-side location offered a safer and cheaper means of transport to market than packhorses or carts. Here he also instigated an innovative system of mass production that broke down the manufacture of a design into distinct stages, which would be undertaken by different workers specially trained for specific tasks. The logical division and specialization of labor were further enhanced by Wedgwood's rationalization of the production process, which included an assembly-line type of manufacturing system. By implementing such a revolutionary means of production, Wedgwood massively increased his factory's input-output efficiency and so extracted surplus value. His ambition did not stop at creating a better and more efficient way of making his goods but also encompassed a desire to find ever more customers for his wares. To this end, Wedgwood introduced new marketing techniques that involved selling his designs through catalogues and in elegant, fashionable showrooms. He also understood the commercial necessity of being constantly à la mode and was one of the very first manufacturers to have the cultural wherewithal to employ some of the period's best artists and craftsmen—most notably John Flaxman—to create designs for industrial production. The forefathers of today's professional designers, these early designers for industry were not only influential in swaying the aesthetic tastes of the time but were also instrumental in the development of a design-based

consumer economy. Wedgwood's dictum "everything gives way to experiment"[8] summed up the ethos of the Enlightenment and the related empiricist mindset, which set the Industrial Revolution on its forward-looking trajectory and was to guide the course of modern design.

↑
The Apotheosis of Homer Vase designed by John Flaxman for Josiah Wedgwood & Sons, 1786.

←
Engraving depicting Wedgwood & Byerley showroom, York Street, St. James's Square, London, published by R. Ackermann, 1809.

Biedermeier and Michael Thonet

O ne of Wedgwood's earliest clients was the designer Thomas Hope, who was a subscriber to the first edition of Wedgwood's Portland Vase, made c. 179–93. One of the great design reformers of the period, Thomas Hope had inherited sufficient money from his Dutch banking family to amass a vast collection of antiques—including ancient Roman statues, Egyptian sculptures, and Greek red-figure vases. Like other young dilettantes, as part of his studies Hope had undertaken an extensive Grand Tour that took in not only the cultural delights of Continental Europe, including Greece, but also, more unusually, Turkey and Egypt. In 1799 he purchased a house designed by Robert Adam on Duchess Street, just off London's fashionable Portland Place, and set about remodeling it with a series of stylistically themed interiors, which were intended as showcases for his various antiques collections. For these extravagant room-sets he created

specially designed furniture, lighting, and *objets*, which were modern interpretations of ideal classical typologies, such as the Greek klismos chair or the large double-handled krater vase, which was used to mix wine and water in ancient Greece. Hope published drawings of these idiosyncratic and strikingly inventive interiors and furnishing designs in his 1807 book, *Household Furniture and Interior Decoration*—the tome that first introduced into the English language the term "interior decoration." Hope's interiors were, like Adam's, most emphatically "designed," with an almost obsessive attention to harmonious proportion and exacting, historically correct detailing, with the resulting whole ultimately being greater than the sum of its individual parts.

The same sense of classicizing order was found in the simplified Neoclassical interiors that became so

←
Model 10 rocking chair designed by Michael Thonet for Gebrüder Thonet, 1866.

↑
Table designed by Thomas Hope, c. 1805, mahogany inlaid with ebony and silver and carved in relief.

↑
"Design of a Room in the Classic Style," plate from *Household Furniture and Interior Decoration* by Thomas Hope (1807).

fashionable in Austria, Prussia, and elsewhere in Central Europe between 1815 and 1848, a period bookended by the Vienna Congress—which marked the end of the Napoleonic Wars—and the year historically famous for the wave of politically charged revolutions across Europe that marked an upsurge of nationalism (most notably in France, Denmark, Germany, Italy, Austria, and Hungary, even spreading to parts of Latin America). This era was marked by increasing industrialization and urbanization, leading to the rise of an urban middle class that enthusiastically embraced the arts in its quest for upward mobility. Affluent members of society were interested in equipping themselves with the latest products, which would in turn give them status and identity, whether it was the fashionable clothes they wore or the household goods they purchased to furnish their newly built homes. The plain and simplified Neoclassical style they adopted would later be known in Austria and the region that would eventually become Germany as Biedermeier—a derogatory term coined in the late 1840s that came to symbolize the stolid reliability of the middle class, formed from the German word *bieder*, meaning honest, respectable, worthy,

and unadventurous, and *meier*, a common German surname, the Teutonic equivalent of Smith.[9] Despite its bourgeois pretensions, Biedermeier was an interesting decorative style in that it shared many of the attributes we tend to associate with the later Modern Movement: simplicity of construction, unadorned surfaces, and clean lines. Perhaps the most remarkable aspect of the Austro-German Biedermeier style was that it was the first design style to be embraced by the newly prosperous middle classes of the emerging industrial age, who wanted not only aesthetic refinement but also affordable practical utility.

One of the greatest proponents of this classical yet common-sense style, especially in Austria, was the

↑
Zimmerbild (chamber painting) by Leopold Zielcke, featuring a typical Biedermeier interior in Berlin, c. 1825, with fitted carpets, unified window and pier-mirror draperies, and framed engravings, all within a restrained classical style.

→
Beech and pine side chair attributed to the circle of Joseph Ulrich Danhauser, c. 1815–20.

The Age of Reason and the Industrial Revolution

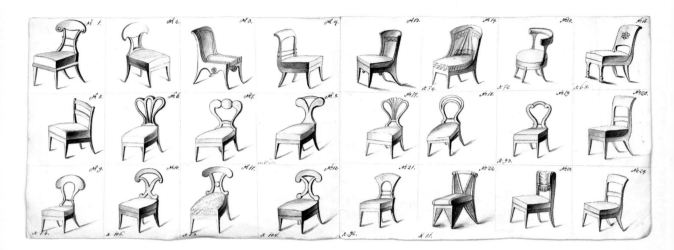

Danhauser Furniture Factory, founded in 1814 by the sculptor Josef Ulrich Danhauser. The company was Vienna's first major furniture-manufacturing business and, as such, strongly influenced the direction of fashionable taste and contemporary design, especially after, as noted at the MAK (the Austrian Museum of Applied Arts), the founder's son Josef Franz Danhauser mounted "an unprecedented, trend-setting advertising campaign featuring a series of interiors . . . reproduced as steel engravings and distributed as a [magazine] supplement."[10] The younger Danhauser became the first to succeed in presenting entire ensembles of furniture to a broad public in an aesthetically sophisticated way, thereby optimally marketing his range of products.

What an astounding range of products it was, with many of the Biedermeier furniture pieces produced by the firm displaying a pared-down, almost sparse proto-modernity. The radical simplification of form adopted by the Danhauser company not only coincided with consumers' desire for relatively plain Neoclassical shapes but also helped to ensure that construction of the furniture pieces was comparatively straightforward and could therefore employ a certain degree of mechanization. Their designs harmoniously combined functional utility with an abstracted, elemental aesthetic that was extremely forward-looking, and, as such, prefigured the language of form espoused by the Modern Movement.

Another furniture manufacturer whose work presaged the advent of truly modern design was Michael Thonet, who took the Biedermeier style's simplification of form and construction to an even greater reductivist level. Around 1830, he began experimenting in his workshop in Boppard am Rhein with laminated wood, using thin veneers that were glued together, placed into molds, and then cured into the required forms. Using this inventive production method, Thonet manufactured a number of innovative bentwood Biedermeier-style chairs. These highly original designs came to the attention of the Austrian Chancellor Prince Metternich, who subsequently invited Thonet to Vienna, where he was granted a patent for his new furniture-making process in 1842. The only problem was that although the laminating process allowed Thonet to produce furniture that was not only lightweight but also elegantly formed, with graceful looping constructions, it was relatively time-

↑
Danhauser Furniture Factory catalogue, showing different chair models designed by Joseph Ulrich Danhauser, 1814–29.

→
Model No. 14 cafe chair designed by Michael Thonet, introduced in 1859.

Early photograph showing the mass-
manufacture of bentwood chairs at the
Gebrüder Thonet factory, c. 1900.

The Age of Reason and the Industrial Revolution

consuming and laborious. After securing the necessary financial backing, Thonet established a furniture workshop with his sons in the suburbs of Vienna in 1849. For the next two years, he concentrated on developing improved manufacturing techniques that would facilitate the mass production of furniture, including the steam-bending of solid wood. Thonet perfected an inventive method of shaping wood using heat and pressure, and in 1851, he exhibited his groundbreaking furniture designs at the Great Exhibition in London, where they were awarded a gold medal.

Michael Thonet's classic cafe chair, the Model No. 14, with its double-looped back, was essentially a Biedermeier form that was stripped of all superfluous ornamentation. Every element of its steam-bent frame and its caned or molded plywood seat was essential for its function: no more, no less. By reducing the chair into the most elemental components, Thonet significantly drove down both the material and the labor costs of its construction, thereby making the pared-down design utterly suited to high-volume production. Sold at very competitive prices, his mass-produced, lightweight yet strong designs heralded a new economic democracy in design—for the first time high-end, cutting-edge furniture was really affordable to the masses, with the firm's Model No. 14 chair costing less than a bottle of wine in 1860. Thonet's ingenious reduction of elements and elimination of extraneous ornament also meant that his designs were eminently suited for export, as they could be space-efficiently boxed in their unassembled state and then simply reassembled with a few turns of a screwdriver once they had reached their destination.

To give an idea of the Model No. 14 chair's exportability, in their unassembled state thirty-six chairs could be transported in a container measuring just one cubic meter in volume. Thanks to their structural resilience, these chairs were suitable not only for domestic use but also in hotels, restaurants, cafes, and bars. By 1891, a staggering 7.3 million Model No. 14 chairs had been sold, a quantity that even by today's standards is impressive. Thonet's humble cafe chair, with its six pieces and ten screws, above

all else demonstrated that the more elemental the construction, the easier and cheaper an object would be to make, and therefore the more suited it would be to industrialized methods of production. That meant selling more and earning more, a point that was not lost on the next generation of would-be design entrepreneurs.

As the first chair designed specifically for high-volume mass production, the ubiquitous yet timeless Model No. 14 holds a special place within the story of design. It introduced so much in terms of design practice and embodied a new kind of rational thinking that was predicated on the idea of a factory system. As the renowned industrial historian Paul Mantoux so insightfully noted in 1928, as modernism was crystallizing into a cohesive design movement: "The object of all industry is the production of goods, or to be more explicit, articles of consumption which are not directly provided by nature. By 'factory system' we therefore primarily mean a particular organization, a particular system of production. But this organization affects the whole economic system and consequently the whole social system, which is controlled by the growth and distribution of wealth."[11] With its elemental construction, Thonet's Model No. 14 chair was one of the very first designs to demonstrate how this new factory system could be successfully exploited for commercial gain. While this radically new way of making products facilitated the provision of affordable design to the masses, it also had the potential for bringing untold wealth to those manufacturers smart enough to understand that industrialized production methods called for a new kind of design thinking whereby products were, above all else, conceived from a rational standpoint.

4

ARMORY PRACTICE AND A NEW SYSTEM OF RATIONALIZED PRODUCTION

Eli Whitney, standardization, and interchangeability

Armory practice and a new system of rationalized production

Though Britain had been the birthplace of the Industrial Revolution in the mid-eighteenth century, America would soon catch up and become its spiritual home. One of the first great inventions of the American Industrial Revolution was Eli Whitney's ingenious cotton gin, patented in 1794. This simple mangle-like machine, which incorporated a toothed cylinder that was turned by hand, made possible the quick separation of cotton seeds from soft cotton fiber, thereby reducing processing time and revolutionizing the cotton industry in the United States. After this foray into the design of a labor-saving machine, Whitney focused his attention on the mass-manufacture of small arms as the US government, fearing an eruption of hostilities with France, was at the time attempting to procure 40,000 muskets from private contractors. At this stage, guns were still made individually and almost entirely by hand, so that each differed slightly from the next, which meant that when a part wore out or broke its replacement required customization by hand in order to make it fit.

After coming up with the idea of mechanizing the production of muskets, Whitney approached the US government for a contract in May 1798, writing to the Secretary of the Treasury, Oliver Wolcott: "I am persuaded that Machinery moved by water adapted to this Business would greatly diminish the labor and facilitate the Manufacture of the Article. Machines for forging, rolling, floating [a kind of filing], boreing, Grinding, Polishing, etc. may all be made use of to advantage."[1] This letter outlining Whitney's concept of industrialized manufacture did the trick, and a government contract was secured the following month to produce 10,000 muskets within a period of twenty-eight months. Later that same year, Whitney acquired a suitable site in Hamden, Connecticut, on which to build a new state-of-the-art armory. He selected a riverside location so that water-power could be harnessed to run the necessary machinery for producing—in theory—such a large quantity of guns. He built his armory on the banks of the Mill River, and also constructed an adjacent village to house his workers, which became known as Whitneyville. In an attempt to fulfill such a large order of arms, Whitney not only built a dam and installed water wheels but also ingeniously developed specially designed water-powered machinery that could be operated by unskilled workmen, and that broke down the muskets' manufacture into separate constituent parts. This meant that a given workman made only a particular section of the gun, and these individual elements were made to conform precisely to the measurements of a standard model. This novel approach to manufacturing allowed the production of musket components that were more or less interchangeable—any part would fit any gun. While this kind of standardization, allowing a degree of interchangeability, had been used previously to make weapons in ancient China and during the Roman period, Whitney was the first to employ it within the context of industrial mechanization. This type of precise replication, pioneered by Whitney in America, meant that time and money were saved both within the still relatively complex production process, with fewer workers able to make more weapons, and on the battlefield, because if a musket part broke it could quickly be replaced and the weapon made usable again. In January 1801 Whitney demonstrated his guns' interchangeability to President John Adams and President-elect Thomas Jefferson by fitting ten different locking mechanisms to the same single musket using only a simple screwdriver. Jefferson immediately

Engraving of Eli Whitney's Cotton Gin, patent applied for in 1794 and approved in 1807.

Previous page: Unidentified soldier in Union Army uniform with three Remington revolvers, two Bowie knives, and a Springfield rifle musket.

Eli Whitney, standardization, and interchangeability

grasped the military benefit afforded by Whitney's new production methods and afterward gave him the necessary time and money to construct more specialized machines and so speed up musket production.

As Whitney had explained to Wolcott before embarking on this manufacturing adventure, one of his primary aims was "to form the tools so the tools themselves shall fashion the work and give to every part its just proportion—which when once accomplished, will give expedition, uniformity, and exactness to the whole. . . In short, the tools which I contemplate to make are similar to an engraving on copper plate from which may be taken a great number of impressions perceptibly alike."[2] Although Whitney did devise new precision machines that made possible an impressive degree of standardized serial-production, his musket parts were never quite as interchangeable as he had hoped: each locking component bore a special identifying mark, which would have been unnecessary if the parts had been truly interchangeable.[3] Despite this shortcoming, however, Whitney's contribution to the story of design has become legendary, for he conceptualized a new system of manufacturing that would eventually allow an unskilled worker to turn out a product of just as high quality as one made by a skilled craftsmen. Whitney was dogged by unforeseen obstacles, such as epidemics and delays in the supply of raw materials, and it took him more than ten years— four times longer than initially anticipated—to fulfill his original government order of 10,000 muskets. But his mechanized and rationalized manufacturing model would eventually be widely adopted by other manufacturers and applied to the design and production of all kinds of consumer goods, both at home and abroad.

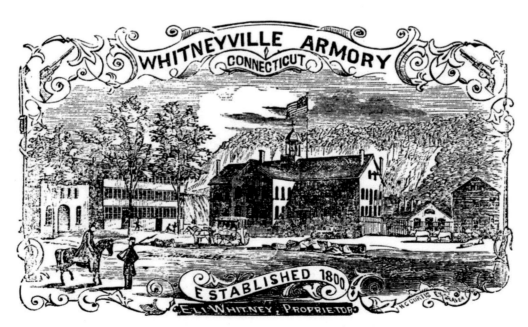

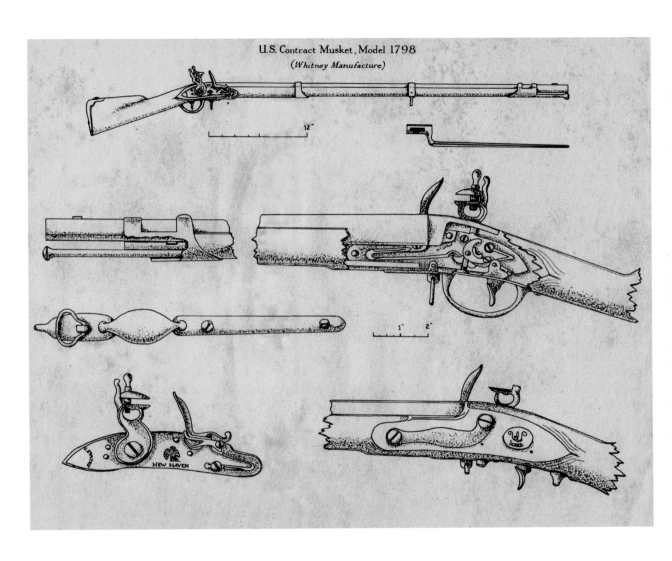

U.S. Contract Musket, Model 1798
(*Whitney Manufacture*)

12"

1" 2"

NEW HAVEN

←
Advertisement for Whitney's Improved
Fire-Arms, c. 1862, showing Whitneyville
Armory in Connecticut.

↑
Drawing of the Whitney Government
Contract Musket, 1798.

The Springfield Armory and the American Civil War

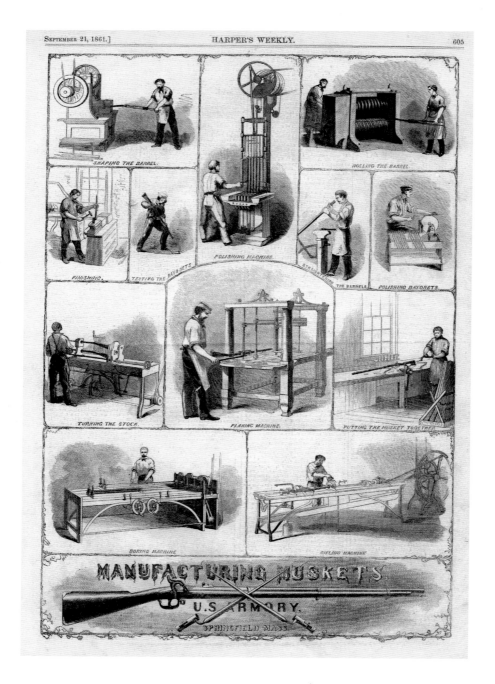

While working at the Springfield Armory in Springfield, Massachusetts, the inventor Thomas Blanchard followed Whitney's pioneering lead to develop two revolutionary machine tools that advanced standardization and interchangeability for arms production even further. His first machine, designed in 1818 and patented the following year, was a "copying" lathe that allowed multiple gunstocks to be produced at the same time, each of which ingeniously replicated the exact turned contours of a standardized model. Blanchard's famous lathe not only enabled the production of standardized rifle stocks, which had precise measurement tolerances, but also significantly sped up the production process, thereby allowing large-scale mass manufacture. The second labor-saving tooling machine that Blanchard developed at the Springfield Armory entered service in 1822. It was another innovative type of lathe that turned rifle barrels and ingeniously changed to a vibrating motion to create the distinctive, finished octagonal shape of the barrel. Blanchard's inventions streamlined the production process to such an extent that mechanized mass-manufacture of any standardized products soon became known as "armory practice."

The adoption of such production methods in the more industrialized economy of the northern states was a major contributing factor to the victory of the Union forces in the American Civil War of 1861–65, because it gave them the advantage of a more plentiful and reliable supply of arms and munitions. While this adoption of rational design principles and production processes won the day on the blood-soaked battlefields, it also heralded a dark new chapter in human history, as the American Civil War became the world's first industrialized war. The wholesale manufacture of efficiently designed arms led tragically to the wholesale slaughter of soldiers—a phenomenon that would be repeated all too often in the century to come, when the power of design was harnessed, it seemed at times, as much for mindless destruction as for mindful construction.

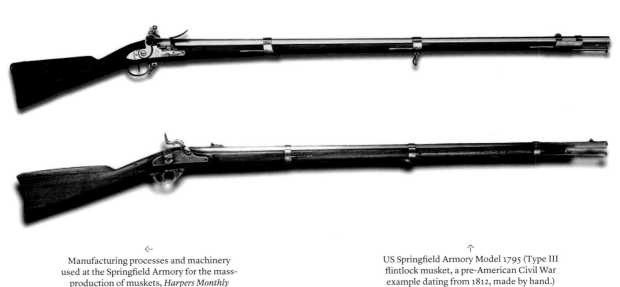

←
Manufacturing processes and machinery used at the Springfield Armory for the mass-production of muskets, *Harpers Monthly Magazine*, September 1861.

↑
US Springfield Armory Model 1795 (Type III flintlock musket, a pre-American Civil War example dating from 1812, made by hand.)

↑
US Springfield Armory Model 1861 rifled musket, dating from 1862, made by machine.

Samuel Colt and the art of marketing

COLONEL COLT.

Inspired by Eli Whitney's manufacturing techniques, Samuel Colt went on to become one of the great American pioneers of mass production and mass marketing, and the most successful patent arms maker of the mid-nineteenth century. As a young seaman bound for Calcutta on a brig called the *Corvo*, Colt had whittled a wooden model of what would later become the most famous handgun ever designed. It took him several more years to develop his idea into a practicable design. His revolutionary repeating firearm, which featured a cartridge cylinder that revolved when the hammer was cocked, was also the first handgun to boast a workable percussion action.[4] He patented this handgun design in Britain in 1835 and the following year received two American patents also relating to its design. That same year, he established the Patent Arms Manufacturing Company in Paterson, New Jersey, in order to produce it. Colt subsequently designed three types of revolver—pocket, belt, and holster models—as well as two rifles. However, he received insufficient orders and his factory closed in 1842, only to reopen five years later when the US government ordered 1,000 revolvers for use in the Mexican War. The contract stated that the revolvers' lock work was "to be made of the best cast or double sheet steel and the parts sufficiently uniform to be interchanged with slight or no refitting."[5] Having neither the time nor the capital to produce these weapons, Samuel Colt subcontracted the order to Eli Whitney's son, Eli Whitney, Jr., on the understanding that he would retain ownership of any specialized machinery needed for the manufacture of his weapons. Crucially for the success of this joint-manufacturing venture, Thomas Warner, who had previously been a master armorer at the Springfield Armory and is generally credited with making the

production of interchangeable parts possible there, oversaw the production of Colt's arms at Whitney's riverside facility. Although systems of mechanized production had been first realized and then expanded at this site, they had not reached the high precision level of the systems that were now in place at the Springfield Armory, and as such a degree of hand labor was still being used in the production of Colt's guns. It was during this period that Colt became convinced that an increased level of mechanization in arms production was the only way to enhance quality and achieve greater uniformity: around half of the Colt guns produced at the Whitney armory failed government standards of interchangeability and were therefore rejected.

The experience of this first government contract taught Colt a very interesting commercial lesson: that he could sell the substandard guns rejected by the War Department to the general public for more money than the government was prepared to pay for first-class ones. In 1848 Colt's machinery and tools were moved from Whitney's factory to an empty textile mill in Hartford, Connecticut. Over the next eight years, this new facility produced Colt revolvers as well as the necessary machine tools for two new Colt armories—one opened in London in 1851, and the other in Hartford. Operational by 1855, this latter facility was equipped with state-of-the-art manufacturing equipment and went on to become the world's largest privately owned armory. Building on Eli Whitney's example, Colt lost no time in developing an increasingly efficient, modern production line to create standardized and interchangeable components, such that within a very short time around 80 percent of the parts produced were made by machine. Colt reputedly declared that "there is nothing that can't be produced by

← Engraved portrait of Samuel Colt holding an early version of his repeating revolver, 1856.

Armory practice and a new system of rationalized production

← Albumen print of a Colt employee demonstrating how to work the barrel rifling machine, c. 1864. This machine was designed by the machinist and inventor Elisha King Root, who was superintendent of the Colt factory from 1849 and built nearly 400 machines to produce interchangeable gun parts. A genius machinist, Root was president the Colt company from 1862 to 1865.

↑ Early photograph of Colt assembly-line workers in the Colt's armory, with machinery being used throughout the workshop, c. 1910.

→ A turret lathe used as part of Colt's firearms manufacturing process, c. 1864.

machine,"[6] and his pioneering advancement of mechanized production methods enabled him to fabricate a remarkable 150 weapons each day by 1856. His revolvers were widely used during the American Civil War, and by the time of his death in 1862, Colt's armories had manufactured over 400,000 firearms.

Colt's success, however, had as much to do with his extraordinary ability to promote his products to potential consumers as with his adoption of rational methods of mechanized production. Having started his career as a traveling entertainer called "Dr. Coult," who regaled his paying audience with chemistry experiments and laughing gas, Colt was an adept showman who well knew the power of self-publicity. After being awarded the honorary title of colonel by the governor of the State of Connecticut for his political support, he styled himself Colonel Sam Colt and had his firearms engraved with "Col. Sam Colt, New York, U.S. America." He also ran early print advertisements and even topped his facility in Hartford with a distinctive onion-shaped dome on which a cast-bronze colt reared heavenward, so that any visitor to Hartford couldn't help but see it and ask about it, and would then hear the success story of Hartford's greatest entrepreneur. As the Colt company history notes, Samuel Colt "was one of the earliest American manufacturers to realize fully the potential of an effective marketing program that included sales promotion, publicity, product

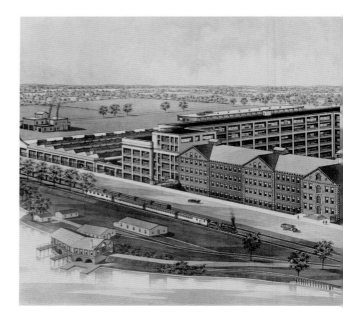

sampling, advertising, and public relations,"[7] and to this extent he helped to alter significantly the course of modern industrial design toward a much more commercial modus operandi. While Sam Colt became famous for perfecting the design, manufacture, and marketing of firearms, it was also his legendary blunt Yankee showmanship that captured the imaginations of other potential design entrepreneurs keen to replicate his success.

←
Colt .45 revolver designed in 1873 (Colt Single Action Army Revolver).

↑
A early print showing the entire Colt complex in Hartford, Connecticut, including the armory, office building, water towers, various other buildings, and the famous onion dome topped with a rearing horse.

→
Colt advertisement showing Uncle Sam pointing out the benefits of Colt's forearms, 1908.

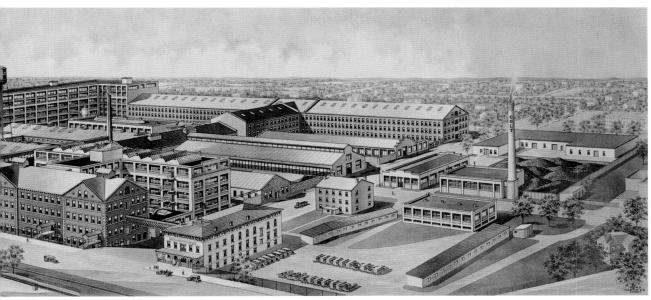

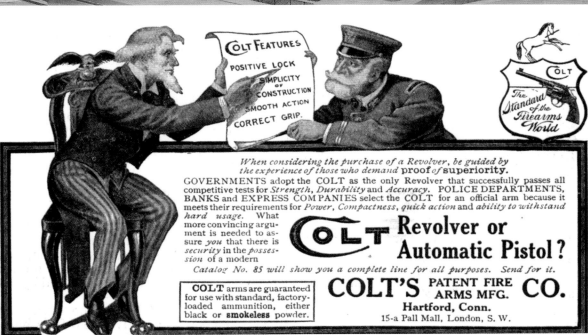

The American system,
from sewing machines to bicycles

In 1831 the aristocratic French chronicler Alexis de Tocqueville undertook a nine-month fact-finding mission to the United States and later wrote up his observations in his book entitled *Democracy in America* (1835). "The American lives in a land of wonders," Tocqueville declared, "in which everything seems to be in constant flux, and every change seems to mark an advance. Hence the idea of the new is coupled in his mind with the idea of the better. Nowhere does he perceive the limits that nature may have imposed on man's efforts. In his eyes, that which does not exist is that which has not yet been attempted."[8] This can-do self-belief and desire for improvement in the United States, as well as the country's increasing adoption of mechanized production systems during this period, can be seen as a direct result of a program initiated by the Kentucky politician Henry Clay in his 1824 tariff scheme to protect American industry. This federal law, which increased import duties, was intended to promote manufacturing independence from Europe in order to defend America's hard-won political autonomy.

The emphasis on manufacturing self-sufficiency considerably bolstered the idea of design innovation, which in turn necessitated the passing of the Patent Act of 1836 in order to protect inventions from infringements. Crucially, the law established the principle of a search to establish that no previous claim had been made before a patent was granted. Prior to this, two inventors could receive patents for the same invention, then have to fight out their intellectual-property claims in the civil courts, which was both financially risky and time-consuming. This important new piece of legislation made the authorship and thereby the ownership of intellectual property far easier to determine and protect and in practice ensured that

original designs were far more difficult for "copyists" to imitate. Consequently, the law made design innovation potentially far more lucrative and had the indirect effect of stimulating an increasing amount of design research and development. It is not particularly surprising that after the passing of the Patent Act of 1836 the number of patent applications filed in America increased dramatically—in 1836, only 702 'utility' patents had been granted in the US, while twenty years later, in 1856, that number had risen to 2,315 'utility' patents and a further 107 for 'design' patents, a more than threefold increase. Importantly for design and manufacturing, this new patent law meant that it was now worth making more of a long-term investment in research and development, since financial rewards resulting from design innovation would be far better protected.

The rapid industrialization of the United States that occurred during the nineteenth century, especially after the Civil War, was boosted by the new patent law but it was also the result of many manufacturers adopting "armory practice" in order to mass-produce a whole range of peacetime consumer items, from textiles and sewing machines to clocks and bicycles. Because of the pioneering production efforts of the small-arms manufacturers clustered around Hartford, Connecticut, and Springfield, Massachusetts, the northeastern states

$\rightarrow$
"Bicycle Room" at the Weed Sewing Machine Company, *Scientific American*, March 1880.

Armory practice and a new system of rationalized production

SCIENTIFIC AMERICAN

[Entered at the Post Office of New York. N. Y., as Second Class Matter.]

A WEEKLY JOURNAL OF PRACTICAL INFORMATION, ART, SCIENCE, MECHANICS, CHEMISTRY AND MANUFACTURES.

Vol. XLII.—No. 12.
[NEW SERIES.]

NEW YORK, MARCH 20, 1880.

$3.20 per Annum.
[POSTAGE PREPAID.]

THE MANUFACTURE OF SEWING MACHINES AND BICYCLES.—THE WEED SEWING MACHINE FACTORY.—[See page 181.]

had a plentiful supply of highly skilled machinists who could conceive and build precision manufacturing tools that increased the production rate of consumer goods. With such a concentration of manufacturing know-how and expertise, the armories' hometowns were to become major industrial hubs. As the English engineer Sir Joseph Whitworth noted in a government-commissioned special report on the Exhibition of the Industry of All Nations in New York (1853–54), Americans "call in the aid of machinery in almost every department of industry. Wherever it can be introduced as a substitute of manual labor, it is universally and willingly resorted to."[9]

Having started out in professional design practice as a machinist, Isaac Merritt Singer was one of the first American entrepreneurs to adopt mechanized production techniques comprehensively for the making of consumer goods—in this case his famous treadle-operated sewing machine. After patenting this revolutionary design in 1851, Singer established I. M. Singer & Co. (which would later become the Singer Manufacturing Company) to mass-produce the machine, which was sold around the world from 1855 onward. During this period, Singer employed a large pool of workers to hand-finish his designs. But in 1863, in order to keep up with growing demand, he began to substantially increase the use of specially designed machinery within his factory, and also to implement a more rationalized production system based on armory-practice techniques. By the early 1880s, the use of automatic and semiautomatic machinery at his plant was so widespread that Singer was finally able to perfect the production of fully interchangeable sewing machine parts. By adopting rational, mechanized production methods and canny marketing techniques, such as pioneering the use of installment-credit plans, Singer grew his company into the world's largest producer of sewing machines, thereby demonstrating the winning commercial formula of marrying design innovation with manufacturing and marketing ingenuity.

E. Remington & Sons also used armory practice to successfully mass-produce another groundbreaking consumer product: the first commercial typewriter. Founded by Eliphalet Remington in 1816 to produce

his famously accurate flintlock rifle, the company later expanded and, in 1828, opened a large factory alongside the Erie Canal. There, Remington and his son Philo pioneered numerous innovations in arms manufacturing, including a lathe for fashioning gunstocks and the reflection method, which was successfully used to straighten barrels. They also developed the first practical, cast-steel, drilled rifle barrel and, in 1847, supplied the US Navy with its first breech-loading rifle. Unsurprisingly for a successful pioneer of large-scale production within the arms industry, the firm eventually began looking to diversify into other areas of manufacture. To this end, in 1873 the Remington factory produced the world's first

commercial typewriter, the Remington No. 1, which was designed by Christopher Latham Sholes and introduced the QWERTY keyboard layout that is still in use today. This machine set the design benchmark for all subsequent typewriters, and many of its features remained essentially unchanged for nearly a century: the cylinder, which featured line-spacing and carriage-return mechanisms; the mechanism that moved the carriage along between each letter; the actuation of the type bars through the use of key levers and wires; and the use of inked ribbon for printing. During the 1870s, the company also began mass-producing sewing machines, showing that technology from the arms industry was now frequently and successfully

↖
Original Singer sewing machine, model patented 1851.

↑
A "classic" Singer Model 99 sewing machine, introduced in 1911, a refined evolution of Singer's earlier design.

←
Lithographic advertisement for Singer sewing machines, showing people of different nationalities using treadle machines, c. 1892.

being transferred to the general production of consumer goods, and that the application of rational manufacturing procedures could enable companies not only to grow exponentially but also to diversify their product lines and so find new markets.

Another American firm that achieved impressive production rates in the late nineteenth century thanks to its adoption of armory practice was the Pope Manufacturing Company, the first bicycle producer in the United States. The firm's first Columbia-brand bicycle was a high-wheeler based on an existing English penny-farthing model, and its manufacture commenced in 1878 in a corner of the Weed Sewing Machine Company factory in Hartford, Connecticut. However, the company's founder, Albert Pope, was determined that, unlike English bicycles, his model would be designed using interchangeable and machine-made parts in order to speed up production and lower unit costs. Critical to Pope's success was the fact that the Weed factory had previously been owned by the Sharps Rifle Company and was still used to produce small arms. Its workers were consequently well versed in the techniques of armory practice. The Pope Manufacturing Company soon introduced its Standard Columbia bicycle, a model that was stripped to its functional bones and available in four different wheel sizes. That same year, the company innovatively established an agency-based retailing model and a uniform pricing system. By 1880 the venture was producing an impressive five hundred bicycles a month, and that year the "Bicycle Room" at the Weed Sewing Machine Company was featured in the journal *Scientific American* because of the groundbreaking techniques for large-scale mass-production practiced there, including rigorous testing for quality control. The technology historian David Hounshell noted:

> Many of the machine tools familiar to New England armories were used at the Weed company for its sewing machine parts and for the Pope bicycle–milling machines, turret lathes, screw machines, grinding machines, drilling and boring machines... It is doubtful whether the Weed company initially built or bought any special-purpose machine tools

for machining bicycle parts; set up differently with special fixtures and cutting tools, the machinery used for sewing machine manufacture fulfilled the requirements for production of the high-wheel bicycle.[10]

In 1881 another article appeared, this one in *Bicycling World*.[11] Entitled "A Great American Manufacture," it too described and illustrated the different stages in the rational, mechanized production of Pope's bicycles. By implementing such a system, the Pope company grew quickly and was eventually able to buy out the Weed company and expand its operations into the whole facility. The Pope Manufacturing Company's great legacy is that it was one of the first businesses in America to apply the principles of armory practice to the making of commercial products other than non-military firearms. Its adherence to testing, quality control, and continuous design improvement also made Columbia not only America's first notable bicycle brand but also, like Singer and Remington, a thoroughly trusted brand name over the succeeding decades.

The mid-to-late nineteenth century also saw the mass production and mass marketing of other landmark American inventions, notably Cyrus McCormick's mechanical reaper (patented 1834), Thomas Edison's electric lightbulb (1879), and George Eastman's first Kodak box camera (1888). As the design historian and critic Sigfried Giedion would later note about the American Industrial Revolution: "Everyone invented, whoever owned an enterprise sought ways and means to make his goods more speedily, more perfectly, and often of improved beauty. Anonymously and inconspicuously the old

tools were transformed into modern instruments."[12] These wondrous new inventions changed millions of people's daily patterns of life and, at the same time, presaged a new modern age in which America would be the envy of the world. During this same period, the design of "advanced" communications and electrical systems, such as Samuel Morse's telegraph (1837), Alexander Graham Bell's telephone (1876), and George Westinghouse's electrical transformer (c. 1886), also had a huge impact on the forging of a shared cultural identity, by stitching the cities and towns of this huge country together for the first time.

↖ Remington typewriter Model 1, 1874. This was the first commercially successful writing machine and was designed by Christopher Latham Sholes, Carlos Glidden, and Samuel Soule, 1866–73. Using the QWERTY keyboard, this revolutionary design began to be produced in quantity by the Remington company in 1874.

↑ Illustration from a Pope Manufacturing Company catalogue showing a Standard Columbia higher-wheeler bicycle, 1881.

← Remington promotional photograph featuring "Miss Remington" with a Model No. 10 Remington typewriter, 1908.

These new technological developments fostered a greater sense of national unification and thereby a better awareness of national identity, and with this came a forward-looking confidence: surely there were no problems that could not be surmounted with a little bit of that famous Yankee design ingenuity.

The Industrial Revolution had truly made America a land of entrepreneurial opportunity, where innovative design and rationalized manufacturing could be put to commercial use to make previously undreamed-of glittering fortunes. The transformative power of design was now being used for commercial rather than military ends, and what had previously been known as armory practice was now known throughout the world as "the American system of manufacturing."

↑
Mechanical reaper and twine binder designed
by Cyrus McCormick, this example 1884.

↑
The Kodak Brownie camera was introduced by
George Eastman in 1900 and sold for $1 (the
example shown is a Model No. 2).

→
Alexander Graham Bell demonstrating his
newly invented telephone in New York City by
calling Chicago, 1892.

Armory practice and a new system of rationalized production

5

THE NEW INDUSTRIAL AGE AND THE GREAT EXHIBITION

An exhibition of all nations

← Previous page: Plate from *Dickinson's Comprehensive Pictures of the Great Exhibition* showing a throng waiting for Queen Victoria's arrival at the Crystal Palace. Elm trees were incorporated into the structure, along with sparrows and sparrow hawks.

↑ Print published by Le Blond showing Queen Victoria arriving to open the Great Exhibition, May 1, 1851, surrounded by emblems of the British Empire.

By the mid-nineteenth century the Western world had been utterly transformed. Not even a century had passed since James Hargreaves's spinning jenny had emerged as the harbinger of so much industrial progress, yet during the intervening period society had witnessed upheaval on an unprecedented scale. The Industrial Revolution's grasping tentacles now spread across Britain into Europe, America, and beyond. Mass urbanization saw countless hordes uprooted from the countryside to find work in the increasingly overcrowded cities; railways now stretched across the land, linking manufacturers to ever-growing markets and factories; and mills spewed dense coal smoke into the smoggy atmosphere and disgorged putrid polluted water into the rivers. Industrial progress had come, but at a price, and the resulting social ills often seemed to outweigh the social benefits that it brought.

The Industrial Revolution made the rich richer and the poor poorer. Among the biggest winners in this game of progress was an entirely new breed of men, the industrialists who had the financial means and entrepreneurial acumen to embrace the vast wealth-generating power of the machine and then control it for their own gain. Apart from these factory kingpins, it was arguably the emerging middle classes that collectively benefited the most from this inexorable change. Aspirational, self-reliant, well educated, and newly affluent, the middle classes found prosperity in the growing cities through mercantile endeavor or civil service, or by being engaged in a profession, such as medicine or law. Increasingly, this new consumer class formed the primary market for the plethora of affordable, industrially produced goods that were being sold enticingly either through mail-order catalogues or in the fashionable department stores that every city now boasted. As home ownership increased, the middle classes bought ever more of the furnishings and domestic wares they needed to fill their personal "castles," yet often the design of these goods left a lot to be desired in terms of both quality and taste.

Somewhere in this heady leap forward into a more industrialized and commercial world, a growing number of social reformers began to question the role of design in society. Surely, they suggested, design could be used to benefit society through the provision of higher-quality wares that would offer better value for money than the shoddy goods being churned out by manufacturers hoping to make a quick profit. At this time, however, most manufacturers viewed design—that is, conception and planning—as just one of the many interrelated aspects of mechanized production and, in the worst cases, almost as an afterthought. Because of this, technical specialists or experts in materials or production methods most often undertook the design of objects instead of professional industrial designers, meaning that design practice at this stage had little, if any, theoretical or philosophical foundation.

Among the great early reformers in this field was Henry Cole, one of the first industrial designers to put theory into practice. Working under the pseudonym Felix Summerly, Cole was awarded a silver medal in an 1846 Society of Arts competition for the design of a white-glazed tea service, notable for its simplicity of form, that was subsequently issued by the Minton Ceramics Manufacturing Company. This success led him to believe that if well-known fine artists could be persuaded to design articles for everyday use, it would help to "promote public taste," by which he meant elevate "good taste" among the masses. In 1965, Cole established Summerly's Art Manufactures, and, as a later article in *Graphic* magazine explained, "he began a series of 'Art Manufactures' with a view to improving the artistic qualities of our industries, an attempt to educate the British workman in art principles, so that he might compete with the foreigners, not only in the workmanship, but the beauty of their work."[1] This design-led enterprise went on to commission a number of accomplished painters and sculptors, notably John Bell, Daniel Maclise, and Richard Redgrave, to create functional wares and Parian figurines specifically for industrialized production. Although the short-lived venture operated for only around five years, it helped to establish the concept of art manufactures and was highly influential in the cause of design reform. Between 1847 and 1849, Cole also organized annual Royal Society of Art exhibitions, again in the attempt to promote art manufactures, and in 1851 he became its chairman.

As part of his design-reform mission, in 1849 Cole also founded the *Journal of Design (and Manufactures)*, edited by Redgrave. In an early issue, Cole wrote:

Design has a twofold relation, having in the first place, a strict reference to utility in the thing designed; and, secondarily, to the beautifying or

The new industrial age and the Great Exhibition

ornamenting that utility. The word *design*, however, with the many has become identified rather with its secondary than its whole signification—with ornament, as apart from, and often as opposed to, utility. From thus confounding that which is in itself but an addition, with that which is essential, has arisen many of those great errors in *taste* which are observable in the works of modern designers.[2]

As Cole correctly identified, the problem was that many manufacturers saw design as the decoration of an object, rather than as an integral part of its conception, planning, and realization. Because of this widely held misconception, design as mere ornamental pattern-making often got in the way of an object's intended function. Another major problem was that surface decoration was frequently used to disguise inferior workmanship or hide poor-quality materials. Quite simply, materials and energy were being squandered when they could have been used instead to create simpler yet better-designed and higher-quality products, in which value was invested in the integrity of the object itself rather than on superfluous surface treatment.

Around this time, Cole and his fellow members of the Royal Society of Art came up with the idea of holding a large international exhibition in London that would not only celebrate the industrial supremacy and prosperity of the British Empire but would also be an instructive exercise for manufacturers and the public alike. This type of exhibition did have a precedent, the successful Exposition Nationale held in Paris in 1844. But Cole et al envisioned something far more ambitious culturally and with an expansive international scope. Queen Victoria's consort, Prince Albert, who was president of the Royal Society, was a high-profile and enthusiastic champion of the proposed Exhibition of All Nations, which would, as he put it, be "for the purposes of exhibition, of competition and of encouragement" to both art and industry. The exhibition became the German-born prince's obsession, and it was his persevering efforts above all others that were ultimately responsible for its realization. In 1848, the prince submitted to the government a proposal drawn up by the Royal Society for a self-supporting exhibition of British industry, to be directed by a royal commission, arguing that such an event would be of huge benefit to British manufacturers.

←
Richard Redgrave, Well Spring carafe for Felix Summerly's Art Manufactures, 1847–51.

↑
Tea service by Felix Summerly (Henry Cole) for Minton, 1846.

↑
Portrait of Henry Cole (a.k.a. Felix Summerly) from *The Illustrated London News*, 1871.

Though the response from members of Parliament was lukewarm at best, Prince Albert was not easily dissuaded, and the following year he delivered a speech at the Lord Mayor's Banquet. Speaking to a supportive audience, he outlined unequivocally the reasons why such an event was not only desirable but also utterly necessary in the name of international unity and industrial progress. He stated

The distances which separated the different nations and parts of the globe are gradually vanishing before the achievements of modern invention . . . thought is communicated with the rapidity and even by the power of lightning. . . the great principle of the division of labor which may be called the moving power of civilization, is being extended to all branches of science, industry and art. . . Whilst formerly discovery was wrapped in secrecy, the publicity of the present day causes, that no sooner is a discovery or invention made, than it is already improved upon and surpassed by competing efforts: the products of all quarters of the globe are placed at our disposal, and we have only to choose what is the cheapest and best for our purposes, and the powers of production are entrusted to the stimulus of competition as capital.[3]

Prince Albert, who was in favor of the event financing itself, went on to argue in this speech that the exhibition would be "a true test and a living picture of the point of development at which the whole of mankind has arrived in this great task, and a new starting point from which all nations would be able to direct their further exertions."[4]

The same year, a meeting at Buckingham Palace saw the formation of a royal commission that raised the necessary funds for the exhibition, some by public subscription and some, more controversially, through speculative underwriting. By the time the commission was ready to invite submissions for the design of the building, in March 1850, the schedule to build a structure of such size—around 700,000 square feet— by the planned opening date of January 1, 1851, was not merely uncomfortably tight but looking virtually impossible. Surely a structure of this magnitude and echoing vastness could not possibly be taken from start to finish in a mere nine months. Nevertheless,

the commission set up a competition and more than 233 architects submitted schemes; none, however, fit the exacting brief. Meanwhile, the commission's building committee had also quietly prepared its own brick-built design, which many condemned on grounds of ugliness alone—and when they put this scheme out to tender, its expense was far more than initially anticipated. The proposal was dropped entirely.

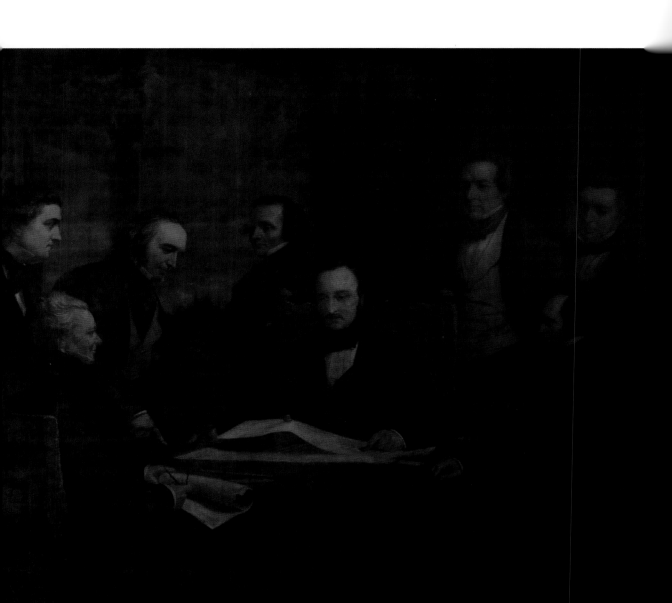

Joseph Paxton's Crystal Palace

The floundering and by now seriously adrift exhibition project was at last saved by "a man of genius, but no architect or engineer,"[5] the remarkably talented Joseph Paxton. As the Duke of Devonshire's head gardener, Paxton had already designed two large greenhouses for the Chatsworth estate in Derbyshire, including the large and innovative Lily House, which was then under construction. The design of Chatsworth's cast-iron-and-glass Lily House, with its inventive ridge-and-furrow roof, was itself inspired by nature, specifically the veined structure of the gigantic pads of the Amazonian water lily species *Victoria regia,* which the conservatory was intended to contain. So impressive was the lily pads' load-bearing capacity that Paxton described them as "a natural feat of engineering." His brilliant idea was to develop his concept for the Lily House into a much larger building constructed on modular lines—a sort of gigantic kit-form greenhouse that would be quick and relatively inexpensive to assemble and that would also be easy to disassemble once the exhibition was over. His proposal was presented to the building committee, whose members were won over by the ingenuity of the scheme; however, in order for it to be adopted, the already-appointed Contractor of Works, the firm of Messrs. James and George Munday, would have to be removed and replaced with a new engineering-specific contractor—a difficult and costly process given that the Munday firm was one of the largest investors in the project. The new firm, Fox, Henderson & Co., specialized in the construction of railway equipment and bridges and, as such, had expert knowledge and understanding of structural ironwork.

Prince Albert, satirized as "the Industrious Boy" and shown holding out his famous tasseled hat for money in the magazine *Punch*, was instrumental in raising the funding shortfall of some £75,000 brought about by the removal of the Mundays. Finally, Paxton's remarkable industrially manufactured building began to take shape in Hyde Park. One of the world's first large-scale examples of prefabricated architecture, the modular iron, glass, and wood building was revolutionary in that machinery was used wherever possible, not only to economize on labor but also to help perfect production. As the historian Hermione Hobhouse comments, "For Londoners it was an Eighth Wonder of the World going up in their midst,"[6] and the general public's interest in the building was certainly piqued by the weekly updates on the progress of its construction in the *Illustrated London News*. Paxton's soaring "Crystal Palace," as it was dubbed by *Punch*, was not only constructed—unbelievably—within budget and on time for the rescheduled opening on May 1, 1851, but was also the perfect expression of the progressive and forward-looking spirit that the event's organizers had wanted to project for this grand-scale exposition of industrialized endeavor. An ingenious building design, the Crystal Palace seemed to encapsulate the future in its soaring construction of tiered girder-work and semicircular ribs made of light cast iron, which covered the old elm trees of Hyde Park to such dramatic effect.

↗

Perspective views of the Victoria Regia House at Chatsworth (Lily House) designed by Joseph Paxton for the Duke of Devonshire, *The Civil Engineer and Architect's Journal*, 1850.

→

The gigantic water lilies at Chatsworth that inspired the construction of Joseph Paxton's Lily House there, as well as the later Crystal Palace, *The Illustrated London News*, 1849.

Fig. 4.--Perspective View of the Exterior.

THE GIGANTIC WATER-LILY (VICTORIA REGIA), IN FLOWER AT CHATSWORTH.

↑ ↗
Engravings showing the prefabricated structure
of the Great Exhibition building being
assembled, *The Illustrated London News*, 1850.

The new industrial age and the Great Exhibition

→
Overleaf: lithograph by Augustus Butler
showing the Crystal Palace viewed from
Kensington Gardens, 1851.

The new industrial age and the Great Exhibition

Joseph Paxton's Crystal Palace

The High Victorian style
and dishonest design

Once the fabrication and construction of the Great Exhibition building was completed, its internal decoration was entrusted to the talented architect and designer Owen Jones, another important theorist, who in 1856 would publish, *The Grammar of Ornament,* a sumptuously illustrated tome that was the first rigorous treatise on decoration. Jones believed that color should be used to help define architectural form. For the decoration of the Crystal Palace, he controversially attempted to put theory into practice by creating a polychromatic scheme of primary colors inspired by historical precedents, or as he put it, "the stupendous monuments of the Egyptians, the Greeks, the Arabs, and other Eastern civilisations."[7] Using a palette of red, blue, and yellow, the scheme formed, as Jones explained, "a neutralised bloom over the whole contents . . . the blending of the three primary colors in the roof nave . . . produced an artificial atmospheric effect of a most surprising kind."[8] Jones's polychromatic painting of the building's interior ironwork helped to create a sense of spatial delineation, producing a feeling of depth and perspective. His coloration also bestowed a visual warmth and beauty that one contemporary commentator, writing in the *Illustrated London News*, compared to the "hazy indistinctness" of Turner's paintings.[9] By visually softening the rather hard-edged, proto-modern industrial structure of the building, Jones presumably made it more palatable to contemporary Victorian taste.

←
Plate from *Art Journal Illustrated Catalogue* showing an ivory statuette and gold and silver objects by Froment Meurice of Paris, 1851.

↑
Plate from *Dickinson's Comprehensive Pictures of the Great Exhibition* showing the India stand and a crystal glass fountain with visitors parading among the tropical plants, elm trees, and exhibits, 1851.

As well as directing the exhibition's interior decoration, Owen Jones was also a superintendent of two of the thirty different classes of exhibits and, as such, was responsible for arranging all the wares in the "Paper, Printing, and Bookbinding" and the "Sculpture, Models, and Plastic Art, Mosaics, Enamels, etc." groupings. More than 100,000 different items were shown in Paxton's vast, echoing space of some thirty-three-million cubic feet; the exhibition's committee did an exceptional job of sorting these wildly varying types of manufacture into logical divisions. Beyond the national sections for overseas exhibitors, there were also sections dedicated to every imaginable endeavor undertaken by manufacturers in Britain, from heavy industrial machines such as marine engines, power looms, steam locomotives, and hydraulic presses to smaller-scale wares such as stained glass, chandeliers,

clocks, and lace. Cleverly presented, the whole two-tiered layout functioned like a covered pleasure garden, with three enormous fountains sited in the north-south transept and the existing trees of Hyde Park enclosed within the glazed space, helping to enhance this effect.

Despite the proto-modern rationality of Paxton's remarkable building, many of the products included in the exhibition were decidedly questionable in taste, design, and manufacture. Even the designs that had been selected as being the best examples of art manufactures for the accompanying *Art Journal Illustrated Catalogue* were almost all encrusted with decoration and florid in style. Heavy ornamentation was for the most part the order of the day, especially in goods destined for the consumer market; the only exhibits that did not display this decorative excess were those industrial machines or agricultural implements that were by their very nature highly utilitarian and functionally driven. Whether it was designs for cutlery or lighting, carpets or furniture, clocks or mirrors, most exhibits were festooned with ornament or heavy pattern. The Italian art critic Mario Praz later used the art-historical term *horror vacui*—fear of empty space—to describe the suffocating clutter of Victorian interiors furnished with such designs. The term could just as well be applied to individual objects themselves, which were for the most part revivalist wares whose decoration teemed with references to every previous style in history, from Rococo, Baroque, and Neoclassical, to the more unusual Assyrian, Eritrean, and Celtic. Such goods encapsulated the then-fashionable High Victorian style, marked by stylistic over-embellishment. Manufacturers of all kinds, it seemed, did not know when to leave well enough alone when it came to decoration. "The more excessive the better" seemed

←
Plate from *Art Journal Illustrated Catalogue* showing a table and other objects by Elkington & Mason of Birmingham, 1851.

↗
Medieval Court by A. W. N. Pugin at the Great Exhibition, 1851.

The new industrial age and the Great Exhibition

to be the pervasive attitude of the day. And the general public was by and large extremely receptive: the restraint of Georgian Neoclassicism must have seemed rather bland and passé when there were affordable "luxury" goods on offer that looked as though they had been expensively handcrafted but were in fact factory-made.

The fundamental problem was that, all too frequently, manufacturers were using decorative icing to cover up shoddy fabrication. By the mid-nineteenth century, Britain was undisputedly the most powerful nation on earth, thanks to her extensive empire and her impressive manufacturing capability. However, as the first country to have undergone an Industrial Revolution, it had no industrial-design blueprint to follow. This meant that the country had to undergo a period of trial by error before a proper understanding of design for industry could be grasped. During this difficult period, the vast majority of manufacturers saw

the machine as a means to create goods more cheaply and more quickly, and so to improve profit margins. They did not realize that rather than being used merely to mimic handicraft, industrialized production methods could be used to make better-quality products that were also more profitable. So-called "fancy goods" became the mainstay of most British manufacturers.

This sorry state of affairs was plain for all to see in many of the designs on display at the Great Exhibition of the Works of Industry of all Nations of 1851. It reflected not only the *nouveau richesse* of a country gorging on its newfound economic wealth but also a manufacturing industry hard at work promoting "stylish" fads and creating a voracious market for them among all classes of consumer. This was of real concern to the exhibition's organizers who had hoped to elevate public taste in design. However, a whiff of reformative spirit did waft through the Medieval Court, which had been designed by the great Gothic Revivalist architect Augustus Welby Northmore Pugin. Reflecting the Victorians' insatiable appetite for inappropriate ornament, these "dishonest designs" pointed to a dire need for both design reform and a better system of education in design. Henry Cole, who had been such a driving force behind the Great Exhibition, was, along with others who had been involved in its inception, determined that the event would leave a lasting, beneficial legacy in this regard.

Luckily, with more than six million paying visitors, the Great Exhibition was an overwhelming success and turned a significant profit. The Royal Commission decided to use £5,000 of this to acquire some of the objects that had been displayed in order to form a collection for the study of design. These instructive objects were housed in the Museum of Manufactures (officially known as the Museum of Ornamental Art), which opened in 1852 at Marlborough House in Pall Mall. A purchasing committee that included Pugin and the artist Richard Redgrave had been set up to select suitably instructive objects for display, and Henry Cole was appointed the first general superintendent of the museum's Department of Practical Art. Cole organized a display of poorly designed objects that was entitled "Decorations on False Principles," but that came to be known as the "Chamber of Horrors." It featured some truly ugly, heavily ornamented objects produced by a variety of British manufacturers. The purpose of this display was twofold: on the one hand it was intended to shame manufacturers into producing better-designed art manufactures; on the other, it was meant to educate the public about the difference between good and bad design. In 1857 the Marlborough House exhibits were used to form the nucleus collection for the new South Kensington Museum, which was eventually renamed the Victoria and Albert Museum. The Government School of Design, which had been established at Somerset House in 1837, was also transferred to this new museum and renamed the Art Training School, later becoming the Royal College of Art. In 1860 Henry Cole became the museum's superintendent. Under his careful guidance, the institution prospered and, over the succeeding years, helped to promote a greater understanding of design principles, which in turn helped to shape modern design practice. It was the human cost of industrialization rather than the tastelessness of manufactured goods, however, that would spur the next generation of design reformers into action.

→
Watercolors by William Linnaeus Casey
showing two rooms of exhibits at the Museum
of Manufactures at Marlborough House, 1857.

The new industrial age and the Great Exhibition

The High Victorian style and dishonest design

H C Maghere chromolith.   M & N Hanhart. Chromolith Imp   F Bogen

1. Spartium Hispaniarum.   2. Cytisus cornutus.   3. Anemone major alba.   4. Genista.   5. Cytisus adulterinus.

6

THE WINDS OF REFORM

A. W. N. Pugin and
the Gothic Revival

H.C. Maguire chromolith.   M. & N. Hanhat Chromolith Imp.   Pugin.

1. Cucumis Turcicus.   2. Ornithogalum luteum.   3. Absinthium album.   4. Narcissus polyanthus Matthioli.   5. Leucoium violaceum.

Even before the Great Exhibition of 1851 there had been stirrings of design reform, notably in Augustus Welby Northmore Pugin's publication of two influential books: *Contrasts; or a Parallel between the Noble Edifices of the Fourteenth and Fifteenth Centuries and Similar Buildings of the Present Day* (1836) and *True Principles of Pointed or Christian Architecture* (1841). The former was intended to show, in Pugin's words, "the present decay of taste," while the latter called for integrity in design and architecture based on three essential attributes: fitness for purpose, truth to materials, and revealed construction—essentially, a moral honesty. Pugin's espousal of the Gothic Revival style had been inherited from his French-born father, Auguste Charles Pugin, an architectural draftsman who had worked in the Gothic style and had himself published several influential books on English Gothic architecture that included analyses of constructions and of the varied interpretations of the style.

For A. W. N. Pugin, the Gothic was far more than just a decorative style: it was a seed from which he believed a truly authentic national style of architecture and design could grow. His form of Gothic Revivalism was essentially an example of National Romanticism, and he argued that Classicism was a pagan style that was inappropriate for a Christian country. During his short but highly prolific career he was an important and divisive figure, guided by deeply held religious beliefs that prompted him, controversially, to convert to Catholicism in 1835. As a fervent believer in what he saw as the true faith, he felt that Gothic architecture was a transcendental expression of Catholicism, stating: "I feel perfectly convinced the Roman Catholic Religion is the only one in which the grand and sublime style of church architecture can ever be restored."[1] For Pugin, the "simple truth" of Catholicism was revealed in the "true principles" of medieval art and design; it was his religious fervor that made him doggedly pursue truth in design and enabled him, almost single-handedly, to establish Gothic Revivalism as the dominant architectural style throughout Victorian Britain.

His largest and most prestigious commission was for the interiors of Charles Barry's magnificent

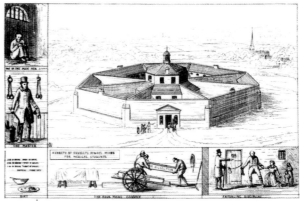

CONTRASTED RESIDENCES FOR THE POOR

← Opposite and previous page: Plates from *Floriated Ornament* by A. W. N. Pugin, 1849.

↑ "Contrasted Residences of the Poor" illustrations, from *Contrasts; or a Parallel between the Noble Edifices of the Fourteenth and Fifteen Centuries and Similar Buildings of the Present Day* by A. W. N. Pugin, 1836.

↑
Lantern slide of the House of Commons
Chamber at the Palace of Westminster
designed by A. W. N. Pugin, 1841.

↑
Waste Not, Want Not bread plate designed by
A. W. N. Pugin for Minton & Co., 1849.

Palace of Westminster (1841), but Pugin also designed numerous churches and houses that were totally integrated projects, in which every detail of a building—from its furniture, metalwork, and stained glass to its wallpapers, textiles, and tiles—were created by him alone. He was also a pioneer designer for industry, creating designs for the ceramics manufacturer Minton & Co., among others. Among his most famous designs for this company was his Waste Not, Want Not bread plate (1849), which revived the medieval encaustic technique of ceramic-making using inlays of different-colored clays, and which, with its incised motto, embodied the essence of nineteenth-century design reform. Through his conviction that Classicism was a pagan and untruthful style, Pugin introduced an ethical dimension into the debate surrounding design and architecture. As his obituary in the *Times* noted in 1852, it was he "who first showed us that our architecture offended not only against the laws of beauty, but also against the laws of morality." Indeed, Pugin preached his doctrine of design reform tirelessly, and such was the impact of his efforts that the English church architect John Dando Sedding would later observe, "we should have had no Morris, no Street, no Burges, no Shaw, no Webb, no Bodley, no Rossetti, no Burne-Jones, no Crane but for Pugin."[2]

Another architect who would have a strong influence on the direction of design was George Edmund Street, who was twelve years Pugin's junior and apprenticed under the other great Gothic Revivalist architect of the day, George Gilbert Scott. From the 1850s onward, Street pioneered an even more muscular interpretation of the Gothic style. In contrast to the Gothick school, which had been influenced by the soaring grandeur of Perpendicular Gothic edifices of the fourteenth and fifteenth centuries, Street was inspired by the plainer early English Gothic buildings of the twelfth and thirteenth centuries. His interpretation of this precedent, however, was more rudimentary than Pugin's, which meant that Street's buildings and furniture designs were less decoratively fussy and more modern looking, with simple, no-nonsense constructions. The circular oak table he designed around 1853–54 epitomizes his purposeful approach

The winds of reform

to the Gothic style. Some of the leading designers and architects of the next generation trained in Street's office, most notably John Dando Sedding, Richard Norman Shaw, William Morris, and Philip Webb. Each of these men applied the underlying principles of Gothic Revival architecture—fitness for purpose, truth to materials, revealed construction—to the creation of everyday wares, such that the German design critic Hermann Muthesius saw in their work "a direct transition to the moderns."[3]

In contrast, the English architect and designer William Burges promoted a far more fanciful, almost fairy tale-esque interpretation of the Gothic style: his work captured the dreamlike world of the Pre-Raphaelites while also anticipating the work of the Arts and Crafts movement. In 1864 Burges gave a series of lectures at the Society of Arts entitled "Art Applied to Industry," in which he argued that there was absolutely no reason for cheap, everyday items to be ugly—for, as he simply explained, "a die or mold of a good design costs no more than a bad one."[4] He also stated that although the serial production of high-end art manufactures was admirable, the best application of art to industry was "when a great many copies are made from an exceedingly good pattern."[5] Burges was no intellectual Luddite, and he believed that the appropriate use of machinery could facilitate the production of high-quality yet inexpensive designs because it would inevitably "reduce pounds to shillings and shillings to pence."[6] He also felt that the best people to design objects for mass production were specially trained designers rather than artists or architects, for they would be educated in both aesthetics and in the technical constraints of industrialized production. Sadly, Burges's design-reform entreaties were largely ignored,

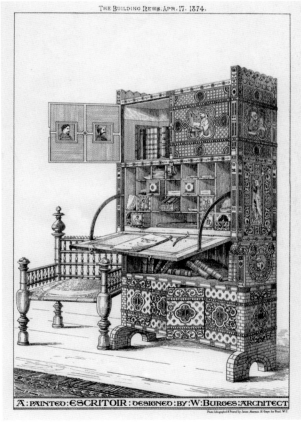

THE BUILDING NEWS. APR. 17. 1874.

A : PAINTED : ESCRITOIR : DESIGNED : BY : W : BURGES : ARCHITECT

↗
Circular table designed by George Edmund Street, c. 1853–54.

→
A painted escritoire and chair designed by William Burges, 1874.

and his own heavily embellished Gothic designs, which seemed rather at odds with what he preached, eventually fell out of fashion. It is only relatively recently that his work and life have enjoyed a revival of interest.

In France, the architect and design theorist Eugène-Emmanuel Viollet-le-Duc also looked to the Gothic style for guidance on design reform. He became famous for his "restorations" of medieval buildings, which often incorporated a certain amount of creative modification of the original structure. Unlike the English art critic John Ruskin, who called for the faithful historical preservation of old buildings, Viollet-le-Duc preferred a more Romantic approach that restored edifices to "a complete state that may never have existed at any given moment"[7]—such as his restorations of the Cathedral of Notre-Dame in Paris and of medieval buildings at Carcassonne. It was Viollet-le-Duc's writings, especially his *Dictionnaire*

raisonné de l'architecture française du XI au XVI siècle (1854), that had the greatest influence on his contemporaries and succeeding generations. Through his research and study of ancient buildings, from Greek Doric temples to medieval Gothic cathedrals, he was able to discern immutable principles that could be applied to the construction of modern buildings—and to the design of objects, too. He championed the idea that the plan of a building should be devised around its function, rather than its layout being fitted into its facade, and that a building should fulfill its purpose as straightforwardly and economically as possible. He also argued that, like the builders of yesteryear, modern architects should embrace new materials and technologies available to them and allow them to guide the fom and construction of buildings. Like Pugin, he also stressed that any ornament should be integral to the construction and, if possible, have an additional functional role. Above all, Viollet-le-Duc called for rationality within design and architecture and urged that form must be the expression of a practical requirement. He also entreated practitioners not to copy the past slavishly but to learn from it in order to apply its relevant principles to the present. Arguably, he had more impact on architecture and design practice than any other design reformer of the late nineteenth century. As Sir John Summerson observed in his essay collection *Heavenly Mansions* (1949): "Should anyone attempt to construct a theory of modern architecture in harmony with the conditions of thought prevailing today, he will discover no starting point so firm, no background so solid as that provided by Eugène Viollet-le-Duc."[8]

↖
Grotesque figure added to the Cathedral of Notre Dame during its restoration by Eugène-Emmanuel Viollet-le-Duc, 1845–64.

↗
View of Carcassonne showing Viollet-le-Duc's restoration of the medieval fortified town, begun 1853 and completed (posthumously) in 1910.

→
The Drawbridge Room at Château de Roquetiallade in Mazères (originally built in the fourteenth century) restored by Viollet-le-Duc and his pupil Edmond Duthoit, 1850–70.

A. W. N. Pugin and the Gothic Revival

Pre-Raphaelitism and the decorative arts

During the mid- to late nineteenth century, another important strand of design reform also emerged with the formation of the Pre-Raphaelite Brotherhood (PRB). This collective started as a fine art group inspired by earlier nineteenth-century Romantic ideals but eventually went on to form the philosophical core of the Arts and Crafts movement. As suggested by the name, the founding members of the Brotherhood—William Holman Hunt, John Everett Millais, and Dante Gabriel Rossetti—sought a purer form of creative expression, believing that art had been sullied over time by the pervasive influence of Raphael and later artists' highly mannered interpretations of Classicism. This kind of overblown and theatrical interpretation of Classicism, which the PRB thought to be overly mechanistic and intellectualized, had over the centuries become a veritable blueprint for the academic teaching of fine art, especially at the Royal Academy of Art in London, founded by Sir Joshua Reynolds, whom the PRB derided as "Sir Sloshua." Looking back to Gothic art, and more specifically to the work of early Italian Renaissance artists such as Fra Angelico, Sandro Botticelli, and Filippo Lippi, the members of the Brotherhood sought to recapture in their own paintings "the feeling of constructive beauty ... not bounded by line or rule, nor taught by theory"[9] that had typified the work of those earlier artists. For the PRB, close observation of the world, both natural and man-made, was the starting point from which to mount their Arthurian "Crusade and Holy warfare against the age."[10] To further its aims, the PRB also published its own short-lived journal, *The Germ*, which featured poetry, literature, and art and was intended to "encourage and enforce an entire adherence to the simplicity of nature."[11] A sense of harmonious proportion, a crispness of line, a purity of color, and an extraordinary level of detail generally characterized the PRB's artwork.

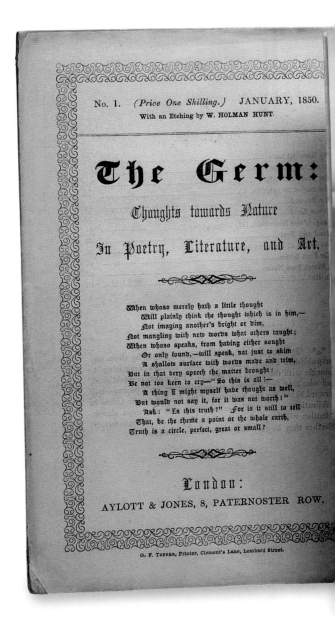

No. 1. (*Price One Shilling.*) JANUARY, 1850.
With an Etching by W. HOLMAN HUNT.

The Germ:

Thoughts towards Nature

In Poetry, Literature, and Art.

When whoso merely hath a little thought
    Will plainly think the thought which is in him,—
    Not imaging another's bright or dim,
    Not mangling with new words what others taught;
When whoso speaks, from having either sought
    Or only found,—will speak, not just to skim
    A shallow surface with words made and trim,
But in that very speech the matter brought:
Be not too keen to cry—"So this is all!—
    A thing I might myself have thought as well,
    But would not say it, for it was not worth!"
Ask: "Is this truth?" For is it still to tell
That, be the theme a point or the whole earth,
Truth is a circle, perfect, great or small?

London:

AYLOTT & JONES, 8, PATERNOSTER ROW.

G. F. TUPPER, Printer, Clement's Lane, Lombard Street.

↓

The Germ: Thoughts Towards Nature, numbers 1
and 3, January and March 1850.

GONERILL: REGAN: LEAR: ROOM: CORDELIA: FRRNCE:

The winds of reform

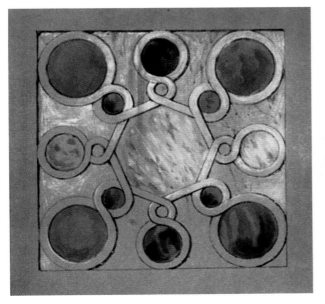

Crucially for the story of design, Edward Burne-Jones and William Morris were strongly influenced by the ideas advanced in *The Germ* while studying theology at Oxford, and they were also morally galvanized by the writings of the Pre-Raphaelites' greatest champion, John Ruskin, the eminent art critic whose book *The Stones of Venice* Morris regarded as a revelation. In this landmark publication, Ruskin explored not only the social damage caused by materialism but also the disconnection of creativity from labor within the industrial system. His ideas are perhaps best encapsulated in the essay "Ad Valorem" (According to Value), in which he stated: "Production does not consist in things laboriously made, but in things serviceably consumable; and the question for the nation is not how much labor it employs, but how much life it produces."[12] Ruskin believed that "common wealth" was not merely a monetary concern but rather meant universal public welfare. So alluring were the Pre-Raphaelite goals, and so potent the argument of Ruskin's

socially motivated writings, that both Morris and Burne-Jones eventually abandoned theology to embark instead on "a life of art."[13] While Burne-Jones pursued painting, Morris initially apprenticed as an architect in George Edmund Street's office, but he was persuaded to hone his painting skills after meeting his hero, Dante Gabriel Rossetti, a charismatic and manipulative painter-poet. Morris struggled with the medium but happily found that he had an aptitude for design when he began decorating his new home, Red House in Bexleyheath, ten miles from central London. Designed by Philip Webb in close collaboration with Morris, Red House was an embodiment of Morris's Pre-Raphaelite dreams of a medieval Arcadia. Furnished with embroidered wall hangings, murals, stained glass, metalwork, and heavy painted furniture designed by Morris and his circle of friends, the home was an artistic triumph that reflected Morris's understanding of materials, texture, color, and pattern.

←
The Red House in Bexleyheath, designed by Philip Webb in close collaboration with William Morris, completed 1860.

↑
Illustrations from John Ruskin's *The Stones of Venice*, 1851–53.

William Morris and the birth of the Arts and Crafts movement

Bolstered by the successful interior decoration of Red House and the camaraderie of like-minded artists it had spawned, and probably also by the ambition of Henry Cole's earlier Summerly's Art Manufactures venture, Morris eventually resolved to establish a new art manufactures firm "where one could either obtain or get produced work of a genuine or beautiful character."[14] Founded in 1861, Morris, Marshall, Faulkner & Co. (or Morris & Co. as it later became known) sought not only to infuse design with art but also to revitalize the age-old craft traditions, which were by now under severe threat from industrialization and mechanized production. The venture had an underlying social mission of rescuing workers from the wage slavery of mindless machine-watching and restoring a sense of "joy through labor" by giving them greater creative control over their work. To this end, Morris tended to shun the machine in favor of handcraft wherever possible, which meant that the designs the firm produced were on the whole relatively expensive. Although Morris wanted to produce affordable items that he described as "Good Citizen's Furniture," his adherence to high-quality handcraftsmanship meant that for the most part he was constantly, in his words, "ministering to the swinish luxury of the rich."[15] He was, however, deeply aware that this latter type of commission work kept his company afloat and his workers in creative, life-enhancing employment. As a deeply committed socialist, Morris was exceptionally reluctant to embrace any form of mechanization that would have seen his skilled craftsmen become mere machine minders. Yet if he had done so, he could have fulfilled his vision of producing affordable, well-designed objects for the many rather than for the few.[16]

Such was the paradox of Morris's design-reforming mission, which aimed toward a then-unachievable goal: affordable yet high-quality goods and creatively engaged workers.

Morris was the first design-reformer to highlight what he saw as the parasitic nature of the Victorian bourgeoisie, who profited from the abject drudgery of the working classes. He asserted that the mindless production of useless luxuries, which he referred to as "slave wares," perpetuated the workers' bondage, and he proposed that all men should be allowed to work worthily. The commercial "fancy goods" he described had indeed become a mainstay of Victorian industry, and only the owners of the factories that made these design fripperies actually profited from them, for the sale of such goods did not benefit the machine-minding workers who executed them nor the consumers who bought them. The idea of fellowship—the sharing of interests among people—was fundamental to Morris's practice of design, for, as he noted, "Fellowship is heaven and a lack of fellowship is hell: fellowship is life, and a lack of fellowship is death: and the deeds that ye do on earth, it is for fellowship's sake that ye do them."[17] This concept of companionship guided Morris's design work and his manufacturing and retailing endeavors, too. Under his hands-on direction, Morris & Co. created products that gave meaningful and satisfying work to those who made them and joy through use to those who could afford to buy them.

Although Morris himself devised many of the wallpaper, textile, and carpet designs retailed by Morris & Co., the firm also produced furniture, stained glass, and tapestries designed by Philip Webb, Ford Madox Brown, George Jack, and Edward Burne-Jones. The younger and highly talented John Henry Dearle was responsible for the design of many other textiles, wallpapers, and carpets, the majority of which we now think of as classic Morris patterns, such as Golden Lily and Compton. The firm also retailed ceramics and tiles by William De Morgan and metalwork by William Arthur Smith Benson. Despite his Arts and Crafts credentials, Benson was far less reluctant to use machines than his contemporaries. By reconciling "art manufactures" with rational mechanized production methods, he was an important and early proponent of modern design—to such an extent that he drew praise from the German architect and author Hermann

←
African Marigold textile (printed cotton) designed by William Morris, 1876.

→
Overleaf left: tea set designed by William Arthur Smith Benson, c. 1885.

→
Overleaf right: table light designed by William Arthur Smith Benson, c. 1900.

The winds of reform

Muthesius, who suggested that Benson's beautiful wares should serve as a model for future German industrial production. Mr. "Brass" Benson, as he came to be known, was also a pioneer of interchangeability of components, whereby various standardized parts were joined together in different combinations to make various types of objects; for example, an element found on one of his teapots might well also have been used to construct a lamp or an inkwell. This mix-and-match assembly enabled Benson to produce hundreds of patterns at his large purpose-built factory, the Eyot Metal Works in Hammersmith, London. Although his brass and copper designs were produced industrially, they did not have an over machine aesthetic and are perhaps best described as having been crafted by machine. With their warm metallic glow and sinuous, unfurling forms, Benson's metalwork designs became an essential element of fashionable New Art interiors during the fin-de-siècle years—especially those created by Morris & Co.

Although by today's standards the interior look promoted by Morris & Co. may seem quite cluttered, in comparison to the High Victorian style it was positively minimalistic. It had a homely, domestic simplicity that contrasted starkly to the overt fussiness of mainstream interior design at the time. As well as putting reforming theory into design practice with his manufacturing and retailing activities, Morris lectured extensively and tirelessly promoted the beliefs that decoration should only be employed if it had a use or a meaning and that the beauty of an object was derived from being in harmony with nature, rather than from mimicking it. For Morris, natural forms possessed an inherent rightness, and purposeful beauty in accord with nature was the ultimate goal of design.

With an almost pantheistic love of nature and a deeply emotional attachment to age-old craft traditions, Morris, like Ruskin, believed in the custodianship of old buildings, whereby they were faithfully conserved for the benefit of future generations rather than creatively

Adoration of the Magi tapestry designed by
Edward Burne-Jones for Morris & Co., 1888
(woven 1894).

The "Morris" adjustable chair designed by Philip
Webb, c. 1870, upholstered in Bird woven textile.

William Morris and the birth of the Arts and Crafts movement

restored as romanticized pastiches. He was so appalled
by the wilful wrecking of old buildings in the name of
restoration during the Victorian era that, in 1877, he
established the influential Society for the Preservation
of Ancient Buildings (SPAB), which was nicknamed
"Anti-Scrape" and was the first institution of its kind.
Morris once stated that "the greatest side of art is the
art of daily life which historic buildings represent"
and went on to note that romance was "the capacity
for a true conception of history, a power of making the
past part of the present."[18] But the socialist historian
John Goode later noted that he was also influenced
by a sense of alienation from his own time and a
romantic idealism, the combination of which enabled
him to envision "the future in the present."[19] While
his desire to preserve the architecture of the past was
undoubtedly spurred by a rose-tinted nostalgia, for
Morris the medieval era in particular also provided a
blueprint for the future of design and manufacturing
practice, in which workers were able to ply their
skills creatively within a protective system of guilds.
Like his Pre-Raphaelite colleagues, Morris dreamed
of creating a utopia inspired by a vision of a rural,
Arcadian idyll in which man and nature were in accord
and craftsmen produced practical and beautiful
objects through, as he put it, "useful work" rather than

"useless toil."[20] This vision inspired the emergence
of the Arts and Crafts movement, and Morris must
therefore be seen as its founding father. The furniture
designer and publisher Gustav Stickley, one of the
chief proponents of the American Arts and Crafts
movement, would later refer to Morris as "the upright
man and the great artist . . . who practiced the most
essential arts and crafts only to transfigure them."[21]

The most popular furniture item made and
retailed by Morris & Co. was the ebonized Sussex
chair, attributed to Philip Webb. This vernacular-style
chair, based on an earlier design typology, was one
of the firm's more competitively priced items, and
its inherent simplicity epitomized Morris's vision for
the betterment of design. As Stickley would note, the
lesson to be learned from Morris's libertarian vision
was that "a real art, created for the people by the
people, is able not only to beautify, but also to simplify
life, to unify the interests of all sorts and conditions
of men, and finally to realize the meaning of the
word commonwealth."[22] Morris's vision for objects
that had a simple functional beauty and were crafted
by creatively engaged workers would become the
guiding aim of the Arts and Crafts movement and its
related guilds, but his own rejection of mechanization
per se would ultimately frustrate the achievement of

THE SUSSEX RUSH-SEATED CHAIRS

MORRIS AND COMPANY
449 OXFORD STREET, LONDON, W.

"ROSSETTI ARM-CHAIR.
IN BLACK, 16/6.

SUSSEX CORNER CHAIR.
IN BLACK, 10/6.

SUSSEX SINGLE CHAIR.
IN BLACK, 7/-.

SUSSEX ARM-CHAIR.
IN BLACK, 9/9.

ROUND-SEAT CHAIR.
IN BLACK, 10/6.

SUSSEX SETTEE, 4 FT. 6 IN. LONG.
IN BLACK, 35/-.

ROUND SEAT PIANO CHAIR.
IN BLACK, 10/6.

truly democratic design. That is not to say, however, that Morris was not a significant figure when it came to the formation of the Modern Movement—he most assuredly was—but it was his emphasis on simplicity as an ethical force rather than his belief in workers' creative fulfillment that was to have lasting influence. His advocacy of a more holistic approach to design and manufacturing for aesthetic, social, and environmental reasons is more relevant than ever in our own post-industrial times.

Textile printing at Morris & Co.'s Merton Abbey works, c. 1890.

Page from Morris & Co. catalogue showing a range of Sussex rush-seated chairs, c. 1880.

The Aesthetic Movement

Like the early Arts and Crafts movement, the Aesthetic Movement was a branch of design reform that stemmed from the Gothic Revival and the Pre-Raphaelite Brotherhood, and that can be seen as a rejection of the Victorian status quo. The Aesthetic Movement was spurred on by the idea of "art for art's sake" rather than "craft for craft's sake." Initially, architects and designers aligned with the movement interwove influences from the fashionable Gothic and Queen Anne revival styles with motifs taken from Eastern influences. Rather than looking to national vernacular precedents for design archetypes, like Morris and his followers, the Aesthetes looked further afield for decidedly more exotic inspirations, from Moorish tiles to Japanese lacquer. One reason for this was that after the success of the Great Exhibition in 1851 there had been a rapid increase in the staging of other such major displays. The International Exhibition of 1862, held in London, was one such notable event. It featured work by the fledgling Morris, Marshall, Faulkner & Co. as well as Charles Babbage's famous calculating machine and marine engines developed by Henry Maudslay's firm. But perhaps even more important, it prominently showcased various Japanese exhibits, giving British designers, artists, and architects their first taste of a design culture that had evolved along very different lines from those in Europe.

A further twenty-four international exhibitions were staged during the 1870s, including four in London, two in Japan, and the Exposition Universelle held in Paris in 1878. The last was infamous for its colonial "human zoo" of 400 "indigenous people." Such events were hugely important for the transfer of culture and ideas from one nation to another, as each country used its dedicated pavilion to highlighty its very best industrial and craft endeavors. The displays in Paris of work from Japan were of special interest, in part because Japanese design and architecture had in effect been hidden behind closed doors for centuries. It was only during the Meiji period (1868–1912), when imperial power was restored, that the country began to become more outward-looking after centuries of introspective feudalism. The arts and crafts of Japan were a revelation to European designers and artists, who found them highly refined, both technically and aesthetically, and admired the fact that even the humblest of objects harmoniously balanced form and function. The great care taken in the execution of Japanese designs was attributable at least in part to the Shinto belief system, which holds that *kami* (spirits) can dwell in objects both natural and man-made. It then makes sense that a culture as immersed in spiritualism and animism as Japan's was far more likely to invest time, money, and energy on objects. Many Japanese objects have a strong formal and aesthetic presence, and there is such reverence for master craftsmen in Japan that the most skilled among them are officially designated as "Living National Treasures." In Paris, the post-impressionist artists were captivated by the bold linearity of Japanese woodcuts. These were subsequently referenced in their own work—the swirling posters of Henri de Toulouse-Lautrec and the boldly outlined, color-saturated canvases of Paul Gauguin being among the best-

→
Edward William Godwin, Anglo-Japanese furniture shown at the Paris Exhibition, *The Building News*, 1878.

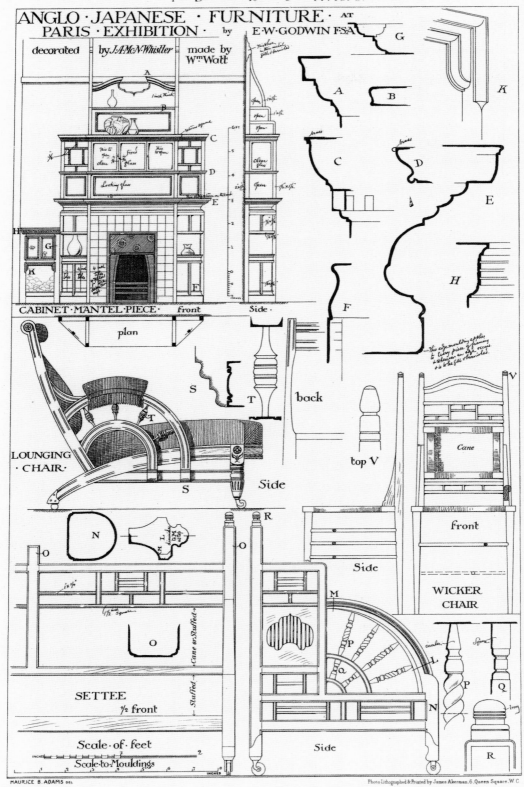

ANGLO · JAPANESE · FURNITURE · AT
PARIS · EXHIBITION · by E · W · GODWIN F.S.A.

decorated by J·A·McN·Whistler made by Wm Watt

CABINET · MANTEL · PIECE · front Side

plan

back

top V

LOUNGING · CHAIR · Side

WICKER CHAIR

SETTEE ½ front

Scale · of · feet

Scale · to · Mouldings

MAURICE B. ADAMS DEL.

Photo Lithographed & Printed by James Akerman, 6, Queen Square, W.C.

known examples. There was a similar interest in all things Japanese in England, where a new generation of designers and architects was entranced by the diversity and decorative richness of Japanese culture, which was unlike anything they had seen before.

In 1862 Farmer and Rogers' Oriental Warehouse opened on London's fashionable Regent Street, becoming one of the first companies to import objects en masse from Japan. This bazaar-like store sold many of the Japanese items that had been displayed at the London International Exhibition the same year. Arthur Lasenby Liberty worked there as the junior manager and, in 1875, founded his own fashionable emporium, Liberty & Co. Initially Liberty retailed silks and *objets d'art* from Japan as well as other decorative furnishing items from China and North Africa.[23] Besides its imported wares, Liberty also sold "Anglo-Oriental" bamboo furniture and Moorish-inspired furniture in the style of the Aesthetic Movement. Another purveyor of such furnishings was the William Watt Artistic Furniture Warehouse (established 1857), which during the 1860s made Gothic Revival and Jacobean Revival furniture designed by the architect Edward William Godwin. In the 1870s the company began manufacturing Anglo-Japanese furniture, created by Godwin in accordance with fashionable taste, alongside "Old English" designs. Godwin also designed various pieces of furniture for production by Collinson & Lock, which similarly captured the spirit of Japan by referencing Japanese motifs and constructions while remaining at the same time very much British "art furniture." Designed around 1867, Godwin's famous Anglo-Japanese sideboard typified this type of artistic furniture, boasting a dramatic grid-like construction of strong vertical and horizontal elements inspired by Japanese screens. It was also highly functional, providing cupboards, shelves, and drawers for storing china and cutlery and even a rack for displaying chargers. With its clean-looking and relatively unadorned surfaces, it was also a very practical and hygienic piece that must have seemed startlingly modern when it first appeared. Godwin also designed wallpaper in the style of the Aesthetic Movement for Jeffery & Co.; ceramics for firms including Minton,

LIBERTY'S NEW SHOPS IN ARGYLL PLACE, REGENT STREET, W.1.

The winds of reform

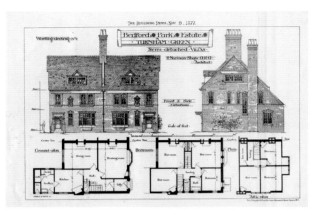

Top: designs for semi-detached and detached
villas for Bedford Park Estate by Edward
William Godwin (left) and Richard Norman
Shaw (right), *The Buildings News*, 1877 and
1879, respectively.

Lithograph of Tower House, Bedford Park,
London by Adolf Manfred Trautschold, 1882.

Model no. 880 andirons designed by Thomas
Jeckyll for Barnard, Bishop & Barnard, 1876.

The winds of reform

Brownfields and Hollins & Co.; and metalwork for Messenger & Co. and Jones & Willis. Many of Godwin's designs anticipated the stripped-down geometric formalism that emerged in the early twentieth century with the Modern Movement.

During the late 1870s, west London became the creative crucible of the Aesthetic Movement. Chelsea was home not only to Rossetti and Godwin but also to the American-born artist James Abbott McNeill Whistler, and Hammersmith was the stomping ground of William Morris and William Arthur Smith Benson. Meanwhile, in the nearby leafy environs of Holland Park, the painter Lord Frederic Leighton built himself a veritable Aesthetic palace—Leighton House—which, rather than channeling the influence of Japanese design, looked to the Middle East for exotic decorative inspiration, for example in its extraordinary Arab Hall tiled with antique Turkish, Persian, and Syrian tiles, installed by William De Morgan alongside his own Arabic-inspired tiles. It was, however, slightly farther to the west of London that the Aesthetic Movement would find its real spiritual home, in the pioneering garden-suburb development of Bedford Park. Speculatively built in Turnham Green, Bedford Park soon became a byword for refined Aesthetic living. Although it was constructed on an informal plan of wide, pleasant, tree-lined residential streets devised by Edward William Godwin, another architect, Richard Norman Shaw, designed the majority of the red-brick, Queen Anne revival-style houses in the development. The height of fashion during the 1880s and 1890s, Bedford Park provided a well-designed "lifestyle" haven for Aesthetes—mainly artists and middle-class professionals—fleeing the dirt and noise of inner-city London. Indeed, Bedford Park became so associated with the Aesthetic Movement that it was later parodied as "Saffron Park" in G. K. Chesterton's novel *The Man Who Was Thursday* (1908), a tongue-in-cheek reference to the color of silk preferred by its inhabitants, who bought their flowing robes from Liberty & Co. "The suburb of Saffron Park lay on the sunset side of London, as red and ragged as a cloud of sunset," Chesterton wrote. "It was built of a bright brick throughout; its sky-line was fantastic, and even its ground plan was

wild. . . The place was not only pleasant, but perfect. . . even if the people were not 'artists', the whole was nevertheless artistic."[24] As a sort of quasi-artistic colony filled with homes tastefully decorated with Morris & Co. wallpapers and De Morgan tiles, Bedford Park functioned as a carefully designed model village of sorts, signaling a new, artistic way of living.

In addition to the Japanese influence, two other decorative motifs recurred in Aesthetic Movement-style interiors such as those at Bedford Park: sunflowers and peacock feathers. These had symbolic meanings that resonated with the movement's concerns, the former alluding to dedicated love and purity of thought and the latter representing beauty and immortality. Yet, despite the impression that might be given by the work of Aubrey Beardsley and other proponents of Aestheticism, the Aesthetic Movement was about far more than exoticism and symbolism. In referencing the stripped-down, formal vocabulary of traditional Japanese architecture and design, the movement heralded a new elementalism[25] that was both highly refined in terms of aesthetics and function and ideal for products intended for mass production: the simpler the product, the easier it was to manufacture. One of

such as a plainly constructed bedroom washstand, were often the best designed. Of course, the formation of these links between quality and utility would help to change taste and, therefore, demand over the coming years, eventually spurring a new proto-modernity in design the following decade. In America a number of leading decorating firms were associated with the fashionable Anglo-Japanese Aesthetic Movement during the 1870s and 1880s, most notably Herter Brothers of New York and, of course, Tiffany Studios. The influence of Japanese design and architecture also seeped into the work of designers now more generally associated with the American Arts and Crafts movement, such as Frank Lloyd Wright and Charles and Henry Greene. As the historian of American visual culture Karen Zukowski insightfully notes, "The aesthetic movement prompted Americans to make the mental leap that beautiful surroundings, in and of themselves, would elevate the soul."[27] This belief helped to bolster the importance of design within the public consciousness and brought the design-reform debate to a wider audience. Though it was a relatively short-lived style, the Aesthetic Movement was an important stepping-stone on the pathway to design reform: essentially a cult of beauty, it was culturally aspirational and international in its outlook and was crucially focused on the look of things in relation to their practical function and underlying symbolism.

the most interesting architect–designers associated with the Aesthetic Movement was Thomas Jeckyll, who produced a large number of designs for the Norwich-based foundry Barnard, Bishop & Barnard, including his sunflower-headed andirons and a plethora of Japanese-inspired fire surrounds. He was also responsible for the extraordinary cast-iron and wrought-iron railings that encircled the Barnard, Bishop & Barnard pavilion at the 1876 Centennial Exhibition in Philadelphia, which received widespread praise for their originality and exacting execution.

Another English designer associated with the Aesthetic Movement was Charles Locke Eastlake, whose book *Hints on Household Taste* (1868) had a widespread influence on public taste in both Britain and the United States. As an accessibly written treatise on interior decoration, it derided the concept of fashionable novelties and instead encouraged the "discrimination between good and bad design in those articles of daily use which we are accustomed to see around us."[26] Eastlake argued that some of the worst examples of design were often to be found in expensive luxury articles, and that the simplest items in a home,

↖
Drawing room of the William H. Vanderbilt residence at 640 Fifth Avenue, decorated by Herter Brothers of New York, c. 1882.

→
Dragonfly table light by Tiffany Studios, c. 1906 (this example). The dragonfly pattern was earlier devised by Clara Driscoll, a brilliant member of Tiffany's design team, and reflected the strong Aestheticism of the studio's early output.

Christopher Dresser: truth, beauty, power

Of the designers associated with the Aesthetic Movement, Christopher Dresser was by far the most significant in the wider context of design reform. As the first person to run a successful design consultancy, he is generally regarded as "the father of industrial design." As an influential design theorist and an accomplished professional designer, Dresser pioneered a pared-down, geometric language that anticipated the Modern Movement, and that was based on his painstaking research into botanical structural forms and his insightful understanding of the art of Japan. Dresser began his design training at the tender age of thirteen, when he attended the Government School of Design based at Somerset House in London. As part of his studies there he specialized in the research of botanical structures. The natural world was at the time seen as a divine blueprint, and there was a growing belief that if the mysteries of natural forms could be unlocked, they would enable designers to emulate their inherent "rightness" within their own work. As a pioneer of what eventually became known as "Art Botany," he went on to contribute a botanical plate to Owen Jones's influential publication *The Grammar of Ornament* (1856), and also lectured and published a number of academic papers on this new design-related subject. Indeed, so far-reaching was the influence of his art-botany writings that in 1859 Dresser was awarded an honorary doctorate by the University of Jena, Germany. Although he had undoubtedly encountered a few Japanese objects during his years of design training, it was not until he visited the 1862 International Exhibition in London that he was fully exposed to the incredibly rich and varied material culture of Japan. Unlike some contemporary designers who ostensibly viewed the Japanese objects on display as little more than fascinating curios of a foreign culture, Dresser immediately grasped that there was much intrinsic merit to Japanese design, which so harmoniously balanced form and function. His designs from the 1860s and 1870s increasingly reflected a Japanese influence in their simplified forms, used to express the unique qualities of the materials.

In 1873, Dresser published the influential book *Principles of Decorative Design*, which explored the relationship between form and function and was intended to aid "the art-education of those who seek a knowledge of ornament as applied to our industrial manufactures." Here he argued that beauty had commercial value and, as such, was an important element of design:

> We may even say that art can lend to an object a value greater than that of the material of which it consists, even when the object be formed of precious matter, as of rare marble, scarce woods, or silver or gold. This being the case, it follows that the workman who can endow his production with those qualities or beauties which give value to his works, must be more useful to his employer than the man who produces objects devoid of such beauty, and his time must be of higher value than that of his less skilful companion.[28]

Three years later, in 1876, Dresser published a follow-up book, *Studies in Design*, which, like Owen Jones's earlier tome, included beautifully executed and richly colored plates intended to show the principles

→
Botanical plate by Christopher Dresser published in Owen Jones' *The Grammar of Ornament*, 1856.

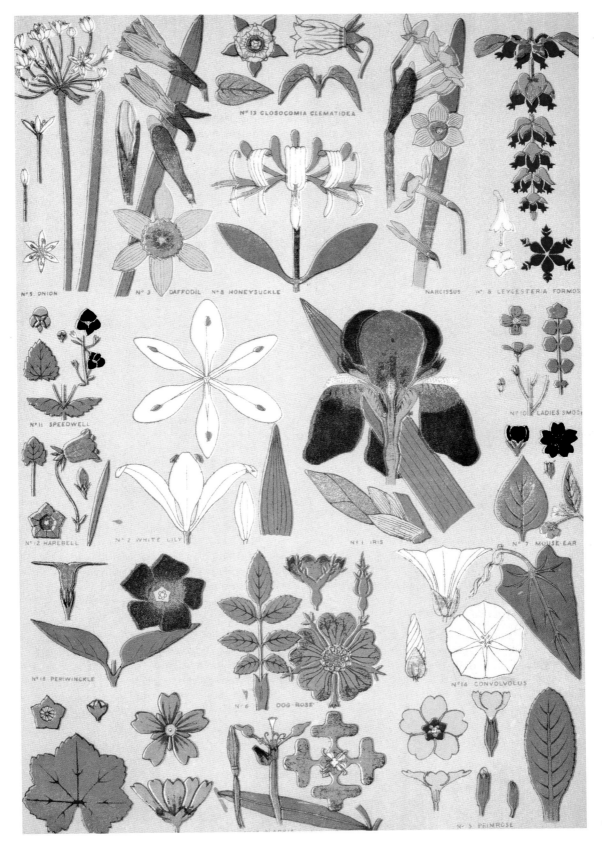

Nº 13 CLOSOCOMIA CLEMATIDEA

Nº 5 ONION Nº 3 DAFFODIL Nº 8 HONEYSUCKLE NARCISSUS Nº 5 LEYCESTERIA FORMOSA

Nº 11 SPEEDWELL Nº 10 LADIES SMOCK

Nº 12 HAREBELL Nº 2 WHITE LILY Nº 1 IRIS Nº 7 MOUSE-EAR

Nº 15 PERIWINCKLE Nº 6 DOG-ROSE Nº 14 CONVOLVOLUS

Nº 5 PRIMROSE

He later published a record of this culturally immersive trip, *Japan: Its Architecture, Art and Art Manufactures* (1882); it was an exhaustive account of the country's various creative endeavors, from an analysis of the different tools used by Japanese carpenters to a detailed and exacting description of how lacquerwork was executed. Dresser was able to apply the design and manufacturing knowledge he had acquired in Japan to his creations on his return to London. For example, his well-known Model No. 2274 lozenge-shape teapot, designed for James Dixon & Sons in 1879, while not in any way replicating a Japanese teapot, was inspired by the elemental geometric formalism found in Japanese design. This rare proto-modern object, though not manufactured in any large quantity, must be regarded as the most significant and revolutionary British silverware design of the nineteenth century, its bold geometry and stripped-down Aestheticism prefiguring the strict formal vocabulary of the Modern Movement.

As the world's first professional industrial-design consultant, Dresser created designs for at least thirty manufacturers, including Minton and Coalbrookdale. Some of his designs were even emblazoned with his autograph—a very early example of an artistic signature used to sell a designed product. Unlike William Morris, Dresser did not distrust the machine but embraced it, recognizing the need for a new, more rational approach to design, harnessing the potential of mass production to create beautiful, useful, and affordable objects for the many rather than for the few. Dresser's designs demonstrated a new formal and functional rationalism that was eminently suited to the demands of mechanized industrial production. His progressive agenda reflected a career-long pursuit of "truth, beauty, power," in which the word "power" implied a strong, energetic force that was ultimately achieved through a thorough working knowledge of the design process, as well as an understanding of materials and manufacturing techniques. For Dresser, design was a discipline that united science and art, and through his considerable influence both as a theorist and as a designer he moved the design-reform debate from the Aesthetic Movement's advocacy of art for art's sake to a standpoint that is best summed up as "art for industry's sake."

of ornament as gleaned from a wide range of historic and foreign sources. Dresser's illustrations had a more abstracted and linear quality that reflected the new reductivist tendency in design that he was introducing.

Hungry to know more about Japan, Dresser undertook an extensive four-month research trip in 1876–77 as a guest of the Japanese government. As the first Western designer to visit Japan officially in order to study its arts and manufacturing, Dresser gained insights into its culture. While in Japan, he kept an illustrated daily diary, and he purchased or had specially taken a thousand reference photographs and small, colored drawings. Apart from visiting about a hundred shrines and temples, Dresser also studied "all forms of art industry" on his two-thousand-mile fact-finding mission, touring sixty-eight potteries as well as many other manufactories and craft workshops.[29]

The winds of reform

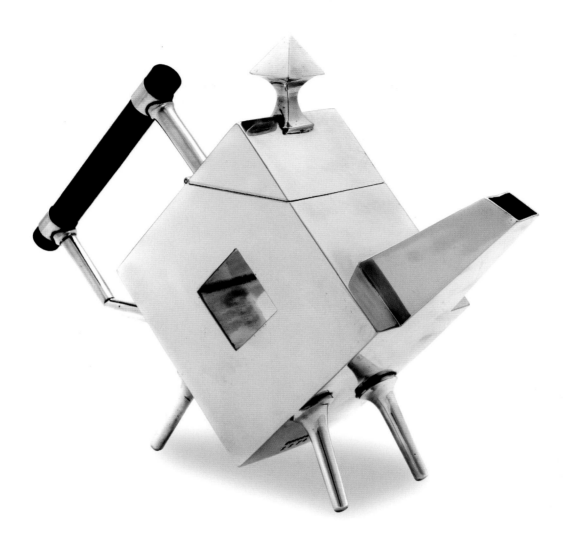

↖

Plate III from Christopher Dresser's
Studies in Design, 1876.

↑

Model No. 2274 lozenge-shape teapot,
designed by Christopher Dresser for
James Dixon & Sons, 1879.

Christopher Dresser: truth, beauty, power

7

THE
NEW
ART

National Romanticism

The flowering of the "New Art" in the 1890s was an international phenomenon that played a key role in the story of design. To understand the developments that gave rise to this progressive new style, which went by a number of other names depending on where it occurred—Art Nouveau, Jugendstil, the Vienna Secession, modernismo, and stile Liberty—it is important to appreciate the background against which these advances took place.

The second half of the nineteenth century saw a seismic shift of power in Europe, with the influence of the British, Russian, Austro-Hungarian, and Prussian empires growing exponentially after France's defeat in the Franco-Prussian War of 1871. The increasing economic and political dominance of what were, in effect, four superpowers, delicately held in balance through royal marital and political alliances, resulted in an escalating sense of national pride within the borders of those nations. At the same time, and in reaction to the growing hegemony of these countries, a similar rise of nationalism occurred in other European states, as well as farther afield, from America to Japan. Parallel with this rising tide of national fervor, the majority of European countries experienced a period of rapid industrialization and, consequently, growing urbanization. Meanwhile, population increased significantly, with advances in medicine and disease prevention helping to double the number of people in Europe over the course of the nineteenth century. This led to a burgeoning middle class, which could now afford to buy more manufactured products. The already established fraternity of design reformers who were deeply troubled by the plethora of badly designed, shoddily manufactured "fancy goods" being cheaply offered to these new consumers sought a more meaningful and moral expression for industrial production, and looked to their national folk roots for inspiration.

The origins of what can best be termed National Romanticism in design can actually be traced back to the preceding century and the Age of Enlightenment, and especially to the writings of the German philosopher Johann Gottfried von Herder. Generally acknowledged as the father of cultural nationalism, Herder believed, as explained by the historian Royal J. Schmidt, that the development of "a national culture upon a native foundation was not only desirable but necessary."[1] Herder considered the present a continuation of the past as well as a bridge to the future, and stressed the importance of ancestry as well as the need for an identifiable sense of character within a nation's culture. It should be remembered that Herder lived in a period when Europe was only just emerging from the stultifying cultural domination of French Neoclassicism. During this time, what we think of as Germany today was still an un-unified grouping of almost tribal, fief-like states. His call for a single nation-state with a single national character is, then, understandable. Little did he know that this rallying cry would find its ultimate expression in the rise of National Socialism in Germany more than a century and a half later.

Herder's ideas and those of other philosophers aligned with the Romantic movement were hugely influential throughout the nineteenth century, especially in its latter half, when there was a growing desire for more intellectually and emotionally meaningful expression in the fine and decorative arts. It could be said that nationalism was born of industrialization, but at the same time it was a response to growing internationalism. Indeed, it was during this period

←
Elbow chair designed by Eliel Saarinen for the State Railway Administration Offices, Helsinki, 1908–09.

←
Previous page: Hera printed-cotton textile for Liberty & Co., 1887—design attributed to Arthur Silver.

that large-scale international exhibitions began to be staged, such as the 1851 Great Exhibition of the Works of Industry of all Nations in London, the 1876 Centennial Exhibition in Philadelphia, and the 1900 Exposition Universelle in Paris. These extravaganzas with their dedicated national pavilions were ultimately showcases of creative endeavor, opportunities for countries to reveal to the world—often for the first time—what was unique about them. As such, they were important barometers of nations' cultural standing upon the world stage, and each participating country was keen to prove the superiority of its cultural output and present its national character in as meaningful a way as possible.

There was a growing recognition among many designers and architects taking part in such events that the decorative and industrial arts had been debased by the bottom line of commercial industrialization, and that wholesale reform was necessary. It was felt increasingly that one solution lay in looking back through time to each country's folk roots in order to identify the essence of its cultural identity. It was generally held that infusing designs with this native character would give greater national authenticity to the work of the present. In addition, it would provide a greater emotive connection between object and user than if a product's design was driven by the ornamental excesses of the mass market.

National Romanticism was not only a reaction against Neoclassicism and the rampant industrialism, urbanization, and social disconnection that the Industrial Revolution had brought. It can also be seen as a rose-tinted retreat into a romanticized and medieval-inspired past that was often more fictional than factual. Intriguingly, it was in Scandinavian countries that a romanticized sense of identity found especially fertile ground. In Norway, National Romanticism as a definable Nordic style emerged around the 1840s and found expression not only in the musical compositions of Edvard Grieg but also in the buildings, furniture, and silverware that were designed in the "Dragon Style," a curious medievalized Viking-revival style. The architect Holm Hansen Munthe's Frognerseteren restaurant (1890–91) in Holmenkollen, on the outskirts of Oslo, is the most famous building in this style to have survived, with its wooden stave roofs terminating in highly mannered dragon motifs. The woven wall hangings of Gerhard Munthe and the extraordinary Viking-style armchair designed by Lars Kinsarvik around 1900 similarly reveal a romantic notion of Norway's past—a sort of "Norwegian Aesthetic Movement"[2] as it has been described by the design historian Widar Halén. The movement reflected the country's desire to break away from the domination of neighboring Sweden, with which it had been formally unified since 1814, and establish national autonomy—which it finally did in 1905.

The New Art

In Finland there was a comparable desire to assert an authentic national identity, though here it was a reaction to Russian domination, as Finland was still at this time a "grand duchy" of the Russian Empire. The most famous product of this nationalistic sentiment was the *Kalevala* (Land of Heroes), an epic poem by Elias Lönnrot published in the mid-1830s. This literary masterpiece, written in Finnish, was based on the country's oral tradition of ancient poetry, songs, and ballads, and inspired by age-old folk tales that had been handed down from one generation to the next. It marked a turning point in Finland's history and became a potent symbol of national consciousness and patriotism. Mystical, heroic, and Romantic, the poem's influence was felt strongly not only in the fine arts but also in Finnish architecture and design.

Perhaps Finland's greatest exponent of National Romanticism was the architect Eliel Saarinen, who pioneered a style of architecture and design that alluded to his country's ancient Karelian culture. His Finnish Pavilion, codesigned with his partners Herman Gesellius and Armas Lindgren for the 1900 Exposition Universelle, took motifs from Nordic folk art and vernacular architecture and transformed them into a building that, with its soaring, trumpet-like spire and boldly arched entrance, articulated the exaggerated stylization of the New Art movement—a new formal expression for the dawning century.

Besides being inspired by their country's folk-art traditions, Saarinen, Gesellius, and Lindgren were strongly influenced by the work of their contemporaries abroad, most notably the Glasgow School and the Vienna Secession. Between 1902 and 1904 the trio designed the Kansallismuseo, the National Museum of Finland, in Helsinki, which with its bold massing of elements was an impressive display of national character interpreted within a proto-modern idiom. It is Saarinen's Helsinki Central Railway Station (initially designed in 1904) that is generally considered the apotheosis of the Finnish National Romantic style. Built between 1910 and 1914, this solidly constructed building, heavily clad in red Finnish granite and adorned with striking neo-Romantic architectural detailing, was a powerful projection of national pride.

↖
Frognerseteren restaurant in Holmenkollen, Oslo, designed by Holm Hansen Munthe in the National Romantic "Dragon Style," 1890–91.

↑
Viking-revival armchair designed by Lars Kinsarvik, c. 1900.

Yet paradoxically, the building also conveyed a new, forward-looking sense of internationalism with its pared-down elemental massing. While it can be considered emphatically a New Art building, it is utterly different stylistically from the oozing organic sensualism generally associated with this style elsewhere in continental Europe. As part of this prestigious commission, Saarinen also designed furniture for the State Railway Administration Offices, including an oak elbow chair with a horseshoe-shaped back and a pierced-heart motif, which revealed the strong influence of the British Arts and Crafts movement, especially the work of Charles Rennie Mackintosh and Charles Voysey. Saarinen emigrated to the United States in 1923, and through his teaching at the Cranbrook Educational Community (which would later incorporate as the Cranbrook Academy of Art) he instilled in the next generation of American designers some of the New Art movement's guiding principles.

↑
Main facade of Helsinki Central Railway Station designed by Eliel Saarinen, initally designed in 1904 and opened in 1914.

↑
Design for a living space by Saarinen, Herman Gesellius, and Armas Lindgren, 1903.

→
Finnish Pavilion designed by Eliel Saarinen, Herman Gesellius, and Armas Lindgren for the 1900 Exposition Universelle in Paris.

National Romanticism

The Arts and Crafts
movement in Britain

In Britain as in Scandinavia, during the closing decades of the nineteenth century there was a desire to create a more meaningful and emotionally resonant language of design. This endeavor built upon design-reform ideas that had been held earlier by A. W. N. Pugin, John Ruskin, and William Morris, and was also an expression of the pan-European National Romantic spirit. In Britain, however, designers were spurred on more by a desire to challenge the ills of unbridled industrialization than by the wish to assert a national identity, as the British Empire was already the world's most dominant political and economic power. In England, Morris's attempts to put ideas of social reform into design practice had a profound influence on the next generation of designers, whose work can best be described as "second phase" Arts and Crafts—a term originating from a show presented in 1888 by the Arts and Crafts Exhibition Society, which was established to promote the ideals of handcraftsmanship and to oppose the increasing industrialization of production.

This younger generation of Arts and Crafts designers quickly came to understand the underlying paradox of Morris's philosophy: his adherence to time-consuming and expensive methods of hand-manufacture prevented him from realizing his goal of creating affordable, well-designed, democratic products. Because of this, they were generally more ambivalent toward industrial mechanization, yet they retained a belief in the physical and moral superiority of handcraftsmanship. This was the generation that came of professional age during the Edwardian era and took Morris's ideas into the new century. They developed a coherent New Art aesthetic that was based on Morris's idea of "The Art of Everyday Life"—practical yet beautiful designs that were intended to remake daily domestic living and thereby transform society.

In 1882, inspired by Morris, the designers Arthur Heygate Mackmurdo and Selwyn Image founded Britain's first important Arts and Crafts group, the Century Guild of Artists. As its statutes declared, the venture was set up "to render all branches of art the sphere no longer of the tradesmen but of the artist" and sought to "restore building, decoration, glass-painting, pottery, wood-carving and metal to their rightful places

beside painting and sculpture."[3] The mission statement continued: "In other words, the Century Guild seeks to emphasize the Unity of Art and by thus dignifying Art in all of its forms, it hopes to make it living, a thing of our own century and of the people."[4] That same year, Mackmurdo designed a highly innovative chair for the guild's dining hall that featured a back splat incorporating an asymmetrical motif of swirling foliage stems. This eye-catching pattern did not look to the past in any way and can be seen as a small green shoot from which the full-blown organicism of the Art Nouveau style would grow and flourish during the following decade.

Among Morris's followers, it was Charles Robert Ashbee who took the great man's socially inspired ideals and advocacy of the simple life to their furthest limit when, in 1902, he relocated his Guild of Handicraft from

←
Decanter designed by Charles Robert Ashbee, 1901/1904–05, executed by the Guild of Handicraft.

↑
Chair with pierced back designed by Arthur Heygate Mackmurdo for the Century Guild of Artists, 1882.

the grimy slums of Whitechapel in London's East End to the ancient Cotswolds market town of Chipping Campden. This experimental collective, which survived for six years, was based on the Arts and Crafts movement's Arcadian vision of a rural community of artistic craftspeople who would find joy in their labor and, at the same time, produce work that was superior in both design and manufacture to that offered by mechanized means. And Ashbee's community of craftsmen—pithily dubbed "Cockneys in Camelot" by John Russell Taylor of the *Times of London*[5]—did produce such work, including various examples of the beautiful decanter previously designed by Ashbee himself in 1901, with its exquisite silver mounts of swirling interwoven floral forms. However, it was sadly destined to fail commercially, as competitors were producing similar designs, often inferior in quality, using more efficient industrial methods, which enable them to undercut the guild's prices. After the failure of his well-intentioned adventure in Chipping Campden, Ashbee turned away from what he deemed the "intellectual Ludditism" of Morris and Ruskin, and later declared that "Modern Civilisation rests on Machinery, and no system for the endowment, or the encouragement, or the teaching of art can be sound that does not recognize this."[6]

In Britain during the fin-de-siècle period, the Regent Street store Liberty & Co. was the most prominent exponent of New Art design and had the greatest commercial influence abroad. The store had opened in 1875 as an emporium of imports from Persia, India, China, and Japan, and it had been at the forefront of taste throughout the Aesthetic Movement. By the 1890s, times had changed and tastes had evolved; as a result, Liberty & Co. began making Arts-and-Crafts-style furnishings conceived by some of the most talented designers of the day.

Among the creative individuals who were commissioned by the store to produce New Art products was Archibald Knox, whose Celtic-inspired designs, like

↑
Oak armchair designed by C. F. A. Voysey, 1902.

↑
Kelmscott Chaucer oak cabinet designed by C. F. A. Voysey, 1899.

←
Cymric clock designed by Archibald Knox for Liberty & Co., 1903.

The Arts and Crafts movement in Britain

those of other second-phase Arts-and-Crafts designers, had a "form-cleansing" aesthetic that made them ideally suited to serial production. Interestingly, when Knox first arrived in London, in the early 1890s, he worked in the design studio of Christopher Dresser, who is generally considered to have been the first industrial-design consultant. From Dresser, Knox gained valuable experience designing "art manufactures" that were suited for serial production or even mass production. His silver Cymric line and his less expensive pewter Tudric line for Liberty & Co. did not have the overt figurative eroticism generally associated with continental Art Nouveau. Rather, they employed highly stylized floral motifs based on ancient Celtic patterns. Knox's use of ornament was integral to the overall form of his designs, which gave his creations a pleasing sense of unity. They also possessed a high degree of formal abstraction and, as a consequence, can be seen to have anticipated the work of the Modern Movement.

In addition to progressive metalwork designs, New Art textiles were a commercial mainstay for Liberty's, and to this end the firm employed many leading practitioners to create patterns during the 1890s and the early twentieth century, although it was company policy not to attribute textiles to specific designers. We know, however, that Arthur Silver of the Silver Studio designed many Liberty textiles, while Lindsay Philip Butterfield, Jessie M. King, Harry Napper, John Scarratt Rigby, Sidney Mawson, Charles Voysey, and Arthur Wilcock, among others, developed patterns for the store as well. As a comprehensive body of work, the textiles produced by Liberty's during this period were characterized by floral patterns that swirled harmoniously across printed cottons and velvets. Unlike the floral chintzes associated with both the earlier High Victorian Style and the majority of contemporaneous French textiles, these new fabrics did not depict flowers realistically, but instead frequently employed highly stylized intertwining motifs. Also in contrast to earlier Aesthetic Movement textiles, whose designs were generally much more controlled and even static, these Arts-and-Crafts fabrics had a strong rhythmic quality. Unsurprisingly, Liberty's bold Art Nouveau patterns became all the rage in England and in continental Europe, and their success soon spawned many imitations, some of which were even sold in France as the "Liberty Style." The Liberty name became so closely identified with Art Nouveau that in

↑
Entrance to the Glasgow School of Art designed by Charles Rennie Mackintosh, 1897–99 and 1907–09.

↑
Library at the Glasgow School of Art.

→
West facade of the Glasgow School of Art.

The New Art

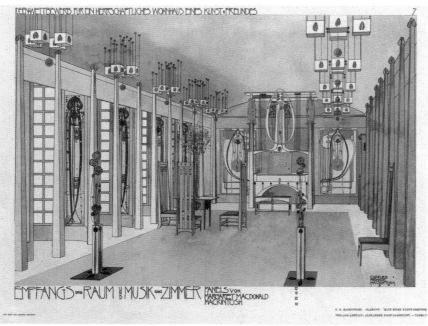

↑
Bedroom at Hill House,
Helensburgh, designed by
Charles Rennie Mackintosh,
1902–04.

←
Music Room designed by Charles
Rennie Mackintosh for the Haus
eines Kunstfreundes (House for
an Art Lover) competition, 1901.

The New Art

Italy the term "stile Liberty" was applied to all Art Nouveau designs, regardless of manufacturer.

Another leading figure in the development of the Arts and Crafts movement was Charles Voysey, without question the most influential British architect and designer of his generation. Voysey looked back to local traditions in building and furniture, designs that can be described as vernacular, to identify ideal forms that had been functionally honed over the centuries. He was also inspired by folk motifs and forms found in nature, and used them to imbue his designs with character and emotional appeal—work conceived for the heart as much as the head.

Voysey's human-centric approach might be seen as a direct result of his upbringing in a family that was deeply religious, though somewhat unorthodox. His father was a controversial Anglican clergyman who founded his own theist church, which was dubbed "the Religion of Common Sense." Throughout his life Voysey's work reflected this humanist philosophy, and his buildings and designs were motivated by an ethical imperative, as encapsulated in his declaration that "Simplicity, sincerity, repose, directness and frankness are moral qualities as essential to good architecture as to good men."[7] Of course, this credo applied equally to his design of objects, many of which were conceived specifically for his architectural commissions. Voysey's promotion of a simple yet modern vernacular style was highly influential not only in his own country, spawning in later decades countless suburbs of cottage-style semi-detached dwellings, but also abroad, both in America and in continental Europe. As the German architect, author, and diplomat Hermann Muthesius was to comment in his three-volume publication *Das Englische Haus* (The English House), Voysey was "the first to achieve a complete synthesis"[8] between the work of the designer and that of the architect, and in so doing created what became known as a *Gesamtkunstwerk*—a total work of art—meaning that an individual was responsible not only for the design of a building but for all its furnishings, too.

Another architect–designer associated with the British Arts and Crafts movement, who would become a great pioneer of the New Art style, was the Scotsman Charles Rennie Mackintosh. His early work was a modern interpretation of earlier types of Scottish architecture and furniture design. During the 1890s, Mackintosh and his associates created buildings and furniture in what became known as the Glasgow School, referencing the Scottish baronial style while appearing, at the same time, proto-modern. Mackintosh's masterwork, the Glasgow School of Art (1897–99 and 1907–09), with its asymmetrical facade and bold massing, was a structure built around its functional requirements. As with other British Arts-and-Crafts buildings from this period, the exterior reflected the configuration of the rooms it contained, in contrast to earlier classical edifices that gave little inkling of the way their interiors were laid out. The art and architecture historian Nikolaus Pevsner wrote of the Glasgow School of Art in his book *Pioneers of Modern Design*: "Not a single feature here is derived from period styles. The facade is of a strongly personal character and, in many ways, leads on to the twentieth century, although the entrance bay with balcony and short turret is deliberately fantastical. . . the rest of the front is extremely simple, almost austere in its bold uniform fenestration."[9] The simple-yet-sturdy furniture Mackintosh designed for the school possessed a similar rustic proto-modernity. The school represented a harmonic synthesis of the traditional and the modern, the beautiful and the utilitarian, the national and the international—and this balancing of opposites characterized not only Mackintosh's work but that of the New Art movement as a whole. Mackintosh's later efforts were even more progressive, as he moved toward a more individualistic style that employed an innovative language of design inspired by the organic found forms of nature.

Like the Glasgow School of Art, Hill House (1902–04) in Helensburgh, a residence Mackintosh designed for the publisher Walter Blackie, was based on a highly functional layout and was a realization of its creator's dogged pursuit of perfectly unified and harmoniously balanced interior schemes. The light-filled rooms of this remarkable dwelling employed both a highly abstracted and stylized organicism, in which forms melded into one another, and a very light color palette that gave the rooms an otherworldly airiness. As

Hermann Muthesius remarked of Mackintosh's "white rooms," like those conceived for Hill House: "At least for the time being, it is hard to imagine that aesthetic culture will prevail so much in our lives that interiors such as these will become commonplace. But they are paragons created by a genius, to show humanity that there is something higher in the distance which transcends everyday reality."[10] The work of "The Glasgow Four"—Mackintosh, his wife Margaret, and his sister-in-law and her husband, Francis and Herbert MacNair—certainly had a strong ethereal quality about it, which earned them the nickname "The Spook School." Their idiosyncratic work was also startlingly progressive and forward-looking, and it is not surprising that in dour Glasgow this was viewed as rather peculiar.

The Four went on to design the "Scottish Room" for the Eighth Secessionist Exhibition in 1900, held in Vienna's sublimely beautiful Secession Building designed by Josef Maria Olbrich (1897-98). This event enabled Mackintosh to establish crucial links with other progressive New Art designers in Vienna, among them Josef Hoffmann and Koloman Moser, with whom he corresponded after the exhibition. Such was the

Glasgow School's influence on designers associated with the Vienna Secession that Muthesius noted of the Four specifically that "they had a seminal influence on the emerging new vocabulary of forms, especially and continuously in Vienna, where an unbreakable bond was forged between them and the leaders of the Vienna Movement."[11] Mackintosh was also commissioned, in the same year as the Vienna show, to design a music salon for Fritz Wärndorfer, the principal backer of the Secessionists and later of the Wiener Werkstätte, a design-reforming enterprise that produced and retailed beautifully designed and executed art manufactures. The following year, he took part in the Haus eines Kunstfreundes (House for an Art Lover) competition, organized by the Darmstadt publisher Alexander Koch, which firmly established MacKintosh's reputation on the continent as one of the most progressive architects of his day. Later, he and his wife designed the Rose Boudoir installation for the Scottish section of the first *Esposizione Internazionale d'Arte Decorativa Moderna* (International Exposition of Modern Decorative Arts), held in Turin in 1902, and a bedroom installation for the Dresdener Werkstätten für Handwerkskunst exhibition of 1903-04. Despite reaping much international acclaim, Mackintosh became increasingly frustrated by the lack of response to his work in the United Kingdom, where he was often regarded more as an eccentric aesthete than as the design genius he undoubtedly was. Nevertheless, his influence on the development of progressive design in Austria and elsewhere cannot be overstated.

The second phase of the Arts and Crafts movement, sometimes referred to as the New Art movement, was to a great extent the British equivalent of the continental Art Nouveau style, and remained popular in Britain

↗
Pair of andirons designed by
Ernest Gimson, 1904

←
The Scottish Room designed by Charles
Rennie Mackintosh, Margaret MacDonald
Mackintosh, Herbert and Francis McNair for
the VIII Wiener Sezession (Vienna Secession)
exhibition, 1900.

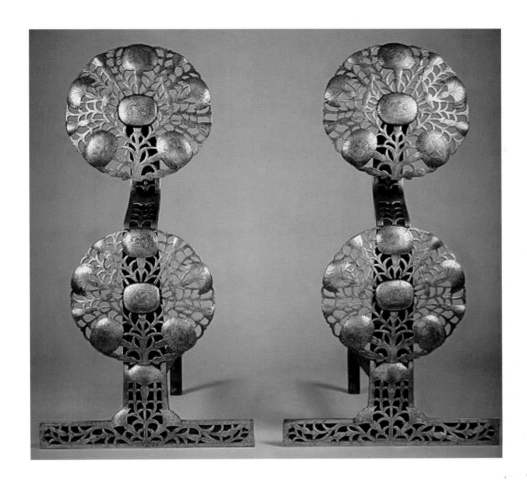

until the outbreak of World War I. Over the intervening years, Arts-and-Crafts furniture in particular became plainer and more utilitarian—as work by Ernest Gimson, Ernest and Sidney Barnsley, and Gordon Russell attests—and expressed a pared-down aesthetic. The British movement's espousal of simplicity, utility, and appropriateness, and its theory that design could be used as a democratic tool for social change, were instrumental in the formation of the Modern Movement, which applied these reforming principles to industrial production. The Arts and Crafts vision of using handcraftsmanship to create affordable, well-designed products was always just a beautiful socially motivated dream; it was only later that designers fully accepted that the only way to achieve truly democratic design was to harness the power of the machine, rather than to reject it.

The Arts and Crafts movement in America

Although it was inspired by the British Arts and Crafts movement's social agenda and democratic ideals, the American Arts and Crafts movement forged its own national interpretation of the New Art style. In the United States, designers took inspiration from the country's can-do pioneering roots and its colonial past to create furniture and other homewares in the so-called Mission Style. This style of design, which was typified by the use of strong vertical and horizontal lines and plain, often unadorned surfaces, supposedly recalled the furnishings used in the missions set up by the Spanish in California during the late eighteenth and early nineteenth centuries. Yet Mission designs often owed very little to their antique antecedents, being based more on romantic nostalgia than historical fact. This notion of the pioneer aesthetic, rose-tinted as it may have been, was the main influence on American Arts and Crafts designers, who focused more on function than decoration. Their rough-and-ready, purposeful approach ensured that they generally produced work that was more muscular and elemental than that created by European exponents of the New Art.

↑
Cover of *The Craftsman* magazine,
January 1904.

←
Side chair designed by Harvey Ellis for Gustav
Stickley, c. 1903.

←
Model 614 oak library table designed by Gustav
Stickley, 1904.

The American Arts and Crafts movement was multi-centered, with various Arts and Crafts societies formed across the country, the first in Boston and Chicago in 1897. The strong socialist undercurrent of the movement in Britain was not so overt in America and inspired the establishment of onyl a few utopian communities, most notably Will Price's Rose Valley Association, founded in Moylan, Pennsylvania, in 1901. That is not to say that William Morris and Charles Ashbee's advocacy of such rural craftsmen collectives did not capture the imagination of designers in America—it certainly did. A number of them sought creative refuge from the rapidly increasing industrialization of their nation, the abuses of which had not only affected the social wellbeing of artisans but also brought about a plethora of poorly designed goods intended mainly for the home. Of course, there were exceptions to this rule, and in America during the nineteenth century a number of machine-made items were of excellent quality, from firearms and bicycles to typewriters and sewing machines. For the most part, however, machines were used by manufacturers to cheaply copy handcrafts and period decorative styles. American were often far less politically dogmatic and more entrepreneurial than their British counterparts in their desire to reform design. One reason why their designs were typically simpler, in both construction and decoration, than their British equivalents, is that the underlying democratic aspects of the movement often appealed more to designers in the US than an emphasis on superlative handcraftsmanship. This trait was also a reflection of the famous Yankee can-do spirit, itself born of a Protestant ethic that saw simplicity as morally superior to complexity.

One designer whose work exemplified the pared-down aesthetic of the American Arts and Crafts movement was Gustav Stickley. Highly influenced by the achievements of the British Arts and Crafts movement, Stickley traveled to Europe and met with Charles Ashbee and Charles Voysey before establishing his own workshop in Syracuse, New York, in 1898. It manufactured rustic Mission-style furniture and lighting. In 1901, Stickley began publishing the highly influential *The Craftsman*, a monthly journal that disseminated his ideas to a wide public and included drawings and plans for Arts and Crafts-style homes and furnishings. As its tagline in its May 1908 issue declared, it was "edited and published by Gustav Stickley in the interest of better art, better work and a better and more reasonable way of living." A 1911 article by Natalie Curtis stated that "there are elements of intrinsic beauty in the simplification of a house built on the log cabin idea."[12]

An associate of Stickley's, Harvey Ellis, also had a strong influence on the development of the Arts and Crafts style in America. The Rochester, New York-based architect began working for Stickley as a designer in 1903, and though they were only together for seven months before Ellis's early death, during this brief period of creative endeavor they pioneered a less rustic style. While Ellis's designs were still inspired by vernacular precedents, they had a lighter and more graceful quality that was stylistically closer to the refinement of continental European Art Nouveau and the artistic excellence of the British New Art movement.

Another American motivated by the design-reforming success of the British Arts and Crafts movement was the designer and entrepreneur Elbert Hubbard. Originally a traveling salesman, Hubbard styled himself "Fra Elbertus" and described himself as an "anarchist" and socialist, but he was in fact a very canny businessman. In 1894 he traveled to Europe to research a series of biographical sketches in booklet form entitled *Little Journeys to the Homes of the Great*. It was during this trip that he claimed to have visited William Morris; whether this actually happened, however, remains a matter of conjecture. On his return to America, he established the Roycroft Press in East Aurora, inspired by Morris's own Kelmscott Press, and

→
Metal workshop at Roycrofters, c. 1909.

The Arts and Crafts movement in America

in 1895 he began publishing his monthly *Little Journeys* booklets profiling famous women, American statesmen, and great philosophers, among others. Hubbard subsequently established his own bindery and leather workshop in East Aurora, New York, and in 1896 added a furniture-making workshop to produce Mission-style furniture. With Elbert Hubbard as its charismatic leader, the Roycroft community of artisans soon became a destination for like-minded freethinking individuals, who came not only to hear Hubbard's socially inspired and often controversial lectures but also to visit the workshops and purchase souvenirs. In fact, Roycroft became such a popular destination for tourists that in 1905 the Roycroft Inn was opened to accommodate their ever-increasing numbers. By 1906 more than four hundred people were working at the community, and in 1909 a metalworking shop was opened. More than anything else, the Roycroft

community, which eventually closed in 1938, demonstrated that it was possible to create a self-sustaining rural crafts collective that could produce art manufactures of a quality superior to those produced entirely by machine. The popularity and overt commercialism of this venture, however, led to accusations of selling out the founding ideals of the Arts and Crafts movement. Whatever one's position, Roycroft was undeniably instrumental in popularizing the movement in the United States and ultimately made the simple forms it espoused fashionable among the wider public.

Various other designers also set up their own Arts and Crafts-inspured workshops: in 1908 Dirk van Erp established the Art Copper Shop in Oakland, California, to produce art metalwork such as his hammered copper lamps, with their distinctive amber-colored mica shades; Charles Limbert established the Holland Arts and Dutch

Copper table lamp with mica shade designed
by Dirk van Erp, c. 1910.

George Ohr in his Biloxi workshop surrounded
by his "No Two Alike" art pottery pieces, 1901.

Crafts Company in Grand Rapids, Michigan, in 1902 to produce furniture that was notable for its use of simple cut-out square and heart motifs and plain slab-like constructions. There was also the Buffalo, New York-based furniture maker Charles Rohlfs, who during the late 1890s and early 1900s created individualistic "artistic furniture" that had an eccentric and fantastical demeanor, with exaggerated forms and highly stylized, organic-inspired decoration. And last but by no means least, there was the "Mad Potter of Biloxi"—the extravagantly bewhiskered George Ohr, who crafted almost paper-thin ceramics that he pinched into distorted naturalistic forms and then sold with the tagline "No Two Alike." Although the outputs of these designers and their workshops, as well as others across the country, were quite distinct, certain characteristics distinguished American Arts and Crafts designs, among them a rustic, unusual style of decoration and the use of simple elemental shapes.

While some took quite a rough-and-ready approach to design and manufacture, others preferred a more refined treatment of materials. Belonging to the latter school was Louis Comfort Tiffany, who received much international recognition for creating innovative designs in the New Art style and whose work was always notable for the exceptional quality of its execution. The son of Charles Lewis Tiffany, who had founded the well-known silver and jewelry firm Tiffany & Co. in 1853, Louis established his own artistic manufacturing venture in Corona, Long Island, in 1892; it was initially known as the Tiffany Glass and Decorating Company and renamed Tiffany Studios in 1900. In 1896 Tiffany began marketing his distinctive iridescent Favrile glassware, which had been trademarked and patented in 1894. Conceived as high-quality "art glass," it was quite unlike anything else then being manufactured in the United States. Characterized by the use of undulating organic forms, Tiffany's Favrile designs—such as his famous Jack-in-the-Pulpit vase of 1907—captured the abstract essence of nature, while their glistening, lustrous surfaces gave them an exotic quality, rather like the shimmering feathers of a peacock. His leaded-glass designs, most notably his "Tiffany lamps," were also highly progressive and boldly extended the parameters

of the age-old craft of stained-glass making. It was his exquisite Magnolia window panels—designed around 1885 for his Madison Avenue residence and later installed in his Long Island country estate, Laurelton Hall—that revealed Tiffany's absolute mastery of his craft and his breathtaking talent for subtle coloring and sublimely balanced composition. These three panels, now in the collection of the Morse Museum of American Art in Winter Park, Florida, even today seem startlingly fresh, using an almost trompe-l'oeil effect to make viewers feel as though they are looking through a window onto real magnolia blossoms. These exquisite panels were the most forward-looking designs of Tiffany's highly prolific career, and demonstrated that American decorative arts could be just as innovative as anything produced in Europe during the late nineteenth century.

In 1894 the Hamburg-born art dealer Siegfried Bing visited Tiffany's Corona-based glassmaking operation. While on this fact-finding trip to New York, he also admired the opulent and exotic Havemeyer

↖
Pink Lotus lamp designed by Louis Comfort
Tiffany and manufactured by Tiffany Studios,
c. 1905.

↑
Magnolia three-paneled window designed by
Louis Comfort Tiffany, c. 1885.

→
Interior of Louis Comfort Tiffany's Laurelton Hall.

Mansion on Fifth Avenue that Tiffany had decorated two years earlier with Samuel Colman. When Bing opened his famous Maison de l'Art Nouveau gallery in Paris the following year, he exhibited Tiffany's glassware and subsequently became his sole distributor in Europe—demonstrating the ever-increasing links being forged during this period between European and American design communities. Yet despite this, most American designers did not embrace the stylistic exuberance of Art Nouveau to the same extent as their European counterparts. Tiffany was an exception to this rule, his work reflecting the influence of Franco-Belgian design tendencies in its motifs and organic forms while also adhering to the underlying principles of the Arts and Crafts movement in its insistence on high-quality manufacturing and hand-finishing by skilled craftsmen. The influence of the Continental Art Nouveau style in America was perhaps felt more acutely in the graphic arts, with the work of Will Bradley having a similar sense of swirling chaotic vigor as the posters of Henri de Toulouse-Lautrec in France or the book illustrations of Aubrey Beardsley in Great Britain.

Like Tiffany, the architect brothers Charles Sumner Greene and Henry Mather Greene also pioneered a uniquely American and more refined interpretation of the Arts and Crafts style, in this instance with their Japanese-influenced residences, such as the Gamble House (1908–9) and the Robert R. Blacker House (1907), both located in Pasadena. These low-slung Californian homes were remarkable not only for the asymmetry, linearity, and extraordinary spatial delineation of their plans but also for the fact that they were conceived as *Gesamtkunstwerk* projects in which custom-designed furnishings contributed to a unified and harmonious whole. Designed for a

↗
Living room of the Gamble House in Pasadena, designed by Greene & Greene, 1908–09.

→
Poster advertising *The Echo* designed by Will H. Bradley, 1895.

The New Art

discriminating and wealthy clientele, these buildings boasted exquisite, coordinated detailing and reflected the philosophy outlined by Charles Sumner Greene in *Western Architect* magazine in July 1908: "The style of the house should be as far as possible determined by four conditions; First, Climate; Second, Environment; Third, Kinds of materials available; Fourth, Habits and tastes—i.e., life of the owner."[13] The Greenes did not always give their clients what they originally thought they wanted, but as Charles Sumner Greene noted the results were "always what they liked," because their schemes were so well considered, thanks to their holistic approach to design, and so exacting in their execution, down to the smallest of details.

Frank Lloyd Wright similarly took enormous care in the minute detailing of his buildings, and more than any other individual he bridged the transition between the Arts and Crafts movement and the later International Style through his unified architectural schemes. Like the Greenes, Wright believed that buildings must not only be designed from a human-centric perspective but also be in harmony with their surrounding environment—an approach he termed "organic." Wright worked for six years in the Chicago architecture firm of Adler & Sullivan and was highly influenced by his mentor, Louis Sullivan, who is remembered for coining the dictum "form ever follows function." Less well known is the fact that Sullivan was a strong believer in transcendentalism, and as such sought to create a "true" and "poetic" architecture based on imagery drawn from nature. He also argued that while it was the decoration of a building that ultimately gave it its "identity" or character, ornament should be an embellishment of structure rather than an extraneous afterthought. Sullivan believed that appropriate decoration was the bridge between nature and science, and also between the organic and inorganic worlds. Galvanized by Sullivan's approach to design and decoration, Wright went on to establish his own architecture practice, first in Chicago in 1893 and then in Oak Park, just west of Chicago. There and in other nearby suburbs, he produced some fifty private residences. These Arts and Crafts houses were built primarily in stone, brick, and wood, and a few of the later projects were designed in the Prairie School style. With their low elevations, projecting eaves, and gently sloping rooflines, Prairie Style buildings were intended to echo the horizontal midwestern landscape and therefore integrate more sympathetically into their surrounding environment. Wright's own house and studio, built in Oak Park in 1889 (and remodeled in 1897–98), demonstrates the remarkable organic unity of his projects, with its custom-designed fixtures and fittings and its harmonious earth-toned palette of warm mustard yellows and dusky sage greens. Unlike the rustic interiors designed by Gustav Stickley, Wright's have a rarefied aestheticism more akin to the later work of Charles Rennie Mackintosh. His buildings similarly reflected the influence of Japanese art and architecture, using screen elements to delineate space and making use of harmoniously unified detailing. Wright's holistic approach went further than architectural fixtures and fittings: he designed matching loose-fitting garments for his wife and also for some of his clients.

→
Architectural drawing showing elevations of
the Gamble House in Pasadena designed by
Greene & Greene, 1908–09.

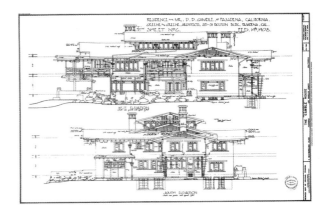

By the opening years of the twentieth century, Wright's buildings had become even more rectilinear and modern looking, as demonstrated by William E. Martin House in Oak Park (1902), with its strong vertical and horizontal planes, stucco facing, and banded windows. It could be said that this late Arts and Crafts building's facade anticipated the work of the later De Stijl movement, having a similar sense of uncluttered geometric purity. The strong rectilinear theme was maintained throughout the house's interior, where for example a reclining oak Morris chair mirrored the sturdy columns and jutting elements of the exterior. Two years later, Wright designed his first significant public work, the Larkin Administration Building, a substantial brick building in Buffalo, New York. With its strict geometric massing, pared-down decoration, and functional delineation of space, the structure was more emphatically modern than any of his earlier projects.

Its highly innovative design and layout were intended to aid the efficient running of the mail-order soap company operating within, and to this end Wright provided an open-plan glass-covered central atrium as well as built-in office furniture. For the office spaces he also designed office chairs made from cast iron, steel, and leather, which had seat backs perforated in a grid pattern that echoed the linearity of the surrounding architecture. This ambitious project's eloquently unified scheme reflected Wright's guiding desire to produce a total work of art, and it certainly helped establish his reputation as a pioneering force within the worlds of architecture and design. In some ways, the Larkin Company Administration Building can also be seen as a transitional work between the New Art movement and full-blown modernism. It was, however, the appearance in 1910 of a two-volume folio comprising a hundred lithographs of Wright's work, published by the Berlin-based publisher Ernst

↑
Interior of the Dana Thomas House in Springfield, Illinois, designed by Frank Lloyd Wright, built 1902–04.

↗
Interior of the Frederick C. Robie House in Chicago, designed by Frank Lloyd Wright, built 1909.

Wasmuth, that would cement Wright's international credentials as a design pioneer, especially in Europe, where his work was a revelation to his peers, who would go on to become the first generation of truly modern designers. More than any other designer working in America around the end of the nineteenth and beginning of the twentieth centuries, Wright was able to evolve the formal language of the Arts and Craftsstyle into something even more aesthetically and functionally progressive, allowing him to create buildings and designs that had a strong proto-modernity about them. Thus we see that the Modern Movement has its roots in the United States, where Arts and Crafts practitioners, looking back to their country's pioneering origins, recognizing simplicity and functionality as the most important aspects of life-enhancing design.

←
Exterior view of the Frank Lloyd Home and Studio in Oak Park, Illinois, built 1889, remodeled 1895.

↖
Exterior view of the Larkin Company Administration Building in Buffalo, New York, designed by Frank Lloyd Wright, 1903.

↖
Workstation designed for the Larkin Company Administration Building by Frank Lloyd Wright, 1903.

8

ART NOUVEAU

The Art Nouveau style

As we have seen, during the fin-de-siècle period spanning the years 1890 to 1914, a new international style emerged, rejecting the slavish historical revivalism of the preceding decades to instead seek inspiration in natural forms as well as in folk-inspired vernacularism. During this heady time, many designers took motifs directly from nature—a furling leaf, a peacock feather, a blossoming rose—and dramatically stylized them in designs that invoked dynamic, swirling growth. Among the leading proponents of this approach in Britain were Charles Rennie Mackintosh and his wife, Margaret, who created furnishings and interiors that had an otherworldly, ethereal quality and also reflected the increasing interest in symbolism and spiritualism of the period. In fact, the Art Nouveau style is seen by design historians as a direct descendant of both the Aesthetic Movement, championed by James Abbott McNeill Whistler and Oscar Wilde, and the Symbolist movement of Gustav Klimt, Gustave Moreau, Odilon Redon, and others.

But it was in France and Belgium that the Art Nouveau style found its most sublime expression, with examples including the extraordinary *Gesamtkunstwerk* (meaning "total work of art") architectural schemes of Victor Horta and the wonderful arching, vegetal Paris Métro entrances designed by Hector Guimard. Unlike the Arts and Crafts movement in Britain and America, which looked back to a historical idyll in order to create a utopian future, there was an altogether less doctrinal interpretation of the New Art style in France and Belgium, where the focus was on ahistorical motifs drawn from the natural world. The use of such patterns was not an arbitrary decorative whim, but rather can be traced to Christopher Dresser's earlier studies of botanical structures, which he had outlined in a series of articles entitled "Botany as Adapted to the Arts and Art Manufactures," published in *Art Journal* in 1857, and to the German biologist Ernst Haeckel, who published his *Kunstformen der Natur* (Art Forms in Nature) lithographic plates in ten installments between 1899 and 1904. Bridging the gap between art and science, these prints of sea anemones, jellyfish, protozoa, and the like were

←
The Salon of Victor Horta's house and studio in Brussels (now the Horta Museum), designed in 1898.

→
Plate showing a variety of sea anemones from Ernest Haeckel's *Kunstformen der Natur*, 1899–1904.

←
Previous page: Cameo glass table light designed by Émile Gallé, c. 1895–1900.

hugely influential on the development of early twentieth-century design and architecture. Interestingly, Haeckel was responsible for coining the word "ecology," in reference to his theory that everything in the natural world is interconnected. His influence is notable in the 1890s work of the Belgian architect Victor Horta, who used vegetal forms that recalled the whirling life force found in Haeckel's lithographs, with all elements of his interiors united by a strong stylistic interrelationship, from the specially designed door handles to the custom-made furniture. One of the best surviving examples of Horta's work is his Hôtel Tassel (1893–94), a *Gesamtkunstwerk* town house built for the Belgian scientist Émile Tassel, generally regarded as the first true Art Nouveau building. The residence was groundbreaking in its use of a steel-and-glass roof that bathed its stairwell core in warm, golden light and the writhing, decorative floral motifs in its staircase, which incorporated structural columns and integrated lighting fixtures to dramatic effect. As the Belgian art critic Sander Pierron, whose own house

Horta had designed, noted in his book *L'École de gravure de Liège* (The printmaking school of Liège) in 1923, the Hôtel Tassel was "the first manifestation of a movement victorious today, the first modernist work, chronologically speaking. All the originality in Victor Horta's talent is to be found in this dwelling: in the plan, in the facade, in the choice and blend of materials of which it is built."[1]

Horta's house and studio, which he built between 1898 and 1901 on the rue Américaine in Brussels, was a similarly progressive project; it is now home to the Horta Museum. Like the Hôtel Tassel, this is an Art Nouveau

↑
Hallway and staircase of the Hôtel Tassel in Brussels, designed by Victor Horta, 1893–94.

→
Dining room of Victor Horta's house and studio in Brussels (now the Horta Museum), designed 1898.

Art Nouveau

The Art Nouveau style

tour de force, its airy, light-filled interiors having a precious jewel-box quality; it is a sublimely beautiful manifestation of the New Art style, which itself reflected the forward-looking spirit of the new century.

Another Belgian architect who had a seminal impact on the development of design and architecture during the first half of the twentieth century was Henry van de Velde. Together with Horta and Paul Hankar, this Antwerp-born designer, who had initially trained as a painter, was a primary exponent of Art Nouveau in Belgium during the 1890s; however, unlike his compatriots, van de Velde had a resounding international influence and in later life became a key figure in the formation of the Modern Movement in Germany. His work was originally inspired by the Arts and Crafts movement in Britain and America, and was stylistically more restrained than Horta's, as attested by the Bloemenwerf chair he designed in 1895 for the dining room of his own house in Uccle. This simple piece, with its flaring back and legs, reflected van de Velde's belief that decoration should always be informed by a design's construction rather than applied as surface ornamentation. As he noted in 1901 in his article *Was ich will* (What I want): "No ornament can be permitted that is not organically absorbed. . . . I wish to replace old symbolic elements, which have lost their effectiveness for us today, with a new, imperishable beauty . . . in which ornament has no life of its own but depends on the forms and lines of the object itself, from which it receives its proper organic place."[2] Unlike designers aligned to the British Arts and Crafts movement, van de Velde saw the machine as a powerful catalyst with which to achieve a new kind of beauty, arguing that engineers were "the architects of the present day."[3] He also called for "a logical structure of products, uncomprising logic in the use of materials, proud and frank exhibition of working processes,"[4] a rallying cry that was later taken up by the association of German designers, architects, artists, and industrialists called the Deutscher Werkbund (German Association of Craftsmen), which was founded in 1907 and of which van de Velde was a member. The British Design and Industries Association, established in 1915, was similarly sympathetic to van de Velde's sentiments. The Belgian designer also believed that the artist's

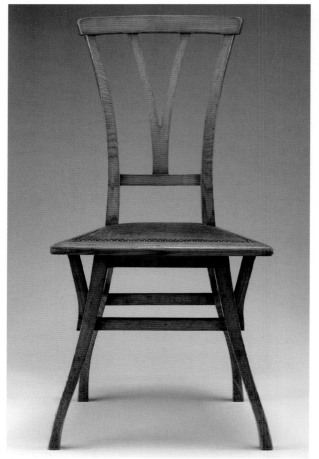

individuality should never be subsumed by the sterile standardization demanded by large-scale industrial production. He was commissioned by the art dealer Siegfried "Samuel" Bing to design the interiors of his upmarket gallery on the rue de Provence in Paris, which became one of the most fashionable centers of the New Art movement.

Like Arthur Lasenby Liberty in London, Bing originally imported and retailed Japanese art and design, both antique and contemporary, and as such was instrumental in the development of Art Nouveau, which was much inspired by the aestheticism of Japanese art. In 1894 the French government commissioned him to produce a report entitled *La Culture artistique en Amérique* (Artistic Culture of America), and on his return

←
Bloemenwerf in Uccle, designed by Henry van de Velde as his own residence, built 1895.

↙
Dining chair for Bloemenwerf designed by Henry van de Velde and manufactured by Société van de Velde & Co., 1895.

↙
Entrance of L'Art Nouveau pavilion at the Exposition Universelle in Paris, 1900.

↓
Advertisement for Bing's Maison de l'Art Nouveau, c. 1900.

abandonment of the eighteenth-century French decorative tradition. For instance, commenting on the store's opening in the Paris newspaper *Le Figaro*, the art critic Octave Mirbeau stated that "All this smacks of the English lecher, the Jewish morphine addict or the Belgian rogue, or a nice salad of these three poisons."[5]

Such damning critiques, however, did not halt the flourishing of the style, which also found fertile ground in other French cities, most notably the Lorraine city of Nancy. In 1901, about ten designers founded the École Nancy to reform design by taking nature as a template—an early example of biomimicry. Among them were Émile Gallé and Louis Majorelle, both of whom ran highly successful workshops that sold their elegant, beautifully handcrafted designs for glass and furniture both at home and abroad. Similarly sensuous, organic forms were also displayed in the oeuvres of Eugène Gaillard and Georges de Feure, both of whom exhibited work in Siegfried Bing's pavilion at the 1900 Paris Exposition Universelle. Another proponent of Art Nouveau in Paris was the German art historian Julius Meier-Graefe, who opened his own rival gallery, La Maison Moderne, in 1899; it was intended for a younger clientele than Bing's and showed work that was even more progressive.

It was, however, the work of Hector Guimard that epitomized the French Art Nouveau style better than any other. Born in Lyons, Guimard studied at the École Nationale des Beaux-Arts in Paris, where he was introduced to the architectural theories of Eugène-Emmanuel Viollet-le-Duc, who argued that it was essential to use materials honestly and that buildings should rationally reflect their construction. The English Domestic Revival of the Arts and Crafts movement also initially inspired him. Despite these ideological influences, it was Guimard's 1895 visit to Victor Horta's Hôtel Tassel that led him to completely reevaluate his approach to architecture and design, helping him to shape his own interpretation of the style. Guimard's Castel Béranger apartment building (1894–98), with its asymmetrical tendril-infested wrought-iron entrance, extraordinary grotto-like foyer, and intricate cast-iron balconies unmistakeably attests to Horta's influence. Yet Art Nouveau in Guimard's hands was treated with an

from his travels in December 1895 he reopened his rue de Provence venue under a new name, the Maison de l'Art Nouveau. Van de Velde's interiors there provided a suitably stylish backdrop for the retail of contemporary artworks, both fine and decorative, produced by Western artists in the Art Nouveau style. The artists and designers whose work was exhibited at the gallery included Georges Lemmen, Édouard Vuillard, Paul Ranson, Pierre Bonnard, Henri-Gabriel Ibels, Félix Vallotton, Henri de Toulouse-Lautrec, and Louis Comfort Tiffany. The store also sold silks by Liberty & Co., wallpaper and textiles by Morris & Co. and metalwork by William Arthur Smith Benson. Although the Maison de l'Art Nouveau became Paris's most stylish emporium for the New Art and there was much enthusiasm for Bing's boutique and the objets d'art it sold, some critics were disturbed by the style's even more flamboyant and vigorously theatrical flair, and his creations had an almost hallucinogenic quality. Although there is no suggestion that Guimard took mind-altering drugs, the use of recreational drugs, especially opiates, was rife during the 1890s and surely had an influence on many designers' creative perceptions. Indeed, the poppy became a recurring motif in Art Nouveau graphics during this period, most notably in Alphonse Mucha's posters.

Above all, it was Guimard's cast-iron entrances to the Paris Métro, designed for the Compagnie du Métropolitain in 1898, that brought him widespread acclaim. These extraordinary street-furniture designs embodied his belief that "For construction, do not the branches of the trees, the stems, by turn rigid and undulating, furnish us with models?"[6] They also led to his name becoming so associated with Art Nouveau that the term "Style Guimard" was coined in France to refer to the style in general. The Métro entrances, with their gigantic swelling and stylized flowering stalks, were constructed using standardized cast-iron components to enable serial manufacture and to ease transportation and installation. For visitors using the new network during the 1900 Exposition Universelle, these curious entrances must have seemed the height of fashionable modernity—and though the taste for Art Nouveau soon began to wane, and was in the process of being replaced by a more restrained aesthetic by the middle of the decade, there were still several years of production within the Art Nouveau style, both in France and beyond.

René Lalique, who designed exquisite jewelry incorporating highly stylized motifs of flora and fauna, must also be mentioned in relation to the Art Nouveau style in France. He created numerous innovative pieces for Siegfried Bing's Maison de l'Art Nouveau gallery, and

Bing also exhibited his work at the Exposition Universelle. His painstakingly executed jewelry designs in enamel studded with gems were stylishly luxurious, characterized by motifs inspired by an array of sources, from wild flowers and insects to magical creatures and classical mythology. For instance, his beautiful gold-and-enamel Dragonfly Woman corsage (c. 1897–98) took the form of a fantastical bare-breasted woman emerging from the iridescent wings of a dragonfly and flanked by golden claws—a piece of finely detailed craftsmanship that exemplified French Art Nouveau's obsession with metamorphosis and eroticism. One English visitor to the Paris exhibition remarked of this exquisite brooch, "Very remarkable and startling to the observer, but is it

↖
Entrance to the Castel Béranger apartment building in Paris designed by Hector Guimard, 1894–98.

→
Advertising poster for Job cigarette papers designed by Alphonse Mucha, 1898.

jewelry?"[7] It most assuredly was, but it was like no design seen before in that medium.

Much the same could be said of the work of the Catalan architect and designer Antoni Gaudí. With their bizarrely biomorphic forms, his buildings and furniture designs were a typically extreme Catalan expression of the New Art style, which in Spain was termed *Modernismo*. This name reflected the style's ahistorical ethos, and although Gaudí referenced past styles in his idiosyncratic work, his designs were still very much an expression of the fin-de-siècle spirit. His Barcelona architecture, from the soaring Sagrada Família church to the Parque Güell, a private residential enclave abundant with gardens, borrowed motifs from Gothic and Moorish architecture and then transformed them into exotic melting forms. As the design historian Nikolaus Pevsner noted of Parque Güell, it went "beyond Western Art Nouveau, and yet can only be understood within the terms of that short-lived style. Here is the frantic desire for the unprecedented, here the faith in the creative individual, here the delight of the arbitrary curve, and here the keen interest in the possibilities of materials."[8] Defying convention, Gaudí used broken tiles as well as old cups and saucers to dress the undulating bench that wraps the development's elevated main plaza, producing a colorful scale-like mosaic effect that was unlike anything that had been produced before. It was playful "art for art's sake" on an unprecedented public scale. He later used the same curious mix of materials for the soaring pinnacles of his Sagrada Família, which looks like a fanciful fairy-tale castle out of sand. More than any other Spanish designer's work, Gaudí's buildings and designs—such as his armchair with a heart-shaped back designed for the Casa Calvet (1989–1904)—possessed an emotionally charged sense of mystical *duende* and

epitomized the sheer theatrical bravado of Spanish Art Nouveau. And they went further than that, too, anticipating at once the collages of the expressionists, with their similarly vibrant patchwork quality, the expressive faux-primitive ceramics of Pablo Picasso, and the joyously surrealistic work of Joan Miró.

The Italian designer Carlo Bugatti also produced fantastical designs within the Art Nouveau idiom, most notably his Snail Room installation for the Esposizione Internazionale d'Arte Decorativa Moderna, which was held in Turin in 1902. Incorporating Moorish-inspired furnishings in the full-blown Art Nouveau style, this "games and conversation room" was based on Bugatti's studies of curvilinear forms found in nature. With its sweeping upholstered banquette, table, and three extraordinary chairs, the forms of all of which were inspired by snail shells, this installation revealed a new and bold Art Nouveau tendency within Italian design, which in Italy became known as the Stile Liberty.

The New Art style also took hold in the Netherlands, notably in the work of Hendrik Petrus Berlage. A student of the German classicist architect Gottfried Semper during the 1870s, Berlage was also influenced by the Gothic revivalist and first theorist of modern architecture, Viollet-le-Duc, who, as we have noted, believed that buildings should directly express their function, materials, and construction techniques. Guided by this honest approach to design, Berlage made buildings and furniture that conveyed an undeniable New Art proto-modernity. Meanwhile, around the turn

↗
Dragonfly Woman corsage designed by
René Lalique, c. 1897–98.

←
Paris Métro entrance designed by
Hector Guimard for the Compagnie du
Métropolitian, 1898.

of the century, the Dutch designer Samuel Schellink produced a series of eggshell porcelain designs for the Rozenburg ceramics factory in The Hague. With their abstract, ballooning organic forms and stylized floral decoration, these pieces were the most overt Dutch expression of the Art Nouveau style.

There were many unifying themes that solidified the various national expressions of Art Nouveau into a distinct international movement: the bold, organic shapes; the adoption of attenuated whiplash forms; the recurrence of a "molten" style, in which elements within a design seemed to merge into one another; the love of intricate pattern-making; and most especially, the strident anti-historicism. It was a style that looked optimistically to the future rather than nostalgically to the past, using as its primary source of inspiration the visually seductive and tactile forms of the natural world. It was also a truly international style that was adopted comprehensively across all realms of the applied arts:

from glassware, furniture, and lighting to jewelry, graphic design, and typography. In this respect, it is now regarded as a "total" style. Yet in many ways Nikolaus Pevsner was correct in his assertion that Art Nouveau was a "blind alley" in terms of the development of the Modern Movement, in that it was primarily a decorative style rather than a functionally driven design movement. This analysis might be too harsh, though, for its practitioners' rejection of historical influences was an important and necessary stepping-stone toward modernism. It could be argued that, because of this, Art Nouveau was the first modern style, that by throwing off the historicizing, decorative shackles of the past it allowed the next generation of designers to seek unencumbered the road to true modernity.

Snail chair designed by Carlo Bugatti for a
"games and conversation room" installation
at the Esposizione Internazionale d'Arte
Decorative Moderna in Turin, 1902.

Interior view of Casa Batlló in Barcelona,
redesigned by Antoni Gaudí, 1904–06.

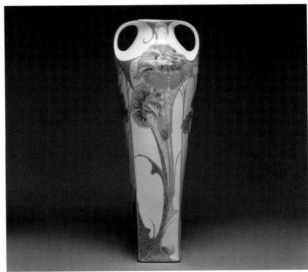

Games and conversation room designed by
Carlo Bugatti for the 1902 Turin exposition,
nicknamed the Snail Room.

Vase designed by Samuel Schellink and
executed by J. Juriaan Kok for Rozenburg, 1902.

Art Nouveau

Jugendstil

Amid the pervasive spread of nationalism in central Europe during the mid-to-late nineteenth century, there was in Germany a strong desire to assert an autonomous cultural identity. This was especially felt after the establishment of the *Kaiserreich* in 1871, which had unified the historically independent states of Germany into a single monarchical entity ruled by the kaiser. It was understood that both art and commerce would be instrumental in the development of an authentic German identity, and as a result a new style emerged that was utterly distinct from other countries' interpretations of the New Art style. The branch that emerged in Germany during the 1890s was termed Jugendstil, which translates as "youth style." Although this name reflected the forward-looking spirit of the movement as well as the youthful optimism of many of its proponents, it was actually drawn from the title of the influential Munich-based weekly magazine *Jugend*. Founded by Georg Hirth in 1896, this cultural journal was largely responsible for popularizing Art Nouveau in Germany. The designers associated with Jugendstil were strongly motivated by the earlier design-reforming ideas and social agenda of John Ruskin and William Morris, and as such had more ideological aims than their Franco-Belgian contemporaries. They not only sought to improve the decorative arts and their related manufacture but also advocated for a return to a simpler and less commercial way of life.

Jugendstil designers had an almost pantheistic reverence for nature and were highly influenced by contemporary scientific research into the workings of the natural world, especially evolutionary theory. *Kunstformen der Natur* (Art Forms in Nature), published between 1899 and 1904 by the renowned German biologist and naturalist Ernst Haeckel, had a profound influence on Jugendstil designers and architects. Like the eminent writer Johann Wolfgang von Goethe, who had led the Romantic movement in Germany during the late eighteenth century, Haeckel stressed the importance of the "spirit" as both a creative and an organizing force. He believed that the evolutionary systems found in nature were not, as Charles Darwin had posited, the result of natural selection, but rather the outcome of organisms interacting with their environment. As Haeckel so concisely put it in his book *Generelle Morphologie* (1866), "The cell never acts; it reacts."[9] The publication of his beautifully drawn, multicolored lithographic plates minutely

←
Jugend magazine cover, May 1896.

→
Cyclamen embroidered panel designed by Herman Obrist, 1895.

↑
Facade and entrance hall, Hofatelier Elvira
photographic studio in Munich, designed by
August Endell, opened 1898.

detailing various forms of land animals, insects, sea creatures, fossils, and plants gave designers working in Germany a rich seam of new subject matter. Essentially, he made much of the previously invisible natural world compellingly visible.

Haeckel had studied at the University of Jena under the German anatomist Karl Gegenbaur, whose pioneering work offered evidence to support the theory of evolution. It is interesting to note that this same institution conferred an honorary doctorate upon the British industrial designer Christopher Dresser in 1860 for his writings on botany and the related natural laws of design. By the 1890s, natural history was considered one of the most worthy areas of scientific study, and the structures and patterns found in the natural world were viewed by architects and designers, especially those in Germany, as blueprints for a universal order from which to learn. Indeed, design teaching there during the latter half of the nineteenth century and the early twentieth century took the study of naturally occurring forms as its basis—so much so that the photographer and artist Karl Blossfeldt's beautiful photographic plant studies were used as design-teaching aids starting around 1906, two decades before they were published.

The swirling vegetal motifs and whiplash forms employed by the Swiss-born German sculptor and designer Hermann Obrist, who had himself formerly studied botany, were almost certainly inspired by Haeckel's botanical drawings, as his hand-embroidered Cyclamen and Grosser Blütentraum wall hangings of 1895 attest. The designer and architect August Endell, a close friend of Obrist, used similarly vigorous and highly stylized quasi-representations of the natural world on the remarkable facade he designed for the Hofatelier Elvira photographic studio in Munich in 1897. This biomorphic fantasy of high-relief stucco, with its bizarre and abstracted central motif, brought Endell instant acclaim as a pioneer of Art Nouveau in Germany, but it was also referred to by one detractor as "Octopus Rococo." The facade articulated a sense of grotesque organicism and powerfully conveyed Endell's ideas regarding the underlying forces of nature. As the design historian Jeremy Howard wrote of this wonderfully inventive wall relief: "It was nothing and everything:

organic and fantastic dynamism; a swerve in grating tones of turquoise and crimson; abstract and real; vital, indeed almost aggressive, in its liveliness."[10] The owners of the studio, Sophia and Mathilde Goudstikker, asked Obrist to design the interior; the scheme he produced was similarly audacious, featuring a remarkable staircase that appeared to be wrought from seaweed and a ceiling in the entrance hall that resembled a gigantic fan of multi-branching coral.

The same year Obrist designed this riotous and rather disturbing expression of Jugendstil, he also cofounded the Munich-based Vereinigte Werkstätten für Kunst im Handwerk (United Workshops for Artistry in Craftsmanship), with the designers Bernhard Pankok, Richard Riemerschmid, Bruno Paul, and Peter Behrens. The founding of this design-reforming enterprise in 1897 was prompted by the success of the decorative arts section at the Seventh International Art Exhibition held in the Glaspalast in Munich earlier in 1897. The new venture sought to establish a sound basis for commercializing the applied arts by promoting greater cooperation among designers and craftsmen. Inspired by the guilds of the British Arts and Crafts movement, the United Workshops was essentially an applied-arts group that not only produced but also retailed and exhibited high-quality "art manufactures." It sold well-considered, practical designs that had a refined elegance, such as Riemerschmid's Music Room chair from 1899 (which was also made in England by Liberty's) and Paul's distinctive spun-brass candelabrum of around 1901. Both of these well-known proto-modern designs had simple, pared-down organic forms that reflected a more restrained and more "modern" interpretation of the Art Nouveau style.

Although the designers associated with the United Workshops did not manually produce their work, they were encouraged to share their technical expertise and oversee the skilled craftsmen who executed their designs. And though the group's commitment to high-quality manufacture meant that its output was relatively expensive to produce, the firm did manage to some extent to meld aesthetic concerns and commercial interests successfully. This achievement meant that United Workshops was instrumental in promoting the

new Jugendstil aesthetic not only in Germany but overseas as well.

Despite its anti-bourgeois undertones, by the late 1890s and early 1900s Jugendstil had become highly fashionable throughout Germany, thanks to its promotion by *Jugend* magazine and two other, similar publications: the satirical weekly *Simplicissimus*, founded in 1896; and the Berlin-based *Pan*, established by Julius Meier-Graef and Otto Julius Bierbaum in 1895. The latter's title paid homage to the youthful Greek god of fertility and passion, and he appeared on the covers of all five of

↑
Music Room installation designed by Richard Riemerschmid for the Vereinigte Wekstätten (United Workshops) and exhibited at the Deutsche Kunstausstellung (German Art Exhibition) in Dresden, 1899.

↑
Behrens Haus designed by Peter Behrens for
his own use as part of the Darmstadt Artists'
Colony in Mathildenhöhe, 1901.

↑
Postcard of Darmstadt Artists' Colony in
Mathildenhöhe showing the entrance of the
Ernst Ludwig Haus, c. 1901.

→
Der Kuss (The Kiss) woodcut created by Peter
Behrens for *Pan*, 1898.

the issues published between 1895 and 1900. The title was a double entendre, also alluding to the Greek meaning of *pan* as "all." Meier-Graefe and Bierbaum intended their journal to be an inclusive publication in which ideas could be gathered from a roster of leading international artists. Although short-lived, *Pan* was an influential organ for Jugendstil graphic design and typography; intentionally provocative, it sought to counter the art-and-design establishment's conservative modus operandi. For example, the journal published *Der Kuss* (*The Kiss*), a woodcut created by Peter Behrens in 1898; perhaps more than any other graphic work, it reflected the inherent erotic sensuality of Jugendstil, with its androgynous lovers kissing as their flowing locks intertwine. The image made an emphatically modern statement, while its boldly outlined, sinuous colored strokes reflected the New Art's tendency toward abstraction and, ultimately, simplification. During the early twentieth century, this abstracted simplicity became increasingly pronounced in Behrens's designs of furniture, textiles, glassware, and ceramics, reaching its zenith in 1907, when he was appointed artistic consultant to the German electricity company, AEG (Allgemeine Elektricitäts-Gesellschaft) and began designing functional household appliances for large-scale industrial production.

The year after *The Kiss* was published, the Darmstädter Künstlerkolonie (Darmstadt Artists' Colony) was established in Mathildenhöhe, Darmstadt, by Grand Duke Ernst Ludwig of Hesse in order to stimulate cooperation between art and industry. It was also hoped that the venture, if successful, might indirectly boost his region's economy. To this end, the Grand Duke recruited seven leading artist-designers—Peter Behrens, Paul Bürck, Rudolf Bosselt, Hans Christiansen, Ludwig Habich, Patriz Huber, and Joseph Maria Olbrich—to take part. Initially, the colony complex comprised a central studio building, known as the Ernst Ludwig Haus, which was designed by Olbrich, and a group of eight artists' houses that included the Behrens Haus, which Behrens conceived as a unified *Gesamtkunstwerk* in which every interior detail, from furniture to drinking glasses was designed site-specifically. Olbrich was responsible for designing the

rest of the artists' houses, which were fully equipped with custom-designed furnishings, although Hans Christiansen contributed to the design of his own house.

The Darmstadt colony's first exhibition, staged in 1901 and titled *A Document of German Art*, was essentially a showcase for these beautiful Jugendstil artists' houses, the atelier, and various temporary constructions. Although the exhibition received much critical acclaim, it was not the commercial success Grand Duke Ernst Ludwig had hoped it would be. Despite this setback, the colony remained in operation until 1914, during which time it staged a further three exhibitions; a total of twenty-four artists designed furniture, glassware, ceramics, silverware, and jewelry for the venture. Many of these designs were featured in Alexander Koch's two influential journals, *Innen-Dekoration* (Interior Decoration) and *Deutsche Kunst und Dekoration* (German Art and Decoration), and as a result they were seen across Germany and elsewhere in Europe. The colony also built two factories for producing glass and ceramics, which helped to stimulate experimentation with industrialized methods in the pursuit of high-quality, high-volume art manufactures. The colony directly inspired the formation of the Wiener Werkstätte in Vienna and was one of the most important centers of proto-modern design in Germany before World War I.

In 1890, a year before the Darmstadt Artists' Colony was established, the cabinetmaker Karl Schmidt set up the Dresdener Werkstätten für Handwerkskunst (Dresden Workshop for Handicraft) in Hellerau.[11] This organization, also inspired by the British design reform movement, was formed to design and manufacture products for everyday use, with the intention of recapturing the home-decorating market from the French *décorateurs* whose work was then at the height of fashion. The Dresden Workshops focused on traditional craft methods of production and, like their British Arts and Crafts counterparts, those associated with this enterprise made work in a neo-vernacular style. Although the workshops had at their inception been committed to handcraft, in the face of commercial realities they soon began to adapt their creative endeavors to be more suited to machine production. To this end, Riemerschmid designed suites of living-room, bedroom, and kitchen furniture incorporating standardized "knockdown" items that could be made by machine and then assembled by hand. These simple and functional proto-modern designs were exhibited as room installations at the third *Deutsche Kunstgewerbeausstellung* (German Arts and Crafts Exhibition) in Dresden in 1906.

It is interesting to note that these room settings also included traditional china, art prints, and even a birdcage—all of which gave them an unpretentious, homely appeal that countered the high-style sophistication of Franco-Belgian Art Nouveau. These items of furniture also revealed the desire among German design reformers for simpler and more functional work that could be produced industrially, yet that was still of a high quality in terms of both construction and overall design. With its advocacy of *Typenmöbel* (type furniture) made from standardized parts, the Dresden Workshops reflected a new, pragmatic approach. By reconciling "art manufacturing" with industrial production, they took a decisive step forward that helped bridge the philosophical divide between the New Art style and the later Modern Movement.

←
Desk designed by Richard Riemerschmid for the Dresdener Werkstätten für Handwerkskunst, c. 1905.

↑
Bedside cabinet designed by Richard Riemerschmid for the Dresdener Werkstätten für Handwerkskunst, 1905.

The Vienna Secession and the Wiener Werkstätte

During the fin de siècle, one city stood before all others as a place of progressive dreams: Vienna, home to forward-looking philosophers, scientists, political intellectuals, musicians, artists, and architects, all of whom were attempting to express through their various endeavors the new spirit of the time. It was the city that gave us the sensual paintings of Gustav Klimt and Egon Schiele, the expressive music of Arnold Schoenberg and Alban Berg, and the revolutionary psychoanalytic theories of Sigmund Freud. It was also the city where the New Art movement ultimately found its most fertile ground. In reaction to the stultifying academic tradition of the conservative Association of Austrian Artists, which was housed in the Künstlerhaus, a group of Austrian artists including the painters Gustav Klimt, Carl Moll, Max Kurzweil, and Josef Engelhart and the architects Joseph Maria Olbrich, Koloman Moser, and Josef Hoffmann founded a breakaway group known as the Vereinigung Bildender Künstler Österreichs (the Union of Austrian Artists) in 1897.

This new group was also called the Wiener Sezession (Vienna Secession), in honor of its members' seceding from the historicism of the Künstlerhaus, and it went on to forge a distinctly Viennese interpretation of the New Art movement. The year the group was founded, Olbrich designed his iconoclastic and now iconic Secession Building, with its large dome of gilded laurel leaves—a suitably imperial motif for the capital of the then Austro-Hungarian Empire. Completed in 1898, this glittering New Art building on Vienna's Karlsplatz provided a permanent exhibition center for the Secession. Above its entrance was boldly inscribed the group's motto, coined by the art critic Ludwig Hevesi: "*Der Zeit ihre Kunst, Der Kunst ihre Freiheit*" (To every age its art. To art its freedom). This rallying cry encapsulated the fin-de-siècle spirit of Vienna, which was at the time the fourth largest city in Europe and without doubt the most culturally progressive. With its stained-glass panels and interiors designed by Moser, this building made a brave new statement of the group's intent to reject historical influence. Although the structure was not finished in time for the first Secession exhibition in 1898, which was staged instead at the Horticultural Hall in Vienna, it would be the

←
Secession Building in Vienna, designed by Josef Maria Olbrich, 1897.

↑
Poster for the seventh Vienna Secession exhibition, designed by Josef Maria Auchentaller, 1900.

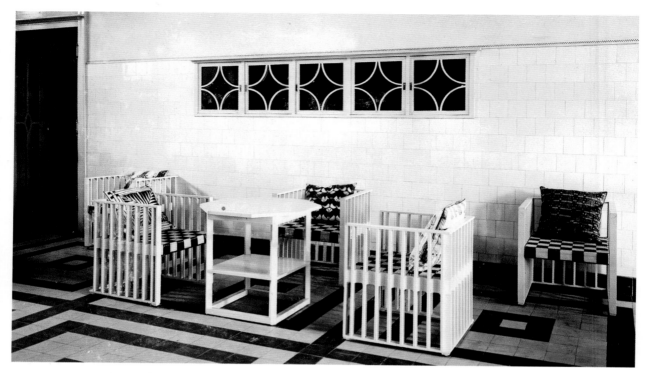

← Dining room at the Hotel Wiesler, Graz,
Austria, designed by Marcel Kammerer, c. 1910.
This room features a Secessionist scheme
complete with a glass mosaic, *Spring*, from the
workshop of Leopold Forstner.

↑ Interior of the Sanatorium Purkersdorf
designed by Josef Hoffmann,
1904–05. This view shows furniture
designed by Koloman Moser for
the project.

↗ Cover of *Ver Sacrum* magazine
designed by Koloman Moser, 1899.

venue for the Secession's subsequent shows. To further publicize its reformist agenda, the Secession also published its own journal, *Ver Sacrum* (Sacred Spring), which, as the first issue of 1898 noted on its cover, was the group's "organ." Although the Secession's early design work essentially fell within the organic canon of Art Nouveau, its output after the eighth Secession exhibition of 1900 became increasingly rectilinear. That landmark exhibition was dedicated solely to the decorative arts and included installations by, among others, Charles Rennie Mackintosh, Charles Robert Ashbee, and Henry van de Velde. There is little doubt that the Secession's subsequent change of direction can be attributed directly to the impact of Mackintosh's geometric forms and pierced motifs.

This unrelenting new rectilinear style was used by Josef Hoffmann in his Sanatorium Purkersdorf (1904–05), and was also echoed in the furniture that Moser designed for that building. This project not only exemplified the post-1900 work of the Vienna Secession; it also anticipated the geometric abstraction that would become a trademark of the Modern Movement in the succeeding decades. Ashbee's influence on the Secession was also significant in that his Guild of Handicraft inspired Hoffmann and Moser to found the Wiener Werkstätte, which they did with the financial backing of the industrialist Fritz Wärndorfer in 1903. This commercial venture produced and retailed New Art designs by members of the Secession, who were stylistically more influenced by Classicism than other reforming groups on the Continent. The Werkstätte had a number of dedicated workshops that oversaw the manufacture of silverware, jewelry, metalware, leatherwork, and furniture. It also had a bookbinding facility as well as an architectural office—which had previously been Hoffmann's—and a design studio.

The Wiener Werkstätte's facilities were notable for their better-than-average working conditions, being both airy and filled with light, and also for the fact that employees enjoyed one to two weeks' paid annual leave—an almost unheard of benefit for the time. The craftsmen's contributions were also acknowledged by the placement of their monograms alongside those of the designers on the works they produced, reflecting the

organization's socially progressive desire to promote equality between its artists and artisans. Like the Guild of Handicraft, the Wiener Werkstätte used only the best available materials and refused to compromise on quality, even if this affected the affordability of its creations. Although this approach led to excellence in both design and manufacture, it also meant that the work was highly exclusive and did not have the democratizing influence it might have had if a more pragmatic, market-driven approach had been adopted. Nevertheless, by 1905 the Wiener Werkstätte had taken over from the Vienna Secession as the leading Arts and Crafts force in Austria, the latter having suffered internal dissension that led several members, including Hoffmann, to leave the group. At this time, the Werkstätte had about one hundred craftspeople in its employ, and its designs were regularly published in the leading design journals of the day, most notably *Deutsche Kunst und Dekoration* in Germany and *The Studio* in England, enabling its work to reach a large international audience. It also staged a number of its own exhibitions and took part in various international expositions, such as the *Werkbund-Ausstellung* (Werkbund Exhibition) held in Cologne in 1914.

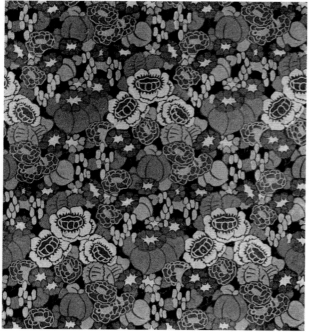

Although more than two hundred designers actually created works for the Wiener Werkstätte during its years of operation, from 1903 to 1932, until around 1914 there was a discernible shared aesthetic based on rectilinear forms and the use of luxury materials. These attributes can be found in Hoffmann's grid-pierced silverware and Moser's inlaid furniture, both produced before 1914, but after backer Wärndorfer's emigration to the United States that year, the Werkstätte's output became more decorative and stylistically eclectic, as demonstrated by the later work of Dagobert Peche. Nevertheless, the Werkstätte was before World War I a bold reforming enterprise that pioneered a new formal language of design based on geometric abstraction and was highly influential on the later Modern Movement.

Another key figure working in Vienna during the fin-de-siècle period was the architect and urban planner Otto Wagner, who became a member of the Vienna Secession in 1897 and subsequently worked within the New Art idiom, albeit with distinctly Neoclassical overtones. His masterwork was the Österreichische Postsparkasse (Austrian Postal Savings Bank) of 1904–06, a remarkable *Gesamtkunstwerk* project that incorporated custom-designed aluminium light fixtures and other architectural fittings as well as bentwood furniture that bespoke a strongly functionalist aesthetic. With its arching, glazed roof and rectilinear facade, this project was astoundingly progressive for its time, and even today is an impressively light and airy space that reflects Wagner's credo: "Nothing that is not practical can be beautiful."[12] He also stated that designs should have "maximum convenience and maximum cleanliness" and went on to declare that "all experiments which do not consider these attributes prove to be worthless, and all artifacts that do not conform to these rules, prove unviable."[13] Wagner taught at the Akademie der bildenden Künste in Vienna, and with his forthright advocacy of a *nutzstil* (commercial style)—or utilitarianism—that dispensed with all forms of superfluous ornamentation, he inspired an entire generation of students. His anti-historicizing approach, which was summed up in his belief that "all modern forms must be in harmony with . . . the new requirements of time,"[14] was also profoundly

influential on later designers of the Modern Movement, who sought a more objective approach to architecture and design after the devastation of World War I. His was not a lone voice of functionalist reason in Vienna, however: in fact, Wagner was quite moderate in his assertions compared to his fellow countryman Adolf Loos, who famously went on to repudiate the decorative excesses of Art Nouveau in his ranting essay of 1908, "Ornament and Crime."

Despite what its contemporary detractors might have thought of it, Art Nouveau was the first truly modern international style. Although its initial agenda for design reform later morphed into a full-blown decorative style, its ahistorical approach was decidedly forward-looking.

By discarding the worn-out pastiches of the past, designers aligned with the movement stylistically unburdened the next generation of designers, allowing them the freedom to seek the *Neue Sachlichkeit* (New Objectivity) of modernism. The earnest yet frustrated attempts of those associated with the New Art style to reconcile artistic handcraft with high-volume manufacture similarly prompted later Modern movement designers to accept the realities of industrial production. Unlike their well-meaning predecessors, they realized that it would only be by harnessing mechanization *and* adopting a rational approach that they could achieve the long-held goal of providing well-designed products for the many rather than for the few.

↑
Interior of the Österreichische Postsparkasse (Austrian Postal Savings Bank) in Vienna designed by Otto Wagner, 1906.

↖
Silver metal and glass vase with handle designed by Josef Hoffmann for the Wiener Werkstätte, c. 1903.

←
Wallpaper design by Erismann & Co. for the Wiener Werkstätte, c. 1912.

The Vienna Secession and the Wiener Werkstätte

BOSCH

9

PUTTING THEORY INTO PRACTICE; FROM ART MANUFACTURES TO INDUSTRIAL PRODUCTS

Adolf Loos, "Ornament and Crime"

Putting theory into practice: from art manufactures to industrial products

Although it is incorrect to talk of Germany as a nation before 1871, the year the various Teutonic *Staaten* or states united to form the German Empire, this region—the bulk of which was made up of a region known as Prussia—had already begun to gear up industrially during the 1840s, as evinced by the construction of railways linking its major cities and the beginnings of what would soon be an impressive steel industry. The German industrial revolution then quickened pace even further during the 1850s as new factories were built at a startling rate, and coal production and exports grew year-on-year. It was not until after unification that this process really consolidated, as various industries were nationalized into state-owned companies. Unlike in Britain, where industrialization had been sparked by individual entrepreneurs seeking personal commercial gain, the main impetus for Germany was the collective desire for a strong and powerful state. Another reason Germany was able to industrialize at such an impressive rate was that it boasted enviable levels of educational attainment among its populace. With one of the highest literacy rates in the world as well as an abundance of excellent universities and technical schools, it was exceptionally well positioned to provide the workforce of scientists, engineers, and technicians necessary for building factories and inventing mechanized production systems, as well as sufficient educated workers for both managerial positions and skilled factory work.

By the late nineteenth century, Germany had become a significant industrial powerhouse: it had the world's foremost chemical industry and was a major exporter of textiles, iron, and steel as well as a notable manufacturer of steam engines and railways. Its industrial might, though, was for the most part based on processes that had been borrowed from British manufacturers; and although the end products were frequently less expensive than British-made goods, they were often of poorer quality, too. As a German delegate to the Philadelphia Centennial Exposition in 1876 noted, "German industry produces only cheap and nasty articles. She has made no progress either in taste or invention."[1] Indeed, during this time the label "Made in Germany" was frequently associated with inferior goods, rather than the excellent quality of design and manufacture with which the term is now synonymous. Because of this sorry state of affairs, there had been distinct stirrings for reform within the German and Austrian design communities throughout the 1890s, when various Jugendstil designers, collectives, and workshops attempted to reconcile art and industry through "art manufactures."

By the early years of the twentieth century, these earnest design-reforming endeavors must have seemed rather backward-looking, with their continuing faith in art manufactures to help preserve craft traditions and keep workers in meaningful employment. Many designers also still held on to the belief that the machine could not match the hand for manufacturing quality. Even when they reluctantly accepted the partial mechanization of certain production processes, they often saw it as a necessary evil and would not embrace the machine's power to produce large quantities of goods more cheaply and efficiently. The Austrian architect and theorist Adolf Loos was one of the first to understand that the only way to mass-produce well-designed objects was to accept the machine as a fact of modern life that was here to stay, and to design specifically for it. In his view, the "artistic" treatment of design advocated by his contemporaries at the Darmstadt Artists' Colony and practiced at the

←
Lantern slide showing Marienhütte ironworks
in Eiserfeld, Germany, 1880s.

←
Previous page: advertisement designed by
Lucian Bernhard for Bosch spark plugs, c. 1914.

Adolf Loos, Ornament and Crime

Munich and Dresden workshops missed the point: design for industry needed a completely different and more rational approach that was based more on standardization than on individuality. In other words, a new approach that was more scientific than artistic and that identified the most logical forms, materials, and manufacturing processes with which to realize designs that could be produced entirely by machine. For Loos, a designed object should not express the soul of the designer who created it but rather the spirit of the machine that made it.

In 1899 Loos devised an interior scheme for the Café Museum, located close to the gilt-domed Secession Building in Vienna. This project introduced the new functionalist spirit of design advocated by Loos: his simple red-painted bentwood chairs, manufactured by J. & J. Kohn, contrasted with the space's light-green walls, which were lit by minimalist light fixtures notable for their display of bare bulbs hanging from simple brass rails. Nicknamed the Café Nihilismus, this comparatively stark space was later described by one of Loos's pupils, Heinrich Kulka, as "the starting point for all modern interior design."[2] It certainly marked a departure from the sinuous whiplash exuberance of Jugendstil style, introducing a more somber reductionist tendency that brought design closer to contemporary styles.

It could be said that the Café Museum served as a cultural seedling from which a new form of design and architecture would grow, one in which practitioners accepted the inevitability of industrialization and were prepared to work with its developments for the benefit of the many rather than the few.

Loos's most influential work turned out to be an essay written in 1908, entitled "Ornament und Verbrechen" (Ornament and Crime). In it he vehemently laid out the case for a more rational approach to design and manufacturing. The essay marked an intellectual turning point that led to the outright rejection of nineteenth-century historicism and the hedonism of the fin-de-siècle Art Nouveau style in favor of a much more purposeful mindset that presaged the unadorned functionalism of the Modern Movement. Loos argued from a quasi-scientific standpoint that ornamentation in design and architecture was retrogressive and, ultimately, responsible for cultural backwardness and degeneracy; he memorably linked tattoos to a proclivity for criminality. Like Morris before him, he understood the human and economic costs of superfluous decoration, yet he was a pragmatist who realized that simplicity needed to be tied to mechanization rather than handicraft. On the insidious effects of decorative excess, he commented:

Putting theory into practice: from art manufactures to industrial products

It is easy to reconcile ourselves to the great damage and depredations the revival of ornament has done to our aesthetic development, since no one and nothing, not even the power of the state, can hold up the evolution of mankind. We can afford to wait. But in economic respects it is a crime, in that it leads to the waste of human labor, money, and materials. That is damage time cannot repair.[3]

He went on to call for a new simplicity in design and manufacture that would eliminate the human costs associated with ornamentation:

The lack of ornamentation means shorter working hours and consequently higher wages. Chinese carvers work sixteen hours, American workers eight. If I pay as much for a smooth box as for a decorated one, the difference in labor time belongs to the worker. And if there were no ornament at all—a circumstance that will perhaps come true in a few millennia—a man would have to work only four hours instead of eight, for half the work done at present is still for ornamentation. . . . Ornament is wasted labor and hence wasted health. That's how it has always been. Today, however, it is also wasted material, and both together add up to wasted capital.[4]

By joining the dots of the design process from initial concept to final economic outcome, and understanding that the machine could be an ally rather than a foe, Loos helped to establish a firm philosophical foundation upon which the Modern Movement could be built. As the trend in Germany was toward ever-increasing state control of the economy, it is not surprising that the country would become the first to attempt put his theories into practice on a meaningful scale.

VORTRAG
VERANSTALTET VOM AKAD. ARCHITEKTEN VEREIN.

ADOLF LOOS: ORNAMENT UND VERBRECHEN.

FREITAG, DEN 21. FEBRUAR 1913, ½ 8ʰ ABENDS IM FESTSAAL DES ÖSTERR. ING. U. ARCH. VEREINES, I. ESCHENBACHGASSE 9. KARTEN ZU 5, 4, 3, 2, 1 K BEI KEHLENDÖRFER

12. MÄRZ: MISS LEVETUS: ALTENGL. KATHEDRALEN. MITTE MÄRZ: DR. HABERFELD: ÜBER ADOLF LOOS.

DRUCK A BERGER WIEN VIII/3

↖
Café Museum interior designed by Adolf Loos, 1899.

←
Color lithographic poster designed by Adolf Loos for his "Ornament and Crime" lecture on February 21, 1913, printed by Albert Berger.

The Deutscher Werkbund

oos's sentiments struck a chord in Germany, where there was already widespread concern among leading design practitioners and theorists that the country's rapid program of modernization had been detrimental to its cultural health. In 1906—two years before Loos wrote his seminal essay—there had already been a notable shift of emphasis at the third *Deutsche Kunstgewerbeausstellung* (German Arts and Crafts Exhibition) held in Dresden. The exhibits there revealed that a more formal language of design, one that placed greater emphasis on functionality, had finally displaced the emotional and artistic expressiveness of Jugendstil. Under the rather festive slogan "A Parade of German Arts and Craft," the designs displayed by the Dresdener Werkstätten für Handwerkskunst, for example, reflected this utilitarian approach to design and manufacture—though they were still far from the stripped-down forms that Loos would advocate. During the period running up to the outbreak of World War I in 1914, there were notable vacillations within the design debate in Germany between the need for standardization and the desire for creative individuality. While many German designers understood the social and economic necessity of mass-produced, machine-made goods, the continuing ideological

influence of the British Arts and Crafts movement perpetuated a deeply held affection for simple yet pleasing art manufactures, executed using a large degree of handcraftsmanship. The design historians Tim Benton and Stefan Muthesius explain that even when attempts to achieve a closer alliance between design and industry were made, they were often thwarted because of "the involvement of people originally trained as artists," which meant there was a strong emphasis on "good quality craftsmanship, the use of simple forms," yet "in most cases these formed a hindrance to the development of design for machinery and mass-production."[5]

As we have seen, it was the Dresden Workshops for Handicraft Art), based in Hellerau, that made the first decisive steps toward a new design-manufacturing rationalism with its standardized *Typenmöbel* (type furniture), created by Richard Riemerschmid and Bruno Paul. The workshop proudly noted in its catalogue that such pieces had been developed "from the spirit of the machine," which, as the design historian Nikolaus Pevsner observed, "was a feat far more revolutionary than it seems to us today."[6] The venture's use of the word "spirit" can be seen as an attempt to humanize industrial production, thus making it seem friendlier to potential customers.

←

Maschinenmöbelprogramm I (Machine Furniture Program I) designed by Richard Riemerschmid for the Dresden Workshops and shown in Dresden in 1906. This group of furniture was designed to be made by machine so that workers could afford it.

↗

Candlesticks, lidded vessels, and silverware pieces shown at the Exhibition of Artists of the German Werkbund at the Gewerbemuseum (Museum of Applied Arts), Basel, 1917.

Putting theory into practice: from art manufactures to industrial products

Although the machine-made furniture produced by the workshop was comparatively plain in form and serviceable in function, it still came from an Arts and Crafts mindset that held that handcraft methods were inevitably superior. As a result, designers associated with the workshop did not initially realize that the process of designing an object for industrial production was completely different from that for craft production, or that plain forms that might be ideal for hand execution were not necessarily suited to machine production. The Dresden Workshop's acceptance of mechanization was, however, an important move toward modernism, and its adoption of increasingly geometric forms were early manifestations of a new machine aesthetic.

It was the founding of the Deutscher Werkbund (German Work Federation) that proved to be the single most important event for the advancement of industrial-design practice in Germany during the years leading up to World War I. The origins of this design-reforming organization can be traced to a lecture entitled "The Meaning of Arts and Crafts," given by Hermann Muthesius in 1907. Muthesius had recently been appointed superintendent of the Prussian Board of Trade for Schools of Arts and Crafts and tasked with reforming the teaching of design in some forty technical schools, with the aim of placing less emphasis on ornamental draftsmanship and spending more time on teaching the "applied arts"—meaning design for industry. Muthesius candidly warned his audience of the dire economic consequences that would befall German industry if it did not abandon its adherence to historicizing ornament and craft-based education. The lecture prompted an outcry of indignation from the Fachverband für die wirtschaftlichen Interessen des Kunstgewerbes (Association for the Economic Interests of the Arts and Crafts), which perceived it as a direct criticism of the quality of German industrial products—which it most certainly was. The ensuing furor resulted in a number of leading members of the association leaving to establish their own design-reforming organization: the Deutscher Werkbund (DWB).

Founded in Munich in October 1907, the Werkbund's initial membership comprised twelve leading architect-designers and twelve enlightened manufacturers—including Olbrich, Muthesius, Richard Riemerschmid, Bruno Paul, and Peter Behrens, as well as the Munich-based Vereinigte Werkstätten für Kunst and the Wiener Werkstätte. It was conceived as a mutually beneficial association that would bring art to industry and industry to art. Its primary intentions were to forge much closer alliances between manufacturers and designers and to promote the teaching of the applied arts, especially as they related to industry, in technical schools across the country. Another of the DWB's central missions was to champion what it saw as "good design" for the benefit of industrialists, retailers and the general public alike, and it did this by running an extensive program of evening lectures that covered topics such as art history and design styles, debated the relative merits of industrial production and handcraft, assessed the inherent qualities of various materials and outlined various production technologies and their associated requirements. Small supporting exhibitions of the exemplars of good design identified in the lectures were often set up. These lectures and shows were staged in numerous towns and cities, which meant the DWB's design-reforming message was spread throughout Germany.

Another way in which the DWB was able to uphold high standards of design practice among its members was that, like a medieval craft or merchant guild, it had a selective vetting system, which meant that any applicant wishing to join had to be approved by a local person as well as by a professional expert. As a result, membership in the Deutscher Werkbund came to be seen as a professional badge of honor, and members had the distinctive DWB logo proudly emblazoned on their stationery. The industrialist Peter Bruckmann was the association's first president, and under his direction membership grew to around five hundred in the first year of operation. Two years later this number had swelled to an impressive 731, including 360 artists, 267 manufacturers and retailers, and 95 experts.[7] Not all academic and industrial bodies were receptive to the DWB's goals, and a certain amount of state-sponsored coercion took place, with master craftsmen being given "state premiums" if they gave their apprentices what the Werkbund deemed to be good training and allowed them time off to attend Werkbund events. The DWB also played on nationalistic sentiment, especially when dealing with trade schools and industries that had no particular interest in reforming their activities, by arguing that it was in the national interest to make Germany more competitive in export markets by adopting better design practices. The association

also promoted its cause by publishing *Jahrbücher* (Yearbooks) from 1912 until 1920 and *Deutscher Warenbücher* (German Production Directories) from 1916. The former publication illustrated objects made by its members that were thoughtfully designed and well executed, though often still quite decorative, while the latter showcased more utilitarian wares, some of which were of faultless simplicity.

In 1909 the Werkbund cofounded an instructional museum of design in Hagen with the German industrialist and collector Karl Ernst Osthaus. Called the Deutsche Museum für Kunst in Handel und Gewerbe (German Museum of Art and Trade Works), its holdings, as Osthaus noted, encompassed "all the objects of commercial life—printed material, advertising articles and packaging . . . a collection of the materials of the applied arts . . . and finally a collection of samples of artistically valuable products such as textiles, tiles, appliances."[8] The museum not only showed prime examples of good design but, like Henry Cole's earlier "Chamber of Horrors," also displayed badly designed objects, perhaps better described as "kitsch"—a word that of course originated in Germany before entering the English language. By showing shoddy wares alongside

↑
Cover of the *Deutsches Warenbüch* (German Production Directory), 1916.

↑
Page from the *Deutsches Warenbüch* showing exemplary household wares, 1916.

↑
Postcard view of the Deutsche Werkbund
exhibition in Cologne, 1914.

←
Poster stamp for the
Deutsche Werkbund exhibition, 1914.

Putting theory into practice: from art manufactures to industrial products

well-designed products, the Werkbund essentially created a "battle of objects" that stimulated debate and helped visitors quickly grasp the differences between kitsch and good design.

By focusing the minds of industrialists on good design as a means of winning new markets, the Werkbund unquestionably helped raise design standards in Germany. Its tireless reforming campaign helped alter public taste and thereby create demand for the types of products made by its members. The Werkbund set itself a wide range of activity: its motto, "*Vom Sofakissen zum Städtebau*" (From sofa cushions to urban construction), reflected its all-encompassing ambitions. Yet despite its progressive vision, within the Werkbund there were two distinct camps of opinion. On the one side was Muthesius, who argued the case for standardization and industrial production, and, on the other, van de Velde, who continued to stress the important contribution that individual creative endeavor could make to design practice. This debate came to a head at the Werkbund's famous first exhibition in Cologne in 1914, which boasted a number of notable "modern" buildings: Bruno Taut's Glass Pavilion, Walter Gropius and Adolf Meyer's model factory, and Henry van de Velde's Werkbund Theatre. All too soon, World War I would eclipse such concerns, as national attention became focused on the pressing need to arm troops in the most efficient ways possible. The Krupp munitions factory led the way in designing and manufacturing German artillery, and the case for modern industrial-design practice was ultimately made on the battlefields of Europe. After World War I, the emphasis of the Deutscher Werkbund's activities moved increasingly toward functionalism. In 1933, with the rise of Nazism, many members left until the Werkbund was disbanded in 1938. It was subsequently revived after World War II, and to this day remains an influential design-led organization in Germany.

↗
Three views of Walter Gropius and Adolf Meyer's model factory at the Deutsche Werkbund exhibition in Cologne, 1914.

→
Bruno Taut's Glass Pavilion at the Deutsche Werkbund exhibition, 1914.

Peter Behrens and AEG

↑
AEG turbine factory in Berlin, designed by
Peter Behrens, built c. 1909.

↗
Top: The world's first four-wheeled motorcar
with an internal combustion engine designed
by Gottlieb Daimler, patented 1885.

↗
Magazine insert poster designed by Lucian
Bernhard for Bosch spark plugs, 1914.

→
Overleaf: early photograph of the
Bosch factory, c. 1910s.

Putting theory into practice: from art manufactures to industrial products

One of the great catalysts of German industrialization had been the invention of the electromagnetic dynamo by Werner von Siemens in 1866–67, which laid the foundations for a new electrical industry. Siemens's innovation instigated a revolution in electrical power, and soon power stations were being constructed to serve towns and cities across Germany—and as more homes gained access to electricity, the market for electrical goods grew exponentially. Another design that must be mentioned in this context is the internal-combustion engine, invented by Karl Benz and patented in 1879. This led to the historic creation in 1885 of Benz's three-wheeled Motorwagen (patented 1886), the world's first car powered by an internal-combustion engine. Later that same year, Gottlieb Daimler patented a four-wheeled motorcar and, the following year, patented with Wilhelm Maybach a more powerful four-stroke engine, which they then mounted on a bicycle to create the first motorcycle. The advent of the internal-combustion engine not only ushered in a transformative era of transportation but also opened a whole new field of design and manufacturing activity, in which Germany led the way. One Stuttgart-based company that became renowned for its production of automotive components was the Werkstätte für Feinmechanik und Elektrotechnik (Workshop for Precision Mechanics and Electrical Engineering), which was established by Robert Bosch in 1886. Bosch had previously worked for Thomas Edison in America, so his firm was one of the first in Germany to manufacture telephones. It also produced early electric household appliances and power tools. In 1902 the company launched its high-voltage magneto spark plug, for which the graphic designer Lucian Bernhard created eye-catching posters and packaging. With its bright colors and bold, abstract treatment, this early exercise in corporate branding demonstrated Bernhard's artistic confidence and also signaled a new, strong, and distinctly modern identity for German industry.

Another German company that exploited the commercial benefits of modern design was Allgemeine Elektricitäts-Gesellschaft (AEG), a pioneer of electrical-transmission systems and an early manufacturer of electric domestic appliances. In 1907 the architect-designer Peter Behrens left the Darmstadt Artists' Colony to take up the directorship of the Kunstgewerbeschule (School of Arts and Crafts) in Düsseldorf. As previously mentioned, that same year

Paul Jordan, AEG's technical director asked Behrens to implement a comprehensive design program for the company. Just as the Wiener Werkstätte brought a coherent character to the decorative objects it produced, Behrens would give AEG a distinctive brand identity that would help to distinguish its products in the marketplace. The strong commercial argument for the use of "industrial art" was not lost on the founder and director of AEG, Emil Rathenau, who was a powerful figure in Germany, both politically and financially. He believed that capitalists should be the prime patrons of art and design—not in the traditional sense of patronage but as a way of improving the products they sold. Under his guidance AEG had previously commissioned the Gothic Revivalist architect Franz Schwechten and the well-known Jugendstil designer Otto Eckmann to create early

Putting theory into practice: from art manufactures to industrial products

logos for the firm. But Peter Behrens's design remit was to be much broader. Although he worked on a freelance-consultancy basis for AEG, Behrens was appointed the company's artistic director in 1907, just a few months before he cofounded the Deutscher Werkbund. In that role, he masterminded the firm's complete implementation of good design. He was responsible for every aesthetic decision involving the firm's buildings, from factories to workers' housing; the products it manufactured, from electric kettles and clocks to toasters and table fans, and also for the company's corporate identity and branding.

This was the first time that a company had employed an individual to advise it on all aspects of design, from architecture to packaging. The results were impressive: with its arching steel frame and use of concrete and glass, Behrens's AEG turbine factory, constructed on the outskirts of Berlin in 1909, was one of the first truly modern industrial buildings erecyed in Germany, or indeed anywhere else. The numerous products Behrens designed for AEG were similarly progressive, incorporating standardized parts that were often interchangeable between products; this rationalized production methods and optimized economic efficiency.[9] Whether it was for arc lights and gas lamps or domestic appliances, Behrens's designs for AEG could in no way be described as art manufactures; they were, rather, industrially produced goods intended for everyday use—though in their stripped-down functionalism they had a decidedly artistic quality. Behrens gave AEG's entire product line a sophisticated "industrial art" treatment that was supported by a thorough understanding of how to tailor designs for efficient mass production. One of the main ways AEG differentiated its products from its competitors' was by promoting them as archetypes of "artistic design" that were in "good taste."[10] This was achieved in part thorough Behrens's work, which included attractive posters and packaging and even storefronts that conveyed the same clean, simple, and essentially forward-looking spirit as the products they advertised or contained.

Behrens occasionally made concessions to contemporary taste: some of the products he designed for AEG clearly imitated Arts and Crafts handcraft, for example his electric kettles, which bore a faux hand-hammered finish. Although this lapse in design truthfulness might have seemed to purists a cardinal

↑
AEG logo designed by Peter Behrens, 1908.

→
Electric table fan designed by Peter Behrens for AEG, 1908.

↓
AEG poster stamp showing table fan designed by Peter Behrens.

Putting theory into practice: from art manufactures to industrial products

↑
Brass electric kettle designed by Peter
Behrens for AEG, 1908.

↗
Advertisement for AEG electric kettles
designed by Peter Behrens, 1910.

Putting theory into practice: from art manufactures to industrial products

ELEKTRISCHE TEE- UND WASSERKESSEL
NACH ENTWÜRFEN VON PROF. PETER BEHRENS

Messing glatt, matt
achteckige Form

PL Nr	Inhalt ca. l	Gewicht ca. kg	Preis Mk.
3588	0,75	1,75	20,—
3598	1,25	1,0	22,—
3608	1,75	1,1	24,—

Kupfer flockig gehämmert
achteckige Form

PL Nr	Inhalt ca. l	Gewicht ca. kg	Preis Mk.
3589	0,75	0,75	22,—
3599	1,25	1,0	24,—
3690	1,75	1,1	26,—

Messing vernickelt, glatt
achteckige Form

PL Nr	Inhalt ca. l	Gewicht ca. kg	Preis Mk.
3587	0,75	0,75	19,—
3597	1,25	1,0	22,—
3607	1,75	1,1	23,—

ALLGEMEINE ELEKTRICITÄTS-GESELLSCHAFT
ABT. HEIZAPPARATE

sin, it actually revealed a rather pragmatic and ultimately realistic approach that the industrial designer Raymond Loewy would later describe as "M.A.Y.A."—Most Advanced, Yet Acceptable. If by slightly humanizing industrially produced goods Behrens made them more desirable to the general public, that must be seen as reflecting a rather sensitive understanding of the culture in which he was operating, rather than a deed to be dismissed on ideological grounds. By creating a distinctive house style for AEG, one that has been described as having a "monumental directness,"[11] he powerfully conveyed the firm's industrial modernity while also capturing the zeitgeist of prewar Germany, which as a young nation was stepping into the new industrial age with a certain amount of bravado. As a pioneer of industrial design who successfully put theory into practice, Behrens changed the perception of the label "Made in Germany." In so doing, he blazed a trail for like-minded practitioners who understood the economic necessity of mechanization as well as the desirability of design practices that would exploit the machine's extraordinary potential to create good design for all—a goal that would become even more pertinent following the dark days of World War I.

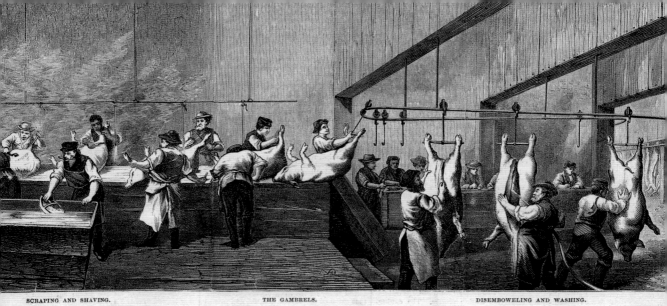

SCRAPING AND SHAVING.   THE GAMBRELS.   DISEMBOWELING AND WASHING.

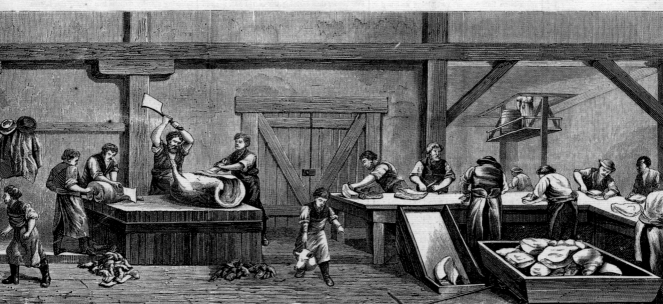

CUTTING-BLOCKS.   TRIMMING-TABLES.

10

THE AMERICAN SYSTEM AND FORDISM

Thomas Edison and the birth of the electric age

As we have seen, the last half of the nineteenth century and the opening years of the twentieth century saw not only the continuing growth of Great Britain's industrial might but also the rise of Germany as an industrial powerhouse. During this period in Europe, the debate about design reform raged while industrialization continued apace, and Gothic Revivalism, Aestheticism, the Arts and Crafts movement, Jugendstil and Art Nouveau were all expressions of such reformist sentiments. This was also a period of rising nationalism, which was likewise articulated in design. Similar concerns about the impact of industrialization and the nature of design for mass production also arose across the Atlantic, especially in the work of architects and designers aligned with the American Arts and Crafts movement, but being a young, forward-looking country that was unencumbered by past decorative or craft traditions, the United States was generally far more receptive to industrial change. Because of this lack of historical baggage, America was actually better able to accept the industrial aesthetic as its own—whether in the design of firearms, bicycles, or sewing machines. According to the national census of 1870, the population of the United States had grown to 35.5 million people, though even at the time this figure was widely believed to be a serious undercount. This meant that there was a large and ready market for homegrown goods, and across America that Yankee can-do spirit spurred countless would-be inventors to try to design what every manufacturer dreams of—a must-have product for all.

This emphasis on the functionally enhanced yet egalitarian product was summed up succinctly in the well-known aphorism of the period, "Build a better mousetrap, and the world will beat a path to your door."[1]

←
Thomas Edison with his phonograph, c. 1877.

←
Previous page: illustration of the "disassembly system" used in the American meat-packing industry, *Harper's Weekly*, 1873.

This quote is attributed to Ralph Waldo Emerson, although what he actually wrote was, "I trust a good deal to common fame, as we all must. If a man . . . can make better chairs or knives, crucibles or church organs, than anybody else, you will find a broad hard-beaten road to his house, though it be in the woods."[2] The gist, though, is the same. The ideals of indispensability and universality were driving forces in America during the late nineteenth and early twentieth centuries, and they lie at the heart of the country's approach to design to this day. The pioneer mindset produced inventors who were good with their hands and enjoyed problem-solving, and unlike in Europe, there was no disgrace in working in trades. These American inventors tinkered in their workshops, turning design concepts into useful products—and they were less concerned with how things looked than with how they worked. The designs that resulted from this type of hands-on development process were often innovative thanks to the dedication of their creators—a commitment that was fueled by the American Dream, which promised success and prosperity to all who were prepared to work hard enough to find them.

After the Civil War ended in 1865, many manufacturers used the ideals of standardization and interchangeability derived from armory practice to diversify their product lines in more commercial ways. In the decade following the war, a reunified United States enjoyed an ever-growing sense of national pride. This was reflected at the Centennial International Exhibition in Philadelphia in 1876, held to mark the centenary of the nation's founding after the Revolution. This first official world's fair held in the United States saw the launch of two much-loved staples of the American diet, Hires Root Beer and Heinz Tomato Ketchup, and also featured two American inventions that would in due time change the course of human history: Alexander Graham Bell's newly patented telephone and Remington's first commercial typewriter. Among the countless exhibitors was also a young but highly gifted inventor by the name of Thomas Alva Edison, who was displaying several new inventions, including his "automatic telegraph system." The same year, Edison—who was prolific not only in his design innovations

but also in filing patents—moved to Menlo Park, New Jersey, to set up an "invention factory." The majority of his time was soon spent experimenting in this state-of-the-art research facility with its sixty employees. Edison worked here for a decade, and often had as many as forty projects running at once. As the "Wizard of Menlo Park" said at a press conference in 1929: "None of my inventions came by accident. I see a worthwhile need to be met and I make trial after trial until it comes. What it boils down to is one percent inspiration and ninety-nine percent perspiration."[3] During this frantically inventive early period Edison was applying for up to four hundred patents per year, and numerous inventions conceived at the Menlo Park laboratories were subsequently transformed into landmark products, including: the wireless telegraph, an improved carbon-button

telephone transmitter, the phonograph, the wireless-induction telegraph and, last but by no means least, the incandescent electric lightbulb.

Today, it is difficult to comprehend the sheer wonderment people must have experienced on witnessing for the first time night being turned into day at the simple flick of a switch. Between the 1850s and the 1870s, numerous inventors had tried to develop the first practical incandescent lamp. The British inventor Joseph Swan eventually became the first to produce a successful lightbulb in December 1878. Earlier that year, Edison had also begun developing his own design with a team of assistants at Menlo Park, and in October 1879 they managed to produce a similarly workable lightbulb. Edison had the commercial wherewithal to patent his invention before Swan and then successfully

The American system and Fordism

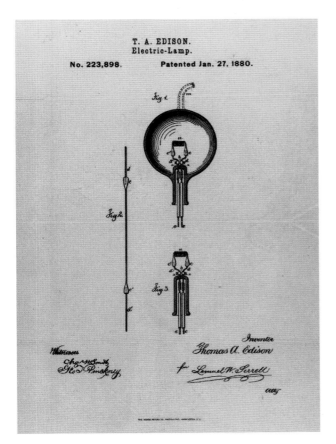

put it into large-scale mass-production. The result of 1,200 trial-and-error experiments, Edison's lightbulb unleashed a new electric age across the world, yet he was not content to rest on the laurels of his already considerable achievements. Instead, he founded the Edison General Electric Company in 1889, which became General Electric in 1892 following a merger. Edison's aim was to develop the necessary infra-structure for large-scale electrification, and installed America's first electrical-power plant in New York in 1882. As electrification became more and more widespread over the succeeding decades, a vast array of electrically powered appliances appeared that would change the very fabric of daily life. These designs would come to express a new machine aesthetic that was a potent symbol of progress.

←
Thomas Edison's laboratory at Menlo Park, New Jersey.

↖
Edison's patent for the incandescent electric lightbulb, granted 1880.

↑
Edison's first lightbulb, 1879.

The Wright Brothers, Henry Ford, and the moving assembly line

While America led the way in electrification and, consequently, in the design of electrical appliances, it also witnessed a revolution in transportation design during the early years of the twentieth century that would have perhaps an equal impact on world history. Orville and Wilbur Wright's first successful airplane flight in 1903 inaugurated a new epoch of air travel—and with it, globalization. While the Wright brothers' legendary flight only covered 120 feet in twelve seconds, they doggedly continued to refine their aircraft designs until, in 1905, they introduced a model that could remain airborne for an impressive thirty-nine minutes. Theirs was a very American approach to problem-solving in design, using a scientific method of painstaking and time-consuming trial-and-error development to discover the most functional solution possible. Eventually, the Wrights so improved their design that, in 1909, they began to supply the US Army with their Model A, the world's first military airplane, which was capable of an average speed of forty miles per hour. More than this, though, the Wrights, through their approach to design, taught man to fly and so permanently altered the way people lived.

Another man whose forays into transportation design had a transformative impact on people's lives was Henry Ford. His Model T automobile of 1908 provided, for the first time, low-cost and reliable car travel for the many rather than the few—it was, as he described it, "a motor car for the great multitude."[4] His creation of a moving assembly line was to have a critical influence on the future design and manufacture of products. The Ford factory in Detroit, had initially adopted armory practice—the mechanized manufacture of interchangeable standardized components—but the rate of production could not keep up with consumer demand for the Model T, which had become an instant success. So Henry Ford looked for other ways to accelerate production flow and lower unit costs. Fortuitously for him, the mechanical engineer Frederick Winslow Taylor had just published *The Principles of Scientific Management* (1911), which proposed applying scientific method to the management of workers in order to increase productivity. Using new photographic technology developed by George Eastman—another great American design innovator—to conduct a series of time-and-motion studies, Taylor demonstrated that productivity could be greatly enhanced if the tasks performed by workers were broken down into their constituent parts and then analyzed in order to eliminate any waste of time or movement. Taylor recommended the application of his common-sense principles to specific tasks, and also to the overall functioning of factories. Ford fully accepted Taylor's advice and began looking for ways to implement it.

By studying the assembly techniques in use at his factory, Ford quickly realized that the stop-start movement of the production line, which involved dragging components from one work station to the next, was extremely time-consuming and needed to be addressed if efficiency was to be increased. Inspired by a conveyor belt he had seen at a grain mill and also by the "disassembly" lines of Chicago and Cincinnati's meat-packing industries—where meat was processed on a very large scale and animal carcasses moved past workers at a steady pace via a system of electrically powered overhead pulleys—he established the world's first factory moving-assembly line in 1913. It brilliantly used pulleys and conveyors to apply the power of electricity to established armory

→
Orville and Wilbur Wright's first
successful airplane flight, Kitty Hawk,
December 17, 1903.

↓
The Wright brothers' Model A
aircraft, 1909.

manufacturing practices—sequential production, standardization, and interchangeability, enabling Ford to radically speed up his factory's workflow. The new system significantly reduced the time taken between tasks: each one performed by a specific worker would flow seamlessly into the next, thereby reducing "set-up time" and eliminating the physical hauling of parts. Ford implemented his first moving assembly line for the production of magneto fly-wheels in 1913. Later that year this more efficient system was also introduced for the building of motors, transmissions, and chassis, whereby these parts of the car were assembled as they were conveyed past stockpiles of components; along the way the manufacturing process was reduced to workers undertaking individual, repetitive tasks. As Ford explained:

> Every piece of work in the shop moves. It may move on hooks or overhead chains going to assembly in the exact order in which the parts are required; it may travel on a moving platform; or it may go by gravity, but the point is that there is no lifting or trucking of anything other than materials. Let the conveyor do the walking. Save ten steps a day for each of the 12,000 employees, and you will have saved fifty miles of wasted motion and misspent energy.[5]

→
History was made as the flywheel/magneto, the first manufactured part built on a moving assembly line, passed by workmen at the Ford Motor Company's Highland Park, Michigan, plant in 1913. Time required to assemble magnetos was reduced from twenty to five minutes; the principle was applied to all Model T assembly operations, and mechanized industrial mass-production was born.

The American system and Fordism

The Wright Brothers, Henry Ford, and the moving assembly line

↑
Reconstruction of the first Ford assembly line at the company's Highland Park plant. Automobile bodies are sent down a ramp, from which they are lowered onto the chassis waiting below, c. 1931.

←
Henry Ford's Model T automobile, 1908.

↗
A 1927 Ford Model T. More that 15 million were built between 1908 and 1927.

The American system and Fordism

The astonishing efficiency of this new production-line system meant that the assembly time of a Model T car's chassis was reduced from twelve and a half hours in October 1913 to ninety-three minutes the following year. As a result, more than fifteen million Model Ts were built between 1908 and 1927, altering the lives of countless families across America and abroad. The success of the car was based on the precepts of good design: practicality and affordability. Meanwhile, Henry Ford's distrust of styling and preference for engineering—as borne out by his well-known but often misquoted quip of 1909, "Any customer can have a car painted any color that he wants so long as it is black"[6]—represented, at least for the time being, the triumph of large-scale manufacture over the fickle nature of fashion. By combining armory practice and a moving assembly line, Ford had, quite simply, revolutionized the capability of factories and made mechanized mass-production truly viable for the first time. Within a very short time, production engineers both in America and abroad adopted his methods. While "Fordism" heralded a brave new world, it also shifted America from being a technocracy—a society based on technological knowledge—toward being a "technopoly"—a society in the thrall of technology. The Ford approach, which involved elaborate planning and synchronization as well as meticulous design and standardization of components, permanently changed not only the manufacturing process but also the way in which products were conceived and designed.

Design in World War I

The mass-production of weaponry perfected in American factories during the mid-nineteenth century changed the face of military conflict permanently, making Civil War of 1861–65 the first instance of modern industrialized warfare. During the fifty years that followed, as American, British, and German industrial might grew exponentially and other countries underwent their own industrial revolutions, military design became increasingly sophisticated and thus much deadlier.

Although World War I was sparked by the assassination of Archduke Franz Ferdinand and his wife by a Serb nationalist in Sarajevo in June 1914, the conflict's origins ran much deeper, in a toxic mixture of nationalist fervor, complex webs of political alliances, territorial disputes, colonial rivalries and economic competitiveness. Added to this, industrialization prompted as each country either attempted to bolster itself militarily or fostered hopes of territorial expansion. Japan had also built up an impressively strong naval industry using a strategy of "copy, improve, innovate,"[7] which involved purchasing vessels from a number of foreign shipbuilders then running them through research trials in order to use key design features and production techniques in the development of its own naval vessels. The Japanese were notable innovators in this field of design. Indeed, in September 1914, they conducted the first ever sea-launched air raid from the *Wakamiya* seaplane carrier, and also boasted the world's most formidable battle cruisers.

A number of other military design firsts appeared during World War I, including chemical weapons such as mustard gas, biplanes used for bombing and aerial reconnaissance, submarines, and tanks. Among the other military materiel used in the conflict were land

Preparation for the flight of an Avro 504K
biplane, the most-produced aircraft to serve
the Royal Flying Corps and the Royal Naval Air
Service during World War I, c. 1915.

The American system and Fordism

mines, trench mortars, grenades, and machine-guns, rifles, and pistols. The German Army's Luger P08 (Pistol Parabellum), one of the first semi automatic pistols to see action, was a tour de force of German design functionality. But it was the huge artillery pieces, or howitzers, that were responsible for the greatest number of battlefield casualties; models included the "Big Bertha," designed and manufactured in Germany by Krupp. The designs for this type of quick-firing field and siege artillery—the twentieth-century's more deadly descendant of the cannon—were honed during the war years to have increasingly longer barrels and wider calibers as well as higher angles of firing trajectory, all leading to enhanced performance.

The British Army's rhomboid Mark I tank, nicknamed "Big Willie," might be the one design most closely linked in our imaginations to World War I, thanks to countless newsreel clips showing its agonizingly slow but decisive advance. It was the first caterpillar-tracked "landship" employed by the British Army in any conflict; interestingly, the word "tank" was originally used to disguise its deadly purpose and make it seem to the enemy as though it was a nonmilitary water-carrier. With its farm-tractor chassis it was unreliable mechanically, but it did have two huge advantages over conventional wheeled vehicles: it could travel over the churned-up and waterlogged terrain of battlefields without immediately getting bogged down, and its 26-foot length enabled it to breach obstacles, most notably wide trenches. Another tracked combat vehicle that first saw action in this war was the armored personnel carrier that carried infantry in the wake of the frontline-breaking tanks. Primitive radio communications were also used—an important innovation that proved invaluable on all sides of the conflicts. As Captain A.P.

Corcoran observed in *Popular Science Monthly* in 1917, the radio-telegraph operator working on the frontline was an invaluable asset. He explained:

> It would be hard to overestimate the importance of his duties. When an enemy trench is being taken, it is he who reports the progress of the encounter—the number of the enemy, the nature of their defense, the amount of the casualties on either side, the condition of the trench when it is finally taken—whether it has been badly damaged by artillery fire, or whether it is practically intact. If a gas attack is coming, it is he who sends the warning to the men behind to put their gas helmets on.[8]

←
A signal officer of the American 42nd Division testing a telephone left behind by the Germans in their hasty retreat from St. Mihiel, France, c. September 1918.

→
The German Army's Luger P08 (Pistol Parabellum), designed and patented by Georg J. Luger, 1898. Its design was then further refined from 1900 to 1945.

← "Big Bertha" howitzer, designed and manufactured by Krupp, introduced in 1914.

↓ The British Army's rhomboid-shaped Mark I tank, nicknamed "Big Willie," introduced 1916.

↗ Young woman working in a Naval seaplane factory in Philadelphia, c. 1917–18.

↘ US Army recruitment poster by James Montgomery Flagg, 1917.

The American System and Fordism

The German military also used radios to guide Zeppelin bombing attacks, but the French soon countered by using similar transmissions to confuse the dirigible pilots.

Although the United States did not enter World War I until April 1917, it played a decisive role in turning the war in the Allied Forces' favor. One way in which it did this was through President Woodrow Wilson's establishment of the War Industries Board (WIB) in July 1917, which managed to increase American industrial production by an impressive 20 percent before its peace-time dissolution in January 1919. Enhanced efficiency was achieved by setting up a system of priorities for the allocation of materials and by encouraging manufacturers to accept large-scale mass-production techniques, as pioneered by Henry Ford, and urging them to implement standardization in order to reduce waste. The acceleration of manufacturing competence ensured that American industry was, after the cessation of hostilities, perfectly positioned to take on the commercial challenges of peacetime.

Rather than technical advances or design innovations, the devastation caused by the so-called war to end all wars would prove to be the conflict's real lasting legacy, especially in the development of modern design. In four exceptionally bloody years, the world had been pulled brutally from the Belle Époque and the gilded age into the modern industrialized age; millions of young lives were lost, the social order universally disrupted, class systems shaken, and gender roles upset. A new and better world needed to be built on the conflict's ashes, and a key part of that task fell to architects and designers.

11

REDUCTIVISM, EXPRESSIONISM, AND RATIONALISM

message that caught their imagination was that matter was the enemy of the spirit; this led them to pursue a dematerialist aesthetic. Echoing the flat, low-lying Dutch landscape, the group employed horizontals and verticals in their paintings, buildings, furniture, lighting, typography, and graphics, believing that a reductivist approach would reveal a spiritual essence or a deeper meaning of life. Through the rationalization of both nature and the man-made into elemental forms, the group aimed, as Van Doesburg wrote in the first issue of *De Stijl*, toward "the development of a new awareness of beauty . . . to make modern man receptive to what is new in the visual arts."[4] Piet Mondrian used the term "Neoplasticism" to describe the group's abstraction of form; this was a misleading translation of the Dutch phrase *nieuwe beelding*, which had been coined by the theosophist mathematician M. H. J. Schoenmaekers, who believed that a rational new world would emerge from geometrically symbolic art. As the design historian Tim Benton later noted: "Mondrian was indebted [to Schoenmaekers] for his conceptual resolve to render meaningful the horizontal and vertical symbols of a fundamental universal rhythm. Schoenmaekers put it in cosmic terms when he spoke of the earth's movement around the sun as a horizontal line of power, and the sun's life-giving rays as vertical."[5] For Schoenmaekers, the colors blue and yellow also symbolized natural forces, the former representing the sky and the latter the sun's rays. In fact, *nieuwe beelding* would have been better translated as "new forming," for the group's goal was to reduce form into the simplest of elements, an essential distillation to achieve spiritual purity.[6] This radical reductivism was expressed in design as well as painting: notable examples include the cover of the first issue of *De Stijl* by Vilmos Huszár (1917) and J. J. P. Oud's remarkable De Unie cafe in Rotterdam (1925). However, it was the work of Gerrit Rietveld that would come to epitomize De Stijl's radical modernity more than that of any other designer. His slatted chair of 1918, later named the Red-Blue chair, is one of the most famous designs of all time, and was a visually powerful three-dimensional realization of the De Stijl group's reductivist approach. The chair was dynamically composed of a square section of "scaffolding" laid out vertically and horizontally that supported the angled seat and back planks. The transparency of its construction suggested

the dissolving of matter and gave a sense of spatial infinity; in this regard it could be read as a piece of abstract sculpture. No concession was made to comfort. In 1923, when at the suggestion of the artist Bart van der Leck it was painted in black and primary colors to enhance its rectilinearity, the Red-Blue chair must have seemed all the more shockingly revolutionary. The best explanation of the chair comes from its creator, who wrote in the second issue of *De Stijl* magazine in September 1919:

> With this chair an attempt has been made to have every part simple and in its most elementary form in accordance with function and material—the form, thus, which is most capable of being harmonized with the whole. The construction is attuned to the parts to insure that no part dominates or is subordinate to the others. In this way, the whole stands freely and clearly in space, and the form stands out from the material.[7]

The extraordinary spatial qualities achieved by this seating design were realized on a much larger scale in 1924, when Rietveld designed his first building, the Rietveld Schröder House in Utrecht. A completely unified *Gesamtkunstwerk* project, this structure was commissioned by the eccentric and recently widowed Truus Schröder-Schräder as a home for herself and her three children. She is believed to have liaised closely with Rietveld to ensure that its unconventional design would promote "active living." While the asymmetrical exterior of the house, with its geometric elements in

←
Gerrit Rietveld sitting in a prototype Red-Blue chair outside his furniture-making workshop in Utrecht, c. 1918—the furniture maker Gerard A. van de Groenekan is standing behind him (center).

←
Elevation of the Rietveld Schröder House in Utrecht designed by Gerrit Rietveld, 1924.

↙
Red-Blue chair designed by Gerrit Rietveld, 1918/1923.

gray, white, and black, had a rather nautical air thanks to its protruding deck-like balconies. The light-filled interiors were notable for their bold primary-color schemes, and also for their interesting delineation of space, attained wih sliding partitions and folding doors. Indeed, one of the most striking things about the house was Rietveld's achievement of an exceptionally multifunctional and adaptable space. As Schröder-Schräder later observed, it was a "modern villa" that reflected Rietveld's hatred of "useless frills." Sshe went on to state: "It is actually a stripped home, there is only that which is necessary for its residents, it's what you call functional."[8] This was a home that functioned like a machine and was intended for modern people. Still, it cannot have been that easy to live in, for its aesthetics were uncompromising. Like other De Stijl designs, it was essentially a statement of intent that offered an enticing glimpse of a utopian future.

Russian Constructivism

Reductivism, expressionism, and rationalism

During the 1910s, members of the Russian avant-garde were influenced by the abstraction of French cubism as well as by the dynamic forcefulness of Italian futurism and its glorification of the machine. Prior to the outbreak of World War I, many Russian artists had traveled to or worked in Western Europe and so were familiar with the latest artistic developments in Paris, Munich, and elsewhere. The war forced many to return home, where, culturally isolated by the conflict, they went on to form their own movement in fine art, architecture, and design, which was based on non-figurative representation and geometric abstraction. Kazimir Malevich's painting *Black Square* (c. 1915) was the ultimate non-representation and exemplified the group's aesthetic, though rather than being a culmination it was the first of a series of abstract paintings that Malevich called "Suprematist." Like the canvases of his De Stijl contemporaries, they juxtaposed geometric forms to create depersonalized spatial compositions. The work of Malevich and other artists associated with the Russian avant-garde, however, favored a more dynamic placement of elements and a greater sense of layering than was found in De Stijl art. Around 1915, the Russian artist Vladimir Tatlin began to experiment with abstracted, three-dimensional reliefs made from different materials that were essentially nonrepresentational constructions. Made from found objects or industrial materials, these early works paved the way for a new art and design movement that would become known as Constructivism.

Like De Stijl, Constructivism had distinctly utopian goals and sought to bring about a new social order by introducing a fresh formal language in art and design. After the Russian Revolution in 1917, Constructivism became the focus of the Russian avant-garde, whose members were looking for a creative expression that would reflect the desire to replace the defunct semi-feudal system of the Tsars with more democratic schemes for the production and distribution of goods. To this end, Tatlin and Malevich, together with fellow artists Alexander Rodchenko, Wassily Kandinsky, Naum Gabo, Antoine Pevsner, and El Lissitzky, began to promote an aesthetic and approach to design that was linked to industrial production. In the early 1920s the group issued two publications heralding the emergence of Constructivism: *A Realistic Manifesto* (1920) by Pevsner and Gabo and *Konstruktivizm* (1922) by Alexei Gan. The adoption of the term "Constructivism" can be traced to a lecture entitled "On Constructivism," which was delivered by Rodchenko's wife, Varvara Stepanova, in December 1921. Believing that the reform of the applied arts could bring about a new social order, the Constructivists began to make utilitarian "production art" and architecture. But the political and economic instability that followed the Russian Revolution meant that few large-scale projects were undertaken, and their output was mainly confined to exhibition design, ceramics, and graphic design.

The Constructivists' most famous work was never built, yet it came to symbolize their ideologically driven reform mission. The *Monument to the Third International*, designed by Tatlin in 1919, was a massive,

↖
VKhUTEMAS lecture hall exhibition of student works on the expression of mass and weight, 1927–28.

→
Black Square by Kazimir Malevich, c. 1915.

Reductivism, expressionism, and rationalism

spiraling tower structure that looked something like a cross between the Eiffel Tower and a helter-skelter. Tatlin conceived it as both a monument and a headquarters building, and it was intended for construction in Petrograd (now St. Petersburg) for the Communist International organization (also known as the Third International), which had been founded by Vladimir Lenin in 1915. Meant to soar one-third heigher than Eiffel's tower in Paris, Tatlin's structure would stand just over 1,310 feet tall and be built from industrial materials such as iron, steel, and glass. The Russian art critic and champion of Constructivism Nikolai Punin provided the best description of this singular symbol of modernity:

> The monument consists of three great rooms of glass, erected with the help of a complicated system of vertical pillars and spirals. These rooms are placed on top of each other and have different, harmonically corresponding forms. They are able to move at different speeds by means of a special mechanism. The lower storey, which is in the form of a cube, rotates on its axis at the speed of one revolution per year. This is intended for legislative assemblies. The next storey, which is in the form of a pyramid, rotates on its axis at the rate of one revolution per month. Here the executive bodies are to meet (the International Executive Committee, the Secretariat and other executive administrative bodies). Finally, the uppermost cylinder which rotates at the speed of one revolution per day is reserved for information services: an information office, a newspaper, the issuing of proclamations, pamphlets and manifestos—in short, all the means for informing the international proletariat.[9]

It was a mad yet brilliant futuristic utopian vision; even the political ideologist Leon Trotsky questioned the practicality of the construction. Too far ahead of its time, Tatlin's famous tower remained a large wooden model that provoked mixed feelings even in those sympathetic to the cause of the avant-garde. As a radical architectural projection, it was also publicized throughout Europe in the various design and architecture journals of the day. The design historian Tim Benton noted that it was seen in Germany to be "the perfect fusion of a radical avant-garde aesthetic

↑
Coffee pot designed by Nikolai Suetin for the State Porcelain Factory, Petrograd, c. 1924.

↑
Constructivist plate designed by Ilya Chashnik for the State Porcelain Factory, 1924.

←
The *Monument to the Third International* architectural model designed by Vladimir Tatlin, 1919-20.

with the vital demands of a revolutionary society—to be interpreted variously as the 'Cathedral of Socialism' given expression in truly twentieth-century form, or as a perfect token of the Machine Aesthetic."[10]

Constructivism achieved some of its greatest design successes in the fields of ceramics and graphics, disciplines that by their very nature did not need large financial investment. The Constructivist plate designed by the artist Ilya Chashnik in 1924, with its asymmetric arrangement of black, brown, and cream lozenges and semicircular black rim, transformed a simple white blank into a bold avant-garde canvas. Other notable ceramic wares produced by the State Porcelain Factory in Petrograd included designs by the artists Wassily Kandinsky and Nikolai Suetin that were similarly

decorated with Suprematist motifs—geometric forms set against plain white backgrounds that conveyed a strong sense of dynamism and modernity.

This same sense of dynamic positioning was to be an identifying feature of the visually stimulating and intellectually engaging graphic design pieces produced by the handful of revolutionary creatives associated with Constructivism. They made propaganda-driven work that celebrated, as the critic Hugh Aldersey-Williams put it, "the anonymous hero-worker of the new communist state."[11]

With its layered elements arranged into complex compositions, the two-dimensional work recalls jutting three-dimensional, steel girders and industrial assemblages. Constructivist graphic design was also

Reductivism, expressionism, and rationalism

innovative in its use of collage that incorporated striking black-and-white photographs taken from unconventional angles. This impressive body of work, from posters to book covers, was a celebration of the modern industrial world seen through the eyes of Soviet doctrine. Yet even removed from the revolutionary zeitgeist in which it was created, the work has an enduring impact, evoking a strong sense of reportage and the strident, pioneering optimism of the early Soviet regime, as epitomized by Rodchenko's *Knigi* (Books) poster of 1924. This dynamic composition features a photograph of the well-known Constructivist muse Lilya Brik—the poster girl of the revolutionary left—calling with her hand cupped to her face into a triangular banner of type.

The Constructivists also established a state-sponsored school of design known as VKhUTEMAS (an acronym for Vyssie Khudozhestvenno-tekhnicheskie masterskie, meaning Higher State Artistic and Technical Workshops). This art and technical institution, founded in Moscow in 1920, had a preliminary course that was compulsory for all students—a sort of foundation program that included, among other subjects, color theory and art history. The school had seven teaching departments: painting, sculpture, architecture, ceramics, metalwork and woodwork, textiles, and typography. Although it was not as well known as Germany's Bauhaus school of art and design, it was actually a far larger enterprise, with many more students. The school held large, open discussions and seminars on a diverse range of topics. As Naum Gabo noted, "these gatherings had a much greater impact on the later development of constructive art than all the teaching."[12] This school evolved from the earlier Svomas, or Free State Art Studios, which had been founded in 1989 following the October Revolution. It promoted "production art" and established contracts with industry with the aim of merging art and craft traditions with modern industrial technology. Although VKhUTEMAS played a crucial role in forging a modern art-and-design ideology in Soviet Russia, the Russian avant-garde associated with it soon ran afoul of the Soviet regime, and in 1930 was shut down in favor of creatively stultifying party-controlled unions.

←
Knigi (Books) poster designed by Alexander Rodchenko for Gosizdat, 1924.

↓
Soviet pavilion designed by Konstantin Melnikov for the 1925 Exposition Internationale des Arts Décoratifs et Industriels Modernes in Paris—a dynamic Constructivist structure.

PAVILLON **U.R.S.S.**
PARIS 1925

The Weimar Bauhaus

Prior to the outbreak of World War I, a number of applied arts groups and workshops were founded in Germany to bring art to industry, with the aims of reforming design and stimulating economic growth. At the same time, a number of creative German groups emerged, among them, in the field of fine art, Die Brücke (The Bridge) and Der Blaue Reiter (The Blue Rider). These groups would coalesce into a movement that in 1913 was given the name "expressionism." Artists aligned with expressionism were more interested in conveying emotion through their work—be it painting, woodcuts, music, theater, or design—than in addressing social needs. This meant that in Germany after the war there was still a noisy debate between those who argued for rationalism and those who championed its opposite, expressionism. It was against the backdrop of this pitting of universalism against individuality that the Staatliches Bauhaus was founded in Weimar in 1919.

The origins of the Bauhaus can be traced back to 1902, when the designer Henry van de Velde was asked by Grand Duke Wilhelm Ernst of Saxe-Weimar-Eisenach to establish a series of industrial-design seminars that would bring local craftsmen and designers together. As part of a wider local design initiative, van de Velde was also engaged as an advisor, and at his instigation a new school of arts and crafts was built in Weimar in 1904–06. Officially known as the Großherzoglich-Sächsische Kunstgewerbeschule Weimar (Grand Ducal Saxon School of Applied Arts in Weimar), this teaching institution was established with the aim of improving design training. In 1907 the school opened a dedicated Institute of Industrial Arts, which was housed in a building specially designed by van de Velde that incorporated his private studio on the top floor. It was in this institute that van de Velde taught students how to design specifically for industry. His position became increasingly difficult in the years leading up to World War I, however, because he was

both Belgian and an avowed pacifist, and was therefore seen as a corrupting influence on German youth.

At the outbreak of the war, van de Velde resigned and returned to Belgium, and the architect Walter Gropius was put forward for the directorship of the Kunstgewerbeschule. It was, however, closed in 1915, before he could take up the position. Nonetheless, Gropius maintained his contacts at Weimar's other art-teaching institution, the Hochschule für bildende Künste (College of Fine Arts). During the war, Gropius served as a soldier, and during this conflict his views became increasingly anticapitalist, leading him to sympathize with the ideals of the Arts and Crafts movement and to draw away from the Deutscher Werkbund's espousal of industrialization. In fact, it was at the front that Gropius formulated his "Proposals for the establishment of an educational institution to provide artistic advisory services to industry, trade, and craft"—the doctrine of the Bauhaus. [13] In 1916 his recommendation that the two Weimar art schools —the Kunstgewerbeschule and the Hochschule für bildende Künste—be merged into a single interdisciplinary school of craft and design was sent to the regional state ministry. In April 1919 the two schools were amalgamated to form the new type of art college Gropius had envisioned, unifying the teaching of art and of technology. Gropius was appointed director of the new Staatliches Bauhaus, and the Bauhaus manifesto was published. The Bauhaus, meaning "building house," sought to reform the teaching of the various creative disciplines and thereby bring an unprecedented unity to the arts. For Gropius, building or making was an important social, symbolic, and intellectual endeavor, and as such, the teaching at the Bauhaus was deeply concerned with concepts of construction. All beginning students had to undertake a yearlong foundation course, after which they entered various workshops situated within

Reductivism, expressionism, and rationalism

the two buildings and trained in at least one craft discipline. These workshops were intended to support themselves financially through private commissions. In acknowledgment of the guild system that had overseen the teaching of craft skills for centuries, the tutors were known as masters—and in fact some of them were members of local guilds—while the students were referred to as apprentices.

Gropius appointed three prominent expressionist artists as the Bauhaus's first faculty members: Lyonel Feininger and Gerhard Marcks were appointed *Formmeister*, or shape master, of the printmaking and pottery workshops respectively, while Johannes Itten was tasked with developing and supervising the preliminary course. Itten was not only a talented painter but also a pioneering color theorist, and under his direction first-year Bauhaus students were taught the basic principles of composition and color theory as well as the inherent properties of materials. As a member of the Mazdaznan cult—a neo-Zoroastrian religion rooted in physical, mental, and spiritual development aimed at enabling humanity to better connect with God—Itten cut an alternative figure; he not only observed a strict vegetarian diet but also practiced meditation as a pathway to creative enlightenment. His mysticism pervaded his teaching: his classes began with breathing exercises and gymnastics and were

↑
Slit tapestry (Red/Green) woven by Gunta Stölzl at the Bauhaus Weaving Workshop, 1927–28.

↓
Teapot designed by Marianne Brandt and manufactured by the Bauhaus Metal Workshop, 1924.

based on principles of "intuition and method" and "subjective experience and objective recognition."[14] To this end, he encouraged his students to study materials carefully so as to reveal their intrinsic qualities and had them make inventive constructions using found objects. The syllabus also included an appreciation of art history, and, believing, like Gropius, that there were natural laws for spatial composition just as there were for musical composition, Itten also stressed the importance of elemental geometric forms such as the circle, square, and cone. He felt that art and design should be infused with the spiritual—and he was not alone, for the Moscow-born artist Wassily Kandinsky, who joined the Bauhaus faculty in 1921, had written a book entitled *Concerning the Spiritual in Art* in 1912 and held similar convictions. Kandinsky believed in the associative properties of color, line, and composition, and cited the Austrian philosopher and social reformer Rudolf Steiner, who promoted "spiritual science," as a major influence. Steiner's belief that "color uplifts the human being from the material to the spiritual"[15] accorded with Itten's views, and many parallels can be drawn between the holistic form of creative education pioneered by Itten at the Bauhaus and Steiner's unconventional yet progressive teaching theories.

Itten's preliminary course at the Bauhaus would become a blueprint for foundation courses at design-teaching institutions around the world, although other courses were not quite as spiritually or mystically engaged. Such was Itten's charisma, with his shaved head and monk-like crimson robes, that his students began to revere him. Several even converted to Mazdaznan, much to the consternation of Gropius, who had now begun to realize that his own authority was being eroded by this guru-like figure. Between 1919 and 1922, Gropius had also appointed a number of other expressionist artists as tutors, including Georg Muche, Paul Klee, and Oskar Schlemmer, but he soon recognized that in order to get back on track the school needed to place much less curricular emphasis on individual creative expression and more on the goals of mass production. Internal differences at the school eventually became untenable, and in March 1923 Itten left to join the Mazdaznan community in Herrliberg on Lake Zurich, effectively marking the end of the expressionist period at the Bauhaus.

↑
Johannes Itten, who supervised the preliminary course at the Weimar Bauhaus.

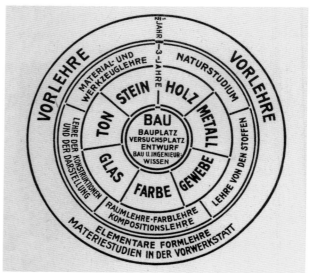

↑
"Scheme for Learning," devised by Walter Gropius for the curriculum at the Staatliches Bauhaus in Weimar, 1922.

Reductivism, expressionism, and rationalism

One of the reasons for Gropius's change of heart was that the Dutch artist Theo van Doesburg moved to Weimar in 1922 in order to extend the influence of the De Stijl group; that same year, the Russian Constructivist painter and graphic designer El Lissitzky visited the Bauhaus. Seeing firsthand the work of artists associated with both of these self-consciously modern groups, and becoming more knowledgeable about their underlying design-reforming motivations, must have been revelatory for Gropius. Around 1923 he began to pursue a new, more purposeful direction at the Bauhaus, fitting the curriculum to the demands of a world that was increasing driven by technology. As part of these changes, he appointed Josef Albers and László Moholy-Nagy as Itten's successors. Although they followed the basic structure of the preliminary course Itten had devised, they rejected his focus on individual creative development. Instead, they favored a more rational and industrialized approach to design and arranged factory visits for their students to help them learn about the design requirements of mass production. The introduction of this pragmatic approach brought about a new creative productivity within the Bauhaus's workshops. A number of truly modern, landmark designs were created around this time, including Marcel Breuer's slatted chair (1923–24), Marianne Brandt's teapot (1924), and Wilhelm Wagenfeld and Carl Jakob Jucker's table light (1923), the last being perhaps the quintessential Bauhaus design. A distinctive formal sobriety and functional utilitarianism were now reflected in the Bauhaus's output, and in 1923 the school staged a major exhibition to display the full scope of its activities and its new, more rational direction.

A highlight of the exhibition was the experimental Haus am Horn, designed by Georg Muche. The goal of this thoroughly modern model dwelling was, as Gropius explained, to achieve "the greatest comfort with the greatest economy by the application of the best craftsmanship and the best distribution of space in form, size and articulation."[16] All of the house's furnishings and fixtures were designed and executed in the school's workshops, including a kitchen designed by Marcel Breuer with an innovative continuous countertop and suspended wall cupboards. With its highly functional layout, this room anticipated the more famous "Frankfurt Kitchen" (1926), a landmark

of rationalist design created by Margarete Schütte-Lihotzky for the architect Ernst May's social-housing project in Frankfurt, which took a scientific-based Taylorist approach to making the most functional kitchen possible within a relatively confined space. Another notable development seen at the 1923 Bauhaus exhibition was the new graphic identity that the school had created for itself. The graphic design now coming from the Bauhaus was highly progressive, and self-onsciously so, incorporating sans serif New Typogaphy to create modern graphics for a modern world.

↓
Table light designed by Wilhelm Wagenfeld and Carl Jakob Jucker and manufactured by the Bauhaus Metal Workshop, 1923—the quintessential "Bauhaus lamp."

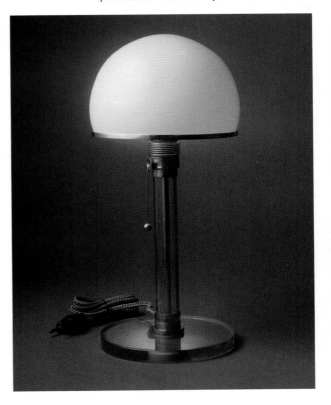

The Dessau Bauhaus
and a New Objectivity

Reductivism, expressionism, and rationalism

Johannes Itten's unusual teaching methods and the underlying socialist ethos of the Bauhaus had already begun to attract local political opposition in Weimar, and the school's days were numbered, despite the critical acclaim that the 1923 exhibition had received. In 1924 right-wing parties won a majority in the Thuringia state elections, and as a result the Bauhaus's state funding was slashed in half. The following year, teachers and students wrote a letter to the local government in Thuringia stating their intention to leave Weimar. In addition, discussions about the school's relocation to Dessau were held with the city's liberal mayor, Fritz Hesse, who promised government funding for the development of a school building and housing for the tutors. Being run by the Social Democratic Party, Dessau's city council was far more receptive to the school's doctrine than Weimar's had been. The city itself was a major industrial center with a better grasp of the value of good industrial-design teaching. By offering the school the funding it so desperately needed, albeit with the understanding that it would partly finance itself through the manufacture and sale of the designed goods it produced, Dessau had thrown the Bauhaus a lifeline.

Completed in 1926, the Bauhaus building in Dessau was a modernist statement in which form was driven by function; it was a structure designed by Gropius along strictly rational lines. This new purpose-built edifice marked a turning point in the school's movement away from craft-workshop ideals and toward full acceptance of industrialized production. Having grown disillusioned with socialism, Gropius now believed that the industrial capitalism pioneered by Henry Ford in the United States could actually benefit workers, and that it was the only approach that might ensure the Bauhaus's economic survival. Now ensconced in

←
Staatliches Bauhaus building in Dessau,
designed by Walter Gropius, completed 1926.

its brightly lit new building, the Bauhaus changed its design ethos entirely, adopting strict functionalism as its guiding doctrine. Designs were now conceived speculatively for large-scale industrial production and consciously promoted a machine aesthetic.

In order to further the school's industrial-design credentials and enable it to raise the necessary funding from the sale of its products, Gropius established a limited company to market the designs produced, with financial support from the wealthy timber merchant Adolf Sommerfeld. Founded in 1925, Bauhaus GmbH published a retail catalogue, though many of the items it featured, despite appearing to be machine-made, were actually unsuitable for large-scale serial production. Even the products that were suited to such production were often too avant-garde in appearance for general tastes, and so were only batch-produced in relatively

limited numbers. There were, however, some outstanding successes, such as Marcel Breuer's furniture designs, which were created from 1925 onward and employed state-of-the-art tubular steel in their construction. These designs reflected the Bauhaus's adoption of *Neue Sachlichkeit*, or New Objectivity—a term coined by the art historian Friedrich Hartlaub in 1925—and in the late 1920s they were licensed to Standard-Möbel and Gebrüder Thonet for mass production. The few licensing agreements that the Bauhaus managed to sign with manufacturers, however, did not bring in the levels of revenue Gropius had been counting on to sustain the school.

In 1928 Gropius became so exasperated with the local political quarrels surrounding the Bauhaus that he decided to step down as director and appointed the Swiss architect Hannes Meyer, who had joined the

Reductivism, expressionism, and rationalism

faculty the previous year, as his successor. By now the Bauhaus bore the subtitle Hochschule für Gestaltung (Institute of Design), which reflected its shift away from teaching fine art toward training for industrial design. As an avowed communist, Meyer believed that products should be affordable as well as functional, so that working-class families could afford to buy them. This desire for cheap, utilitarian, democratic products led the Bauhaus to adopt an increasingly scientific approach to design. During Meyer's tenure, the Bauhaus also became increasingly politicized, the school site becoming a hotbed of Marxist student activism. This again threatened the Bauhaus's very survival, and under pressure to depoliticize the school the architect Ludwig Mies van der Rohe was brought in to take over from Meyer in 1930. Under Mies's guidance the preliminary course became optional, and the study of architecture was given far greater emphasis; although the design workshops continued to operate, their task was now only to create products suitable for industrialized mass production.

The winds of political change were gathering in Germany, and in October 1931 the National Socialists swept to power in Dessau. Hostile to everything the Bauhaus stood for, they voted in August 1932 to close the school. After decamping to Berlin, Mies briefly reestablished the Bauhaus as a private school in a derelict telephone factory, but on April 11, 1933, the Gestapo came to the school and closed it by force, loading anybody without the proper identification papers onto trucks and driving them away. That July, the masters elected to dissolve the Bauhaus officially, thereby marking the end of this ideologically troubled yet remarkably forward-looking institution, which had swung like a pendulum from expressionism to rationalism within the space of fourteen short years. It was a bitter ending for an institution that had lit a creative spark in its gifted students and alumni, enabling them to come up with innovative approaches that in later decades would be hailed as masterpieces of modern design. Even more important, though, the Bauhaus had been a powerful modernizing force: it transformed design education and thereby profoundly influenced the story of design.

↖
B3 "Wassily" armchair, designed by Marcel Breuer, 1925.

↑
Sintrax coffee percolator, designed by Gerhard Marcks and Wilhelm Wagenfeld for Jenaer Glas, Schott & Gen., 1932.

The Weissenhof exhibition

STUTTGART. Weißenhof-Siedlung

While the 1920s roared in America and Paris enjoyed being the center of the fashionable world, during that decade Germany struggled with hyperinflation and the imposition of the harsh war reparations by the 1919 Treaty of Versailles. A by-product of German economic troubles was a severe housing shortage, which inspired members of the Deutscher Werkbund to work on an exhibition on the theme of *Die Wohnung* (the dwelling). It just so happened that the city of Stuttgart had already earmarked 1.5 million reichsmarks for the construction of public housing, and when the mayor, Karl Lautenschlager, learned that the Deutscher Werkbund was planning to stage its *Die Wohnung* exhibition in his city, he and other local politicians gave their approval for Werkbund-associated architects to design forty flats or houses as part of the proposed program of a hundred new public-housing units.

The same year, Lautenschlager and the Deutscher Werkbund president Peter Bruckmann issued a joint memorandum outlining the intentions of the exhibition: "Efficiency measures in all areas of our lives do not stop where housing is at issue. The economic conditions of today prohibit any kind of waste and demand the maximum effect with minimum amount of means, requiring the implementation of such materials and technological appliances which will lead to lower building and operational costs, and will lead to a simplification of households, and to improvements of living itself."[17]

Reductivism, expressionism, and rationalism

The aim of the exhibition, staged from July to September 1927, was to rationalize the building of public housing in order to minimize waste in both construction and upkeep. The exhibition took the form of a model modern housing estate called the *Weissenhofsiedlung*, comprising twenty-one prototypical buildings that contained sixty "dwellings" designed by leading Modern Movement architects of the day, including Walter Gropius, Bruno Taut, J. J. P. Oud, Ludwig Mies van der Rohe, Le Corbusier, Josef Frank, Mart Stam, Peter Behrens, and Hans Scharoun. This ambitious project, overseen by Mies van der Rohe, comprised a mixture of terraced housing, detached houses, and apartment buildings. There was a strong stylistic consistency in the designs, even though the buildings had been designed by a variety of European architects. The structures were typified by the use of plain, unadorned facades, flat roofs, open-plan interiors, prefabricated constructions, and, most of all, a strong geometric formalism. The estate was an architectural showcase for what would eventually become known as the International Style.

While the main focus of the *Die Wohnung* exhibition was on the buildings on the Weissenhof housing estate, the event also displayed the latest developments in industrial design; for example, AEG had a stand of its latest electrical products in the main hall. The interiors of the model dwellings were also noteworthy in that they showcased the idea of "modern living," incorporating tubular metal furniture by designers including Mies van der Rohe, Marcel Breuer, Mart Stam, and Le Corbusier. These room installations were featured widely in design journals and led to a greater acceptance of modernism in Germany and abroad. Starkly furnished yet well lit, these uncompromisingly modern interiors reflected the contemporary obsession with health and hygiene and revealed the increasing internationalism of the Modern Movement. While the Werkbund's earlier exhibition *Form ohne Ornament* (Form without Ornament), held in 1924, had focused on the design of functional products that were denuded of all superfluous decoration, the *Die Wohnung* exhibition essentially stripped the concept of the home down to what Le Corbusier called "a machine for living in."[18] The brave new world of Modern design pioneered by the Dessau Bauhaus and showcased at the Weissenhof exhibition was founded on rationalism. Yet in their ideologically driven quest for universality, the Modernists often forgot that people were not machines and failed to comprehend that a sterile machine aesthetic could be spiritually and emotionally alienating.

←
Poster for the Deutscher Werkbund's *Die Wohnung* exhibition held in Stuttgart, 1927.

↖
Postcard showing a general view of the Weissenhof Housing Estate in Stuttgart, 1927.

12

ART DECO AND INTERPRETATIONS OF MODERNISM

The 1925 Paris Exposition, from Art Deco to modernism

Boudoir of the Hotel d'un Collectionneur at the 1925 Exposition Internationale des Arts Décoratifs et Industriels Modernes in Paris, designed by Émile-Jacques Ruhlmann and epitomizing the opulent Art Deco style.

Previous page: The German Pavilion at the 1929 Barcelona International Exposition, designed by Ludwig Mies van der Rohe— a masterwork of the International Style.

During the 1920s, two major stylistic threads ran through design: the extravagant Art Deco style and the uncompromising modernist "avant-garde" style, as it was then known. The former emerged during the late 1910s but did not reach its zenith or stylistic maturity until the early 1920s. The latter had also initially appeared at the end of World War I, with the work of the De Stijl movement in the Netherlands and the opening of the Weimar Bauhaus in 1919, but did not become a truly international phenomenon until the late 1920s and 1930s. As is always the case, the economic conditions of the time were a major influence on the development of design, and Art Deco, with its connotations of luxury, became a major international style during the boom years of the early 1920s. After the stock market crash of 1929, however, the modernist cause, with its stress on manufacturing efficiency and utilitarianism, gained considerable ground.

One country did not enjoy the boom years of the 1920s but instead struggled economically: Germany. Through financial necessity, the country became the crucible of modernism. During the interwar period avant-garde architects and designers there adopted a strident, forward-looking agenda that was reflected in their pursuit of *Neue Gestaltung* (New Design), *Neue Bauen* (New Architecture) and *Neues Wohnen* (New Living). The reason for this attitude was not just economic but also socio-political: Germany's immediate past was too painful to look back on, and only the future appeared to offer any hope. During this period, Germany's obsession with the new became quite catching, spreading particularly to France during the latter half of the 1920s, when there was a similar desire to throw off all remnants of the past and embrace a brighter, more modern way forward. However, the French interpretation of modernism was quite different from that found in Germany.

Although Art Deco was truly international during the early 1920s, its epicenter was Paris. There, numerous talented architects and decorating firms were able to call upon the skills of small specialist workshops to execute their unashamedly luxurious designs for furniture, metalwork, glassware, lighting, textiles, and wallpapers. Thanks to the stock market-fueled prosperity of the Roaring Twenties, there was also a sufficient number of wealthy clients both in Paris and overseas who could afford to lavish seemingly limitless amounts of money

on creating homes that were the height of fashionable luxury. Unlike the preceding Art Nouveau style, which was consciously antihistorical in its preference for motifs drawn from the natural world, Art Deco drew its references from an eclectic range of historic sources, from African tribal art to ancient Egypt, with motifs inspired by Howard Carter's sensational discovery of Tutankhamen's tomb in 1922. It was also influenced by contemporary artistic developments, most notably French cubism and Italian futurism.

In France during the early 1920s, the decorative arts—furniture, lighting, ceramics, textiles, metalwork, glass, and so on—were dominated by the respected decorating firms based in Paris, which was seen as the hub of sophisticated and elegant living. These firms worked in the long-established French *ébéniste* tradition of superlative cabinetmaking and often employed luxurious materials, such as rare and exotic hardwoods, ivory, mother-of-pearl, and shagreen (shark's skin). Most often, they provided a full decorating service for their well-heeled clientele, and as such, buildings were frequently designed as *Gesamtkunstwerk* projects, unified in everything from furniture and lighting to textiles, wallpapers, and carpets. These firms relied on private patronage, most notably from French fashion designers such as Paul Poiret and Jacques Doucet, and used labor-intensive production methods and costly materials.

↓
Hotel d'un Collectionneur (House for a Collector) for the 1925 Exposition Internationale des Arts Décoratifs et Industriels Modernes in Paris, designed by Émile-Jacques Ruhlmann.

So Art Deco was a relatively short-lived style that was inevitably superseded by more progressive approaches. The designers associated with it, though, were not industrial Luddites. As the designer Émile-Jacques Ruhlmann, a leading figure of the Art Deco movement, memorably noted, nothing that could be done by machine should be done by hand.[1] Yet despite this acceptance of mechanization, most high-end Art Deco furnishings created in Parisian workshops needed highly skilled craftsmen for at least some of their execution.

Although as a style Art Deco had been prevalent during the first half of the 1920s, the term itself was coined slightly later and derived from the title of the landmark exhibition Exposition Internationale des Arts Décoratifs et Industriels Modernes held in Paris in 1925. As its name suggested, this well-received and highly influential event showcased Art Deco interiors alongside a few more progressive Modernist room schemes. The event's two most influential installations were Ruhlmann's interiors for the Pavillon du Collectionneur, designed by the architect Pierre Patout, and the Pavillon de l'Esprit Nouveau, designed by the Swiss-born architect Charles-Édouard Jeanneret, better known as Le Corbusier. Ruhlmann's "house for a collector" epitomized the Art Deco love of opulence and applied decoration. With its large living room, dining room, and bedroom, the installation skillfully brought together the creations of nearly forty artists and craftsmen who worked under Ruhlmann's creative direction to achieve this harmonious interior design. Exuding a shameless spirit of luxurious decadence that was inventive yet also respectful of the French decorative tradition, Ruhlmann's theatrical suite of rooms deliberately appeared to counter the modernist currents that had already begun to run through design by the mid-1920s.

In striking contrast to the exuberant style of Ruhlmann's work, Le Corbusier's pavilion was restrained, possessing a stylish utilitarianism. With its airy spatial quality and sparse, functional furniture, including mass-produced bentwood Thonet chairs, this avant-garde space reflected the Modern Movement's obsession with health and hygiene as well as the unrelenting progression of the modern industrial age. Much to the consternation of the exhibition's organizing committee, the pavilion provocatively rejected the traditional decorative arts; through it, Le Corbusier attempted to demonstrate that "the sphere of architecture embraces every detail of household furnishing, the street as well as the house, and a wider world still beyond both."[2] Le Corbusier bore an undisguised contempt for the decorative arts tradition, his overriding intention being to show that standardized industrial production by necessity created pure forms that carried intrinsic value. The Pavillon de l'Esprit Nouveau was essentially a cell-like unit for modern living, and its furnishings were intended to function more as equipment than as traditional furniture. The space reflected Le Corbusier's belief that "a house is a machine for living in,"[3] and marked a turning point in the evolution of modernism by demonstrating that the "scientific" approach to design espoused by the Dessau Bauhaus could be used to create Modernist interiors that were quite chic in a hard-edged, minimalistic way. Certainly Le Corbusier's work had, as he put it, the "esthétique de l'ingénieur"[4] (aesthetic of the engineer). In a 1921 article with that title, he had urged, "Let us heed the advice of American engineers. But let us fear American architects."[5] The pioneering aesthetic of his pavilion caught the imaginations of many of his peers who visited it, such as the Danish architect Arne Jacobsen, and became the impetus for what in a few years would become known as the International Style.

Another less well-known design presented at the 1925 Paris exposition that also provoked considerable controversy was the Soviet pavilion, designed by the Constructivist architect Konstantin Melnikov. This visually striking building was built to a rhomboid plan and had two staircases that dynamically sliced its structure into a pair of acute triangles. Here was one more blatant riposte to the bourgeois luxury of Western decorative art, so abundantly displayed in many of the surrounding pavilions. While these buildings exuded capitalist opulence in their theatrical rooms, furnished with beautiful and exquisitely made objets d'art, the Soviet pavilion was a piece of revolutionary architectural propaganda. Despite its uncompromising modernist form, Melnikov framed the building with wood rather than steel, presumably because it was a cheaper and therefore more proletarian material. Although Melnikov's structure won the Grand Prix, Le Corbusier's pavilion was to have a greater legacy, acting as a powerful catalyst for the widespread acceptance of modernism, at least among designers and architects.

Art Deco and interpretations of modernism

↑
Exterior of Le Corbusier's Pavillon de l'Esprit
Nouveau at the 1925 Exposition Internationale
des Arts Décoratifs et Industriels Modernes
in Paris.

→
Interior of the Pavillon de l'Esprit Nouveau,
designed by Le Corbusier (with
Pierre Jeanneret and Charlotte Perriand)
for the 1925 Exposition Internationale.

1925 Paris Exposition, from Art Deco to modernism

The Maison de Verre
and tubular metal

ust three years after the 1925 Paris exhibition, the furniture and interiors designer Pierre Chareau began the three-year project of planning and building the extraordinary Maison de Verre (House of Glass) in Paris. It was breathtakingly innovative in its use of industrial materials, including steel beams, translucent glass bricks, perforated sheet metal, and rubber flooring tiles. Commissioned by Dr. Jean Dalsace, a cleanliness-obsessed Parisian gynecologist who was an influential member of the French Communist Party, this overtly modernist structure was an ingenious infill building wedged between two eighteenth-century buildings and squeezed beneath an existing top storey. On the ground floor was a progressive, clinical-looking suite of medical rooms. The building's layout and all of its fixtures and fittings were designed with health and hygiene in mind—with tiling that was easy to clean and long rows of windows to provide adequate ventilation. A dramatic open-backed staircase rose to link the ground-floor workspace to the first-floor living area above. This level incorporated a two-story living room with exposed steel beams as well as other rooms, including a solarium. There was also a retractable "ladder" to the second floor, where the bedrooms and bathrooms were located. Throughout the house were numerous built-in features that not only saved space but also offered a high degree of functional flexibility, such as sliding sheet-metal screens and metal closets that served as walls between the various rooms. Yet despite its emphatic industrial aesthetic, this extraordinary dwelling had a surprising visual warmth thanks to Chareau's clever juxtaposition of industrial materials with dove-gray carpeting, gleaming blond-wood paneling, and amply upholstered furniture covered in tapestries and warm-toned velvets. The house revealed a far more moderate interpretation of avant-garde design than Le Corbusier's Pavillon de l'Esprit Nouveau, and so it is no wonder that Chareau's masterpiece has since become a place of pilgrimage for the architecturally informed.

Other architects who pioneered a more tempered form of modernism in France during the late 1920s and 1930s included René Herbst, Robert Mallet-Stevens, and the Irish émigré Eileen Gray. Their work can be seen as an avant-garde interpretation of the Art Deco

style—often more modernistic than truly modern. And yet, by making modernism chic they also made it more palatable than the sterile utilitarianism promoted by the Dessau Bauhaus. In fact, modernism became such a strong and divisive force in French interwar design and architecture that in 1929 about twenty members of the conservative Société des Artistes Décorateurs left to form their own association, the Union des Artistes Modernes (UAM), which promoted design over decoration. This alliance tirelessly advanced its agenda by participating in the numerous salon exhibitions held during the 1920s and 1930s. Some of the younger UAM members, most notably Jean Prouvé and Charlotte Perriand, pioneered a slightly more utilitarian look during this period, but their work was still imbued with a sense of French modishness.

Making modernism stylish was not just the preserve of French designers and architects. Ludwig Mies van der Rohe, an architect born in Germany, memorably created the German Pavilion at the 1929 Barcelona International Exposition. This was one of the great landmark buildings of twentieth-century architecture, harmoniously blending radically modern elemental forms and industrial materials such as steel and glass with materials more traditionally associated with luxury, namely marble, red onyx, and travertine. With its chromed-steel columns supporting a floating roof, this open-plan structure was not about everyday function but rather about creating a modern space that conveyed a positive message about contemporary Germany. It was built as a temporary facility, with no function other than to host the king and queen of Spain while they signed a visitors' book at the opening of the exhibition. It was furnished with site-specifically designed chromed-steel and buttoned leather seats—Mies's famous Barcelona chair—that were essentially reinterpretations for the modern age of the *sella curulis*, a type of chair used in ancient Rome by high-ranking members of society. The sparsely appointed space was a dramatic composition that gracefully confirmed Mies's famous dictum: less is more.[6] In addition to its other qualities, the German pavilion was a place of meditative calm with a striking de-materialist aesthetic, complete with two reflecting pools and Georg Kolbe's *Alba* (Dawn) statue. Overall, the pavilion vividly demonstrated that industrial materials and modern construction methods handled

←
Facade of the Maison de Verre (House of Glass) in Paris, designed by Pierre Chareau, 1928.

The Maison de Verre and tubular metal

↑
First-floor living room of the Maison de Verre (House of Glass) in Paris, designed by Pierre Chareau, 1928

→
L'équipement d'une habitation (equipment for the home) model apartment installation designed by Le Corbusier, Pierre Jeanneret, and Charlotte Perriand for the 1929 Salon d'Automne.

↗
The German Pavilion at the 1929 Barcelona International Exposition, designed by Ludwig Mies van der Rohe

→
Interior of the German Pavilion showing the Barcelona chairs Mies designed for this project.

deftly could produce results that exuded a strong sense of the spiritual. At one stroke, Mies had elevated modern design and architecture to a new aesthetic plane and released it from associations with utilitarian worthiness.

A similar transformation was under way in furniture design. As we have seen, World War I had concentrated the minds of both designers and manufacturers on design's role in society, and there had been a feeling among designers associated with the Bauhaus that a radical *Neue Sachlichkeit* (New Objectivity) was urgently needed, both in society as a whole and more specifically within art and design. This reforming zeitgeist was powerfully realized in three-dimensional form when Marcel Breuer designed his Model B3 "Wassily" armchair in 1925. Although it was not specifically designed for the artist, Wassily Kandinsky admired the design and used it in his house at the Bauhaus in Dessau. The production of seamless tubular metal was pioneered in Germany, where Max and Reinhard Mannesmann had patented processes for its mass production in 1885. One of the material's first successful applications had been in the construction of bicycles. Reportedly, the handlebars of Breuer's recently purchased Adler bicycle inspired him to make furniture with this modern industrial material. Apart

from its high-tensile strength, tubular steel was a very hygienic material that was easily wiped clean. Even before World War I, there had been huge interest in improving public health, as reflected in the 1911 international hygiene exhibition held in Dresden. But in the 1920s it became an even more pressing issue. In this climate of heightened medical concern, tubular-metal furniture seemed to be a healthful solution, being less likely to harbor germs and infestations of pests and parasites than traditional upholstery. Tubular steel was also a low-cost material when produced on

an industrial scale, which meant that in theory it could be used to mass-manufacture inexpensive furniture for the multitudes. Breuer's Wassily chair was the first to employ a supporting frame of tubular steel. Thanks to the material's springy resilience, the design provided comfort without the need for traditional padded upholstery. Instead it employed leather slings, which gave it a strong spatial quality rather like Gerrit Rietveld's earlier Red-Blue chair. Around the time of its design, Margaretha Reichardt developed, in the Bauhaus weaving workshop, a durable fabric made from heavy-duty woven cotton treated with paraffin wax and reinforced with metal thread. Known as *Eisengarn* (iron yarn), it proved to be the perfect durable material for sling seats; it was subsequently used by Marcel Breuer as well as other designers in their tubular-metal seating designs.[7]

At a 1926 meeting of Deutscher Werkbund architects participating in the design of the Weissenhof housing estate—the centerpiece of their *Die Wohnung* exhibition in Stuttgart the following year—the Dutch architect Mart Stam discussed with his peers a radical new chair with an innovative cantilevered construction that he had recently made by welding together iron gas pipes. He also made a sketch of his groundbreaking design, which inspired Breuer and Mies to develop their own more refined versions of Stam's cantilevered chair—the B 64 Cesca chair (1928) and the Model No. MR10 Weissenhof chair (1927), respectively—which employed tubular steer instead of rigid pipes. In contrast to the age-old four-legged arrangement, the cantilever shape provided a marked increase in springiness, as did marrying the

resilience of tubular metal with the flexibility of woven rattan or *Eisengarn* canvas. This proved the perfect formal and material combination to achieve maximum comfort with a minimum of means.[8]

These new tubular-metal seating designs marked a watershed in the story of design and introduced a new and unequivocally modern style to the furnishing of interiors. By the late 1920s and early 1930s, tubular steel had become the material of choice among most modernist designers—Le Corbusier, along with his cousin Pierre Jeanneret and his colleague Charlotte Perriand, created a number of landmark tubular-metal furniture designs, including the well-known B 306 chaise longue of 1928; it was regarded by Le Corbusier as a *machine de repos* (machine for resting) and was shown as part of the trio's *L'équipement d'une habitation* (equipment for the home) model apartment installation at the 1929 Salon d'Automne. René Herbst also used tubular metal in his furniture designs, which, like the work of Le Corbusier, Jeanneret, and Perriand, were de luxe Art Deco interpretations of modernism. Herbst used elasticated straps known as sandows for the seats of some of his chairs, which gave them a distinctive industrial chic. The tubular-metal furniture created by French designers bore a Parisian modishness that was removed from the socially conscious utilitarianism of German design of the time. By giving modernism a touch of Parisian glamour, these French designers made it more attractive to consumers and contributed to a greater acceptance of the machine aesthetic during the 1930s, when the Depression made the implementation of Modern design and architecture ever more pressing.

During the 1920s and 1930s, modernism's influence was not confined to architecture and product design but also acted as a powerful stimulus on graphic design. This was made evident, as we have seen, in the Bauhaus's introduction of New Typography at its landmark 1923 exhibition in Weimar; after the school clsosed in 1933, the modernist baton was taken up by a number of Swiss graphic designers working in Zurich and Basel. This coterie became known as the Swiss School and included Ernst Keller, Theo Ballmer, and Max Bill. It was influenced by the typographic theories and asymmetrical layouts of the Bauhaus as well as by the Russian Constructivists' use of photomontage and De Stijl's spatial principles. Bringing these elements together in their own work, these designers pioneered a distinctive graphic language. Espousing a reductivist aesthetic, Swiss School design was typified by the use of sans-serif typography, white space, and "objective photography," meaning realistic imagery. Direct, precise, and clinical, such work was intended to be easily deciphered: a universal language of modern visual communication. Displayed at the Swiss national exhibition in 1939, the Swiss School's brand of uncompromising modernism went on to become the International Typographic Style; to this day, it influences graphic designers, many of whom either admire its message-carrying clarity or despise what they see as its formulaic blandness.

←
Model No. MR20 Weissenhof chair designed by Ludwig Mies van der Rohe, 1927—an armchair version of the Model No. MR.10.

↙
Neues Bauen (New Building) poster for Deutsche Werkbund exhibition at the Kunstgewerbe Museum, Zürich, designed by Theo Ballmer, 1928.

↓
Travel poster for the Swiss Tourist Board, designed by Herbert Matter, 1925— a masterwork of Swiss School graphic design.

STOCKHOLMSUTSTÄLLNINGEN 1930.

50 — EXPOSITION INTERNATIONALE
DES ARTS DÉCORATIFS — PARIS - 1925
PAVILLON NATIONAL de la SUÈDE (Carl S. Bergsten architecte)   A. P.

promote links between artists and manufacturers, with a view to improving the design of industrially produced goods. The results of this design-reforming venture were shown two years later at the 1917 *Hemutstallningen* (Home Exhibition), and many of the exhibits satisfied Key's desire for beautiful everyday objects. These mass-produced wares had simple yet pleasing forms informed by functional considerations. Wilhelm Kåge's *Liljeblå* (Blue Lily) dinner service (1917), produced for the porcelain company Gustavsberg, featured folk-inspired decoration and came with an affordable price

↑
Postcard showing the 1930 Stockholm Exhibition at night, with its Functionalist buildings reflecting a new rational direction in Swedish Design.

↑
Swedish Pavilion designed by Carl Bergstein at the Exposition Internationale des Arts Décoratifs et Industriels Modernes in Paris, 1925.

tag, factors that combined to make it such a commercial success that it came to be known as the *Arbetarservisen* (Worker's Service). Many of the honest, utilitarian designs promoted by the Svenska Slöjdföreningen, though, were not particularly well received by the working classes for whom they were intended, who found them too expensive or just too plain, given that "simple" household items were still widely associated with low socio-economic status. Nevertheless, the Home Exhibition did focus attention on the pressing need for inexpensive, well-designed products, and also provoked a spirited debate about the appalling slum conditions that existed in Sweden's rapidly expanding cities and how this problem could be tackled.

In 1919 Gregor Paulsson, the director of the Svenska Slöjdföreningen, published a pamphlet entitled *Vackrare Vardagsvara* (More Beautiful Everyday Objects), which was essentially a design manifesto aimed at manufacturers. It made the case for creating wares for a then largely overlooked part of society, low-wage earners, but its message fell mainly on deaf ears. As a result, the Swedish Pavilion at the landmark Exposition Internationale des Arts Décoratifs et Industriels Modernes in Paris in 1925 was a mishmash of contradictory design tendencies: handcraft versus industrial manufacture, individualism versus universalism, primitive versus modern. The objects on display did, though, share a graceful simplicity that led the British design critic Philip Morton Shand to coin the term "Swedish Grace" to characterize these designs, which were predominantly modernistic rather than truly modern. Yet within five years, there would be a sea change within Swedish design, thanks to the 1930 *Stockholmsutställningen* (Stockholm Exhibition), which showcased the work of architects and designers associated with the *Funkis* (Swedish Functionalist) movement, notably buildings by Erik Gunnar Asplund and Sven Markelius. The exhibition was masterminded by Paulsson, who was still heading the Svenska Slöjdföreningen, and had been inspired by his visit to the Deutscher Werkbund's Weissenhof housing estate at the 1927 *Die Wohnung* exhibition in Stuttgart, whose functionalist goals he shared. Codirected by Asplund, the show embodied the Swedish Functionalists' credo that purposeful design is beautiful. The prevailing spirit of the event was summed up in its slogan: *Acceptera!* (Accept!)—a clear plea for the wholehearted embrace

Art Deco and interpretations of modernism

of modernity: its functionalism, its standardization, its industrial production, its social change.

Meanwhile in Finland, a similar yet less dogmatic spirit of design reform could be detected in the work of the designer Aino Aalto and her architect husband, Alvar Aalto. Together they provided a much needed reinterpretation of Modern Movement functionalism that was based on a holistic and human-centric approach to design. Married in 1925, the Aaltos collaborated closely on many projects, including the development of techniques for laminating and bending wood, starting around 1929, which led to the manufacture of numerous landmark chair designs during the 1930s. They were also talented glassware designers, as shown in Aino's 1932 line for the Karhula-Iittala glassworks, which featured ribs of rippling glass, and Alvar's well-known Savoy vase (1937), reportedly inspired by the shorelines of Finnish lakes.[12] Capturing an abstracted essence of nature with its fluid undulating form, this latter piece anticipated the amorphous objects that would become so popular after World War II, from kidney-shaped coffee tables to blob-like glassware. Aalto felt that design should be a humanizing force, and he therefore rejected the severe geometric vocabulary of form so beloved by his contemporaries in Germany, France, and Sweden. He disapproved of the use of tubular metal on similar grounds, and instead created modern furniture from laminated wood and plywood that could be bent into curves that conformed to the human body and that were warm to the touch. Aalto's comfortable yet functional seating signaled a new direction in modern design in which the alienating steel-and-glass aesthetic was rejected in favor of more natural materials and forms. His well-known Model No. 41 armchair (1931–32), designed as part of his *Gesamtkunstwerk* scheme for the Paimio Sanatorium, epitomized his work, its organic form providing visual pleasure as well as ergonomic comfort. This was beautiful, democratic design, rather than prescriptive utilitarian design for the low-paid worker. With its emotionally compelling, soft-edged aesthetic, the Aaltos' work offered a highly influential new vocabulary of organic form that ultimately provided a more palatable version of modernism than those that had emerged so far.

↑
Glass pitcher designed by Aino Aalto for the
Karhula-Iittala glassworks, 1932.

↑
Model No. 41 armchair designed by Alvar Aalto
for Artek, 1931–32, also known as the "Paimio" armchair
because it was originally designed for the
Paimio tuberculosis sanatorium.

British modernism
and its social agenda

World War I catapulted Britain out of its cozy Edwardian idyll and into the modern world, a jolt that brought with it enormous social change. As on the Continent, victory had come at a heavy cost both financially and in human terms, with over seven hundred thousand young lives lost. The economic stagnation of the postwar years saw British design and manufacturing in almost complete stasis, but the introduction of the Austin 7 automobile in 1922 reflected a new postwar social order, being Britain's first affordable car for the everyman. Another item that epitomized British design during the 1920s was the Lygon cabinet, designed by Gordon Russell for the 1925 Exposition Internationale des Arts Décoratifs et Industriels Modernes in Paris. Painstakingly executed by highly skilled craftsmen, it featured exquisite dovetail joints, laburnum veneers, ebony handles, and brass hinges, reflecting a continuing adherence to the ideals of the Arts and Crafts movement, which still existed in Britain. Yet in the cabinet's plain symmetry, one can detect the first inkling of British modernism. Although designers such as Russell followed the developments of the progressive Modern Movement in Continental Europe, they still saw France as the major driving force behind it. It was not until the late 1930s that greater awareness grew of the Bauhaus, when many of its members fled to London on the eve of World War II.

America's stock market crash of October 1929 had devastating consequences for Britain, as elsewhere, and by the early 1930s the country was in the grip of an economic depression, with unemployment rising to 20 percent in 1933. As the economy worsened, the financial argument for modern industrial design grew. During this so-called devil's decade, there was an increasing acceptance of modernism in Britain, and a machine aesthetic was beginning to emerge in products for the market. While social idealism blossomed, clean modern lines that reflected a new industrial functionalism became part of the country's design vocabulary, as can be seen in items ranging from George Carwardine's innovative Anglepoise lamp (1932) to Wells Coates's gleaming Bakelite Ekco AD-65 radio (1934). Similarly, in graphic design, Henry Beck's diagrammatic remodeling of the London Underground map (1933) and Edward Young's covers for Penguin Books paperbacks (introduced in 1935) revealed a purposeful modernity. The looming threat of war with Germany also focused attention on the development of state-of-the-art military materiel, leading Reginald J. Mitchell to design the ingenious Supermarine Spitfire, a single-seat fighter aircraft that first flew in 1936.

In 1933 the Modern Architectural Research Group was established to promote the cause of modernist architecture in Britain: Philip Morton Shand, Wells Coates, and Maxwell Fry were among its founding members. It was, however, the influx of avant-garde architects and designers fleeing Nazi Germany—who included Marcel Breuer, Walter Gropius, Erich Mendelsohn, and Serge Chermayeff—that really helped to galvanize acceptance of modern design in Britain. These highly talented émigrés worked alongside

←
Anglepoise task lamp designed by George Carwardine for Herbert Terry & Sons, 1932.

→
Lygon cabinet designed by Gordon Russell for the 1925 Exposition Internationale des Arts Décoratifs et Industriels Modernes in Paris.

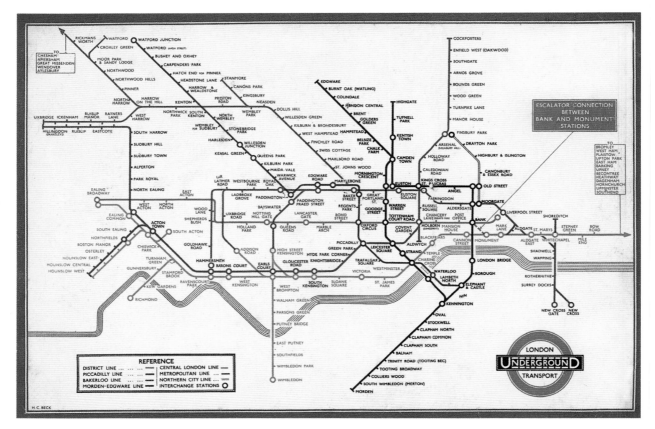

↑
Henry Beck's diagrammatic redesign of the London Underground map, 1933.

←
Ekco AD-65 radio designed by Wells Coates for Ekco, 1934.

→
Plywood lounge chair designed by Gerald Summers for Makers of Simple Furniture, 1933.

↗
A standard-format Penguin Books paperback cover, originally designed by Edward Young in 1935 and subtly adjusted by Jan Tschichold in the late 1940s.

Art Deco and interpretations of modernism

established British architects, and as a result they left a strong ideological legacy that remained long after their departure to other shores, most frequently America. The tubular-steel designs produced by the London-based furniture manufacturer PEL (Practical Equipment Ltd.), for example, showed not only an acceptance of Bauhaus-style functionalism but also a rejection of the craft ideal that had been central to the development of British design during the early years of the twentieth century. This same seemingly strident modernist stance was also reflected in the bold geometric forms of Keith Murray's ceramics for Wedgwood and Enid Marx's durable moquette textiles for London Transport. Yet at their core these designs were born of a craft tradition and were therefore a gentler, less austere expression of modernism. Scandinavian modernism was also a strong influence on British designers during the 1930s, particularly through the work of the Finnish architect Alvar Aalto, whose iconic molded-plywood furniture was imported to the UK and retailed by Finmar Ltd. This type of soft-edged, organic design did not have any worryingly Teutonic connotations; its direct influence is clearly visible in Gerald Summers's remarkable plywood lounge chair of 1933.

During the 1930s British design practice became increasingly professionalized; one clear example of this is Milner Gray and Misha Black's foundation, in 1934, of the Industrial Design Partnership, which was a forerunner of the Design Research Unit. The government, too, was mindful of the importance of good design in relation to industrial production, and was highly active during this period in its promotion of arts allied to industry, leading to the establishment in 1933 of the Council for Art and Industry—the forerunner of the postwar Council of Industrial Design. By the late 1930s, thanks to its excellent system of design education and the government's tireless promotion of good design, Britain boasted a sizeable body of highly talented design professionals who were creatively ready to solve the many design challenges that the nation would face after war was declared in 1939.

Italy: futurism, Novecento, and rationalism

The origins of modern design in Italy can be traced to the publication of Filippo Tommaso Marinetti's *Manifesto del Futurismo* (Futurist Manifesto) in 1909.[13] In this incendiary manifesto, Marinetti asserted that "the world's magnificence has been enriched by a new beauty: the beauty of speed."[14] He went on to call for an authentic modern expression of industrialized life that renounced Classicism as well as Arte Nuova (the Italian take on Art Nouveau). Instead, he celebrated the technological marvels of the day: factories, bridges, steamers, locomotives, airplanes, and—especially—fast cars. Marinetti's rallying cry was echoed by musicians, poets, writers, and filmmakers, and also by designers, who saw futurism as a means of disassociating with the past and embracing modernity. It was the first cultural movement to distance itself from nature and instead glorify the energetic flux of the metropolis. To this end, futurist designers such as Fortunato Depero used fragmented cubistic forms as a means of evoking acceleration and speed.

A leading instigator of futurism, Depero established the Casa d'Arte Futurista (House of Futurist Art) in 1919, which produced not only works of fine art but also tapestries, toys, carpets, windows, and posters. The architect Antonio Sant'Elia also joined the movement and provided an unabashedly utopian vision of the future with his designs for the *Città Nuova* (New City), which featured astonishingly forward-looking proto-Brutalistic buildings. The New City proposals were visual expressions of the ideas outlined in his 1914 *Manifesto dell'Architettura Futurista* (Manifesto of Futurist Architecture), in which he argued for the abolishment of decoration and for transience in design and architecture. "Every generation must build its own city," he proclaimed.[15] Attempting to subvert the prevailing bourgeois culture of Italy, futurism—which was aligned to Fascism—expressed an aggressive machine-age aesthetic and sought to create order through radicalism. As such, it must be seen as the first truly radical design movement, not only in Italy but anywhere in the world.

←
Moka Express espresso maker designed by Alfonso Bialetti for Bialetti Industrie, 1933.

↑
The Città Nuova (New City) urban-planning proposal designed by Antonio Sant'Elia, 1914.

↑
Casa del Fascio (Fascist Headquarters)
in Como designed by Giuseppe Terragni,
constructed 1932–36—an extraordinary Italian
rationalist gesamtkunstwerk.

←
Follia chair designed by Giuseppe Terragni
for the Casa del Fascio in Como, 1934 (later
reissued by Zanotta).

→
Luminator floor light designed by Pietro Chiesa
for Fontana Arte, c. 1933.

Art Deco and interpretations of modernism

Another new design movement, known as Novecento, was officially launched at an exhibition in Milan in 1923. Although it, too, was aligned with Fascism, Novecento—meaning "Twentieth Century"—was diametrically opposed to the futurists in its goals, seeking to revitalize Classicism within a modern idiom. Essentially an Italian manifestation of Art Deco, its most notable contributions were the 1933 Moka Express espresso-maker designed by Alfonso Bialetti and the Neoclassical ceramics designed by the architect Gio Ponti for the ceramics manufacturer Richard Ginori. Of far greater influence was *Domus* magazine, launched in 1928 by Gio Ponti and the publisher Gianni Mazzocchi. *Domus* publicized the work of designers aligned with the Novecento movement. Although it was initially produced as a lifestyle magazine, under Ponti's editorship it soon became the authoritative voice on design and architecture in Italy. It was so strident in championing Italian design both at home and abroad that it became known as the "Mediterranean megaphone."

Another design and architecture movement pioneered in Italy during the 1920s and 1930s was rationalism, which sought to reconcile the functionalism of the European avant-garde with Italy's Classical tradition. Like the Novecento, rationalism had its own mouthpiece, *La Casa Bella* magazine (later renamed *Casabella*), which was founded in 1928 and edited by the architect Giuseppe Pagano from 1933. Rationalism essentially occupied the middle ground between the industrially inspired designs of the futurits and the overtly neoclassicist work of the Novecento. One of the most notable manifestations of this new style was Giuseppe Terragni's Casa del Fascio (Fascist Headquarters Building) in Como, completed in 1936. Using a severe, geometric formal vocabulary and state-of-the-art materials, including reinforced concrete and glass block panels, its totally unified scheme was equipped with suitably progressive furniture, such as Terragni's Follia chair (1934). The Fascists initially embraced rationalism, seeing themselves as champions of a new world order and so sympathizing with its forward-looking machine aesthetic. Eventually, though, they opted instead for the more grandiose Novecento style, with its more overtly Classical and imperialistic connotations.

CONVERTIBLE

While this battle of design styles was being waged during the 1930s, Italian industry developed rapidly. As a consequence, a number of noteworthy designs intended for mass production appeared, revealing the beginnings of an identifiably Italian approach to design. Among these were the elegant Luminator floor lamp (1933) by Pietro Chiesa for Fontana Arte, the diminutive Fiat 500 Topolino (1936) by Dante Giacosa, and the plastic molded Model No. 574 radio (1938-39) by Livio Castiglioni, Pier Giacomo Castiglioni, and Luigi Caccia Dominioni for Phonola—all of which reflected a uniquely Italian approach to design that effectively clothed function in elegant form. It was, however, only after World War II that Italian design would blossom fully and become a major force on the international scene.

↑
Fiat 500 Topolino, designed by
Dante Giacosa, 1936.

→
Model No. 574 radio designed by
Livio Castiglioni, Pier Giacomo Castiglioni,
and Luigi Caccia Dominioni for Phonola,
1938-39.

Art Deco and interpretations of modernism

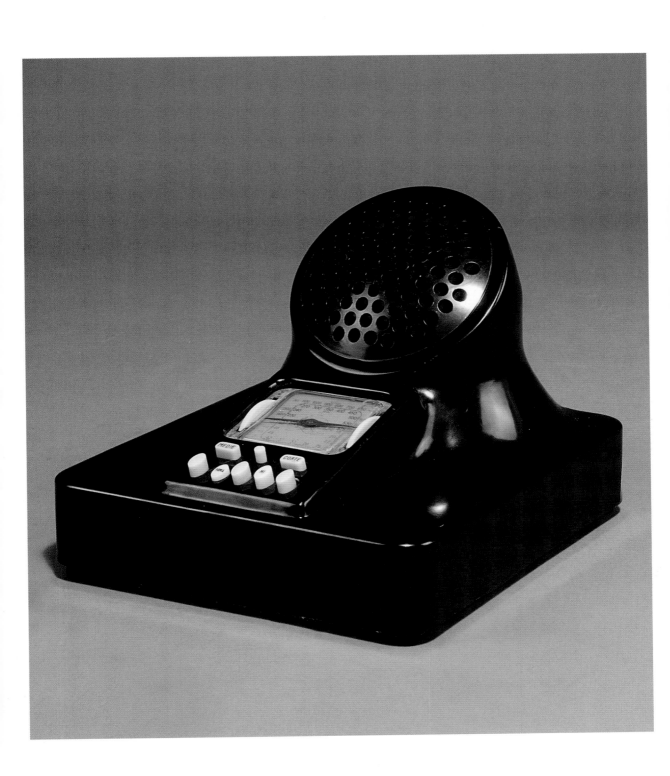

Art Deco: from boom to bust

Because the United States did not enter World War I until April 1917—having remained neutral for almost three years—its industrial might was intact when the conflict ended in November 1918. If anything, its industries were in better shape than they had been before the war, which meant that Americans enjoyed an abundance of consumer goods during the 1920s, as wartime production transitioned to peacetime manufacture. The expansion of American industry was further helped by a surplus of raw materials and the high duties slapped on foreign imports. Some businesses also enjoyed government subsidies, which further enhanced their profitability. The Roaring Twenties was a period of prosperity and optimism, and also an era of growing national pride, as embodied in the towering Art Deco skyscrapers that were being built in the larger cities across the country. These glittering edifices celebrated American technological innovation and surging corporate strength. During this period, the United States also underwent rapid urbanization. At the same time the percentage of white-collar workers making up the nation's workforce increased significantly, and it was perhaps this sector of society that most enjoyed the consumer-goods revolution that brought about widespread car ownership and a burgeoning advertising industry. This era also saw the arrival of the country's first radio network, NBC, in 1926, and the advent of motion-picture "talkies" in 1927, which together created a shared media culture, binding the nation together socially with its embrace of modernity and its promotion of an array of new products that offered consumers a starring role in modern American life.

Despite Prohibition, the Jazz Age of the 1920s brought greater gender equality and sexual freedoms. The optimism, confidence, and social liberation of the times were reflected in the bold geometric patterning and massing found in fashionable Art Deco products and buildings. For many Americans, it must have

seemed that the American Dream, which promised success through hard work, had at last been fulfilled by the abundance of affordable luxury goods. As America's economy boomed, the soaring skyscrapers mirrored the ever-upward trajectory of the buoyant stock market. In this era of flagrant materialism, chain stores began to dominate the market, making the acquisition of goods easier and cheaper thanks to their economy of scale, while the introduction of installment purchasing further stimulated product consumption. Now that cars, household appliances, radios, phonographs, pianos, and furniture could all be bought on credit, there really was no need for delayed gratification. Yet in buying such "big ticket" items on credit, many households saddled themselves with high levels of debt that would eventually come back to haunt them.

Unlike earlier American design, which was often characterized by a practical utility, Art Deco objects tended to rely more on "eye appeal" than function.[1] Many Americans were captivated by the idea of affordable luxury and aspired to the glamorous lifestyles that were beginning to be portrayed on Hollywood's silver screen. Luxury was no longer seen as morally decadent but rather as a normal feature of modern American life. With greater spending power, many Americans could now afford nonessential products such as cocktail shakers and "fancy" glassware, and numerous manufacturers across America began to produce party wares that were relatively cheap to mass-manufacture yet looked

←
Previous page: 20th Century Limited streamlined locomotive designed by Henry Dreyfuss for the New York Central Railroad, 1938.

→
The Chrysler Building in New York City designed by William Van Alen, constructed 1928–30—the ultimate skyscraping expression of the American Art Deco style.

The Great Depression and the Moderne style

Art Deco: from boom to bust

expensive.[2] By the mid-to-late 1920s, consumers had also come to expect wider product choice, and manufacturers, especially in the automotive industry, now regarded color as a business asset, since it allowed them to offer more purchasing options to potential customers. Even Henry Ford, whose famous quip "Any customer can have a car painted any color that he wants, so long as it is black"[3] reflected his commitment to a one-size-fits-all form of standardization, was forced to redesign his highly successful Model T car in 1927 into a new model with a more appealing streamlined appearance and in various color options, in a bid to regain market shares.

During the 1920s it was believed that consumption bred progress, and increasing the availability of material goods was viewed as an essentially democratizing action. Manufacturers were keen to sell consumers everything their hearts desired. As the radio announcer Helen Landon Cass explained to a convention of salesmen in Philadelphia in 1923:

> Sell them their dreams. Sell them what they longed for and hoped for and almost despaired of having. Sell them hats by splashing sunlight across them. Sell them dreams—dreams of country clubs and proms and visions of what might happen if only. After all, people don't buy things to have things. They buy things to work for them. They buy hope— hope of what your merchandise will do for them. Sell them this hope and you won't have to worry about selling them goods.[4]

In that atmosphere, manufacturers made luxury commonplace, employing professional designers who understood the emotional attraction of fashionable goods. During this decade of overindulgence, stylishly designed department stores throughout the country brought a plethora of voguish deluxe items to the average consumer, and in so doing were instrumental in changing the notion of purchasing: rather than being seen as a mundane necessity, it was now viewed as an enjoyable leisure pursuit. As the then-Brooklyn Museum curator Stewart Culin noted: "The stores, not churches, are the greatest influences for culture and taste that exist today."[5] He went on to observe that these sparkling palaces of merchandise, filled with objects of desire, "make it possible for us all to participate in the creative thought of a new and revolutionary era."[6]

The good times were, nevertheless, running out. Throughout the decade, America's financial markets had experienced rapid growth, which enticed many people to borrow large sums in order to speculate on the stock market—profits from share investments being seen as a "sure thing." For several years everything went swimmingly. Fortunes were made, often overnight, as the Dow Jones Industrial Average soared from sixty in August 1921 to four hundred in September 1929, providing more than a sixfold return on investments. Trying to cool the overheated market, the Federal Reserve raised interest rates several times, but to no avail; by the fall of 1929, the bull market was rapidly turning into a bear market. The seismic shock of the Wall Street crash on October 24 reverberated across America, spurring panic selling and runs on many banks by savers, which prompted their collapse. Overnight the American Dream had evaporated into thin air, replaced by the waking nightmare of pervasive financial crisis on a previously unimaginable scale.

↖
Illustration of the Ford Convertible Cabriolet, *Ladies' Home Journal*, 1929— the colorful successor to the Model T.

↑
Skyscraper cocktail shaker designed by Louis W. Rice, c. 1928.

↑
No. 2A Beau Brownie camera designed by Walter Dorwin Teague for Kodak in 1928 (patented 1930).

Moderne in the Design Decade

The bursting of Wall Street's financial bubble tipped America into the Great Depression, which saw mass poverty ripple across the country. While millions of jobs were lost and countless families became homeless, manufacturers either went to the wall or desperately struggled to cut costs in order to survive. The economic downturn during the Depression years of the 1930s meant that manufacturers needed to give their products added value in order to stand out within a now very competitive marketplace. The fledgling profession of industrial-design consulting flourished during this period, because manufacturers suddenly found themselves needing help in differentiating their products from those of their competitors: after all, if two companies' products had the same functionality and cost, the customer was likely to purchase the more attractive one. Also, this first generation of American industrial-design consultants—many of whom had initially worked in advertising agencies or as stage designers—not only knew how to give products greater surface allure, thereby increasing sales, but also in some cases had the necessary design skills to reduce factory unit prices. They did this by following a process-driven approach to design, whereby the most efficient use of the manufacturing process was analyzed and then used to inform the construction and final form of the product.

Thanks to the economic importance placed on design during this period, the 1930s became known as the Design Decade in the US, and large corporations courted prominent consultants such as Raymond Loewy, Henry Dreyfuss, Lurelle Guild, Harold van Doren, Walter Dorwin Teague, John Vassos, George Sakier, and Joseph Sinel to redesign their entire product lines. Although these Americans were obviously aware of developments within Europeanmodernism, including the theories emanating from the Bauhaus, they did not subscribe to any one theory of design. As the design historian Jeffrey Meikle has noted, "In the American tradition of practical eclecticism, they took whatever seemed modern and transformed it for commercial use."[7] Their products were often more modernistic than modern, in that they relied on surface styling to give the appearance of innovation rather than truly innovating through functional design. Before this period there had been various "art industries" in the US, mainly manufacturing Arts and Crafts-style domestic items such as ceramics, glassware, furniture, leatherwork, textiles, carpets, and wallpapers. During the Depression, however, manufacturers from what the designer and critic George Nelson called the "formerly artless industries"[8]—for example, the producers of vehicles, washing machines, sewing machines, stoves, locomotives, refrigerators, pens, clocks, and food packaging—turned to celebrity designers to give their products an "artistic treatment." And no wonder, considering the added value generated

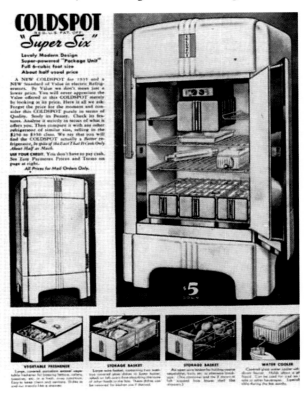

←
Mock-up of Raymond Loewy's office at the Metropolitan Museum of Art, New York, with the designer posing near a Hupmobile model, 1934.

→
Advertisement for a streamlined Coldspot Super-Six refrigerator designed by Raymond Loewy for Sears, Roebuck, 1934.

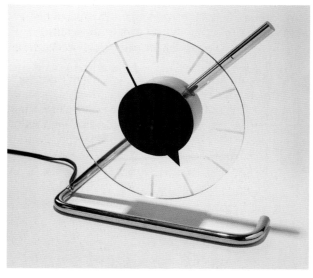

↑
Insulated pitcher (Model No. 549), designed by
Henry Dreyfuss for Thermos, 1935.

↑
Z Clock (Model No. 4090) designed by Gilbert
Rohde for the Herman Miller Clock Company, 1933.

→
Petipoint electric iron designed by
Clifford Brooks Stevens and Edward P.
Schreyer for the Waverly Tool Company,
c. 1940, patented 1941—the ultimate
streamlined household product.

by these consultants. For example, Harold van Doren's streamlined redesign of a weighing scale for the Toledo Scale Company increased sales by a staggering 900 percent while reducing manufacturing costs; similarly, Lurelle Guild's redesigned Kensington Ware aluminium coffeepot for the Aluminum Company of America (Alcoa) boosted sales by 40 percent, while also lowering production cost.[9]

These professionals, with their large offices, commanded high fees for their services. For instance, Henry Dreyfuss's consultancy rate was $50 per hour, which translates to about $680 today; meanwhile Raymond Loewy worked on annual retainer fees of $10,000–$60,000 per company, which would be $135,000–$815,000 today. This handful of celebrated professionals was so in demand that their yearly incomes averaged around $150,000 each—a princely sum when one considers that the average American weekly wage in 1934 was just $19.12.[10] Yet for companies such as Westinghouse, Sears, Roebuck and Company, Philco, WearEver Aluminum, Eastman Kodak, DeVilbiss, and the Radio Corporation of America, these first "superstar" designers earned every cent of their fees by designing products that could, in effect, sell themselves in a market that had all but collapsed. As an article in the February 1934 issue of *Fortune* magazine explained:

> These men came to redesign the surface of the product, [and] often stayed to suggest practical improvements—sometimes gadgets, sometimes fundamental changes. The shelf of an oven might be made to slide out without the risk of burning the cook's fingers, a penny-in-the-slot scale might be made so that loungers could not look over the shoulder of the lady being weighed and read her poundage, certain parts of a stove might be standardized.[11]

Moreover, these industrial-design consultants often saved the manufacturers significant amounts in tooling costs by making a few seemingly insignificant changes in their redesigns. They also changed materials—say, from metal to plastic—which made products cheaper to manufacture and, in some cases, more functional.

The Great Depression and the Moderne style

Dreyfuss, for example, streamlined the model 150 vacuum cleaner for Hoover (1936), housing its internal mechanism in a sleek Bakelite and lightweight magnesium-alloy casing. Manufacturers also found that designer cachet helped sell products; as a result, portraits of these professionals were often featured in advertisements; some even went so far as to emblazon the designer's signature on the product, the most notable example being Dreyfuss's Model No. 549 insulated pitcher (1935) for Thermos.

Whereas hard-edged geometric motifs, especially those alluding to Egyptian ziggurat forms, had been fashionable in the 1920s, during the 1930s more curvaceous shapes flourished, as was seen in the furnishings of Gilbert Rohde's Design for Living house, exhibited at the Century of Progress International Exposition held in 1933–34 in Chicago. Manufactured by Herman Miller, Rohde's furniture had clean, modern lines and was often multifunctional, in recognition of the space constraints of urban living spaces. His desktop clock designs for the Herman Miller Clock Company—which were also exhibited in the Design for Living house—were perhaps even more extraordinary, boasting bold, streamlined forms. Streamlining brought connotations of modernity and speed and was symbolic of the machine age. Although aerodynamic, streamlined forms can certainly improve the performance of cars, trains, and planes, in the 1930s most industrial designers were using such curves less for functional reasons and more to make household products look sleeker and thereby more tempting to the consumer. As Harold van Doren observed: "Streamlining has taken the world by storm. We live in a maelstrom of streamlined trains, refrigerators, and furnaces . . . The manufacturer who wants his laundry tubs, his typewriters, or his furnaces streamlined is in reality asking you to modernize them, to find the means for substituting curvilinear forms for rectilinear forms."[12]

Using clay models, designers essentially sculpted sweeping modern-looking forms for a whole range of consumer items, including radios, cameras, telephones, and household goods. Many of these products featured casings made of Bakelite or Catalin, thermoset plastics suited to being molded into flowing,

streamlined forms.[13] A versatile material, Bakelite offered previously undreamed-of possibilities to both designers and manufacturers; within a very short time, innumerable applications had been found for this wondrous and economical plastic, marketed as "the material of a thousand uses." In terms of product design, Bakelite and other phenolic plastics were excellent electrical-insulating materials, and as such they were ideal for molding appliance housings, as in Fredrik Ljungström's Ribbonaire table fan for the Singer Sewing Machine Company (1931). From the mid-1930s onward, numerous landmark "Depression Moderne" designs in plastics were mass produced for the American market, for example Walter Dorwin Teague's miniature Baby Brownie camera for Kodak (1934) and Executive (Model No. 114) desk lamp for Polaroid (1939). Catalin, which could be colored to produce an onyx-like effect, was also used widely, especially for radios such as those produced by the Emerson Radio & Phonograph Corporation.

In 1934 Loewy's streamlined Coldspot refrigerator for Sears, Roebuck became the first domestic appliance to be marketed for looks rather than performance. Later in his career, Loewy even went so far as to suggest the criterion of good design was no longer function but rather "an upward-sweeping sales curve."[14] The commercial benefits of streamlining and "consumption engineering" made them rivals to advertising in their efficacy at selling products. As a result, the practices

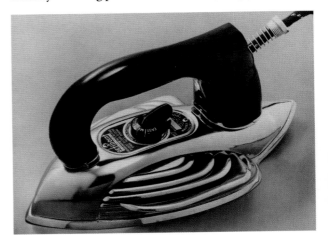

The Great Depression and the Moderne style

soon became widespread, and designers who used such methods were celebrated as purveyors of luxurious yet affordable modernity—none more so than Loewy, who was viewed as a veritable guru. As a consultant to more than 140 companies during his career, the majority of them large, well-known corporations, Loewy had an enormous influence on design practice. Ever a pragmatist, he had, he claimed, "a fifth sense about public acceptance"[15] and practiced an approach to design that he eventually termed MAYA, standing for "Most Advanced Yet Acceptable." As he explained in his 1951 book *Never Leave Well Enough Alone*, the designer's natural desire is always to give the customer the most advanced product possible. But there is a consumer "shock zone" where the desire to buy flattens or even decreases. Therefore, Loewy concluded, if a product is to be really successful in the marketplace it is essential for the designer to be sensitive to the public's taste threshold and never to go beyond it.

Designers such as Dreyfuss, Bel Geddes, and Teague, who worked in what became known as the Moderne style—essentially a modernistic interpretation of late Art Deco style—were, like Loewy, finely attuned to the likes and dislikes of the American consumer, using streamlined shapes and gleaming chromium and aluminium surface finishes to give their designs an alluring appearance. Many products, from table lighters to toasters, were also adorned with the classic Moderne motif of three incised lines, which emphasized the sweeping form of the glinting surfaces and suggested speed. On this subject, Edgar Kaufmann, Jr., Director of the Industrial Design Department at New York's Museum of Modern Art and a tireless champion of good design during the postwar years, stated in 1944: "Streamlining is not good design. Its theme is the magic of speed, expressed by teardrop shapes, fairings, and a curious ornament of parallel lines—sometimes called speed whiskers. The continued misuse of these devices has spoiled them for most designers."[16]

Yet who could fail to be impressed by the sumptuous interiors and furnishings designed by Donald Deskey for Radio City Music Hall, which perhaps best reflected the streamlined Moderne style's association with celebrity glitz. The optimistic opulence and forward-looking nature of the style offered a respite, albeit illusory, from the social havoc of the Great Depression, and it came to characterize a more glamorized version of the American Dream that was appropriate for the dawning machine age. This coming era of remarkable technical progress saw the advent of mass-market advertising as well as the growth of large corporations that could exploit their economies of scale in order to buy the best design talent available, thus providing better-designed and cheaper products to lure the cash-strapped consumer.

←
Bluebird 566 radio designed by Walter Dorwin Teague for Sparton, 1935–36—with what Edgar Kauffman, Jr., called its "speed whiskers."

→
New York apartment for the manager of Radio City Music Hall designed by Donald Deskey, 1933.

Restyling, planned obsolescence, and the world of tomorrow

In America, despite the boom years of the 1920s, there had been a growing problem for manufacturers: market saturation. There were only so many products individual consumers could reasonably buy, so the challenge was how to entice them to discard the products they already had and purchase newer ones. Traditionally, manufacturers had worked hard to make products that lasted, but this meant that consumers were less likely to buy replacement goods if the ones they had were still perfectly serviceable. Manufacturers began to realize that the best way to lessen a product's lifespan was to replace it with another, making consumers feel that their existing toaster, cooking appliance, or car was old-fashioned in comparison to the latest, heavily advertised replacement, one that was always just a bit sleeker, a bit more alluring, and a bit more stylish. Around this time designers were often referred to as "industrial stylists," and they were mainly tasked with streamlining the surfaces of existing products so as to make them appear new.

By the early 1920s, there were few limitations on industrial productivity, but the market for consumer goods was growing increasingly competitive. General Motors chairman Alfred Sloan, realizing that aesthetics would play an increasingly important role over the coming years in differentiating products, invited the prodigiously talented car stylist Harley Earl to Detroit in 1925. Before this, Earl had devised an innovative modeling-and-styling technique using clay—which would become standard practice among car manufacturers, and was then taken up by other industries—that enabled him to make the car bodies he worked on more sculpturally expressive. Earl's first brief for GM was to bring "something" to the new LaSalle brand, which was pitched between the upscale Buick and luxurious Cadillac models. The resulting 1927 LaSalle was the first mass-produced car whose body shape was created by a stylist rather than an engineer or builder; as such, it ushered in a new era of automotive styling. Sloan realized that the company would profit even more if it could produce new cars each year that differed from the previous year's model. This idea of annual cosmetic changes to promote stylistic obsolescence led to the creation of General Motors' Art and Color Section in 1928. Prior to that, the design of car bodies in America had been primarily the responsibility of engineers. Earl became supervisor of the unprecedented department, renamed the Style Section in 1937, and began to lower and lengthen models in order to rid them of their boxy appearances. "My sense of proportion tells me that oblongs are more attractive than squares," he noted, "just as a greyhound is more graceful than an English bulldog. Happily, the car-buying public and I consistently agree on this."[17] Earl also used female stylists in the department in order to reach the increasingly important women's market. In addition, he oversaw the development of the very first concept car—the 1938 Buick Y-Job—which boasted trailblazing two-tone paintwork, a wraparound windscreen, and a "fishtail" rear fender.

As the cultural commentator Stephen Bayley observed, "Without quite realizing it . . . General Motors' executives had summoned up the genie of styling."[18] As everybody knows, when a genie is released from a bottle, it is well-night impossible to put it back in—and so it was with the capricious styling genie. Competing automobile manufacturers soon initiated similar annual restyling programs, and this practice was adopted by other industries as well. Working as industrial stylists, designers around this

↑
Top: LaSalle car designed by Harley Earl for
General Motors, 1927.

↑
Buick Y-Job designed by Harley Earl for
General Motors, 1938.

time created, as we have seen, streamlined forms suited for production on an industrial scale, often without thinking too much about the item's utility. More often than not, surface aesthetics were more important than functionality.

The journalist and author Christine Frederick, who was famed for writing best-selling manuals on household efficiency, and her husband, George, who ran a publishing company called Business Bourse that specialized in business-related market research and data, were early champions of the type of planned obsolescence that was pioneered at General Motors. Essentially, the concept centered on curtailing a product's lifespan so that it would be replaced sooner than would otherwise be expected. The Fredericks came up with the delightful euphemism "creative waste," arguing that if products' life cycles could be accelerated, consumers would buy more things, which would benefit not only manufacturers but the economy as a whole. In a nutshell, more products meant more jobs. At this stage there was no real concept of environmental sustainability nor of the finite nature of natural resources, and as a result this type of consumer manipulation was seen as a legitimate way of promoting economic growth. As a prominent evangelist for consumption, Frederick noted in her influential book of 1929, *Selling Mrs. Consumer*: "Consumption is the name given to the new doctrine; and it is admitted today to be the greatest idea that America has given to the world; the idea that workmen and the masses be looked upon not simply as workers or producers but as *consumers*. Pay them more, sell them more, prosper more is the equation."[19]

By deliberately accelerating the stylistic obsolescence of products that were still serviceable, manufacturers had shifted their focus from the costly process of researching and developing universal, timeless products to superficially remodeling fashionable ones. Having abandoned Louis Sullivan's dictum, "Form ever follows function," designers were now creating ever more extreme variations of products. This marketing ploy cynically played to the consumer's childlike love of novelty, and, for the first time, linked designed goods to seasonal fashions. This trend-driven practice was widely embraced. As Christine Frederick further observed:

There isn't the slightest reason in the world why materials which are inexhaustibly replenishable should not be creatively "wasted." . . . We have subscribed wholeheartedly to the revolutionizing consumer idea that goods should not be consumed up to their last ounce of usability . . . in an industrial era Mrs. Consumer is happiest and best served if she consumes goods at the same approximate rate of change and improvement that science and art and machinery can make possible. . . It increases general income, whereas clinging to the old goods decreases it.[20]

The consumerist approach to design and merchandising, which later came to be known as "planned obsolescence" or "built-in obsolescence," and it was directly responsible for the rise of America's throwaway culture. Echoing Frederick's sentiments, the leading advertising executive and copywriter Earnest Elmo Calkins, further rationalized the approach in economic terms:

Obsoletism is another device for stimulating consumption. The element of style is a consideration in buying many things. Clothes go out of style and are replaced long before they are worn out. That principle extends to other products— motor-cars, bathrooms, radios, foods, refrigerators, furniture. People are persuaded to abandon the old and buy the new to be up-to-date, to have the right and correct thing. Does there seem to be a sad waste in the process? Not at all. Wearing things out does not produce prosperity, but buying things does. Thrift in the industrial society in which we now live consists of keeping all factories busy. Any plan which increases the consumption of goods is justifiable if we believe that prosperity is desirable.[21]

The respected British economist John Maynard Keynes also saw the Depression as a failure of consumer confidence, and in his book *The General Theory of Employment, Interest and Money* (1936) argued that the lack of consumer demand and rising unemployment could be solved by significantly increasing government expenditure to stimulate the national economy. To this interventionist end, the US Government used low interest rates to encourage people to borrow money to

renovate and furnish their homes. Franklin Roosevelt's New Deal cultural programs also helped create jobs within the design sector through commissions for public information posters, murals for hospitals, schools, and other public buildings. The Federal Art Project's Index of American Design, an enormous undertaking, documented thousands of colonial designs and early examples of American folk art with exquisitely executed watercolor renderings. The concept of "saving by buying" also gained currency during this period, most notably through the greater accessibility of radios, which provided cheap home entertainment, and the increasing availability of refrigerators, which meant that householders could save money by buying food in bulk. During the Depression, spending money on stylish designer goods such as radios, refrigerators, cars, and furniture was seen as an important patriotic duty that would ultimately pull the country out of its economic morass. And yet, despite interventionist economic policies that brought about a 70 percent increase in government

spending, and aggressive design-and-marketing techniques devised by manufacturers hungry for sales, it was the threatening spectre of Nazi aggression in Europe that finally boosted American employment figures and thereby the nation's economy in the late 1930s. The government introduced a massive rearmament program, with generous contracts that guaranteed manufacturers a healthy profit on the war supplies they produced. In fact, the economic paralysis of the Great Depression never really ended but was instead subsumed by the mobilization of American

↑
Model 115 radio manufactured by the Fada Radio & Electric Company, first introduced in 1941—the quintessential streamlined American Moderne radio.

industry for military ends.

Around the time America was gearing up for the war effort, the country saw a large influx of influential European avant-garde architects and designers who had been driven to emigrate in order to escape Nazi persecution. Amongst these talented figures were Walter Gropius, Marcel Breuer, and László Moholy-Nagy (all of whom arrived 1937), who were to become the three most important promoters of Bauhaus modernism in the United States. Both Gropius and Breuer subsequently taught at the Harvard Graduate School of Design, while Moholy-Nagy established the New Bauhaus in Chicago, which was later known as the Institute of Design. Although the influence of their teachings was not felt particularly during the 1930s, one cannot underestimate their impact on the development of American design during the succeeding decade as their students came of age professionally. For example, the eminently talented Florence Knoll studied under Mies van der Rohe at the Armour Institute and was mentored by him, going on to put his classic furniture designs into production under the auspices of Knoll Associates in the late 1940s, and to pioneer her own

interpretation of the International Style. Many other European-born designers also arrived in America during this time, too, and collectively they later became well known "American" postwar designers.

The theme of the 1939–40 New York's World Fair, clearly reflecting a growing desire to distract Americans from the country's recent and persistent economic woes, was "Building the World of Tomorrow"; it encapsulated two powerful national traits, optimism and futurism. The exhibition emphasized that American society was about to be profoundly altered by advances in science and technology, and the event's forty-five million visitors appear to have embraced its futuristic vision of the coming technological age with much enthusiasm. Many of the exhibits offered tantalizing glimpses of high-tech marvels, from televisions to robots, or speculated on futuristic modes of living. The renowned Broadway-stage designer and industrial-design consultant Norman Bel Geddes was responsible for the Futurama centerpiece of General Motors' Highways and Horizons pavilion and the acknowledged highlight of the whole fair. Futurama used early multimedia presentational

←
Bakelite Plastics exhibit at the New York World's Fair, 1939–40. A woman tests Hoover's streamlined Model 150 vacuum cleaner, designed by Henry Dreyfuss in 1936.

→
Entrance ramp of General Motors' Highways and Horizons exhibit at the 1939–40 New York World's Fair.

The Great Depression and the Moderne style

techniques to give the viewer an unforgettable ride into the future. Bel Geddes drew on both his theatrical flair and his industrial-design skills to construct his spectacular 35,000-square-foot diorama from 408 highly detailed sectional models that showed his extraordinary, prophetic vision of 1960s American jet-age transportation and living; it incorporated half a million minutely detailed buildings, intersecting elevated motorways, and gleaming, illuminated skyscrapers. The breathtaking detail of the models was achieved using aerial photography and maps; a circular moving conveyor with seats known as the "magic carry-go-round" allowed some 28,000 visitors a day to get a 360-degree view of this remarkable three-dimensional projection of future living. As they toured the exhibit, a recorded message invited spectators to "come tour the future," and explained the benefits of the replanned modern cities and an advanced national highway system that would allow faster travel. Meanwhile, the most iconic structures of the New York World's Fair were the gleaming spire-shaped Trylon, housing the world's longest escalator, and the gigantic ball-like Perisphere. This highly futuristic structure held the Democracity diorama, designed by Henry Dreyfuss, which speculated on what a utopian American city would look like in 2039, with skyscrapers at its heart and suburbs and parks and freeways radiating from its center. The fair opened in April 1939, only four months before Hitler invaded Poland—an event that was to annihilate any hope of realizing the utopias conjured up by these exhibits at the Building the World of Tomorrow fair.

14

DESIGN
FOR WAR

Military designs
of World War II

While the effectiveness of military weaponry and hardware is perpetually improved as a result of technological progress, the primary criteria for military design have remained the same for centuries, namely: durability, strength, fitness for purpose, functionality, transportability, and ease of maintenance and repair. Successful military designs, as we have already seen, also rely on constructions that are both rationalized and standardized, making them comparatively easy to manufacture; in wartime, suitability for high-volume production is always important. The functionality of weapons is also frequently a decisive factor, and it is essential to have state-of-the-art equipment. This has meant that there has long been a culture of military-design development, which over time has led to increasing specialization. This field of design can be broken down into five main categories: offensive, defensive, transport, communication, and detection. The interwar period and World War II saw enormous design progress in all these areas, which helped to determine the conflict's outcome.

Although the Great War of 1914–18 prompted ideological change in design and ultimately led to the increasing acceptance of modernism in all its guises, it can be argued that World War II had an even more profound impact on the story of design. The reason for this is that it brought about a rapid acceleration of research and development; after the war designers and manufacturers had a plethora of new materials and technologies at their disposal for peacetime applications. Between 1919 and 1945, various designs that had been introduced in the 1914–18 conflict were improved considerably; this was especially true in the case of aircraft and tanks. Battlefield communications had also become increasingly sophisticated, with the design of field telephones in particular facilitating command and control of troops. The aircraft carrier came of age as well, bringing a completely new dimension to naval warfare. In addition, the design of aircraft became increasingly specialized. Daylight bombers such as the Boeing B-17 Flying Fortress (first flight 1935) required the development of long-range fighter escorts such as the North American P-51 Mustang (first flight 1940). Similarly, the compact and agile Japanese Mitsubishi A6M "Zero" fighter (first flight 1939), with its excellent aerobatic-style handling, was perfectly suited to the restricted takeoff and landing area on the Japanese Imperial Navy's aircraft carriers.

Tanks also played a crucial role in providing armies with greater maneuvrability and the possibility of punching holes through enemy lines—the Russian T-34 tank (1940) might not have been the most sophisticated armored fighting vehicle on the battlefield, but it became one of the most decisive weapons in World War II, mainly because it was designed for large-scale mass production, showing that sometimes in war quantity is more important than quality. Before and during World War II, several nations, including the United States, Germany, and Britain, had also secretly developed object-detection systems that used radio waves to track enemy aircraft and ships. In 1940 the US Navy coined the word "radar"—an acronym based on "Radio Detection and Ranging"—to describe these state-of-the-art tracking systems. Prior to the war, Britain and the US had also been developing underwater sound propagation equipment, christened by the Americans "sonar"—"Sound Navigation and Ranging"; these were first deployed by the Allied navies to detect the stealthy threat of German U-boats.

Although many countries were involved in the conflict, there were essentially five major players—Britain, Germany, the United States, the Soviet Union, and Japan—responsible for most developments in military design during the period. In Britain there were two aircraft designs that have entered the pages of history as iconic war-birds: the Supermarine Spitfire

Top: P-51 Mustang fighter-bomber aircraft,
first flight 1940.

Mitsubishi A6M "Zero" fighter aircraft,
first flight 1939.

Design for war

(first flight 1936) and the Avro Lancaster (first flight 1941). The Spitfire fighter, designed by the aeronautical engineer Reginald Joseph Mitchell, had a purposeful elegance that embodied the attributes of British design better than any other aircraft. With distinctive elliptical wings and a monocoque fuselage, this low-wing single-seater aircraft underwent many changes throughout the war. [1] Yet as the aviation annual *Jane's All the World's Aircraft* noted in 1944: "The soundness of the basic design has been proved in six years of war, throughout which the Rolls-Royce-engined *Spitfire* has, in its many progressive developments, remained a first-line fighter."[2] Renowned for its aerodynamic airframe and impressive maneuvrability at high altitudes, the Spitfire played a decisive role in the Battle of Britain as a superb defense interceptor. While the Spitfire was nimble, the Lancaster was an altogether different type of beast: a heavy bomber that packed an impressive payload and could carry the Royal Air Force's heaviest blockbuster bombs, weighing up to 12,000 pounds each. Although predominantly used on night bombing raids, the Lancaster was also employed as a daylight precision bomber—and was memorably modified to carry the famous bouncing-bomb designed by Barnes Wallis that was used to destroy the Möhne and Edersee dams in Germany.

Despite these two landmark aircraft designs, Britain's war materiel was generally inferior to Germany's. Germany had undertaken much more research and development before the war, and so its arms industry was considerably more advanced. The Tiger I heavy tank designed and manufactured by Henschel and Sohn, for example, was arguably the best such vehicle to appear during the war. It was highly engineered and had a fairly complex design, however, making it expensive and time-consuming to produce. Only 1,347 were built between August 1942 and August 1944. With its initial development worked on by the renowned German automotive engineer Ferdinand Porsche, the Tiger I was notable for its impressive firepower, which came courtesy of a mounted 88 mm gun, and for its welded rather than riveted armor, which was made of high-performance steel alloy. A landmark of tank design, the Tiger boasted the speed and mobility of other tank designs on the battlefield despite being a much heavier vehicle, weighing in at more than 11,000 pounds. In the skies, Germany boasted the extraordinary Messerschmitt Me 109 (first flight 1935), which was one of the first truly modern fighters, its various advanced features including a metal monocoque construction, retractable landing gear, a closed canopy, and a fuel-injection engine. This advanced low-wing cantilever monoplane, designed by Willy Messerschmitt and Robert Lusser, was based on the latter's "lightweight construction" principle, whereby the elements making up the airplane were kept to an absolute minimum. Having fewer parts made it easier to mass-manufacture, which in turn made it the most produced fighter aircraft of all time: an astonishing 33,984 units rolled off the production line between 1936 and 1945. Yet this workhorse of the Luftwaffe was trounced in terms of design innovation by the formidable Messerschmitt Me 262 (first flight with jet engines 1942). The world's first jet-powered fighter, it had a groundbreaking bullet-like body and swept-wing layout designed by the pioneering aerodynamicist Ludwig Bölkow.[3]

On the battlefield, German soldiers also benefited from better-designed small arms and support weapons than their opponents. These included: the cutting-edge MP44 Sturmgewher assault rifle (the blueprint for postwar weapons such as the legendary Russian AK47), which featured the gas-operated firing mechanism of a machine gun but the selective firing capacity of a rifle; and the MG42 machine gun, generally credited as one of World War II's most effective weapons owing to its stunning rate of fire, reliability, and ease of operation. On a larger scale, the German Army also had at its disposal the dreaded 88mm artillery piece known in Germany as the *Acht-acht* (Eight-eight), an anti-aircraft and anti-tank gun designed and manufactured by Krupp. One of the most easily recognized German weapons of the war, this "flak" gun was not only used to support ground troops but was also a key weapon for coastal defense. Relatively lightweight in comparison to other similar artillery guns, the 88 was consequently far easier to site and, once in place, took only two-and-half minutes to set up for firing; it was this enhanced maneuvrability and speed that made it such an effective weapon.

Design for war

← Boeing B-17 Flying Fortress heavy bomber, first flight 1935.

↑ Tiger I heavy tank designed and manufactured by Henschel and Sohn, 1941.

↙ Avro Lancaster heavy bomber designed by Roy Chadwick, first flight 1941.

↓ T-34 tank designed by the Kharkiv Morozov Machine Building Design Bureau, 1940.

Military designs of World War II

←
Messerschmitt Me 109 fighter designed by
Willy Messerschmitt and Robert Lusser,
first flight 1935.

↓
Messerschmitt Me 262 designed by the
pioneering aerodynamicist Ludwig Bölkow,
first jet-powered flight 1942.

The Germans also pioneered self-propelled guided-missile systems with the design of the Fieseler Fi 103 flying bomb, better known as the V-1, which was introduced in 1944. The design of this remote, unmanned projectile—the antecedent of today's cruise missile—was overseen by two highly talented engineers, Robert Lusser of the Fieseler aircraft works and Fritz Gosslau of Argus Motoren. Fired from "ski" launch sites along the French and Dutch coasts, the V-1 was powered by a pulse-jet engine and became known as the "Doodlebug" or "Buzz Bomb" thanks to the distinctive noise it made as it flew overhead, the engine pulsing fifty times per second. Despite its relatively simple construction of welded sheet metal for the fuselage and plywood for the wings, the V-1

was a terrifying and highly efficient weapon. Even more powerful and deadly, however, was the V-2 (officially called the Aggregat-4), which was designed by the engineer Wernher von Braun, the acknowledged father of rocket science. As the world's first successful short-range ballistic missile, the V-2 could carry a warhead weighing a massive 2,200 pounds, marking a paradigm shift in military technology that would play out during the Cold War years.

Two other German designs were far lower-tech but equally important: the pressed-steel jerrycan fuel container and the *Stahlhelm* (steel helmet), both of which reflected an understanding of the Modern Movement's dictum "Form follows function." The former design proved to be almost impossible to

MG42 machine gun manufactured by Mauser, 1942.

MP44 Strumgewher assault rifle designed by Hugo Schmeisser, 1942.

improve upon: its robust construction featured stamped indentations that not only gave it extra strength but also provided a greater surface area, allowing the container's volatile contents to expand and contract safely when placed in hot or cold conditions. The *Stahlhelm* was a very early example of ergonomic design by Dr. Friedrich Schwerd of the Technical Institute of Hanover. His 1915 study of head wounds suffered early in World War I led him to develop a better-fitting helmet, introduced in 1916, that was loosely based on a

close-fitting sallet helmet used in the fifteenth century. Schwerd's helmet was further improved to provide soldiers in World War II with far greater protection than either military caps or the traditional spiked helmets previously used by the German army.

Across the Atlantic, American manufacturers were also producing a remarkable range of state-of-the-art military hardware, which, thanks to large-scale industrialization, could be manufactured on a truly impressive scale. This proved to be a critical factor in

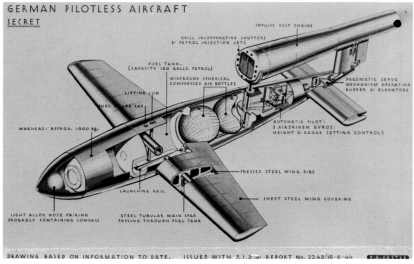

The 88mm "Acht-acht" (Eight-eight) anti-aircraft and anti-tank gun designed and manufactured by Krupp.

→

A cutaway and annotated drawing of the Fieseler Fi 103 flying bomb (better known as the V-1), introduced in 1944.

→

V-2 (officially called the Aggregat-4) designed by Wernher von Braun.

Design for war

the war's outcome. Among the highly advanced American military designs of the war years was Boeing's B-29 Superfortress, the first aircraft to feature a pressurized cabin; it could fly at much higher altitudes than other war planes, making it perfect for daytime bombing missions. Widely used in the Pacific Theater, it was employed to firebomb Japan and to carry the atomic bombs that were fatefully dropped on Hiroshima and Nagasaki in August 1945, leading to the end of World War II. The atomic bomb heralded a new era of nuclear warfare that upped the stakes of destruction so high as to become the ultimate deterrent. The A-bomb was the progeny of the US government's top-secret Manhattan Project, dedicated to the research and development of nuclear warheads, which was famously undertaken in Los Alamos, New Mexico, as well as other secret locations.

Although the A-bomb was the most awe-inducing and destructive weapon in America's imposing arsenal, other essential items of military kit used by US ground troops were also highly innovative, such as the standard issue M1 Garand semiautomatic rifle, described by General George S. Patton as "the greatest battle implement ever devised."[4] Developed by the French-Canadian inventor John Garand at the US Army's Springfield Armory in 1926 and further modified up until its introduction in 1934, the M1 was a simple yet ingenious gun weighing less than 9 lbs and very well balanced, which improved accuracy. It also had a comfortably contoured wooden stock that made it perfect for shoulder firing when either standing or kneeling as well as suitable for extended firing from a prone position. Even after the war, the M1 still saw many years of active duty, notably as a standard service rifle in the Korean War and later as a sniper rifle. One of the main reasons for the M1's great success and longevity was that its simplified design made it comparatively easy to mass-manufacture: the civilian contractor used for its production, the Winchester Repeating Arms Company, made over half a million units during the war, while the Springfield Armory manufactured an incredible 4,000 units a day at the peak of production. In fact, a total of more than four million M1s were made during the conflict, and thanks to a sliding economy of scale, production costs dropped from an initial $200 per rifle in 1936 to a mere $26 in 1945.[5]

Another piece of American military hardware that could be mass-produced efficiently, was easily repaired in the field, and proved to be perfectly adapted to the various difficult conditions it was thrown into was the US Army Jeep. Patriotically described by Army Chief of Staff General George C. Marshall as "America's greatest contribution to modern warfare,"[6] the Jeep was a rugged, lightweight, and fast all-purpose vehicle that took terrain challenges in its stride. The origins of its design go back to 1940, when the US Army issued specifications for an all-terrain reconnaissance vehicle and invited 130 automobile manufacturers to present working prototypes within just forty-nine days. Only three manufacturers responded to this seemingly impossible challenge, and while Batham won the initial pre-production contract by agreeing to deliver a prototype model within the specified period, it was Willys-Overland who subsequently won the next, far more important, order for 16,000 vehicles. The visually distinctive, robust four-wheel drive vehicle he designed, which boasted a powerful Willys L134 "Go Devil" engine, was capable of carrying a 660-pound load, making it ideal for ferrying troops or carrying the wounded. Perhaps its greatest asset was that, thanks to its simple design, it could be easily disassembled for transportation and then quickly reassembled for rapid deployment—making it an essential workhorse of the US Army. As Willys's chief engineer Barney Roos

noted, "It is purely a combat vehicle, designed with simplicity, to do a specific job. It makes no concessions to art, and damn little to comfort."[7]

↑
M1 Garand semiautomatic rifle designed by
John Garand at the Springfield Armory, 1926,
patented 1934, and further modified up to its
introduction in 1936.

↑
Willys-Overland Jeep, 1940.

Design on the British home front and Organic Design in home furnishings

During the war all design and manufacturing activity in Britain was by necessity focused on the war effort and the production of military materiel. Because raw materials were in such short supply, the government also had to introduce strict rationing, and it introduced utility schemes for the design of clothing and furniture in 1941 and 1942, respectively. It was not until 1951, well after the cessation of hostilities, that the Utility Furniture Scheme was completely lifted. The Board of Trade's utility specifications outlined the quality and amount of materials permitted and gave a range of statutory designs that had been thoughtfully conceived by an advisory committee, one of whose members was the furniture designer Gordon Russell. These standardized "home front" furniture pieces, intended to make a little go a long way, were guided by an Arts and Crafts sensibility yet also by a Modernist ethos. Solid and highly serviceable, these pieces had basic constructions that used simple manufacturing techniques, which enabled them to be produced throughout the country by more than two hundred different manufacturers. Embodying the worthy

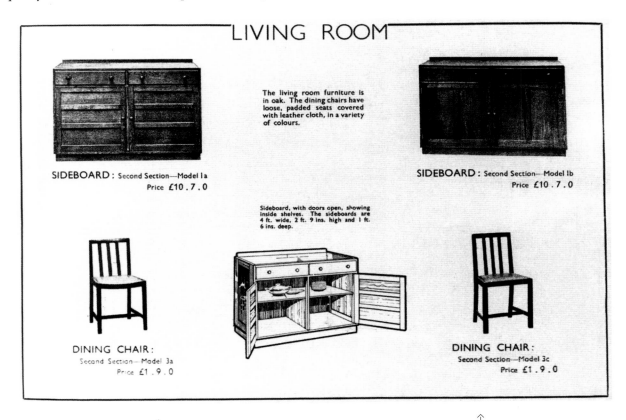

LIVING ROOM

The living room furniture is in oak. The dining chairs have loose, padded seats covered with leather cloth, in a variety of colours.

SIDEBOARD : Second Section—Model 1a
Price £10.7.0

SIDEBOARD : Second Section—Model 1b
Price £10.7.0

Sideboard, with doors open, showing inside shelves. The sideboards are 4 ft. wide, 2 ft. 9 ins. high and 1 ft. 6 ins. deep.

DINING CHAIR :
Second Section—Model 3a
Price £1.9.0

DINING CHAIR :
Second Section—Model 3c
Price £1.9.0

←
BA chair designed by Ernest Race for Race Furniture, 1945, made of resmelted aircraft scrap.

↑
Catalogue page showing living room furniture made under the Board of Trade's Utility Furniture Scheme.

principles of Good Design, the Utility Furniture Scheme was highly prescriptive and reflected the wartime socialism of the day. Although the pieces were well made and of high quality, considering the material restrictions imposed on them, they were seen by the general public as rather too utilitarian—adequate given the needs of the time but not particularly loveable. In 1943 a design panel headed by Russell was set up with a view to extending the Utility Scheme into the postwar period; this resulted in three new ranges being launched in 1946. After the war, rationing restrictions slowly loosened and previously unobtainable materials became increasingly available. The general public, sick of imposed restrictions on what it could and couldn't have, demanded greater consumer choice, and on the whole opted for more stylish designs such as Ernest Race's BA chair (1945) made of resmelted aircraft scrap.

In contrast to utilitarian Britain, during the early 1940s a more consumerist approach continued to manifest itself in American design, though tastes had changed since the prewar period. Rather than using sweeping streamlined forms that had futuristic connotations, designers influenced by new tendencies in contemporary fine art began to explore free-form biomorphic shapes that were intended to express the abstract essence of nature. The pioneering organic designs of the Finnish architect Alvar Aalto—whose work had been exhibited at New York's Museum of Modern Art (MoMA) in 1938, and who had also, as we have seen, designed the Finnish Pavilion at the 1939-40 New York World's Fair—profoundly influenced the new generation of young American designers. Aalto's holistic, human-centered approach offered an enticing alternative to the hard-edged modernism that was synonymous with the Bauhaus, and also to the superfluous styling that became the trademark of the previous generation of American industrial-design consultants. This new direction was revealed in several of the entries submitted for MoMA's international Organic Design in Home Furnishings competition, held in 1940. The winning entry was a proposal for a group of ergonomically refined furniture designs by Charles Eames and Eero Saarinen; it included sculptural armchairs that used state-of-the-art technology to construct single-form, compound-molded, plywood seat shells announcing a new direction in furniture design. Sadly, the intended mass production of the furniture group was not realized, because America's entry into World War II in December 1941 following Japan's bombing of Pearl Harbor brought about wartime restrictions on materials.

↑
Finnish Pavilion at the 1939-40 New York
World's Fair, designed by Alvar Aalto.

↗
View of Charles Eames and Eero Saarinen's entries
for MoMA's international Organic Design in Home
Furnishings competition, held in 1940.

→
High-backed molded-plywood armchair designed by
Charles Eames and Eero Saarinen for MoMA's Organic
Design in Home Furnishings competition, 1940.

→
Cover of the catalogue for the Organic Design in
Home Furnishings competition, 1940.

museum of modern art new york

ORGANIC DESIGN

Design on the British home front and Organic Design in home furnishings

The American war effort

Having been reluctant to enter the conflict, the United States eventually did so with steely determination. Many factories were turned over to full-scale military production, meaning that there were fewer consumer goods available. On the American home front, most citizens readily accepted the inconvenience of wartime restrictions in the knowledge that they would hasten the return home of troops. A system of rationing was implemented that used books of coupons, similar to those used in Europe, which were needed to purchase numerous items and commodities such as tires, cars, shoes, nylon, sugar, petrol, heating fuel, coffee, meat, and processed foods. The Office of Price Administration (OPA) also regulated rents and administered price controls in order to stabilize food prices. Despite such short-term privations, the war actually helped to create huge opportunities for long-term economic growth in the United States, while also assisting the expansion of American political might and industrial-design authority.

Throughout World War II, increasing attention was given to the development of new technology. As part of the deadly arms race being played out among the countries actively engaged in the conflict, the US government established various top-secret research facilities that were to play a decisive role in the war's outcome, including the previously mentioned Los Alamos Scientific Laboratory near Santa Fe, New Mexico, where the first atomic bomb was built. Apart from these highly classified programs, the war effort also had a massive impact on the evolution of the less high-tech aspects of American design, as government dollars flowed into the hands of manufacturers to spend on time-consuming and costly research and development. After two decades of styling-driven products, there was now a huge swing back to functional design basics in order to create tools that performed better at war. Automobile companies, arms producers, aircraft fabricators, and many civilian manufacturers were all now engaged in the production of military equipment—from Jeeps and tanks to gunsights and radio antennas. Federal government cash accelerated the development of numerous state-of-the-art materials, including various types of plastics and exotic metal alloys, which dramatically expanded the functional and aesthetic boundaries of design. Many new production technologies were also advanced, which led to copious novel applications for existing materials. For instance, Charles and Ray Eames would later use the high-frequency electronic bonding techniques that had been developed for aircraft manufacture to adhere connecting rubber shock mounts to their chairs' plywood seats and backs, and to their steel or laminated wood supporting frames.

The war effort also heralded an unprecedented construction program that included cutting-edge defense plants and factories as well as many large communities of new, modern-style homes for factory workers to live in; these were prefabricated from lightweight materials using innovative production technologies. In fact, this large-scale housing-construction program fundamentally reoriented the lives of many Americans by introducing them to modern modes of living. Wartime also brought about a marked increase in the technical training of women, who were to play a vital role in running manufacturing plants while their husbands and brothers were off fighting in Europe or the Pacific. "Rosie the Riveter," who was immortalized by Westinghouse Electric's famous poster, became a national cultural icon whose

←
Photograph by Alfred Palmer of a worker at the Douglas Aircraft Company plant in Long Beach, California constructing a Plexiglas bombardier nose for a B-17F "Flying Fortress," 1942.

slogan, "We Can Do It!," encapsulated the hands-on determination of wartime America. The practical, manual training of women was crucial in creating a greater sense of gender equality, and it is not surprising that during the immediate postwar years a greater number of American women entered the design profession on more equal terms. Many men and women at the forefront of American architecture and design also received valuable hands-on experience by developing products for military use during these years of global conflict. Charles and Ray Eames, for example, designed innovative molded-plywood leg-splints and stretchers for the US Navy, and R. Buckminster Fuller's galvanized steel Dymaxion Deployment Units (1940) were used as emergency accommodation for troops. Such forays into military design were hugely informative, allowing many designers both to experiment with new materials and technologies and to gain real experience and the ability to respond to exacting design briefs using a purposeful approach to problem solving.

←
"We Can Do It!" wartime propaganda poster designed by J. Howard Miller for Westinghouse Electric, 1943, featuring "Rosie the Riveter," who became a national cultural icon.

↗
Galvanized steel Dymaxion Deployment Units designed by R. Buckminster Fuller, 1940.

→
Molded-plywood leg-splint designed by Charles and Ray Eames for the US Navy, 1942.

Homemaking and the designed American Dream

One cannot overestimate the impact that the materials and technologies developed during wartime were to have on postwar design, especially in the United States. Unlike Europe, America emerged from the war stronger and more confident that ever, having reinvigorated its enormous industrial might and shaken off any vestiges of the Great Depression. The factories that had churned out aircraft, tanks, munitions, and other war materiel in truly impressive volumes were now ready to gear up for the mass production of consumer goods on an unprecedented scale. At the same time, peacetime inspired a strong "nesting" instinct in the general populace—unsurprising given the physical disconnections and emotional uncertainties that people had endured during the war years. Once hostilities ceased and peace reigned, the American Dream was transformed into a familial vision of suburban homemaking: a mainly white, middle-class utopia of stay-at-home moms; smiling dads with secure white-collar jobs in large, benevolent corporations, and well-behaved, healthy kids—all living happily together in modern, spacious homes with contemporary furnishings, the latest appliances, and, of course, a large station wagon parked out front. Although this image of carefree affluence remained a dream for many Americans, it reflected a widespread yearning for a lifestyle that involved unparalleled levels of consumption; one championed by a highly sophisticated advertising industry that linked aspiration to a perpetual desire for new and seemingly improved goods.

←
Previous page: Photograph by Julius Shulman of Case Study House No. 20 designed by Buff, Straub, and Hensman, 1958.

←
Westinghouse publicity photograph for a Laundromat washing machine, late 1950s/early 1960s.

↗
LCW chair designed by Charles and Ray Eames for Herman Miller, 1945—this red-analine-dyed option was part of the Eameses' compound-molded plywood chair series designed in 1945–46.

→
DAR armchair designed by Charles and Ray Eames, 1948–50, part of their groundbreaking Plastic Shell Series chairs.

One of the first American designs to make waves on the postwar international design scene was Charles and Ray Eames's landmark series of compound-molded-plywood chairs, designed in 1945 and 1946, which pioneered the adapting of that material into seductive ergonomic form and was directly informed by the Eameses' development of plywood leg splints and stretchers for the US military during the war. Dirk Jan De Pree, legendary chairman of Herman Miller— the Zeeland, Michigan-based firm that manufactured the line of molded-plywood chairs—described this range as, "Beautiful, comfortable, easy to move. It's unimprovable. It's a national treasure that ought to be made available."[1] But at least initially, the postwar market for home goods was flooded with high-priced, poor-quality items—the very antithesis of the Eameses' chairs.

In fact, when the American public was faced with a glut of shoddy, marketing-driven goods, the role of design became a topic of wide and earnest debate, and organizations such as the Museum of Modern Art (MoMA) in New York sought to promote better-designed products. To this end, in 1948 Edgar Kaufmann, Jr., the museum's Director of Industrial Design, published a damning yet highly influential article, "Borax, or the Chromium-Plated Calf," in the *Architectural Review*, condemning the superfluous, ornamental nature of streamlining, especially when it was used on fundamentally static objects.[2] He also decried the prevalence of marketing-driven design and argued for a return to the true functional principles of modernism. "Borax" was a derogatory term thought to derive from the showy product promotions of the Borax soap company; it was used to deride the then-popular aesthetic of flashy modernistic designs, which according to Kaufmann had been "elevated on the altar of sales, [with] statistical magnificats [. . .] sung in its honor."[3] He went on to note that "star" designers were increasingly using personal publicity to promote their work to the general public, but that their appeal to corporations was actually based on far firmer foundations. These designers, he wrote,

. . . have evolved ways of relating design directly to sales, not only after the event, but by plausible preliminaries that have all the earmarks of a sound dollar investment. They refuse to make or sell fanciful sketches showing how they think the client's

product ought to look, designing only after careful investigations. They study the sales records and financial statements of the company; they compare its product with competitive ones for quality, price and style; they examine the retail distributor through whom the product reaches the public and learning his servicing problems; they make it a point to gain the friendly cooperation of company designers, engineers and sales staff, and for this reason it is rarely announced that a particular product is designed by a particular industrial design office. Further, these designers limit themselves to contracts whose least duration is one year, and they work with only one manufacturer at a time in a particular field [. . .] In building this relationship to their clientele, the big design offices have had to put "results," that is sales, first. Their gloss on the text "form follows function" is "style follows sales."[4]

In 1948, the same year his scathing "Borax" article appeared, Kaufmann organized MoMA's landmark International Competition for the Design of Low-Cost Furniture, which sought to counter the approach of America's industrial-design celebrities. The event was also intended to stimulate a global return to the tenets of the Modern Movement, and was part of a wider reform program known as "Good Design." The competition, according to a press release distributed by MoMA, was "the first time an entire industry—manufacturers, retailers, and designers—have banded together on a nationwide scale in a single project to produce well-made furniture within the average man's income."[5] The response to this competition—which awarded winners in the various categories prizes and research grants totaling the princely sum of $50,000—was extraordinary: nearly 3,000 entries were received from more than thirty countries, many from the United States. A further incentive of the competition was that the manufacturers associated with the event would put the prize-winning designs into production and retail them in some two hundred stores across the country, giving the designers a royalty income on all sales generated. The winners were announced in early 1949. The storage category was won by the British design duo of Robin Day and Clive Latimer, whose sleek "new look" modular units were highly adaptable, reflecting the postwar need for multifunctional, space-saving furniture.

It was in the competition's seating category, though, that the most interesting and unusual entries were submitted—including some that bordered on the positively bizarre. Although the first prize for this section was awarded jointly to the Berlin-based designer Georg Leowald and Don Knorr of San Francisco, the real star of the competition was actually a group of Eames chairs that shared second prize. Developed in conjunction with a team of engineers and specialists from Herman Miller, from Zenith Plastics of Gardena, California, and from the engineering department of the University of California, Los Angeles, the Eameses' seating included an armchair and a side chair, both of which employed single-form seat shells made of molded, glass-reinforced plastic (fiberglass). But it was not only the choice of this state-of-the-art material that made these chairs groundbreaking, nor simply the use of pioneering technology; it was also the fact that they were based on the concept of a universal seat shell that could be used in conjunction with a wide range of interchangeable bases to provide numerous variations. One of the very first completely integrated seating systems, the Shell group was also the first to be mass-produced in unlined plastic. Indeed, they were among the first such plastic consumer items to be mass-produced.

↑
Edgar Kaufmann, Jr., standing amid the prize-winning designs of the International Competition for the Design of Low-Cost Furniture (*Life* magazine, May 8, 1950).

Good Design

As a highly respected arbiter of taste, Edgar Kaufmann, Jr., also found other ways, through his activities at MoMA, to promote the idea that "Good Design" was based on recognized aesthetic, technical, and functional precepts generally associated with the European Modern Movement. He tirelessly argued that this approach was the best way forward in the creation of safer and more democratic products. MoMA had organized various traveling Useful Objects exhibitions since 1938 that featured exemplars of affordable American home-furnishings design. But it was not until 1950, thanks to Kaufmann's efforts and the sponsorship of The Merchandise Mart in Chicago, that the first of five annual shows entitled *Good Design: An Exhibition of Home Furnishings* was held. This presentation, designed by Charles and Ray Eames, included a selection of 256 pieces deemed to fit the criteria of Good Design by jurors from the national home-furnishings wholesale markets held in Chicago. This first show included items by Edward Wormley, Ray Komai, Eero Saarinen, Don Knorr, the Eameses, George Nelson, Pipsan Saarinen Swanson, Paul McCobb, Bernard Rudofsky, Benjamin Baldwin, William Machado, Paul Rand, Dorothy Liebes, Marianne Strengell, and Anni Albers—the very cream of America's enviable crop of midcentury modernist designers. The selected products were later sold in shops across the country, adorned with labels bearing the distinctive Good Design logo created by the Chicago-based designer Mort Goldsholl in 1950.[6] These items, like others selected for later Good Design exhibitions, were characterized by pure forms, practical function, appropriate use of materials, restrained use of color, high-quality construction, and good value for money. Over time such designs came to be synonymous with good taste, and many were acclaimed internationally for their aesthetic excellence and functional integrity. At long last, American design had joined the avant-garde, thanks largely to an organic approach to modernism pioneered by designers such as the Eameses, Eero Saarinen, George Nelson, and Isamu Noguchi. This type of contemporary design was now a crucial element of a new and authentically American cultural movement that also included experimental jazz, beat poetry, and Abstract expressionist art. These designers' work was not only distinctively homegrown but also well-suited, both functionally and aesthetically, to the more casual lifestyles of the postwar period.

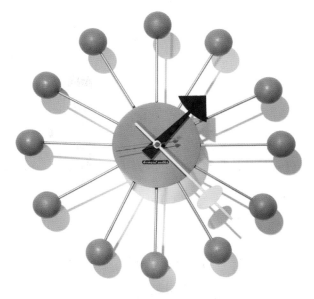

↑
Ball Wall Clock (Model No. 4755) designed by George Nelson Associates for the Howard Miller Clock Company, 1949.

↑
Good Design logo created by Mort Goldsholl, 1950.

←
Good Design display of Charles and Ray Eames's DKX-2 chair with "bikini" upholstery, Sol Bloom's Scoop chair, and George Nelson's Bubble lamp, early 1950s.

'Another champion of Good Design was *Arts & Architecture* magazine. Under editor John Entenza it spearheaded the famous Case Study Houses project, which ran intermittently from 1945 until 1966. The purpose of this ambitious initiative was to challenge the architectural community to come up with postwar housing solutions that, both in their construction and in their furnishings, used the new materials and manufacturing techniques that had resulted from wartime research and development. With the magazine acting as sponsor, each home would be built for either a real or a hypothetical client and would take into account their specific housing requirements. The project eventually produced designs for thirty model homes, and although just under a third of them remained unbuilt, they all appeared in the pages of the magazine. The most famous was Case Study House No. 8 (1949)—now better known as the Eames House—in Pacific Palisades, the self-designed home of Charles and Ray Eames. The brief for this specific house was for a married couple working within the design field whose children had left home. Featuring a revolutionary prefabricated construction, this home was essentially a kit house made of modular elements, with transparent glass and solid colored panels placed in a De Stijl-like grid arrangement

↑
Case Study House No. 8, designed by Charles and Ray Eames, 1949—better known as the Eames House—in Pacific Palisades, California.

→
Photograph by Arnold Newman of Charles and Ray Eames at home, showing the interior of their Case Study House No. 8.

on a supporting steel frame of vertical struts and horizontal beams. The building also reflected the influence of Japanese architecture in its use of screens and its harmonious relationship with the garden that surrounded it and also its wider environment. Filled with the Eameses' idiosyncratic collections of toys from around the world and colorful kites, as well as furniture they had designed for Herman Miller, the homey yet stylish light-filled Eames House was the apotheosis of midcentury American modern living.

The two furniture companies that were in the vanguard of American design during this period, and have remained there ever since, were Herman Miller and Knoll Associates: the former boasted the Eameses, Nelson, and Noguchi in its stable of designers, and its output is perhaps best described as stylishly sculptural. The designs manufactured by Herman Miller were governed by its founder, Dirk Jan De Pree, whose criteria for Good Design were: durability, unity, integrity, inevitability, and beauty.[7] Sharing many of the same values, Knoll also produced avant-garde designs along modernist lines. This New York-based company counted among its designers many of America's leading creative lights, notably Eero Saarinen, Harry Bertoia, Jens Risom, and Florence Knoll, the wife of founder Hans Knoll. The firm was associated with a more stylishly "arty" aesthetic than Herman Miller. Knoll's interpretation of the International Style came to epitomize the look of corporate America in the 1950s. Both companies also used eye-catching graphic design to create distinctly contemporary corporate identities for themselves. Irving Harper, who was then a member of the design team at George Nelson Associates, developed the classic red "M" Herman Miller logo. During the late 1940s and 1950s, Irving also created most of the furniture company's trade advertisements, which conveyed an up-to-date, casual look. The Swiss-born graphic designer Herbert Matter, who had gained widespread renown for his Swiss National Tourist Board posters in the mid 1930s, also contributed to the early Herman Miller look, after first working with Charles and Ray Eames. In 1946 Knoll Associates appointed Matter as its art director, and for the next two decades he pioneered the use of photo-collage graphics to create bold, dynamic artwork for the company, often infused with a sense of surprise or subtle humor. The graphic designer Paul Rand also came to prominence by creating a distinctive new logo for IBM (International Business Machines) in 1956. That same year, the company had hired Eliot Noyes—an architect and former curator of the Industrial Design department at MoMA—as its design consultant, and at his instigation a comprehensive corporate-design program was introduced, under which Rand's logo was produced and all aspects of the company's look—from core products to marketing materials—were overhauled. As Noyes, who called

↓
IN-50 coffee table designed by Isamu Noguchi for Herman Miller, 1944 (introduced 1948), an early example of the artist's sculptural tables.

↘
Coconut lounge chair designed by George Nelson for

↗
Knoll showroom at 575 Madison Avenue, 1951, photographed by Robert Damora.

→
The Pedestal Collection designed by Eero Saarinen for Knoll, 1957.

The American Dream and Good Design

↑
Cover of *Arts & Architecture* magazine designed by
Herbert Matter, 1946, incorporating an image of leg
elements from the Eameses' LCW chair.

↑
Logo for IBM devised by Paul Rand, 1956.

↑
Selectric electric typewriter, designed by Eliot Noyes for
IBM, 1961, which incorporated a "typeball."

himself a "curator of corporate character," noted, "In a sense, a corporation should be like a good painting; everything visible should contribute to the correct total statement; nothing visible should detract."[8]

Another American corporation that was very concerned with its image, and in particular with associating its brand with innovative design, was General Motors. In 1958 the company produced a short documentar, *American Look*, which was intended as a tribute to "the stylists of America who work in lines, forms and textures and colors to give us beauty, charm and elegance in the conveniences, comforts and necessities of our daily living."[9] This populuxe film functioned as a kind of soft-sell infomercial showcasing beautiful everyday goods created by a roster of leading American designers; all of these had a distinctive sculptural quality, whether it was the Diamond Chair by Harry Bertoia, the Womb Chair by Eero Saarinen, an electric toaster from General Electric, or a vacuum cleaner from Hoover. While a dream modern kitchen was featured, the voiceover announced, "By the way things look as well as the way they perform, our homes acquire new grace, new glamour, new accommodations, expressing not only the American love of beauty, but also the basic freedom of the American people, which is the freedom of individual choice"; this really meant the freedom to consume.

It was not just the American home that received the designer treatment: all kinds of consumer goods were now sold in bright, colorful, expertly designed packaging. The 1950s was the decade of the brand, and while Madison Avenue advertising executives taught companies how to sell not only products but also to trust in their names, design consultancies such as Raymond Loewy and Associates and Landor Associates became specialists in creating attention-getting packaging and comprehensive corporate identities, from logos to store design. The American white-collar workplace also got a serious makeover, and offices increasingly were open-plan, filled with light and modern-style furnishings that conveyed a sense of casual sophistication. Indeed, a company's offices often said as much about its goals and aspirations as did its logo: while these new workspaces provided a more pleasant and efficient environment for employees, they also had the added benefit of being a positive projection of a firm's corporate identity—and large blue-chip corporations in particular were very well aware of this fact.

In the United States, the 1950s were a period of mounting abundance, driven by the new culture of designed consumption. The prosperity of rapidly expanding metropolitan areas overshadowed the poverty that was still found not only in citites but also in many rural communities, especially among immigrant and ethnic populations. Designers and manufacturers appealed to customers' growing expectations by producing ever-more forward-looking designs to embody the American Dream: objects of desire that were the antithesis of the "make-do-and-mend" ethos of the depressed 1930s and the war-constrained 1940s. During this decade of dream cars, dream kitchens, and dream homes, the mass media—from billboard advertising and magazines to radio and especially television—helped to foster a national culture in which consumption was viewed as a pleasurable social act as well as an economic necessity. It was the era in which what we today call popular culture was born: here for the first time were television ads with catchy jingles, convenience TV dinners, fast-food restaurants, cars with tail fins, youth fashions, and rock'n'roll music. The success of all these phenomena can be seen as the result of a desire of the burgeoning middle classes to exercise their freedom of choice in consumerist terms rather than in political or social ones—a desire to gain empowerment and identity through their purchases. As the Pulitzer Prize-winning journalist David Halberstam explained:

> In that era of general goodwill and expanding affluence, few Americans doubted the essential goodness of their society. After all, it was reflected back at them not only by contemporary books and magazines, but even more powerfully and with even greater influence in the new family sitcoms on television. These—in conjunction with their sponsors' commercial goals—sought to shape their audience's aspirations. However, most Americans needed little coaching in how they wanted to live. They were optimistic about the future.[10]

Unsurprisingly, the postwar optimism and prosperity translated into a rush to have children, as many young people's lives had been put on hold during the war. Their children, the so-called baby-boomers were brought up as perfect mini-consumers in a society of plenty in which nearly ever product in their daily lives—from the sugar-encrusted cereal they ate in the morning to the toys they played with in the afternoon—had been designed by corporations. During the 1950s, competition in the consumer-goods market and the sheer scale of production focused attention on design: in order to succeed, products had to be impeccably conceived. Increasingly, large corporations had in-house design departments that were specialized to their needs, rather than employing more generalized industrial-design consultants. This had the effect of making American design increasingly corporate—a trait that remains to this day.

↑
General Motors' Motorama automobile show at the Waldorf-Astoria in New York, 1950, with "A Pillar of Progress" displaying advances made within the automobile world, surrounded by the latest GM models.

American culture was now heavily driven by mass consumption. People's identities were increasingly linked to what they bought, and nowhere was this truer than in the realm of car ownership. One of the greatest symbols of America's new culture and its industrial ascendancy was General Motors (GM), which during the 1950s became the first corporation ever to gross a billion dollars a year. Throughout that decade, under the design leadership of Harley Earl, the company subjected its cars to more and more fanciful yearly restyling, the results of which were debuted with great fanfare at its annual Motorama shows, staged between 1949 and 1961. Also displayed at these extravaganzas were revolutionary concept cars, such as the Firebird XP-21 (1954). Unashamedly futuristic, these vehicles were intended to whet the general public's appetite for ever greater novelty while boosting sales of GM's current models by association. This marketing-driven venture into excessive styling reached its zenith with the unveiling of the 1959 Cadillac, its extraordinary tail fins terminating in red rocket-shaped lights. Here was the ultimate car on which to speed down the American highway into a futuristic present, for the foundation of the National Aeronautics and Space Administration (NASA) the previous year had heralded the advent of the great American Space Age. The 1959 "Caddie" and other seminal automobile designs of the decade, such as the 1951 Hudson Hornet Club Coupe, the 1953

Chevrolet Corvette, the 1955 Ford Thunderbird, the 1957 Chevrolet Bel Air Coupe, the 1957 Ford Fairlane Skyliner, and the 1959 Buick Electra 225 Convertible, were daring embodiments of this gleaming new futuristic Space Age style. They symbolized the somewhat naively optimistic view that the American life of full employment, plentiful leisure time, and widespread prosperity was here to stay. Yet already by the mid-to-late 1950s, America's policy-makers were taking steps toward greater involvement in the Vietnam War—a conflict that would come to haunt the country in the following decade and that would ultimately lead to a widespread questioning of the status quo, including the suburban idyll of the American Dream. This fundamental challenge to convention would change the very goals, and so the course of modern design.

↑
General Motors's publicity photograph of the
1959 Cadillac Coupe de Ville.

←
Detail of 1959 Cadillac tail fin.

Anthropometrics
and Organic Design

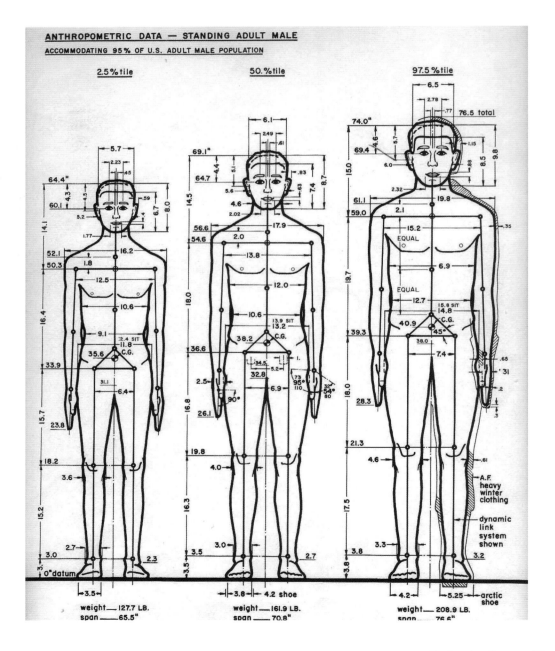

During the postwar years, another aspect of American design evolved out of wartime research into "human factors": called anthropometric design, it would become increasingly important within professional circles. The pioneer in the field was the industrial designer Henry Dreyfuss, who in 1955 published a highly influential book on the subject, *Designing for People*. In it, he introduced "Joe and Josephine," two diagrammatic characters based on the concept of the "average Joe." They were the result of years of painstaking research undertaken by Dreyfuss's office, in which he and his staff analyzed median human measurements between physical points, such as the distance between wrist and elbow, or knee and ankle. As Dreyfuss explained:

> Merely assembling average measurements from anatomical drawings would not have been difficult. However, the concern of the industrial designer is with the mass public, and it was necessary to determine the extreme dimensions, for we must consider the variations from small to large. After all, people come in assorted rather than average sizes.[11]

This new, more ergonomic approach broke ground and would subsequently inform the development of all kinds of products, from large hand-operated machinery and John Deere tractors to Bell telephones and office chairs. By using these Mr and Mrs More-or-Less Average

two-dimensional models, industrial designers now had at their disposal an improved methodology by which to solve problems, the results of which could for the first time be empirically justified. This more scientific method based on "human factors" introduced greater universalism in manufactured products, and as a result began to erode national tendencies within the practice of modern design.

Although the term "International Style" had been coined in 1932 by the architect Philip Johnson and the architectural historian Henry-Russell Hitchcock, it was really only after World War II that modern design was embraced on a global scale. Postwar modernism, however, was markedly different from prewar modernism, not only because of the different materials and technologies it exploited but also because the rigid geometric formalism of the Bauhaus and Le Corbusier was replaced by a more emotionally engaging language of organic form. This freer interpretation of modernism, which became known as Organic Design, was less ideologically driven and more aligned to movements within contemporary fine art. It was informed by ergonomics and influenced by the gentler Scandinavian approach to modernism, as typified by Alvar Aalto's pioneering work in the 1930s, and offered a more holistic understanding of what constituted Good Design. Fundamentally, Organic Design was about fostering better functional, intellectual, and emotional connections between object and user through a more mindful, human-centric approach to problem solving.

←
Anthropometric diagrams from Henry Dreyfuss's *Designing for People*, 1955.

→
La Chaise lounger designed by Charles and Ray Eames for the Museum of Modern Art's International Competition for the Design of Low-Cost Furniture, 1948–49 (reissued by Vitra from 1990).

As Eliot Noyes had outlined in the catalogue that accompanied MoMA's 1941 Organic Design in Home Furnishings competition, this new approach was about "a harmonious organization of the parts within the whole, according to structure, material and purpose. With this definition there can be no vain ornamentation or superfluity, but the part of beauty is none the less great—in ideal choice of materials, in visual refinement, and in the rational elegance of things intended for use."[12]

↑→
TWA Terminal at Kennedy Airport, New York,
designed by Eero Saarinen, built 1956–62,
detail of exterior and view of interior.

The practical application of Organic Design was not confined to products: it also found architectural expression, most notably in Eero Saarinen's TWA (Trans World Airlines) Terminal (1956–62) at New York's Idlewild Airport (now John F. Kennedy Airport), whose free-flowing curves suggested flight. The success of Organic Design, meanwhile, prompted the rise of biomorphism, which, rather than attempting to capture the abstracted essence of natural forms, distorted them for purely decorative purposes. This resulted in some of the designs most closely associated with the kitsch look of the 1950s, for example asymmetrical kidney shapes. Yet despite this unintended consequence, the organic approach brought a new clarity to the function and goals of design. The postwar years consequently saw a remarkable new flowering of modern design in Europe, America, and Japan.

The reconstruction of Italy
and the flowering of Italian design

↑
Vespa 150 scooter designed by
Corradino D'Ascanio for Piaggio, 1955.

During the war years the development of any non-military design was put on hold in Europe. This was especially true in Italy, which saw many of its factories destroyed by Allied bombing; its main industrial cities, Milan and Turin, were repeatedly targeted. After Italian partisans executed Benito Mussolini in April 1945, Italy was freed from the Fascist grip that had dominated its social, political, and cultural life for more than twenty years. At the same time Allied forces closed in on Milan, making it the first of the major Axis-controlled centers to fall. After five long years of war, Italy was a country on its knees: it had lost almost half a million civilians and soldiers as well as much of its vital infrastructure.

Italy emerged from World War II both physically exhausted and spiritually demoralized, and the situation on the ground was pretty dire, with more than three million homes destroyed and essential commodities and raw materials either in short supply or nonexistent. At this stage Italy's economy was still primarily rural, but a number of enlightened manufacturers, such as Fiat, Olivetti, and Pirelli, recognized that if the country was to recover from the war, a comprehensive program of industrial rationalization would have to be implemented. These manufacturers likewise realized it was vital to produce goods for export, and so bring in much-needed foreign revenue to help fund the reconstruction of the nation.

Over the next five years, Italy emerged from poverty and soared into postwar prosperity thanks to a number of initiatives adopted by the anti-Fascist coalition government formed in 1946. The new policymakers made it easy for private companies to trade overseas, and simultaneously introduced measures to protect the home market's interests. The state also boosted Italian industry by offering it cheap credit and inexpensive energy and steel. In addition, the Istituto per la Ricostruzione Industriale (Institute for Industrial Reconstruction) was tasked with regulating Italy's publicly owned industries, from airlines and telephone networks to car manufacturers and machine-tool companies. But perhaps the single most important contributing factor to *La Ricostruzione* (The Reconstruction) was the government's "low wages" policy, which kept pay low, enabling Italian industries to manufacture competitively priced export goods that could be exchanged for much-needed foreign income.

American aid in the form of the Marshall Plan, officially known as the European Recovery Program, also helped Italy's reconstruction considerably, bringing in around $1.2 billion in grants and loans. Italy also

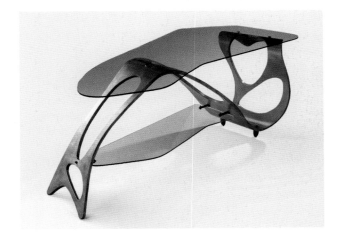

↗
Arabesque table designed by Carlo Mollino and executed by Apelli and Varesio, 1949.

→
Lady armchairs designed by Marco Zanuso for Arflex, 1951.

received $2.2 billion in fuel and food aid from America. This injection of financial goodwill, together with a growing middle class eager to buy consumer products after the deprivations of the war years, proved to be the perfect tonic for economic recovery. Luckily, Italy also had a surfeit of highly trained architects, industrial designers, and engineers, who were able to design stylish, innovative goods not only for the new homeowners in Italy but also for America's postwar homemaking generation.

Initially, designers and architects focused on styling rather than on technological innovation, primarily because they did not have sufficiently advanced technology at their disposal and were therefore forced to use their imaginations, making do with the materials and low-tech production methods that were available. Through this reliance on styling was born the "Italian Line," which, like American streamlining, was used to enhance products' visual appeal. The Italian Line often compensated for technical deficiencies with visual charm, and helped give a product an emotionally compelling edge over competing ones. This focus enabled manufacturers to create goods that were desired around the world, and as such was a key driver of *il miracolo economico* that transformed Italy into a major exporter and industrial power.

One of the primary factors in Italy's design-led recovery was that it still had a large number of highly specialized workshops, for example the Turin joinery shop of Apelli and Varesio, which executed many of Carlo Mollino's furniture pieces. During the years immediately after the war, the small-scale, high-

quality production offered by these largely family-run businesses helped minimize manufacturing risk and enabled the production of aesthetically progressive designs. The inherent flexibility of small-scale production proved to be Italy's greatest asset, for it allowed manufacturers to adapt their product lines quickly in response to the latest fashions.

At the same time in Italy there was a continuing struggle of styles between the neo-rationalist and the anti-rationalist camps. Franco Albini championed the left-wing, utilitarian cause of the former through his writings for *Casabella*, while Gio Ponti, as editor of *Domus*, promoted the right-wing design agenda of the latter, which sought to imbue products with a greater sense of artistry. After the left-wing Popular Front lost its place in the coalition government and the more centrist Christian Democrats gained political control, winning a majority in the general election held in 1946, there was a shift both politically and within design, with designers now increasingly in accord with Ponti's call for quality over quantity. One designer who agreed with Ponti's stance was his good friend Carlo Mollino, who created flamboyant furniture and lighting that reflected his belief that "everything is permissible as long as it is fantastic."[1]

Many other designers followed Gio Ponti's "gentle manifesto," especially as his less utilitarian approach made sense commercially in a society where middle-class consumers preferred a stylish, sculptural look to bland rationalism. This focus on creative artistry meant that Italian design, which encompassed everything "from the spoon to the city"—as the architect Ernesto

Rogers memorably noted—became widely associated with a very particular, stylish, and sophisticated visual identity. During the early 1950s, a host of Italian products exemplified this contemporary, fashionable look, among them Marcello Nizzoli's Lettera 22 typewriter (1950), Marco Zanuso's Lady armchair for Arflex (1951), Corradino D'Ascanio's Vespa 125 motor scooter (1951), and Osvaldo Borsani's P40 lounge chair (1954). Many of these products were characterized by the use of sensuous curves and undulating forms, marking a new sculptural confidence in Italian design that reflected the influence of American streamlined "body-shell" shapes. Arguably, though, it was the sculptural bodywork of the Ferrari 250 TR racing car (1957), created by Sergio Scaglietti in Maranello, that marked the high point of 1950s Italian styling.

The influence of the United States was not only felt in the streamlined style and aid money. During this period, Italian industry crucially benefited from American industrial know-how, which saw the implementation of Fordist assembly-line mass-production methods. The American film industry also did much to publicize Italian postwar design during the 1950s; in the mind of the American moviegoer it became the style of sophistication—with *Roman Holiday* (1953), *Three Coins in the Fountain* (1955), and a host of other films capturing the apparently *dolce vita* lifestyle

of postwar Italy. The launch of the Compasso d'Oro ("Golden Compass") awards by the La Rinascente department store in 1954, at the instigation of Gio Ponti, likewise added momentum to the development of Italian design, by publicly rewarding manufacturers for innovative designs while at the same time promoting the award-winning products through a related annual exhibition. Among the recipients of Compasso d'Oro awards during the 1950s were the Fiat 500 Nuova by Dante Giacosa, the Cifra 3 alarm clock by Gino Valle, the Luminator floor lamp by Achille and Pier Giacomo Castiglioni, the Zerowatt table fan by Ezio Pirali, and Bruno Munari's Zizi toy monkey—all innovative products with forward-looking aesthetics. By the mid 1950s there was optimism and confidence. Having put Marshall Plan dollars to good use, the country was reaping the benefits of free-market capitalism, and its industry had begun to use design as a tool for economic and cultural change. In so doing, it catalyzed the modernization of Italy.

↖
Ferrari 250 TR racing car designed by
Sergio Scaglietti, 1957.

↓
Fiat 500 Nuova designed by
Dante Giacosa, 1957.

Good Form and the
West German economic miracle

Like Italy, Germany emerged from World War II as a shadow of its former self—a nation torn asunder between the Soviet East and the capitalist West. This once-mighty industrial powerhouse had lost not only the war, but also its national self-belief. It now found itself in economic chaos and, thanks to Adolf Hitler's scorched-earth policy and Allied bombing, facing a severe housing shortage. It was also forced to face up to the terrible truths of its recent past: ideologically driven genocide nightmarishly implemented on an industrial scale. Guilt-ridden and economically crushed, West Germany was in a cultural morass. But rather than look back on a past that was too painful, it looked to build a better future once it became politically independent, in 1949. With its newly elected Christian Democratic government choosing the pathway of free enterprise, the country's industrialists and industrial designers, as in Italy, began using design to help build a new nation. By putting its faith in the transformative power of *Gute Form* (Good Form), West Germany eventually became a major exporter of beautifully designed and engineered products that brought about the *Wirtschaftswunder*—the economic miracle of the mid-1950s.

Unlike Italy, Germany already had an esteemed history of industrial design achievement, from Peter Behrens to the Deutscher Werkbund to the Dessau Bauhaus, and so after the war it was able to resume its modern design practices for peacetime production. West Germany was at this time also benefiting hugely from a veritable flood of US dollars thanks to the Marshall Plan. As a result, an American-like mindset had begun to take hold. In fact, postwar America served as a sort of template for the rebuilding of damaged societies across Western Europe. This was particularly noticeable in the seductive styling of Ferdinand "Ferry"

Porsche and Erwin Komenda's Porsche 356 sports car of 1948, a vehicle built for driving pleasure rather than everyday utility.

West Germany's severe postwar housing shortage was among the country's most pressing concerns, leading architects and designers to turn to new social housing solutions in the years immediately following the war. Reflecting this spirit, the 1949 exhibition entitled *Wie wohnen?* (How to Live?), held in Stuttgart, heralded Germany's reentry onto the international stage and revealed a "New Look" for German design. The centerpiece of the show was a modest four-room home designed by Egon Eiermann, furnished with simple, multifunctional furniture pieces including his well-known E10 basket chair made of woven rattan. That same year, Eiermann also designed his classic SE 42 chair—the first entry in a range of seating that would become the Teutonic answer to Charles and Ray Eames's earlier plywood chairs; it was subsequently manufactured by Wilde+Spieth. These seats had a softer, more sculptural sensibility that marked a new stylistic departure for German design. Similarly, Wilhelm Wagenfeld's Max and Moritz salt and pepper shakers (1953) for WMF revealed a far more organic approach to design, and their title, taken from characters in a children's book by Wilhelm Busch, reflected a more lighthearted approach to everyday

←

Porsche 356 sports car designed by Ferdinand "Ferry" Porsche (son of Ing Ferdinand Porsche), 1948, its bodywork styled by Erwin Komenda.

↗

Model No. 367/6046 wall clock designed by Max Bill for Junghans, 1956–57.

Max and Moritz salt and pepper shakers designed by Wilhelm Wagenfeld for WMF (Württembergische Metallwarenfabrik), 1952–53.

↓

Biomorphic ashtray and vase designed by Fritz Heidenreich for Rosenthal, 1950s.

→

Ulm stool designed by Max Bill and Hans Gugelot, 1955.

Reconstruction and a spirit of optimism

wares. During this period, the ceramics manufacturer Rosenthal also produced housewares with a strongly biomorphic quality, designed by Fritz Heidenreich, a sculptor and ceramicist who headed the firm's design department in Selb from 1946 until 1960. Yet even these items contained at their heart the DNA of Bauhaus-style functionalist modernism.

The legacy of the Bauhaus was further bolstered with the founding of the Hochschule für Gestaltung (College of Design) in Ulm in 1953. Its aim was to revive the Bauhaus's socially inspired design doctrine, which had been so abruptly interrupted by the National Socialists in the 1930s. The idea for this school was first mooted at a meeting in 1947 between the Bauhaus-trained Swiss designer Max Bill and the German graphic designer Otl Aicher and his future wife, Inge Scholl, who had been a leading member of the nonviolent Weiße Rose (White Rose) resistance group during the war. When the Ulm School officially opened, Bill was appointed its first

director, and many of its staff members had taught at the Bauhaus, most notably Johannes Itten, Josef Albers, and Ludwig Mies van der Rohe. The following year, Hans Gugelot was made director of the school's product-design department. Under his guidance a functionalist approach to design that relied heavily on engineering expertise was adopted. This new science-based, process-driven method resulted in functionally and technologically persuasive products with an essentialist aesthetic, designs trimmed of all decorative excess.

Meanwhile in industry, Dieter Rams was taking a similarly functionalist approach at the electronics manufacturer Braun. Rams began working for the firm in 1955 as an interior designer, architect, and exhibition designer and moved into its product-design section the following year. Among his projects was the Phonosuper SK4 radio-phonograph (1956), which he codesigned with Hans Gugelot. Nicknamed "Snow White's Coffin" by Braun's competitors, this design radically reimagined

Reconstruction and a spirit of optimism

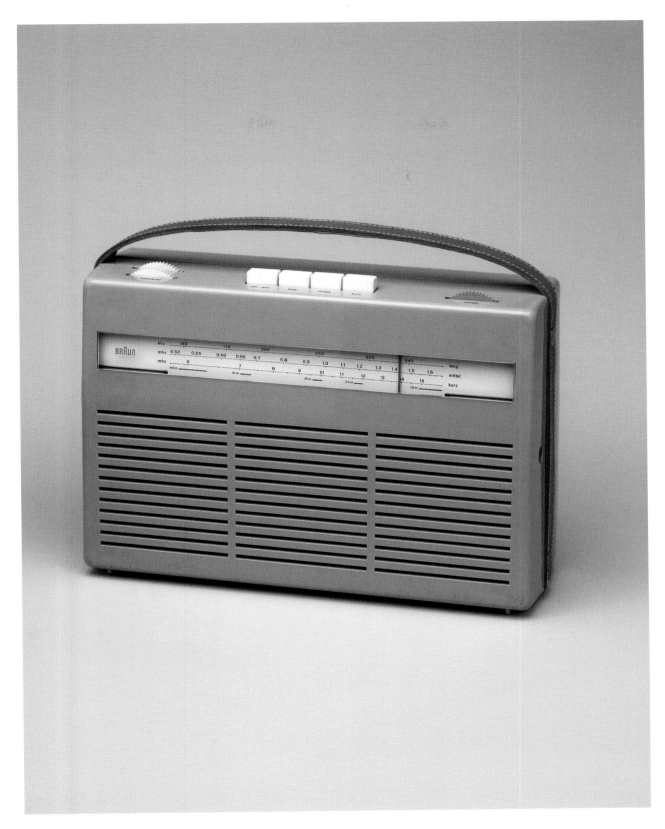

products in its category, using a white housing, a clear plastic top, and a simple, functional layout. It was not an immediate commercial success, being too far ahead of popular taste. Yet the SK4 was soon celebrated by the design cognoscenti for its fresh essentialist vocabulary of form, and it helped establish Braun as one of the world's leading consumer-electronic brands. Rams also designed other audio products for Braun, such as the T41 pocket radio (1956) and the P1 portable record player (1959), that had a similar essentialism and clarity of layout and that embodied the practical, ordered approach that had been born at the Bauhaus Dessau and was now being advanced by the Hochschule für Gestaltung (HfG) in Ulm. In 1961 Rams was appointed head of Braun's design department, and under his guidance during the decades that followed the firm produced an impressive body of work that epitomized Good Design and reflected his well-known motto, "Less, but Better."

Another designer who created objects that were remarkable for their functional simplicity was Max Bill. Perhaps best-known is his multifunctional *Ulmer Hocker* (Ulm stool) (1955), which he codesigned with Hans Gugelot for students to use at the HfG. Its striking Spartan quality anticipating the hard-line minimalism of the 1970s, this simple piece could be used as either a stool or a side table, and embodied the HfG's functionalist doctrine. Bill's wall clocks, kitchen timers, and wristwatches designed for Junghans during the 1950s are now similarly regarded as icons of West German postwar design. Highly refined in their engineering and with clear, minimalist layouts, they revealed Bill's adherence to the formal abstraction pioneered by the Concrete Art movement as well as his rare gift for harmonious composition. But perhaps Bill's greatest contribution during these postwar years was his instigation of the *Die gute Form* (Good Design) campaign, the origins of which can be traced back to a Schweizerischer Werkbund (Swiss Werkbund) conference speech he made in 1948 on "beauty as function and based on function."[2] Following this talk, the Swiss Werkbund commissioned him to prepare

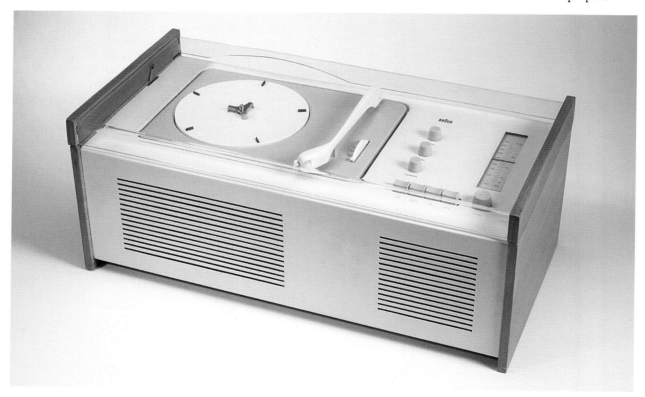

an exhibition of Swiss exemplary designs that would "show the principles of pure functional form organized systematically."[3] This *Die gute Form* touring exhibition of 1949 led the Swiss Werkbund in 1952 to introduce its annual Gute Form prize. A year later the Rat für Formgebung (German Design Council) was established, with the mandate to promote *gute Form* for reasons both economic and cultural.

Perhaps more than any other product of this period, the Volkswagen Beetle, designed by Ferdinand Porsche, reflected postwar Germany's newly found democracy: compact yet practical, it was an affordable auto for the everyman. And although the design of this "people's car" had been commissioned by Adolf Hitler in the late 1930s, it was not until after 1945 that it was manufactured in significant numbers. The VW Beetle was the kingpin of Europe's postwar *kleinwagens* (small compact cars), and a potent expression of West Germany's design-led economic miracle as well as the younger generation's new sense of egalitarian freedom.

←
SK4 record player designed by Dieter Rams and Hans Gugelot for Braun, 1957, nicknamed "Snow White's Coffin."

←
Previous page left: TP1 portable radio and phonograph designed by Dieter Rams for Braun, 1959.

↑
Volkswagen Beetle designed by Ferdinand Porsche, 1938, only produced in significant numbers after World War II.

←
Previous page right: T24 portable transistor radio designed by Dieter Rams for Braun, 1956.

Japanese postwar design

Japan experienced a rapid cultural transformation while under the occupation of the Allied Powers between 1945 and 1952. The Empire of Japan was officially dissolved, and in 1947 a constitutional democracy replaced it. Like its wartime allies Germany and Italy, Japan was compelled to transform itself from a military power into an economic one, though the country had undergone its industrial revolution relatively early in comparison to other non-Western countries. The inventor and industrialist Sakichi Toyoda had designed Japan's first steam-powered loom in 1896, and it had been instrumental to the growth of Japan's modern silk industry. As we have seen, this coincided with a huge increase in exports to the West, and by World War I Japan was a leading industrialized nation. Its industry had continued to grow throughout the interwar period, thanks not only to another invention by Toyoda—the world's first automatic loom capable of replenishing the shuttle during continuous operation (1924)—but also to the Japanese government's desire to become a significant military power.

The Japanese defeat in World War II came as a severe blow to this essentially inward-looking society. The effects were felt in all areas of life, but they were especially strong in the manufacturing sector. For decades most of these major companies had supplied military materiel to the Japanese government, and now they had suddenly lost their most important customer. In order to survive, they had to convert their production to consumer goods for civilians. To do this, they needed first to decide which types of product to manufacture and then to learn how to design them, or at least work out how to copy successful products made abroad. And even if Japanese manufacturers accomplished all of this, they faced another problem, which was that although they were often competitive on price, they had a long-established reputation for poor-quality manufacture—the term "Made in Japan" being widely associated with shoddy goods. The situation needed urgent redress, and fortuitously for Japanese manufacturers a book was published in 1951 that answered their prayers: the *Quality Control Handbook*, written by the Romanian-born American management consultant and engineer Joseph M. Juran. The book soon came to the attention of the Japanese Union of Scientists and Engineers (JUSE) and made a lasting impression. It laid out the "economics of quality of design," explaining how to implement control systems and exacting standardization in the mass manufacture of goods, and also how to introduce a procedural culture of organization and planning. Among other things, the book detailed processes for the selection and rigorous testing of materials, the specialized training of a workforce, the maintenance of strict financial controls, and the monitoring of quality standards throughout the manufacturing process.

All of this made Juran a veritable guru to Japanese manufacturers, given the problems they were then addressing, and in 1952 the JUSE invited him to Japan. He made his first of ten visits to the country in 1954, and while there he gave seminars to top-ranking and mid-level executives from ten companies, including Nikon and the Noritake chinaware company. Juran's first series of seminars was so well received that JUSE and the Japanese Standards Association asked him to deliver more lectures on subsequent trips. Put simply, his message was that by introducing quality-control systems, firms could increase customer satisfaction, produce more saleable goods, be more competitive, increase market share, and enjoy better income and margins—and that while higher-quality products often cost more in the short term, they reaped a much better return on investment in the long run. His message soon spread throughout Japanese industry, and in time the larger firms set up their own internal quality-control training programs. Such was the impact of Juran's pioneering work in quality control that Japanese national radio began to offer related courses for foremen, and booklets on the subject were sold at newspaper kiosks.

The transformative influence of Juran's work on Japanese design is vividly illustrated by a comparison of the output of Nikon in the late 1940s and in the late 1950s. In 1948 the company, then known as Nippon Kogaku, launched a compact camera known as the Nikon I, which was not only its first camera but also the first product to bear the Nikon name. This design was inspired by the successful top-of-the-line Leicas then being produced in Germany. A decade later, Nikon introduced its own groundbreaking high-end camera, the Nikon F—the company's first interchangeable-lens SLR (single-lens reflex) model. This design, with its boldly styled, distinctive casing, offered numerous innovations, including the first exposure meter to be fully coupled with an aperture and the first practical application of a motor drive. It was this type of technically persuasive and beautifully engineered product that transformed "Made in Japan" into an indicator of design innovation and manufacturing quality. Thanks to Juran, the tables had turned within a very short period of time.

Another Japanese firm whose name became closely associated with the country's postwar design revolution was the Toyota Motor Co. Ltd. The company had been established in 1937 by Kiichiro Toyoda, eldest son of the famous power-loom inventor, Sakichi Toyoda. During the war years, the firm undertook extensive research into and development of, among other things, batteries, diesel engines, alternative fuels, forge-processing techniques, and steel alternatives. Then, on August 14, 1945, its main plant in Koromo was hit in an air raid and a quarter of the factory was destroyed. The

Nikon I camera, launched 1948.

following day, the emperor's broadcast announced the end of the war, and Toyota was immediately tasked by Vice President Hisayoshi Akai with resuming truck production, which was seen as essential to Japan's postwar reconstruction. Although the Allied Powers issued a memorandum the following month prohibiting the manufacture of passenger cars, they still allowed the production of trucks and also certain types of electrical equipment such as boat engines, small motors, radios, and various household appliances. Toyota, therefore, diversified its product range to encompass such products. But while the production of passenger cars was banned by the occupying administration, research and development into their design was not, so Toyota busied itself in that area. The results were plain to see when its first postwar car was launched in October 1947. The Model SA (1947), retailed under the Toyopet" brand, was a family sedan, the brainchild of Kiichiro Toyoda, who had taken to heard his father's entreaty to "stay ahead of the times."[4] Its aerodynamic body, predominantly the work of the engineer Kazuo Kumabe, can be traced to prewar German models; the reason for this was that Kumabe, together with other Toyota engineers, had traveled to Germany before World War II to study the automotive technology and styling then being pioneered by the talented engineers at Auto Union (Audi), Porsche, and Volkswagen. In contrast the

first Toyota Crown, introduced in 1955, reflected the influence of American styling; unsurprisingly, it was successfully exported to the United States during the late 1950s.

Nissan, another Japanese car manufacturer, also became a successful exporter to America. Having entered this overseas market in 1958, it had established dealerships across the country within a year. In 1960 it began selling the all-new Datsun Bluebird 310 through these dealerships. This marked the beginning of a tremendously successful period for Nissan in America: in 1971 alone, it sold an astonishing 255,000 automobiles, demonstrating convincingly that Japanese manufacturers had managed to overthrow any doubts about their design and manufacturing credentials by creating products that the whole world wanted to buy. The power of design had yet again been harnessed to create national industrial wealth and, with it, national industrial pride.

More than any other company, Sony was responsible for the extraordinary rise of modern design in Japan during the postwar period. In the first few months after the war ended, there had been a huge surge of demand for radios, fueled by a population eager for news from around the world. In September 1945, spotting the opportunity that this demand represented, a young engineer named Masaru Ibuka opened a small office in Tokyo. Rather grandly named the Tokyo Tsushin Kenkyujo (Tokyo Telecommunications Research Institute), the business functioned as both a research lab and a repair center for war-damaged radios and sets whose shortwave units had been disconnected by the military police to prevent their being tuned in to enemy propaganda. The fledgling company also manufactured innovative adapters that allowed short-wave units

↖
Nikon F camera, 1959.

↗
Toyota Model SA, 1947, retailed under the Toyopet brand.

→
Nissan's Datsun Bluebird 310, 1959—this model from 1962.

Reconstruction and a spirit of optimism

to be converted into all-wave receivers. These short-wave adapters were featured in the "Blue Pencil" column of the respected *Asahi Shimbun* newspaper, and this led the physicist Akio Morita to reconnect with his old friend Ibuka. Together they went on to found their own company the following year. Known as the Tokyo Tsushin Kogyo Kabushiki Kaisha (the Tokyo Telecommunications Engineering Corporation), this venture was set up to research and manufacture telecommunications equipment and measuring devices. Initially, its best-selling product was an electrically heated cushion. But in 1950 it launched the first Japanese-made magnetic recording tape, dubbed Soni-Tape—hence the name "Sony." That year they also released the first Japanese reel-to-reel audio device, which was used by the Supreme Court and various other government agencies to record evidence, thereby earning it the nickname "G Type"—G for government.

A sales trip to America taken by Ibuka in 1952 propelled the young Japanese company into an exciting new sphere of electronics manufacture. Having read an article in an American magazine about the invention of the transistor by W. B. Shockley, J. Bardeen, and W. Brattain at Bell Laboratories in 1948, Ibuka was skeptical about its practical application. Nevertheless, while in America he heard from a friend based there that Bell Laboratories' parent company, Western Electric, was going to license the manufacture of transistors to interested parties on a royalty basis; his interest was piqued. During a night of jet-lagged restlessness, an idea flashed though Ibuka's mind: maybe his company could license the manufacture of transistors, and then his highly trained staff could work hard to perfect their commercial application. Unable to secure a deal with Western Electric on this first visit, Ibuka doggedly persisted. Eventually, he received a letter announcing that the US company would be happy to license its patent to Ibuka and his team. This was a major coup, and Ibuka's partner Morita was assigned to close the deal, which he did during another fact-finding

Reconstruction and a spirit of optimism

trip to America. On the same trip Morita visited various European countries, among them the Netherlands, where the Philips electronics company inspired him to believe that his company too could go from very humble beginnings to worldwide sales.

Having finally obtained the license to produce transistors in 1954, Ibuka observed: "As long as we're going to produce transistors, let's make them for a product that anyone can afford to buy. Otherwise we'll be wasting our time. What I have in mind is a radio. Let's work on a transistor radio from the beginning, regardless of any difficulties we may face."[5] This was a formidable challenge considering that transistor technology at this stage was still fairly basic, using only low frequencies; this meant that early transistors were suitable for hearing aids and not much else. Within a year, though, Ibuka's company had introduced the first Japanese transistor radio, the TR-55 (1955), which, measuring only 3½ x 5½ x 1½ inches and weighing less that 20 ounces, was an unprecedented feat of miniaturization—a major theme in design that would become increasingly associated with Japanese products in the coming years. With its colorful plastic housing, eye-catching tuning dial, and stamped aluminium speaker grille, inspired by the dashboards of Lincoln automobiles, the TR-55 had an appealing futuristic quality that undoubtedly

contributed to its success. It was also emblazoned with the distinctive Sony logo, which had been used on some of the company's earlier products.

In 1957 the firm launched another revolutionary product: the TR-63 radio, which similarly incorporated transistor technology, allowing its internal mechanism to be much more compact. As the world's first pocket-sized radio, it introduced the concept of listening to the radio on the move. This diminutive item measured just 4 7/16 x 2 13/16 x 1¼ inches and incorporated a dial that also functioned as the tuner. It was almost minimalist in style, with a strong functional clarity that made it an intuitive product to use. The TR-63 was the first full-fledged Sony-branded product exported to America, where it became a massive hit despite its premium price tag of $39.95 (the equivalent of about $315 today). The diminutive radio was available in four colors—yellow, red, green, and black. In total, more than 100,000 units were sold in the US alone. In 1958 the company changed its name to the more westernized Sony Corporation and launched another pocket radio, the TR-610, which—with its slightly more upmarket styling—proved an even bigger hit in America and Europe, selling more than half a million units worldwide. Yet around this time, despite Sony's extraordinary commercial success, Ibuka, mindful of the necessity of staying ahead of

↖
Sony's G Type reel-to-reel tape recorder, 1950.

→
Sony's TR-55 transistor radio, 1955.

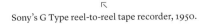

the electronics game, declared, "The days of radio are over. The future lies in television." Soon afterwards, Sony launched the first fully transistorized television, the TV8-301 (1960)—a model designed to be highly portable, demonstrating once again the ability of Japanese manufacturers to miniaturize technology into compact "personal" electronic products. This small, soft-edged TV, with its distinctive Sony logo, showed just how far Japanese consumer-product design had come since the end of World War II. The country had transformed itself from an ill-reputed producer of poorly made, replicated goods to a nation at the very forefront of design innovation, pioneering commercial applications for cutting-edge technologies. This single-minded commitment to design and manufacturing excellence was key to restoring national pride to Japan. It also stimulated a buoyant economy with which to build the infrastructure of a new, democratic, and far more outward-looking society. It might be said that a country's designed products can determine its cultural standing in the world—and this was especially true of Japan during the 1950s.

←
Sony's pocket TR-63 radio, 1957.

↑
Sony's TV8-301 television, 1960–
the world's first fully transistorized TV.

Postwar Britain
and the Festival of Britain

↑
Antelope chair designed by Ernest Race
for Race Furniture, 1951.

↗
Festival of Britain catalogue showing the
Festival's logo designed by Abram Games,
1951.

Reconstruction and a spirit of optimism

Although jubilantly victorious at the end of World War II, Britain remained in the grip of shortages and rationing in the years that followed. This era, though, marked the beginning of a new chapter in British history as well as in the story of British design. Like other European nations exhausted by the war, Britain needed to adapt its industries quickly from military production to peacetime manufacture, and to generate revenue from exports in order to fill its war-depleted coffers. This was an uphill battle given the scarcity of raw materials, but British designers and engineers put their famed ingenuity to good use and produced innovative products from whichever materials they could find. Ernest Race's BA chair of 1945, for example, was made from resmelted aluminium aircraft scrap. This design, and around 4,000 others, was included in the 1946 *Britain Can Make It* exhibition at the Victoria and Albert Museum. Critics cynically referred to it as the "Britain Can't Have It" exhibition because, thanks to rationing, most of the products on view could only be sold abroad.

The goal of the exhibition was, according to Sir Stafford Cripps, then-president of the Board of Trade:

> To prove that industrial design is by no means an impracticable and idealistic matter. Industrial design has, in fact, the most intimate connection with the comfort and happiness of our daily life. Good design can provide us in our homes and working-places with pleasant articles which combine good construction and fitness for their purpose with convenience in use and attractiveness in shape and color.[7]

The exhibition had a two-pronged agenda: it aimed to establish foreign markets for well-designed British products and to educate the public about the moral and economic benefits of Good Design. The Design Research Unit—established in 1943 by Misha Black and Milner Gray, among others, as Britain's first multidisciplinary design consultancy—was responsible for the creation of one of the show's most important displays, "What Industrial Design Means." In order to demonstrate clearly the entire stage-by-stage process of designing an object for industrial production, the installation traced the development of an eggcup from initial concept to finished product. It ended with a speech bubble emerging from the eggcup:

So you see designing me,
Is as tricky as can be:
A thousand other problems lie,
In every object you may buy.[8]

The Council of Industrial Design (CoID) also publicized Good Design through its monthly journal, *Design*, first published in 1949. Besides the magazine, the CoID produced a range of educational materials for use in schools, including classroom posters and portable mini-exhibitions containing artifacts that children could handle. During this period the CoID aimed to show adults and children alike that "Good Design can be Good Fun."[9]

A lighthearted approach to design education was certainly taken at the 1951 Festival of Britain, which marked the centenary of the famous Great Exhibition by celebrating national accomplishment in the sciences and arts. Patriotic to its core, the yearlong festival was

a much-needed morale boost, and it acted as a catalyst for modern design. After coming through two battering world wars and a prolonged interwar recession, Britain was ready to look to a brighter and more modern future. This was most emphatically demonstrated at the festival's centerpiece, the South Bank Exhibition overlooking the River Thames. Here the newly built Royal Festival Hall, the futuristic Dome of Discovery, the soaring Skylon sculpture, and an assortment of modern pavilions introduced a new postwar look to British design and architecture.

During the festival the South Bank Exhibition attracted nearly 8.5 million visitors, and many of them visited the Design Review display, a curated selection of British-designed products that met the exacting standards of Good Design. As the director of the CoID, Gordon Russell, wrote:

> An avowed aim of the Festival of Britain is to show a high standard of industrial design. How shall we define this? I would say that a well-designed industrial product would be made to serve a particular and useful purpose. It would be designed so that it could be made economically, of good and suitable materials, by normal machine processes and sold through normal trade channels. [. . .] It should give pleasure in use. Design [. . .] is recognized as an integral part of quality, which can no longer be thought of as good workmanship and good material only. In fact, good design should be regarded as one of the consumer's guarantees of quality."[10]

The Design Review section spotlighted every conceivable area of design endeavor, from furniture, lighting, and domestic appliances to machinery, commercial vehicles, and communications equipment. All of the exhibits reflected the CoID's desire for well-made, mindful, practical designs, but it was Ernest Race's Antelope chair—designed for the outdoor terraces of the South Bank Exhibition, with a looping steel-rod construction and curious atom-like ball feet—that best encapsulated the festival's "New Look."

The postwar generation of British designers, many of whom had either recently graduated from the Royal College of Art or were still studying there, were inspired by the designs they saw at the festival, and also by the underlying message about the importance of Good

↑
Calyx textile designed by Lucienne Day
for Heal & Sons, 1951.

↑
Pride cutlery designed by David Mellor, 1954.

↗
Sideboard designed by Robert and
Dorothy Heritage for G. W. Evans, 1954.

Reconstruction and a spirit of optimism

Design. After the success of the festival there was a far greater acceptance of modern design in Britain, and over the following few years a distinctive design style emerged in the country expressing a modern aesthetic. Whether it was Lucienne Day's Calyx textile, Robin Day's furniture for Hille, David Mellor's Pride cutlery, Robert Welch's stainless-steel tea-sets for Old Hall, Terence Conran's chinaware, or Robert and Dorothy Heritage's sideboard decorated with a cityscape, these new items shared the youthful, optimistic look. In 1957 Prime Minister Harold Macmillan made a memorable speech at a Conservative Party rally, in which he famously stated, "Most of our people have never had it so good." It was certainly true that the grim years of austerity and utility had been followed by a consumer-led age of growth and employment, of bright textiles and modern furnishings, of televisions,

and modern, labor-saving appliances. And yet Britain, like other countries in Europe, never wholeheartedly adopted the marketing-led consumer culture found in postwar America. One of the reasons for this was that European economies were not nearly as buoyant, and therefore disposable incomes were not as high, meaning that there was not as much money to buy fashionable products. And even if there had been, there might not have been the same appetite for novelty in Europe, where repeated cycles of hardship over long and often turbulent histories had increased the appeal of well-designed, durable products. Also, as the cradle of the Modern Movement, Europe was home to design practitioners and design-led manufacturers who had been weaned on the ethics of Good Design. This moral dimension underpinned their whole understanding of design practice.

The Scandinavian approaches

After World War II, Scandinavian designers built on the region's prewar successes to make it one of the most influential forces on the international scene. There is a tendency to group the work of Swedish, Danish, Finnish, and Norwegian designers together under the banner "Scandinavian," but this classification is no more useful than grouping the work of British, French, Italian, and German designers under the rubric "European." There were in fact notable distinctions between the design outputs of the Nordic countries. But despite their underlying differences, these four nations all produced well-designed, beautifully executed objects during the postwar period—objects that exemplified the precepts of Good Design and the very Scandinavian belief that everyone had a right to well-designed products that enhanced life.

In Sweden the socialist concept of the *Folkhemmet* (people's home),[11] which had emerged before the outbreak of war, was translated into a comprehensive welfare state, complete with a state-controlled housing policy that had an influential and lasting impact on the structure of its society. Modernist ideals were built into the Swedish homemaking dream, and the concept of design as lifestyle gained increasing popularity in the country's design community. Even beyond the design community, there was a widely held conviction that everyday life could be improved by the implementation of modern design, as demonstrated by an exhibition of Swedish design held in Zurich in 1949, *Vom Stadtplan zum Essbesteck* (From Town Plan to Cutlery). During the postwar era Swedish designers began to develop a gentler form of modernism than the one advocated by their functionalist forbears in the 1930s. This reinterpretation was reflected in the homey informality of postwar interiors, with their blond-wood furniture, patterned curtains, and woven rugs. As Sweden's economy grew more prosperous, the need for rigorous functionalism lessened, to such an extent that even the nation's greatest advocate of standardization, Gregor Paulsson, eventually had to admit, "The choice of goods is a choice of lifestyle."[12]

In 1955 many of the designs shown in the landmark *H55* exhibition in Helsingborg worked within this reinterpretation of Swedish modernism, which was characterized by sensual, organic forms, warm earth tones, and the use of natural materials. Although such craft-inspired, industrially produced designs might have been construed as marking a return to traditionalism, they had an underlying rationalism, and the use of natural materials was often driven as much by their ready availability as by any design ideology. During the 1940s and 1950s Swedish engineers and designers also began to develop a variety of innovative industrial-design solutions that fulfilled the Svenska Slöjdföreningen's (Swedish Society of Industrial Design) long-held goal of producing goods that were recognizably of the Machine Age. Working with state-of-the-art materials and manufacturing processes, this new throng of professional consultants, which included Sixten Sason, Ralph Lysell, Carl-Arne Breger, and Sigvard Bernadotte, designed an array of products—from vehicles, power tools, and washing machines to typewriters, cameras, and vacuum cleaners—for a host of Swedish companies, such as Ericsson, Electrolux, Gustavsberg, Hasselblad, Husqvarna, Saab, and Volvo. Although they were inspired by 1930s American streamlining, Swedish industrial designers often used aerodynamic forms not for stylistic purposes but as a means of creating better products, most notably Sixten Sason's Saab 92 (1942), which featured a sweeping,

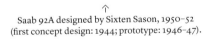
Saab 92A designed by Sixten Sason, 1950–52
(first concept design: 1944; prototype: 1946–47).

→

Ericofon telephone designed by Hugo Blomberg
and Ralph Lysell for Ericsson, 1956.

→

Plastic watering can designed by Carl-Arne
Breger for Gustavsberg, 1957–58.

aerodynamic monocoque body that set new standards in automotive design. Likewise, Hugo Blomberg and Ralph Lysell's Ericofon telephone for Ericsson (1956) innovatively integrated the earpiece, mouthpiece, and dial into a single unit, with an ergonomically refined, sculptural form. Carl-Arne Breger, who became known as Mr. Plastic, also worked with thermoplastics, extending the aesthetic and functional parameters of their use for the design of everyday objects. His plastic watering can (1957–58) was a sculptural tour de force.

In 1957 the Society of Swedish Industrial Designers (SID) was established to raise the profile of Swedish industrial design both at home and abroad. By emphasizing the aesthetic qualities of their own manufactured goods, Swedish designers forged a distinctive identity. At the same time, companies that prized design, such as Volvo, were building international reputations for superlative manufacturing quality as well as ethically driven design. The much-loved Volvo Amazon, released in 1956, was the company's first "democratic" car, affordable for the average man; it also introduced numerous safety features, including the world's first three-point safety belt and a padded dashboard. In comparison to the styling-led car designs being built in Detroit around the same time, the Amazon was by far the more progressive, in terms of aesthetics, safety, and quality. It can be seen as another concrete expression of Scandinavian Good Design.

The concept of Good Design also permeated Danish production in these years. To this day Denmark, more than any other nation, is associated with high-quality, well-designed products that have timeless appeal. One of the main reasons for this is that in Denmark, Good Design has long been linked to the search for "ideal forms," and this was especially true during the postwar period. This singular aspect of Danish design can be traced to the architect and furniture designer Kaare Klint's pioneering research into anthropometrics (the systematic collection and correlation of body measurements), conducted in the 1920s and 1930s. Through his detailed studies,

Klint revived the timeless ideals of Neoclassicism and established a humanistic approach that formed the fundament of postwar Danish modernism. By devising a system of average measurements based on actual human proportions and then applying it to the design of furniture, Klint hoped to develop ideal furnishing solutions. In this pursuit of the essential, Klint and his students also carefully studied the dimensions of various historically successful furniture types. Denmark also had a long and illustrious cabinetmaking tradition, and the craft skills that had been honed over decades in the various workshops were employed in developing modern designs for mass production. This craft-based knowledge of materials and construction techniques, married to an early understanding of ergonomics and a thorough analysis of successful precedents, set Danish design apart.

Many of the country's designers, such as Børge Mogensen and Hans Wegner, continued Klint's search for ideal forms and produced modernist reworkings of numerous vernacular types of furniture. Mogensen's Shaker chair (1944) and Wegner's Chinese and Peacock chairs (1943 and 1947, respectively) epitomized this evolutionary approach to design practice. By studying "classic" antecedents and updating them within a modernist idiom, they advanced a less dogmatic and more accessible form of modernism. Congenial and informal, and often using warm-toned woods rather than modernistic steel and glass, Danish postwar furniture design became a firm favorite among both tastemakers and homemakers throughout Europe and America in the 1950s and 1960s.

In general, the postwar period was a democratic one in design, in which greater emphasis was placed on producing furniture and other domestic products that

←
Volvo Amazon designed Jan Wilsgaard, introduced 1956.

↑
Peacock chair designed by Hans Wegner for Johannes Hansen, 1947.

↑
Bowl designed by Finn Juhl and executed by Magne Monsen for Kay Bojesen Modeller, c. 1950.

were suitable for smaller living spaces and could be afforded by the average family. By using high-quality, machine-aided craftsmanship, Danish modernism exemplified Good Design and in due course came to be seen as epitomizing good taste, too. Its reputation was significantly bolstered by various influential exhibitions held in America and Britain, as a result of which, by the midcentury, "Design from Denmark" was internationally sought after. Denmark also owed much to the extensive importation of teak from the Philippines during the 1950s. During World War II, teak had been logged on these islands in order to clear roads for military operations, and as a result there was a surplus of it as a reasonably priced material following the war. This superior, closely grained hardwood, with its distinctive rich tone, was so widely employed by Danish furniture designers such as Finn Juhl, Hans Wegner, and Peter Hvidt that the term "Teak Style" was coined to describe their work. Teak was also widely used for Danish housewares, notably Jens Quistgaard's ice bucket for Dansk Design (1960), and also toys, such Kay Bojesen's characterful wooden monkey of 1951.

Although teak was the wood of choice for many Danish postwar designers, the architect Arne Jacobsen instead chose to explore the formal and functional potential of molded plywood, which was more suited to producing furniture for the mass market. The resulting Model No. 3107 chair from Jacobsen's landmark Series 7 line (1955) became one of the best-selling chairs of all time, and like his earlier Ant chair (1951–52) marked a complete break from Denmark's evolutionary approach to design. Similarly revolutionary were Jacobsen's Swan and Egg chairs (1957) for the SAS Royal Hotel in Copenhagen. These seating designs introduced a sculptural confidence to Danish design and anticipated the progressive work of another Dane, Verner Panton, whose playful K3 Heart and K1 Cone chairs (1959 and 1958) bridged the organic approach of the 1950s and the Pop art aesthetic of the following decade.

Finnish design also underwent an extraordinary revival of fortunes during the postwar period. But while Swedish designers embraced industrial-design consultancy and their Danish counterparts explored the manufacturing potential of ideal sculptural forms, Finnish designers tended to prefer a more expressive approach. After the hardships of World War II and the burden of war reparations, there emerged in Finland a powerful desire to boost national self-confidence. Indeed, the promotion of a distinctive Finnish identity in the applied arts, from ceramics and glassware to textiles and furniture, yielded a general feeling of optimism and renewal in the 1950s. During these years designers such as Tapio Wirkkala, Timo Sarpaneva, Antti Nurmesniemi, Ilmari Tapiovaara, and Maija Isola reimagined Finnish design, bringing their work to a new high of aesthetic expression. This ascendancy was recognized in 1951 with the so-called Milan Miracle:

↖
NV48 armchair designed by Finn Juhl, 1948.

←
Teak ice-bucket designed by Jens Quistgaard for Dansk Design, 1960.

Reconstruction and a spirit of optimism

↑
Egg and Swan chairs designed by Arne Jacobsen for
Fritz Hansen in Copenhagen, 1957, originally created
for the SAS Royal Hotel, Copenhagen.

←
Model No. 3107 chair designed by Arne Jacobsen for
Fritz Hansen, 1955, from Jacobsen's landmark
Series 7 line.

→
K3 Heart chair designed by Verner Panton
for Plus Linje, 1959 (reissued by Vitra).

various Finnish designers, most notably Wirkkala, won six Grand Prix awards at the IX Milan Triennale exhibition. Wirkkala designed the Finnish section of the X Milan Triennale in 1954; on display there were a variety of objects, including award-winning glassware, that emphasized the fresh sculptural bravado of Finnish design. One commentator described the look as "a mixture of primitive daring and incredible elegance."[13] Success at these Milan exhibitions attracted widespread recognition of the boldly individualistic work of Finnish designers, who explored the formal properties of their materials using organic sculptural forms. But what really distinguished Finnish design was its emotional appeal, derived from the use of shapes and patterns found in nature—from Tapio Wirkkala's Kantarelli (Chanterelle) vase for Iittala (1947) to Maija Isola's Unikko (Poppy) textile for Marimekko (1965). And while the youthful vitality of Finnish furniture, textiles, ceramics, and glassware embodied the spirit of the postwar era, it also anticipated the defining feature of design in the mid- to late-1960s: artistic expression.

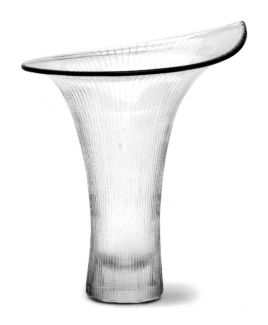

↖
Leaf dish designed by Tapio Wirkkala for Soinne et Kni, c. 1951.

↖
Lancet III art object/vase designed by Timo Sarpaneva for Iittala, 1955.

←
Tapio Wirkkala's Kantarelli (Chanterelle) vase for Iittala, 1947.

→
Unikko (Poppy) textile designed by Maija Isola for Marimekko, 1964.

Reconstruction and a spirit of optimism

The plastics age

Pop design and the counterculture

The first years of the 1960s were very similar to the 1950s, but around 1963 there was an ideological seachange as various sociopolitical events began to alter public attitudes. Being a powerful social barometer, design mirrored the emerging "sixties" outlook. The previous year, the Beatles had recorded their first single, "Love Me Do," at EMI's Abbey Road studios in London; the *Sunday Times* had become the first British newspaper to print a color supplement; Rachel Carson's eco-concern book *Silent Spring* had been published; the Cuban missile crisis had provoked widespread anxiety about potential nuclear conflict; and the term "personal computer" had its first mention in the media. All of these events were to have an effect on the practice of design, some sooner, some later. In January 1963 America's military supremacy also suffered a severe dent when the Viet Cong won their first major victory at the Battle of Ap Bac, provoking growing unease about what American soldiers were doing half the world away, in another country's war of independence. Soon a spirit of antiwar protest was in the air, as the singer-songwriter Bob Dylan noted the following year in his song "The Times They Are a-Changin'," which would become an anthem for the disaffected younger generation. It was these very same individuals who were now also beginning to enjoy the sexual freedoms brought about by the increasing availability of oral contraceptives, which had first been approved by the US's Food and Drug Administration (FDA) in 1960 but were only now becoming widely available. "The pill" unquestionably spawned a more casual approach to life in all sorts of ways, and this laid-back, anything-goes mindset became a defining feature of the period as well as of its designs.

The ensuing years of the 1960s saw unprecedented social and political change that proclaimed a new era of gender and racial emancipation and sexual permissiveness. Among the most important factors of change were the questionable ethics of the Vietnam War, which led to an increasing erosion of trust in the establishment and its political elite during the period, both in America and Europe, in turn provoking a shift in public attitudes, especially among young people. This demographic increasingly rebuffed the establishment's authority and became ever more determined to undermine the status quo through proactive subversion. Rejecting the cozy, predominantly patriarchal suburban home-making that had come to define the American Dream, this idealistic generation sought a less restrictive vision of the future, bolstered by economic boom, moral conviction, and recreational drugs. The fashions of the day reflected these utopian ideals, from the Space Age aesthetic of the mid- to late-1960s through to the nature-inspired hippie look of the late 1960s to early 1970s. And they also found an expression in the era's design and architecture.

By the 1960s new plastic materials and their related manufacturing technologies, many of which had been researched and developed during World War II, were widely available and were enthusiastically added to the design toolbox. These new synthetics included a wide array of thermoplastics, which, unlike earlier thermoset plastics, could be repeatedly reheated and remolded. This meant that, once the high tooling costs had been met, they could quickly and cheaply be injection-molded using heat and pressure into complex, three-dimensional forms. Designers reveled in these wondrous polymers, creating futuristic shapes that encapsulated the youthful spirit of the day. During the early 1960s, technical

←
Previous page: Capitello chair designed by
Studio 65 for Gufram, 1971.

←
Zanotta publicity photograph for the
Blow chair designed by De Pas, D'Urbino,
and Lomazzi, 1967.

developments within the plastics industry produced a host of new synthetic materials, from durable, colorful polypropylene to hard, glossy acrylonitrile butadiene styrene (ABS). These new thermoplastics, many of which were suitable for high-volume injection-molding processes, captured designers' imaginations, especially in Italy, which already had a mature plastics manufacturing industry thanks to the Milanese chemist Giulio Natta's pioneering discovery of catalysts that could be used to polymerize polypropylene in 1954. In and around Milan there were numerous small, highly specialized design companies, as well as a pool of highly trained engineers who were able to transform designers' sketches into three-dimensional products. This provided fertile territory for the development of groundbreaking products, many of which had a Space Age aesthetic, and Italian companies such as Artemide, Kartell, Poltronova, and Zanotta gave their designers free rein to create visions of the future using their substantial economic and technical resources. The products that emerged from these "concept factories," with their unfettered creative freedom, were some of the most progressive in the history of design. Among them were Ettore Sottsass and Perry King's Valentine portable typewriter (1969), which revolutionized office equipment; Marco Zanuso and Richard Sapper's Grillo folding telephone (1965); the Sacco beanbag (1968–69) by Gatti, Paolini, and Teodoro, which gave new meaning to the idea of laid-back living; and, of course, De Pas, D'Urbino, and Lomazzi's inflatable Blow chair (1967), which transformed the humble chair into an object of playful fun and ephemeral sculptural beauty. Plastics democraticized avant-garde design, making it so affordable that for the first time in history it became part of the mass market.

In France, Pierre Paulin and Olivier Mourgue similarly exploited the sculptural potential of man-made materials, namely polyurethane foam and stretch jersey fabric. Paulin created a range of visually stunning and very comfortable seating furniture for the Dutch manufacturer Artifort, and Mourgue's Djinn seating series memorably furnished the Hilton lobby of the space station featured in Stanley Kubrick's epic sci-fi film, *2001: A Space Odyssey* (1968). Over in Scandinavia, Verner Panton and Eero Aarnio also used synthetic materials to create groundbreaking seating designs, notably the landmark S-shaped single-form, single-

The plastics age

↑
Panton chair designed by Verner Panton for
Vitra, 1959-60.

↑
Prydan bowls designed by Hans Skillius for
Hammarplast, 1974.

↑
Ball chair designed by Eero Aarnio
for Asko, 1963.

↑
Model No. 1099 pitcher and Model
No. 9644 mugs designed by Sven-Eric Juhlin
for Gustavsberg, 1969-70.

Pop design and the counterculture

material Panton chair (1959–60) and Aarnio's Ball chair (1963), which provided a womb-like space of padded comfort in which to retreat from the world. These designs, however, did not have the playful expendability of their Italian counterparts, but were instead intended to be long-lasting, a quality achieved through the skillful use of durable plastics. In Sweden during this period, companies such as Gustavsberg and Hammarplast invested considerable resources in the development of "plastic design." The resulting products, among them Carl Arne Breger's Duett jug and citrus press (1967), Sven-Eric Juhlin's Model No. 1099 pitcher and Model No. 9644 mugs (1969–70), and Hans Skillius's Prydan bowls (1974), were remarkable for harnessing plastics to create life-enhancing products for the home. This was the very antithesis of the hedonistic, throwaway Pop culture celebrated by the glossy magazines and Sunday supplements of the period. And yet such products were in a very real sense "popular," in the sense of being commercially successful, democratic designs with up-to-date aesthetics. Plastics also lent themselves to more sculptural forms thanks to their inherent moldability, which enabled designers to produce objects that expressed the oozing, flowing properties of the materials. As the design critic Nigel Whiteley later noted, "What we were witnessing was going beyond the Modernist 'truth to materials' principle to a stage at which the associations of plastics became part of the 'meaning' of the product: plastic was, in a way, both form and content."[1]

But perhaps the most successful "plastic design" of this period was based on a problem-solving approach to material and process: Robin Day's ubiquitous Polyprop chair (1960–63), which has sold fourteen million units across the globe since its debut. For this design, Day essentially took the idea of a universal seat shell with different types of interchangeable bases, first put into practice by the Eameses, and skillfully translated it into injection-molded polypropylene. More than any other design of the 1960s, the Polyprop revealed the democratizing influence of plastics, showing that far from cheap and nasty, as they had previously been perceived, they were in fact noble materials that could be employed to mass produce inexpensive, high-quality, durable products. It was this potential that made the decade from around 1963 to 1973 a veritable golden age of plastics in design.

↑
Polyprop chair and variants designed by Robin Day for Hille, 1960–63.

Design goes Pop

The origins of Pop as a cultural phenomenon can be traced to the formation of the Independent Group in London in 1952. The group, which included the artist Richard Hamilton, the sculptor Eduardo Paolozzi, the architecture critic Reyner Banham, and the architects Peter and Alison Smithson, was established to examine the technical achievements of American industrial production and its by-product, popular consumerist culture. Rejecting modernist doctrine, the Independent Group controversially drew inspiration from the "low art" of advertising, packaging, and comics. The term "Pop" was coined to describe this new tendency in the creative arts, and in 1957 Hamilton famously wrote a letter to the Smithsons in which he defined Pop art as:

Popular (designed for a mass audience)
Transient (short-term solution)
Expendable (easily forgotten) -
Low cost
Mass produced
Young (aimed at youth)
Witty
Sexy
Gimmicky
Glamorous
Big Business[2]

By defining Pop and raising popular culture to the level of serious academic debate, the Independent Group laid the theoretical foundations upon which a design movement would flourish in the 1960s. And all of the attributes of Pop art outlined by Hamilton applied equally to Pop design, for Pop was a mindset that was born of its times.

←
C&B Italia publicity photograph of the Up Series designed by Gaetano Pesce, 1969.

While the advertising industry grew in scale and professionalism in both New York and London during the early 1960s, the music and fashion scenes underwent a demographic shift toward a more youthful audience. This generational displacement of power and influence initially saw London becoming the epicenter of the Swinging Sixties, to be rivaled by San Francisco later in the decade. The design historian Fiona MacCarthy has observed of London in the early 1960s that "There was an obvious feeling of the new day dawning and a sudden, reckless, very general enthusiasm, even among erstwhile caretakers of purism, for the fashionable, ephemeral and zany [. . .] The style of the times was, at its most apparent, a rather knock-out style of ostentatious verve and jollity."[3]

Crucial to the Pop zeitgeist in Britain was the introduction in 1962 of the *Sunday Times* color supplement, the first of its kind. In its quest for new and exciting content to fill its pages each and every week, the *Times* supplement, along with other lifestyle journals, helped to promote a stylistic pluralism that rejected the dominance of good taste and state-promoted Good Design in favor of bold and eye-catching consumer products. The tantalizing glimpses of new designs in each issue also helped to create a surge in consumption. The British public had simply become bored with sensible rationalism; it no longer wanted or required "definitive" design solutions. Driven by the tastes of a younger demographic, manufacturers now began to produce a steady stream of inexpensive, expendable products that suited their customers' more casual lifestyles. The earthy tones and "teak-look" of the 1950s were unceremoniously junked in favor of bold patterns and shiny, brightly colored designs. In 1964 Terence Conran's first Habitat store opened on London's Fulham Road; its warehouse-like retail space stacked with affordable flat-pack furniture and a bazaar-like array of constantly changing kitchen goods and accessories epitomized this spirit. It could reasonably be argued that Conran and his fashionable emporium did more to bring modern design into British people's everyday lives than the previous decades of commendable Good Design promotion had ever done.

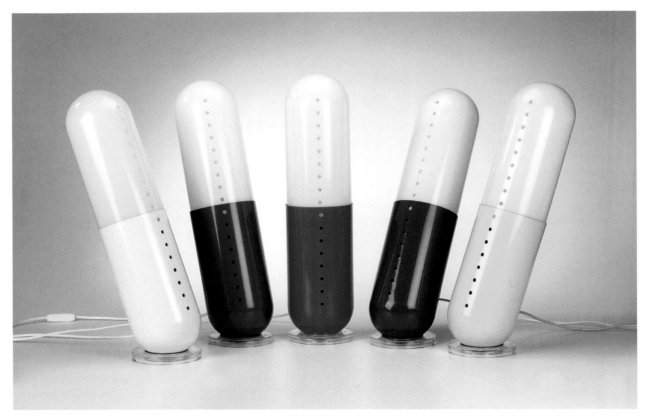

↑
Pillola table lights designed by Cesare Casati
and Emanuele Ponzio for Ponteur, 1968.

←
Basilico teapot from the Indian Memory series
designed by Ettore Sottsass and executed by
Alessio Sarri Ceramiche, 1972.

→
Superbox furniture unit prototype designed by
Ettore Sottsass for Poltronova, 1966, intended to
give "a ritual weight to the design of objects."

Pop design and the counterculture

Continental Europe saw a similar rejection of the worthy rationalism of modernism, especially in Italy and France, where the Pop art sensibility was visible in young designers striving to find new avenues for creative self-expression. Mainly working outside the industrial mainstream, they created avant-garde pieces that were often batch-produced in limited numbers and sold in galleries in much the same way as pieces of fine art. And the parallels with contemporary fine art did not stop there: pieces such as Studio 65's Capitello chair (1971), Cesare Casati and Emanuele Ponzio's Pillola table lamps (1968), and Gaetano Pesce's gigantic molded polyurethane foam foot, Up 7 (1969) echoed the outsized and out-of-context sculptures of Claes Oldenburg. Experimental lighting design was also particularly dynamic, and many products of the period functioned more as ambient sculptures than as practical lighting solutions. In another sign of the increasing crossover between art and design, established artists such as Victor Pasmore and Eduardo Paolozzi dabbled in product design, while designers such as Ettore Sottsass began to create pieces intended for limited-edition production, such as his Indian Memory series of sculptural teapots (1972) and his monolithic Superbox furniture prototypes covered with boldly patterned Abet plastic laminates (1967). Archizoom's series of Dream Beds (1967), whose kitschy glamour was the antithesis of Good Design, similarly functioned more as design-art installations than as real-world bedding.

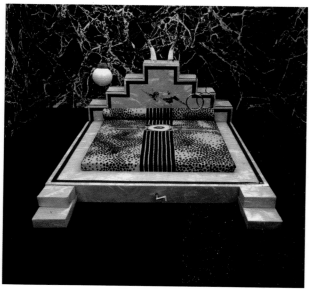

Naufragio di rose (Shipwreck of Roses) bed
and the Presagio di rose (Omen of Roses) from
the Dream Bed series designed by Archizoom,
1967.

The increasingly nomadic lifestyles of younger consumers also prompted the rise of inexpensive flat-pack furniture, which was easily transported and reassembled; Terence Conran's Habitat was again one of the leaders in this field of design in Britain. The Swedish company IKEA also grew from strength to strength during this period, thanks to its affordable self-assembly furniture and its introduction in 1968 of inexpensive, durable, and easy-to-process particleboard. Virtually every year that followed saw the company expand into another country. By the late 1960s, contemporary designs were widely available at affordable prices, and although the quality of goods was often not as high as in previous decades, the majority of customers didn't seem the least bit concerned. The design historian Nigel Whiteley has described this attitude as an "enjoy-it-today-sling-it-tomorrow philosophy"[4]: durability and permanence had come to be regarded as quaintly old-fashioned and essentially outmoded. Most young people in Western Europe and America were instead interested in keeping up to date with rapidly changing trends in music, fashion, and design.

Amid such change, the international design establishment continued to promote the cause of modernist design through conduits such as the Museum of Modern Art (MoMA), the Alcoa Industrial Design Awards, the Industrial Designers Society of America, and the Design Centre in London, though their efforts achieved little. MoMA, in fact, largely turned its back on design, hosting far fewer design-specific exhibitions in the 1960s than in the previous decade. The only significant such exhibition it held during the Pop era was 1972's landmark *Italy: The New Domestic Landscape*, a swansong of sorts for this period of creatively unfettered, radical change in design. Five years earlier, in 1967, the head of the Design Council in London, Paul Reilly, had acknowledged in an article called "The Challenge of Pop" that:

We are shifting perhaps from attachment to permanent, universal values to acceptance that a design may be valid at a given time for a given purpose [. . .] All that means is that a product must be good of its kind for the set of circumstances for which it has been designed. For example, in this age of accelerating technology to refuse to take notice of the transitory or to reject the ephemeral *per se* is to ignore a fact of life.[5]

The following year, Peter Murdoch's paper furniture won a Design Council Award, showing that disposability in design was now acceptable even to the British design establishment, which had been a strong champion of modernism since the founding of the Design and Industries Association (DIA) in 1915, and had long been guided by its slogan "Fitness for Purpose."[6] The purpose of design seemed to have been turned on its head, for better or worse.

Expendability being a strong Pop theme, it is no surprise that this was the period in which inflatables became an international phenomenon in design and architecture, aided also by the increasing availability of PVC (polyvinyl chloride), which could be heat-welded to create playful pockets of air. Various designers and design groups produced inflatable designs, but it was the French-Vietnamese designer Nguyen Manh Khanh, known as Quasar, who developed the very first line of inflatable furniture, the Aerospace collection, in 1967. Mobility was another theme of Pop, inspiring designs such as the Quasar Unipower (1968), a motorized glass cube that was intended to be a Parisian urban vehicle, and the Italian designer Mario Bellini's bright-green mobile conversation pit/sleeping area, the Kar-a-Sutra (1972), a collaborative project between Citroen and Pirelli that reflected the informality of early 1970s lifestyles. Bellini's design also revealed the extraordinary creative freedom enjoyed by European designers during this period, especially in Italy, where companies such as C&B Italia, Zanotta, and Poltronova saw the publicity and commercial benefits of being seen as champions of cutting-edge design.

In the United States, however, the picture was a little different. American design had become increasingly corporate, and as a result had lost the avant-garde edge it had enjoyed during the 1950s. Most large corporations now had in-house design teams, and the prevailing culture was safe and conservative. As a result, American homeware design of the 1960s and early 1970s was subsumed into middle-of-the-road markets epitomized by Sears catalogues and La-Z-Boy recliners. In fact, most of the high points of American design during this period were found in car manufacturing, in icons such as the Chevrolet Corvette

↑
Spotty chair designed by Peter Murdoch for Peter Murdoch, Inc. (backed by International Paper, Inc.), 1964.

↑
Aerospace collection chair designed by Nguyen Manh "Quasar" Khanh for Quasar, 1967.

Sting Ray coupe (1963) and the Ford Mustang fastback (1965), and, later, muscle cars, such as the Chevrolet Camaro (1967), the Hemi V8-powered Dodge Charger (1968), the Plymouth Road Runner (1968), and the third-generation Plymouth Barracuda (1970). Several US military aircraft designs also became milestons, especially the Bell "Huey" helicopter (first flight 1956), which is permanently associated with the Vietnam War, and the stealthy Lockheed SR-71 "Blackbird" reconnaissance airplane (1964), designed by Clarence "Kelly" Johnson. All of these designs were born of deep-pocketed commitment by their respective manufacturers and teams of skilled designers, engineers, and technicians working together to produce the best possible design solution within the given constraints: this was design in the age of American big business.

A number of notable designs created in America during this period were developed solely for offices and institutions, which, as many manufacturers had figured out, were far more lucrative sectors than the home-consumer market. These products included Robert Propst's revolutionary Action Office II system for Herman Miller (1971), David Rowland's GF 40/4 stacking chair (1964), and Eliot Noyes's IBM Selectric typewriter (1961). There were, of course, a few successful designs that skillfully bridged the domestic and contract markets, such as Michael Lax's Lytegem

task lamp for Lightolier (1964), the ubiquitous Trimline phone designed by Henry Dreyfuss and Donald Genaro for Bell Telephone Laboratories (1962–65), and Richard Schultz's Leisure Collection of outdoor furniture (1966). Products such as these shared a rather sober esthetic that resulted from their corporate origins.

In stark stylistic contrast, a small number of American designs reflected the growing influence of Pop culture. These were executed outside the industrial mainstream and included Jack Lenor Larsen's swirling and vibrantly colored Firebird textile (1966), Wendell Castle's Molar sofa (1969), Milton Glaser's Bob Dylan poster (1967), and Wes Wilson's neo-Art Nouveau music posters and flyers, which brought psychedelic art to graphic design and stood in diametric opposition to the modern movement's insistence on universal clarity, white space, and compositional order in graphic design. Although Pop designs such as these never managed to gain a particularly strong foothold in the United States, thanks mainly to the prevailing conservatism of most American companies, these few examples were every bit as progressive as their European counterparts.

Three key designs expressed the cultural changes afoot in the 1960s and early 1970s better than any others. The first was Alec Issigonis's small but perfectly formed Morris "Mini" Mark I (1959), a feat of automotive miniaturization with an ingenious, space-saving transverse engine, a diminutive boxy form, and zippy handling. This was both a trendsetter and the first truly classless car; it could equally have been driven by a housewife, a famous celebrity, or a hip member of the British aristocracy. The second design, the Boeing 747 jetliner (1969), was innovative in its unprecedented scale and passenger-carrying capacity. Nicknamed the "jumbo jet," it could carry two-and-a-

↖
Kar-a-Sutra mobile conversation pit/sleeping area designed by Mario Bellini, 1972.

↗
Ford Mustang fastback, 1965.

→
Plymouth Road Runner "muscle" car, 1968.

Pop design and the counterculture

Design goes Pop

↑
Robert Propst's Action Office II system for
Herman Miller, 1971.

→
Michael Lax's Lytegem for Lightolier, 1964.

Pop design and the counterculture

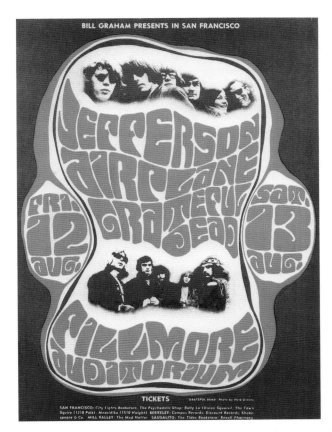

→
Jefferson Airplane/Grateful Dead
concert poster designed by Wes Wilson
and Herb Greene, 1966.

↓
Firebird textile designed by Jack Lenor Larsen,
1966.

Design goes Pop

half times the number of passengers than the earlier Boeing 707, and so had a huge impact in bringing low-cost air travel to the masses in the 1970s. Mass tourism meant true globalization, which helped popular culture to transcend national borders. The third landmark design of the 1960s was perhaps the most crucial of them all: the System/360 computer, introduced by IBM in 1964, was the first family of commercial mainframe computers to use interchangeable software and peripheral equipment. These colossal, whirring machines ushered in a new era: over time, the course of design would be altered and computers would transform everyday experience into an interconnected, 24–7, globalized phenomenon.

↑
Morris "Mini" (Mark I) car designed by Alec Issigonis for British Motor Corporation, 1959.

Pop design and the counterculture

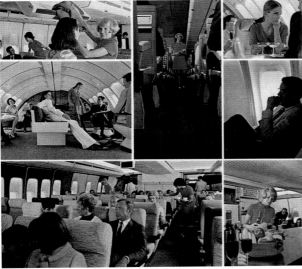

↑
Boeing 747 passenger jet, first flight 1969,
nicknamed the "jumbo jet."

↑
Views of the 747's interiors used in a
Boeing advertisement, 1970s.

→
System/360 mainframe computer
manufactured by IBM, 1964.

Space Age visions and Radical Design

Most of the designs emerging from Italy during the Pop era, which spanned a period of roughly ten years between 1963 and 1973, were highly futuristic, and were directly inspired by the age's cultural fixation on space travel and lunar research. This decade-long obsession began when the Soviet cosmonaut Yuri Gagarin became the first man in space in 1961, which prompted John F. Kennedy's famous "moon speech," given at Rice University in September 1962. The president threw down a formidable design and engineering challenge with the prophetic words:

> We shall send to the moon, 240,000 miles away from the control station in Houston, a giant rocket more than 300 feet tall, the length of this football field, made of new metal alloys, some of which have not yet been invented, capable of standing heat and stresses several times more than have ever been experienced, fitted together with a precision better than the finest watch, carrying all the equipment needed for propulsion, guidance, control, communications, food and survival, on an untried mission, to an unknown celestial body, and then return it safely to earth, re-entering the atmosphere at speeds of over 25,000 miles per hour, causing heat about half that of the temperature of the sun—almost as hot as it is here today—and do all this, and do it right, and do it first before this decade is out.[7]

The space race had accelerated. Naturally, the particular requirements of space travel influenced the work of designers on the National Aeronautics and Space Administration's (NASA) human space-flight program, but the phenomenon also inspired those working in much more (literally) down-to-earth areas. Many designers looked to the future optimistically and created products for a space age in which everything would be shiny, clean, and bright; the visions they conjured offered a much-needed respite from the Vietnam War and other earthbound troubles. The undisputed maestro of such forward-looking design was the Italian architect and designer Joe Colombo, who during his prolific but sadly all-too-short career created a host of designs and environments that captured the utopian aspirations of the late 1960s and early 1970s. His designs were intended for, as he put it, "the environment of the future."[8] Yet despite their visionary, Barbarella-like quality, they also had an underlying Modernist functionality—for instance, his Visiona 1 installation, commissioned by the German chemical and plastics company Bayer as part of the *Interzum* exhibition at the 1969 Cologne Furniture Fair, used a variety of Bayer's plastics to create a range of workably integrated "living units." These included the Central Living Unit (a sofa with integrated storage and table above which a television was suspended); the Night Cell (a capsule with sliding screens and a round bed that also included a practical bathroom unit); and the Kitchen Box (complete with a compact sink, small stove, space-saving cupboard with sliding doors, a handy serving hatch, and a variety modern labor-saving appliances). Colombo explored the idea of

capsule living further for the 1972 MoMA exhibition *Italy: The New Domestic Landscape*, in which he showed the even more integrated Total Furnishing Unit (1971–72), which provided everything needed for a home in a single compact module. On the four sides of a rectangular monobloc unit were: a fully fitted kitchen behind a screen, a living space complete with a drop-down table and an integrated television, a bedroom area with an extendable bed and built-in storage compartments, and a compact bathroom capsule. These designs took Le Corbusier's idea that a house was a machine for living into a new dimension: they were utopian visions made from bright, shiny plastics rather than steel and glass, but they were as rationally conceived as their modernist antecedents.

Bayer was also responsible for another very different, more sculptural vision of a Space Age future through its sponsorship of Verner Panton's Visiona II installation. Positioned onboard a Rhein pleasure cruiser at the 1970 Cologne Furniture Fair, this was a hallucinogenic fantasy of riotous colors and unconventional forms; its series of cave-like rooms furnished with inviting latex-foam-upholstered furniture and sculptural lighting reimagined ways of living. Above all else, Panton wanted the installation to provide an unforgettable sensory stimulus, and each room had, as his wife Marianne Panton observed, its "own sound and color atmosphere, its own smell."[9] This widely publicized display also helped the promotion of Bayer's Dralon, a stretchy, 100 percent polyacryl fabric that would became a ubiquitous feature of 1970s living rooms, showing that avant-garde design often has a trickle-down effect on the mainstream—rather like the influence of haute couture on high-street fashion.

With hindsight it is little wonder that designers looked to space for inspiration when there was so much unrest on Earth. Another outcome of this disenchantment was the rise of Radical Design, which

<table>
<tr><td>

⬉

Visiona I installation at the Cologne Furniture
Fair designed by Joe Colombo for Bayer AG,
1969.

</td><td>

↑

Visiona II installation at the Cologne Furniture
Fair designed by Verner Panton for Bayer AG,
1970.

</td></tr>
</table>

Space Age visions and Radical Design

rejected the precepts of the modern movement and attempted to incorporate political dialogue into the design of objects. The movement gained force and recognition during the late 1960s and early 1970s, thanks to the attention-grabbing activities of various Italian groups, notably Archizoom, Superstudio, UFO, Gruppo Strum, and 9999. These groups contended that modernism was no longer a cultural driving force because industrial interests had contorted its original goals into a consumerist marketing ploy. Rejecting consumerism and advanced technology, Radical Design instead pursued the "design of evasion," which was advocated by Superstudio and others as a means through which to explore the irrational and the poetic and to counter the blandness of products that came from the modern movement's "less is more" doctrine. In the view of Radical Design groups, messy complexity offered far more potential for creative and intellectual engagement, and "negative utopias" such as Archizoom's *No-Stop City* and Superstudio's *Monumento Continuo* (Continuous Monument) architectural projections (both from 1969)

sought to demonstrate that rationalism, taken to its logical conclusion, became absurd. As one of Archizoom's founders, Andrea Branzi, noted, "Criticism of the Modern Movement was also and above all expressed by taking rationalism to an extreme, with the intention of exposing the underlying contradictions of the movement, along with the fragile nature of its apparent unity of research."[10] The Radical Design groups also mocked accepted notions of good taste, and by inference Good Design, by referencing kitsch. Archizoom's faux-leopard-skin Safari seating unit (1968) and its plastic palm-tree-shaped San Remo floor lamp (1968) were perhaps the best examples of this subversive camp tendency.

The aforementioned MoMA exhibition, *Italy: The New Domestic Landscape*, curated by the Argentine architect and industrial designer Emilio Ambasz, exposed the opposing themes running through Italian design and design more generally. Here, engineering-oriented design intended for mass production met semantic counter-design that gleefully announced the demise of modern design. This latter category was itself divided into playful anti-design with a Pop sensibility and its more theoretical, politicized, and experimental cousin, Radical Design. The intellectually contentious work of the Radical Design groups laid the philosophical bases for the Global Tools collective (founded in 1973), as well as for the later Studio Alchimia (1976–91) and Memphis (established 1981) design collectives and, ultimately, for the emergence of postmodernism as an international style in the early 1980s.

↑
No-Stop City architectural projection designed by Archizoom, 1969.

↗
Il Monumento Continuo (The Continuous Monument) dystopian architectural projection designed by Superstudio, 1969.

→
Poltronova publicity photograph of Safari seating unit designed by Archizoom, 1968.

Pop design and the counterculture

Eco-awareness
and product morality

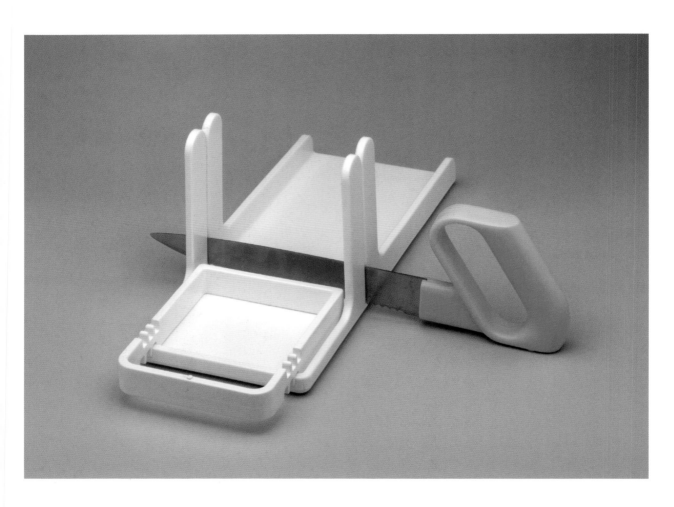

Designers questioning the precepts of modernism had, as we have seen, opened up new creative and intellectual opportunities that were explored largely in Europe from the early 1960s until the early 1970s. But where did this spirit of inquiry come from? The answer can be traced to a seminal book published in 1957, *The Hidden Persuaders*. Written by the American journalist Vance Packard, this damning critique revealed the "hidden" or subliminal techniques of psychological manipulation employed by the advertising industry to encourage consumers to buy products that they often did not need. This book, which went on to sell more than a million copies, bred a growing distrust of modern marketing techniques. It planted in the minds of many consumers the idea that the new car, the updated washing machine, or the colorful box of cereal being cleverly peddled to them might not be what they seemed. As the media studies professor and author Mark Crispin Miller notes of this pioneering publication: "Although it had no obvious political effects (nor did its author call for any), this anomalous exposé encouraged a new mass attentiveness to all of modern marketing, the ads included—a critical alertness, or heightened wariness, that is still perceptible (albeit less prevalent) today."[11]

By exposing the dark arts of the advertising industry, Packard also revealed the darker side of consumer culture, in which advertising executives spun apocryphal tales to help their clients to shift more products. He had exposed the consumerist American Dream for what it really was—a fantasy conjured up in the smoke-filled offices of Madison Avenue ad men—and in so doing fundamentally shifted public opinion, helping to create a countercultural spirit of enquiry.

Perhaps more pertinent to the story of design is Packard's follow-up book, *The Waste Makers* (1960). This work exposed the deeply cynical practice of planned obsolescence, which was employed to fuel consumption and so keep manufacturers in the black—often driving their customers into debt in the process.

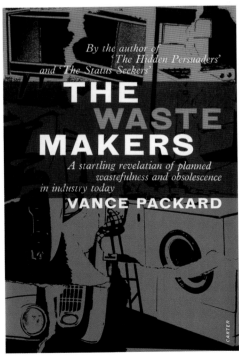

↖
Kitchen knife and cutting board designed by Ergonomidesign (Maria Benktzon and Sven-Eric Juhlin) for RFSU Rehab, 1973, a seminal design for (dis)ability.

↗
Cover of Vance Packard's *The Hidden Persuaders*, 1957.

→
Cover of Vance Packard's *The Waste Makers*, 1960.

This publication charted the rise of American consumer culture and predicted ever-growing numbers of disposable consumer goods in what Packard described as the "Cornucopia City" of the future.[12] It also predicted the dire environmental, financial, and even spiritual consequences of planned obsolescence, and revealed the techniques used by manufacturers and advertisers to convince consumers to buy more, more often. These included the now well-established custom of Detroit car manufacturers annually introducing new models that were updated only in style, as well as more covert practices such as furniture manufacturers setting "death dates" for products by incorporating elements into their construction that were "built to break down within a few years."[13] Packard wrote:

> The pressures to expand production and consumption have forced Americans to create a hyperthyroid economy that can be sustained only by constant stimulation of the people and their leaders to be more prodigal with the nation's resources. This presents us with another specter [. . .] the dangerous decline in the United States of its supply of essential resources [. . .] once fabulously rich in these, the United States is now a have-not nation becoming more so every month.[14]

It is startling that in 1960 American manufacturers were using the lion's share of the world's natural resources—some 50 percent—for the benefit of just 6 percent of the global population. From any angle, consumerism American-style seemed unsustainable, both materially and morally.

Packard's early wake-up call about the evils of planned obsolescence was bolstered by the marine biologist Rachel Carson's bestselling book *Silent Spring* (1962), which highlighted the ecologically devastating consequences for birdlife caused by pesticides, especially DDT (dichlorodiphenyltrichloroethane), which was then widely used as a spray for killing mosquitoes. Bringing a new eco-awareness into public consciousness, *Silent Spring* had an important if indirect influence on design, making designers and consumers alike more aware of mankind's potentially devastating effect on the natural environment.

It was a young Princeton-educated attorney by the name of Ralph Nader who first emphatically stated the ethical issues surrounding design, manufacture, consumer protection, and design safety. His first attack on safety measures in car design and manufacturing appeared in an article, "The Safe Car You Can't Buy," published in the left-leaning *Nation* magazine in 1959. In this early lambast of the automotive industry, he

Pop design and the counterculture

wrote, "It is clear Detroit today is designing automobiles for style, cost, performance and calculated obsolescence, but not—despite the 5,000,000 reported accidents, nearly 40,000 fatalities, 110,000 permanent disabilities and 1,500,000 injuries yearly—for safety."[15] That was the crux of the matter: the automotive giants were more interested in making money than in the safety of their customers.

Nader followed this article up with a carefully researched book on the subject, *Unsafe at Any Speed: The Designed-in Dangers of the American Automobile* (1965). His chief target in this highly influential publication was General Motors's sporty mid-engine Chevrolet Corvair (1960), which, thanks to faulty rear suspension, had a tendency to skid violently and roll over when turning corners. Despite being aware of this inherent flaw, GM launched the car and continued to produce it for four years before making modifications. Nader noted that such corporate negligence was "one of the greatest acts of industrial irresponsibility."[16] In fact, in 1964 GM spent only $1 million—0.05 percent

of its $1.7 billion profit—to fund external automobile-accident research. Nader also showed that the company spent around $700 per car on styling but only a derisory amount on safety features—approximately 23 cents. Also highlighted in the book was the fact that many of the fatalities on America's roads were not the result of poor driving, as the car companies so often inferred, but rather of inherent design and engineering flaws, such as rigid steering columns and instrument-panel hazards. Rather than trying to mend its ways, GM launched a dirty tricks campaign against Nader, which, once exposed, made him a major public figure, a widely recognized "people's champion" and consumer advocate; as a result, his cause achieved far greater publicity. Nader's damning exposé of GM led Congress to pass twenty-five different pieces of consumer legislation between 1966 and 1973 that opened the floodgates for product-liability lawsuits in the United States and in turn made manufacturers far more mindful of safety issues.

Custom Features for the CORVAIR

1960

A New Concept in American Motoring

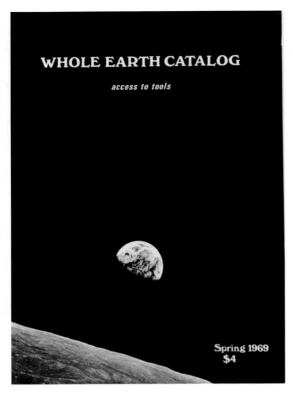

WHOLE EARTH CATALOG

access to tools

Spring 1969
$4

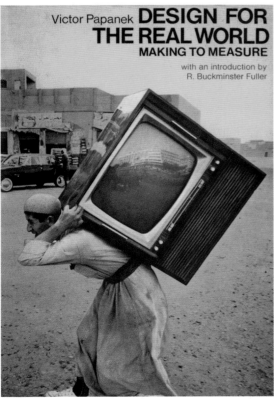

Victor Papanek **DESIGN FOR THE REAL WORLD**
MAKING TO MEASURE

with an introduction by
R. Buckminster Fuller

The 1967 "Summer of Love," which saw the hippie revolution burst onto the streets of the Haight-Ashbury district in San Francisco, made bohemian counterculture a major international force—one that would alter, among other things, ideas about the very purpose of design. The following year, the first *Whole Earth Catalog* was published, curiously subtitled "access to tools," while the cover of its second issue bore the hugely influential "Earthrise" photograph taken from outer space by the astronaut William Anders in 1968 during the *Apollo 8* mission, the first manned voyage to orbit the moon. The *Catalog*'s editor, Stewart Brand, had the right countercultural credentials: he had studied biology at Stanford University then design at San Francisco State College, and had been a willing guinea pig for LSD research held in Menlo Park, near San Francisco. Under his direction, the *Whole Earth Catalog* essentially functioned as an alternative mail-order catalogue. While it did not sell the various goods advertised in its pages, it acted as a conduit between potential customers and suppliers of early ecological designs and other ethically oriented products. Among the items on offer, there was a strong bias towards those that helped achieve a more independently sustainable lifestyle. Crudely printed on pulpy paper, the *Catalog* issues had a wholesome, earthy feel that suited the "tools" they were promoting. Each issue had a different theme; for example, the September 1969 issue included "The Unanimous Declaration of Interdependence," which was based on the idea of "interconnectedness," and also included articles on model communities and low-cost housing solutions. The "tools" changed constantly, ranging from actual implements for jewelry making, enameling, woodwork, and blacksmithing, to books on pressing environmental issues such as population control, to a host of how-to

↖

Cover of the second issue of the *Whole Earth Catalog*, spring 1969.

←

Cover of Victor Papanek's *Design for the Real World: Human Ecology and Social Change*, first published 1971 (UK edition, shown here, bore an altered subtitle).

↗

Geodesic dome structures and "Zomes" in Drop City, near Trinidad, Colorado, founded in 1965.

guides that offered advice on just about everything the average hippie wanted to know, from how to live in a tepee to mushroom-hunting tips. Although many of the designs shown in the *Whole Earth Catalog* were fairly eccentric, its do-it-yourself ethos proved a powerful influence on design practice in the later 1970s, especially in the emergence of the Craft Revival.

Another expression of this DIY spirit was Drop City, founded in 1965. This hippie commune in rural Colorado became famous for its construction of "zomes"—geodesic domes and other habitable structures built along the same geometric lines—which went on to win Richard Buckminster Fuller's Dymaxion award in 1967. In many ways, though, the Drop City experiment in alternative living was indicative of the counterculture movement as a whole: it started out full of youthful "peace-and-love" enthusiasm, but tensions and personal conflicts soon grew between the earnest back-to-nature fraternity and newcomers attracted by its notoriety, who were often more interested in mind-altering substances. Nevertheless, the community reflected the desire of its early participants to create a more ethically sustainable society out of the scraps of a wasteful, consumerist society—metaphorically and quite literally, as some of the zomes' panels were made of metal recycled from old cars.

The same ethical outlook characterized Victor Papanek's seminal book *Design for the Real World: Human Ecology and Social Change*, first published in 1970. Curiously, although Papanek lived and worked as a designer and design educator in the United States, the book first came out in Swedish, and was only made available in English the following year. Nevertheless, it quickly became a bible for designers around the world, especially in Sweden. Calling for moral and social responsibility in design practice, Papanek highlighted numerous "real," non-consumerist issues, from automobile safety and pollution to design for (dis) ability and the Third World. Undoubtedly inspired by Papanek's plea for socially responsible design, two Stockholm-based design groups, A&E Design and Ergonomidesign,[17] began to specialize in the development of innovative, life-enhancing products for people with disabilities, which went on to receive many awards and widespread recognition as real designs for real needs. This reflected the spirit of the day: it had been widely acknowledged that design practice needed to change for the better, and this need became all the more pressing when the global oil crisis of 1973 abruptly burst Pop's bubble. The ensuing economic downturn brought with it a new sense of functional purpose within the international design scene.

High-Tech, Craft Revival, and ergonomics

Rationalism versus craft

In October 1973, members of the Organization of the Petroleum Exporting Countries (OPEC) issued an oil embargo in response to the US government's decision to resupply the Israeli military during the Yom Kippur War; as a result, oil prices quadrupled. Drastically higher oil prices of course made plastic—the favorite material of the previous decade—much more expensive. Beyond that, all manufacturers felt the pressure of higher energy, transportation, and production costs. Most were forced to slash their research-and-development budgets, spelling an end to Pop and unfettered experimentation in product design. As home and export markets contracted and costs soared, conservative, low-risk design became the norm. In furniture design, for instance, bright plastics fell out of favor and were replaced by wood, steel, and glass.

The pervasive conservatism in mainstream design during the mid-to-late 1970s felt, in many ways, like a return to modernism. In fact, in these years there was a general reevaluation on the part of the design cognoscenti of the modern movement's achievements, and modernist design icons such as Marcel Breuer's Wassily chair and Le Corbusier's chaise longue became increasingly common features of interiors. This same back-to-basics mindset also prompted a rather uninspiring form of 1970s rationalism, which was typified by the use of geometric forms and muted earthy tones, all of which were in stark contrast to the exuberant colors and sculptural forms of pre-oil-crisis design. Indeed, within the car industry as well as in the furniture market, most designs looked as though they had been created using a setsquare, and the truth of the matter was that they probably had been. Certainly within automotive design there was an increasing emphasis on masculine boxy forms, which

← Trolley from The Service Range designed by Johan Huldt and Jan Dranger for Innovator Design, c. 1967.

← Previous page: Tizio desk lamp designed by Richard Sapper for Artemide, 1972.

↑ Toyota Corolla advertisement for the American market, 1974.

↑ Willis Faber and Dumas headquarters, Ipswich, England, designed by Norman Foster, built 1971–75.

continued well into the mid-1980s. Another effect of the oil crisis was to prompt American car manufacturers to explore more fuel-efficient "compact" models, although Japanese car manufacturers, who had already positioned themselves in this market with models such as the Toyota Corolla and the Datsun Sunny (both 1966), went on to dominate it, with both of those selling in impressive numbers around the world.

This rationalism in international design also found expression in the industrial-chic aesthetic of the new High-Tech style. The first stirrings of this style had been felt in architecture during the late 1960s, when British architects such as Richard Rogers and Norman Foster were inspired by the problem-solving approach of the design-engineer and futurist philosopher R.

Buckminster Fuller—a relationship of which Foster later noted: "I was privileged to collaborate with Bucky for the last 12 years of his life and this had a profound influence on my own work and thinking. Inevitably, I also gained an insight into his philosophy and achievements."[1] In 1968 Fuller had published *Operating Manual for Spaceship Earth*, a book that in addition to popularizing the term "spaceship earth," raised awareness about the finite nature of fossil fuels. As an early environmentalist, he had also argued that design could be used more mindfully, to devise more eco-efficient solutions. But Fuller was no Luddite: rather, he advocated doing more with less—a classically Modernist ethos that chimed with the financially straitened times brought about by the oil crisis.

↑
Bauhaus textile designed by Collier-Campbell
for Liberty, 1972.

↓
Super Erecta trolley designed by Louis Maslow
for Metro, c. 1970–75.

As Rogers, Foster, and another British architect, Michael Hopkins, incorporated unadorned industrial elements such as exposed steel beams, pipework, and vent shafts into their High-Tech buildings, the style began to find its way into mainstream interior design. Starkly utilitarian equipment and fittings manufactured for use in factories and institutions, such as metal trolleys, rubber flooring, clamp lighting, Metro's Super Erecta shelving units, and Kee Klamp scaffolding poles, all featured in these interiors, which often used bold primary-color schemes in homage to the earlier De Stijl movement. These industrial-furnishing elements had the added benefit of being relatively inexpensive, having been created for high-volume, contract usage; this had a certain appeal in the midst of a recession. As well as "found" elements, the High-Tech interior also frequently featured Rodney Kinsman's Omkstak chair (1971), which became an icon of the time. Also popular in 1970s interiors was Collier-Campbell's Bauhaus textile for Liberty, which reflected the renewed interest in

Omkstak chair designed by Rodney Kinsman
for OMK, 1971.

↖
Hopkins House in Hampstead, London,
designed by Michael and Patty Hopkins, 1976

designs from the modern movement, being itself a colorful reinterpretation of a Bauhaus tapestry.

Around this time there was also an increasing awareness about the role of ethical design in society. This was expressed in the democratic work of the Swedish design duo Johan Huldt and Jan Dranger, who established their own company, Innovator Design, to produce and market their work anonymously in order to counter the cult of designer products. Using tubular metal, sheets of perforated metal, and canvas, Huldt and Dranger developed a range of colorful, inexpensive, and highly practical furnishings—including chairs, tables, trolleys, and shelving—that exemplified Swedish egalitarianism and also signaled a new internationalism in Scandinavian design. Innovator's products were hugely successful throughout the late 1970s and early 1980s, and were even retailed by the likes of Habitat and IKEA. While the roots of Huldt and Dranger's furniture can be found in 1930s Swedish functionalism,

these designs were also quintessentially of the High-Tech school. The style also found fertile ground in the United States, where the well-known interior designers Joseph Paul D'Urso and Ward Bennett incorporated salvaged industrial materials into their interior schemes. In 1978 Joan Kron and Suzanne Slesin published a book on the design phenomenon, *High-Tech: The Industrial Style and Source Book for the Home*, though by this stage the style was already on the wane. Rather than dying out completely, though, it morphed into the short-lived Matte Black style of the late 1970s and early 1980s, which was distinguished by a macho, modernistic aesthetic, as presaged by Richard Sapper's Tizio desk lamp (1972) or seen in the earliest work of Philippe Starck, such as his Mac Gee bookshelf (1979). Like its older brother High-Tech, Matte Black was uncompromisingly industrial.

Paradoxically, while High-Tech was enjoying its brief starring role in international design, a major return to craft in design also occurred during the 1970s. The Craft Revival, as it came to be known, was not only the antithesis of the High-Tech style but also ran counter to the overt consumerism of the previous two decades. Craft revivalists such as John Makepeace in Britain and Wendell Castle in the United States attempted to preserve the craft traditions in wood, which had suffered so much from the dominance of industrial production—though their work, like that of their spiritual predecessor William Morris, was time-consuming to produce and thus expensive. One main reason for the flourishing of the Craft Revival was reduced employment in the design industry as a whole: as companies' research-and-development budgets contracted, so did the number of jobs for professional designers. Even those who did find work saw that the conservative mood of the recession left

←
Mitre armchair designed by John Makepeace, 1978.

↗
Music stand designed by Wendell Castle, 1972.

Rationalism versus craft

little room for creative engagement. As a result, during the 1970s a great number of designers were effectively excluded from industry, by lack of employment or lack of inclination, and many of them embraced the polar opposite of the industrial process: handicraft. With little financial outlay other than the cost of raw materials and an appealingly low-tech, do-it-yourself ethos, the Craft Revival enabled practitioners to reengage with the hands-on process of making, and to make that process a form of creative expression. The movement also reflected a growing eco-awareness, which had first emerged in the previous decade: the environmental impact of individual designer-craftsmen making bespoke objects is, of course, far less than that of industrial manufacturing systems. Perhaps the greatest driver of the Craft Revival, though, was its power to foster emotional connections between objects and users—something that was sorely lacking in the disposable-design gimmickry of the 1960s and the sterile industrial production of the 1970s mainstream.

The social mission of design, as expounded by Victor Papanek in his book *Design for the Real World* (1971), also became a theme of the mid-to-late 1970s, most notably in the increasing use of ergonomics in design practice, with the goal of creating better-performing, safer, and more user-friendly products, especially in the case of equipment destined for the work environment. One of the main drivers for this was President Richard Nixon's establishment in 1970 of the Occupational Safety and Health Administration, whose mission was to "assure safe and healthful working conditions for working men and women by setting standards and by providing training, outreach, education and assistance."[2] Other countries were also creating public bodies to oversee the introduction of health and safety standards around this time, and companies were coming to realize that better-designed workplaces could lead to increased efficiency and productivity. One of the pioneers in this field was the American industrial designer Niels Diffrient. While working in the offices of Henry Dreyfuss, he coauthored the *Humanscale 1/2/3* manual (1974), which became the industrial designer's bible of ergonomic data.[3] It contained three double-sided plastic data tables

relating to the sizes of people, seating considerations, and requirements for the elderly and disabled. The calculation guides also included measurement wheels that could be turned to give precise information on, for instance, the optimum heights for lumbar supports, armrests, tabletops, and so forth, which were determined by the height of the user.

This more scientific understanding of the human form helped designers create products that worked in better harmony with—and were more comfortable for—users. Emilio Ambasz and Giancarlo Piretti's Vertebra chair (1975), for instance, was one of the first office chairs designed from an ergonomic standpoint, and the first to respond automatically to the user's movement, thereby maintaining continuous contact and support. Another early ergonomic office chair was Fred Scott's Supporto (1976–79), manufactured by Hille, which managed to combine comfort based

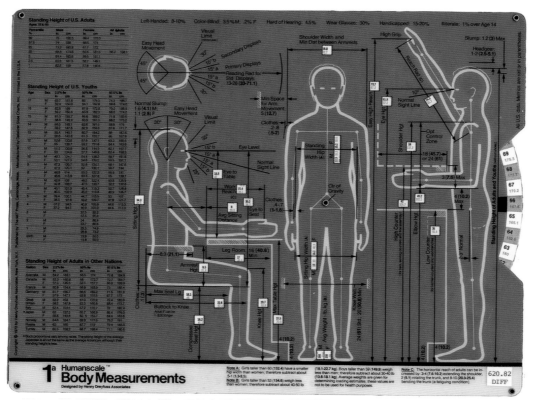

Left-Handed: 8-10%   Color-Blind: 3.5% M; .2% F   Hard of Hearing: 4.5%   Wear Glasses: 30%   Handicapped: 15-20%   Illiterate: 1% over Age 14

1a Humanscale™
Body Measurements
Designed by Henry Dreyfuss Associates

Note A: Girls taller than 60 (152.4) have a smaller hip width than women; therefore subtract about 5-1 (1.3-2.5).
Note B: Girls taller than 53 (134.6) weigh less than women; therefore subtract about 40-50 lb

(18.1-22.7 kg). Boys taller than 59 (149.9) weigh less than men; therefore subtract about 30-40 lb (13.6-18.1 kg). Average weights are given for determining loading estimates; these values are not to be used for health purposes.

Note C: The horizontal reach of adults can be increased by: 3-4 (7.6-10.2) extending the shoulder, 2 (5.1) rotating the trunk, and 8-10 (20.3-25.4) bending the trunk (a fatiguing condition).

620.82 DIFF

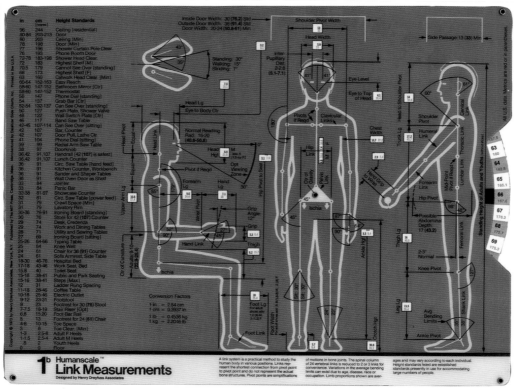

1b Humanscale™
Link Measurements
Designed by Henry Dreyfuss Associates

A link system is a practical method to study the human body in various positions. Links represent the shortest connection from pivot point to pivot point and do not represent the actual bone structures. Pivot points are simplifications of motions in bone joints. The spinal column of 24 vertebral links is reduced to 2 or 3 links for convenience. Variations in the average bending limits can exist due to age, disease, race or occupation. Limb proportions shown are averages and may vary according to each individual. Height standards tested are established standards presently in use for accommodating large numbers of people.

442

on science with stylish, High-Tech good looks: it was a commercially winning combination. Scandinavian designers made some notable contributions to healthy seating design, too, among them the Norwegian Peter Opsvik, who developed the first ergonomic posture chair, the Variable balans (1979) for Stokke, and the Finn Yrjö Kukkapuro, whose Fysio office chair (1978) had a distinctive high back that followed the contours of the user's spine. Ergonomic design clearly had roots in social ideas related to health and inclusivity, but it was also a manifestation of the wider return to rationalism in design. Trimmed of all decoration, these items were pure expressions of function, shaped by data rather than creative intuition. The only drawback was that, for all their enhanced performance, they were rarely what might be considered visually exciting.

←
Niels Diffrient's *Humanscale 1/2/3* manual, designed by Henry Dreyfuss Associates, 1974.

↖
Vertebra office chair designed by Emilio Ambasz and Giancarlo Piretti for Anonima Castelli, 1975.

↑
Supporto office chair designed by Fred Scott for Hille, 1976-79.

Radical Design reemerges

Mainstream design of the mid-to-late 1970s was, on the whole, rather dull, even in Italy: manufacturers produced bland products and consumers bought them. Yet fermenting under the surface was the Italian Radical Design movement, which had emerged during the late 1960s and now had a lot more to rail against, in the midst of such banality in mass-produced objects. The architect, designer, and artist Riccardo Dalisi had already undertaken experiments with *tecnologia povera* (poor technology) in the late 1960s, and had later organized workshops for underprivileged children in the Traiano district of Naples in 1973 in an attempt to bring personal and spontaneous creativity back to design practice. His research inspired the establishment, in January 1973, of a "school" of counter-architecture and counter-design in the editorial offices of *Casabella* magazine in Milan. This new collective, known as Global Tools, was founded by some of Italy's most avant-garde practitioners: Archizoom Associati, Remo Buti, Riccardo Dalisi, Ugo La Pietra, Gruppo 9999, Gaetano Pesce, Gianni Pettena, Ettore Sottsass, Superstudio, Gruppo UFO, and Zziggurat. In the magazine's March 1973 issue, the group defined itself as "a system of workshops for the propagation of the use of natural materials, and the relevant behaviors," and explained that its objective was "to stimulate the free development of individual creativity."[4] Armed with a do-it-yourself ethos and a left-leaning political agenda, Global Tools sought to creatively connect ordinary people with the design process. For its two years of operation, it was the central forum of Radical Design. Its disbanding in 1975 marked the end of Radical Design's first phase in Italy.

←
Casabella cover, January 1973, featuring the members of Global Tools.

↑
Lassù chair designed and symbolically burnt by Alessandro Mendini, 1974.

Paola Navone, and Michele De Lucchi. The studio's name, which alluded to chemistry's pseudo-scientific predecessor, was a jibe at the scientific rationale underlying modernism. It also alluded to alchemy's association with magical transmutation, and the transformation of existing designs became a defining feature of the studio's output. The best-known examples of this approach were Mendini's redesigns of iconic furniture pieces: he decorated Marcel Breuer's Wassily chair with colorful organic forms reminiscent of camouflage; gave Joe Colombo's Universale chair a faux-marble finish; and attached ensigns to Gio Ponti's Superleggera chair in a nod to the traditional fisherman's chair that had inspired it. More famous, though, was Mendini's Proust armchair (1978). Here, an everyday antique-style chair was transformed into an ironic statement by the addition of innovative colors and/or applied motifs. Mendini decorated the armchair in a pointillist style, with multicolored dabs of paint. Studio Alchimia's Bau.Haus 1 and Bau.Haus 2 collections of 1978 and 1979, respectively, pointedly ridiculed what these designers saw as the banality of the prevailing modernist aesthetic. Andrea Branzi explained Studio Alchimia's central—and rather

New mutating shoots of Radical Design had appeared a year before Global Tools broke up, when the designer Alessandro Mendini set fire to two identical archetypal chairs outside the offices of *Casabella*, where he was editor-in-chief. Both chairs bore the name Lassù (Up There), and the act of burning them was intended to blur the boundaries between art and design. Later that same year, another Lassù chair was taken to a quarry and placed on a flight of steps before being engulfed in flames and photographed. This incendiary act was intended to reenact the legend of the phoenix, allowing new designs to rise from the ashes of old.

In 1976, the architect Alessandro Guerriero founded Studio Alchimia, which would become the main champion of this provocative new form of intellectually challenging counter-design, best described as the second phase of Radical Design. Although first intended as a gallery space for exhibiting pieces that were not constrained by industrial mass production, Studio Alchimia soon became an influential studio that produced avant-garde work by designers including Ettore Sottsass, Alessandro Mendini, Andrea Branzi,

pessimistic—premise by stating that "operations of redesign consisted of touching up found objects or famous products of design to illustrate the impossibility of designing something new in respect to what has already been designed."[5] Highly semantic and self-consciously elitist, intellectual, and politicized, Studio Alchimia's facetious, subversive work, and that of the second wave of Radical Design from which it came, paved the way for the emergence of the Memphis design group in the 1980s.

Radical culture was also stirring in Britain, where the deep recession and high unemployment of the 1970s produced a disenfranchised generation that was deeply skeptical of the establishment. Punk was the natural expression of this disaffection, emerging in fashion and music around 1974 and soon making the leap to graphic and product design, in, for example, Jamie Reid's anarchic 1977 cover for the Sex Pistols' *God Save the Queen* and, slightly later, Daniel Weil's *Radio in a Bag* (1981). British interior design, at the time typified by Habitat and its by-then phenomenally successful flat-pack furniture, fluffy duvets, and chicken bricks, also felt the effects of punk, in the anarchic Creative Salvage movement it spawned in around 1981.

↖
Wassily chair redesign by Alessandro Mendini for Studio Alchimia, 1978.

↙
Proust armchair designed by Alessandro Mendini for Studio Alchimia, 1978.

↑
Radio in a Bag designed by Daniel Weil for Parenthesis (UK) and Apex International Company (Japan), 1981.

←
The Sex Pistols' *God Save the Queen* album sleeve, designed by Jamie Reid, 1977.

The electronics age

While mainstream design was, for the most part, not as "happening" in the 1970s as it had been in the previous decade, there was one notable are of exception: consumer electronics. In fact, it could be said that the decade saw a revolution in this manufacturing sector, with Sony launching its first videocassette recorder, or VCR, in 1971, and the Dutch electronics company Philips introducing a competing model the following year. A battle of videotape formats later raged between JVC's VHS and Sony's Betamax from the mid-1970s into the 1980s, with the former famously emerging as the victor. Whichever side consumers chose, during this period they were able, for the first time, to record television programs and watch them at their own convenience. They could also buy or rent videos, meaning their homes were now far more entertaining places. The videocassette recorder, though technically primitive in comparison to today's electronic gadgets and streaming capabilities, was an important first step toward the design of more personalized entertainment-delivery systems.

The year after the VCR was introduced saw—as any gaming enthusiast will know—the launch of the first really successful arcade video game, Pong. Designed by the American games developer Atari, Pong opened the floodgates to a whole new area of design endeavor and birthed an industry that would eventually come to rival the older entertainment markets of film and television. Less well known is that 1972 was also the release year of the first video-game console for the home, the Magnavox Odyssey. The American inventor and engineer Ralph Baer, now widely regarded as the father of video games, was behind this new family of home-electronics products; prototypes had been developed in the late 1960s, and the final working prototype, produced in 1968, was known as the "Brown Box." Magnavox first publicly demonstrated the Odyssey in May 1972 and released it in August of that year, predating Atari's Pong home console by three years. (And as a footnote in gaming history, it should be noted that Pong was actually inspired by the Odyssey's earlier table-tennis game.) The gaming industry truly came of age, though, with the Atari 2600, which was released in 1977 and was the first console that, rather than being programmed with a set number of games, could be used to play an unlimited number of games cartridges.

←
VP-1100 videocassette recorder launched by Sony in 1971.

→
Magnavox publicity photograph for the Odyssey home video-game console, 1972.

↑
Top: Magnavox Odyssey games console
designed by Ralph Baer, released 1972.

↑
Atari 2600 console, released 1977 (this "wood
veneer" version dates from 1980-82).

Rationalism versus craft

←
Early version of Motorola "Brick" DynaTAC
mobile phone designed by Martin Cooper,
c. 1973

↑
First Sony Walkman (TPS-L2),
launched in 1979.

The following year brought the much-played Space Invaders arcade game, and with it a new sophistication in gaming design; when it was released for home use in 1980, it sent sales of the Atari 2600 console rocketing and cemented home gaming as a lucrative market. The development of video games did not stop with the console but involved the design of the games, too; along with other types of software programming, this considerably widened the scope of design practice. Traditionally, designers had created objects; now they also operated in the digital realm and were pioneering the design of interfaces that connected the real and the virtual.

In the early 1970s, Motorola began to experiment with cellular radio technology, and the results of those tests went on to revolutionize communication devices. In 1973 the company tested the first "portable radio phone" in New York. It was a hefty device, though still mobile, known as the DynaTAC. The model was refined and, after gaining approval from the Federal Communications Commission, finally went on sale in 1983. For obvious reasons, it quickly gained the nickname "the brick." Mobile phones were unsuitable for consumer use until after 1978, when the first automated cellular networks were launched, so it was not until the 1980s that the world really began going mobile. The Sony Walkman was also developed in the late 1970s; the first model, the TPS-L2, was released in 1979 and achieved iconic status until the 1980s. It was a key lifestyle product of that decade, despite its rapid battery drainage and limitation to the single function of playing a cassette tape. The mobile phone and the Walkman were pathbreaking in their miniaturization of technology and introduction of two brand-new types of personalized, mobile electronic products to the market. This area of design was soon to have a transformative effect on society and would, of course, eventually lead to the creation of a single device.

19

POST MODERNISM AND INTER NATIONALISM

Memphis and postmodernism

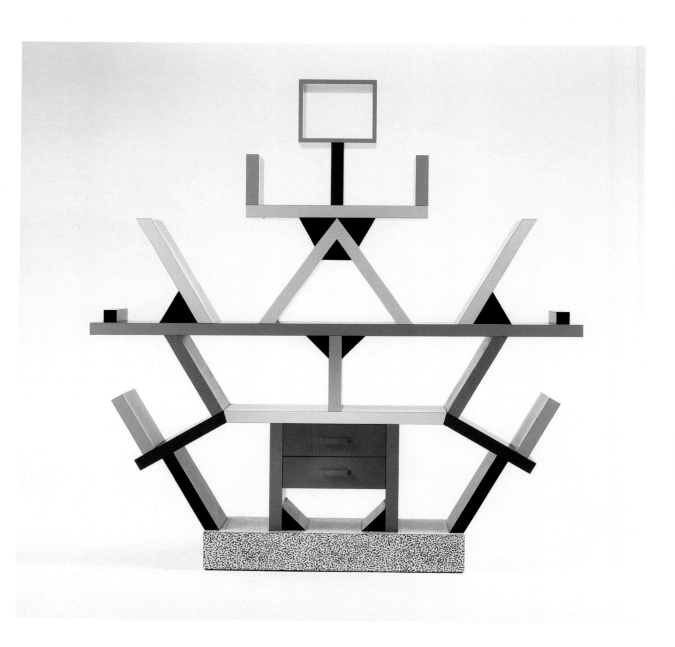

The 1980s was a highly significant decade in the story of design, in which the new international avant-garde style, postmodernism, boosted the profile of the discipline exponentially, and digital tools emerged that would increasingly come to shape it. After the economic woes of the angst-ridden 1970s, it seemed as though a page had been turned to a new chapter of history, giving innovative design an opportunity to flourish once again. A resurgence in right-wing political thinking—as espoused by Britain's first female prime minister, Margaret Thatcher, and her American presidential counterpart, Ronald Reagan—and the changes this brought in its wake, from the privatization of nationalized companies, to the breaking of the unions' grip on industrial production, to the loosening of financial market regulations, saw the global economy finally pull itself out of recession and begin to surge upward.

The go-getting culture of the day brought with it an increase in homeownership and widespread dabbling on the stock market, as well as a renewed feeling of optimism among many people, who felt that a free-market economy would lead to a better future. The paternalism that had so shaped governments' economic policies in the West from the late 1930s to the late 1970s, as advocated by the British economist John Maynard Keynes, had been replaced by a very different doctrine, one radically opposed to interventionist "big government." The new economic mood was inspired by the American economist Milton Friedman's argument that the well-meaning interventionist policies of the US Federal Reserve during the Great Depression had actually made matters worse, and that a laissez-faire approach might have worked much better in lifting America out of its financial malaise. With the world still in the grip of a protracted economic downturn during the late 1970s and early 1980s, both Reagan and Thatcher seized upon Friedman's ideas, believing that the society of free enterprise and lower taxation, less regulation, and restrained public spending that he advocated might be just what was needed to start the economy's cogs turning once again. This message focused on the power of individuals, rather than government or society, to effect change—an empowering theme for young entrepreneurs. The ideas of freedom from intervention and self-motivation advocated during this period lie at the very heart of the American Dream, and in Britain as in America at this time, the message was that hard work, ability, and persistence would be rewarded with social mobility.

So how did this mindset alter design practice? The most notable effect was the more entrepreneurial streak that became increasingly apparent in designers and design companies. Another was that there was far more disposable income floating around for the acquisition of "design," which became a subject of increasing public interest, academic study, and debate. After the relative stasis of design practice in the mid- to late 1970s, during which the Italian Radical Design movement, innovative though it was, remained a minority interest, there came a sudden surge of change as a new wave of avant-garde design broke on the scene in the early 1980s. Such was its effect that the 1980s came to be known as "the designer decade." For the vast majority of people, however, "design" meant "designer labels"; the term was generally used for fashion items such as jeans, sunglasses, sneakers, and even underwear. Some other "lifestyle accessories" were also given this appellation, among them Zippo lighters, Dualit toasters, Bang & Olufsen stereos, and Rolex watches. It was not until

←
Previous page: Tea and Coffee Piazza designed by Aldo Rossi for Alessi, 1983.

←
Carlton bookcase/room divider designed by Ettore Sottsass for Memphis, 1981.

→
Official photograph of the Memphis group in 1981 showing the collective's members relaxing in the Tawaraya boxing ring cum conversation pit designed by Masanori Umeda in 1981.

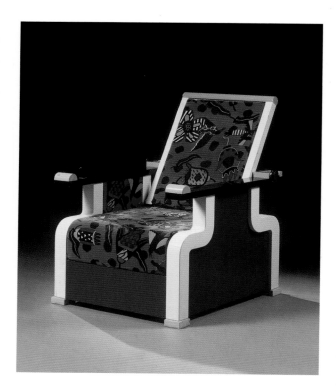

the 1990s that the general public was reminded that "design" was not just a noun but also a verb—that it is a process of problem-solving.

The origins of what was then termed New Wave design, but that also became known as postmodernism, can be traced to December 1980, when Ettore Sottsass hosted an informal gathering of designers at his apartment on Milan's Via San Galdino—an event that would come to be woven into contemporary design lore. At sixty-four years old, Sottsass had already achieved considerable success in industrial design and was an acknowledged leader of the Italian Radical Design movement, but he had no plans to slow down. He invited a number of talented designers, all in their twenties, to discuss his plan to produce a new line of furniture to be executed by his old friend Renzo Brugola, who owned a cabinetmaking workshop in Milan. Even in the early 1980s, the craft skills that had been such an important factor in Italy's postwar economic miracle were still very much in evidence,

and Sottsass had realized that they offered a means of creating innovative design outside mainstream industrial production. Although he had collaborated with Studio Alchimia and contributed his Svincolo floor lamp, among other designs, to its first collection, he found the group's focus on redesign and "banal design" too pessimistic and creatively restrictive. Sottsass had a vision of something far more attuned to the emerging optimism of the 1980s: a sort of neo-Pop that was visually loud and colorful but that, like the work of Studio Alchimia, was infused with layers of symbolism. As the design guru discussed his idea for a line of furniture that he dubbed "The New Design" with his youthful acolytes—Martine Bedin, Aldo Cibic, Michele De Lucchi, Matteo Thun, and Marco Zanini—Bob Dylan's song "Stuck Inside of Mobile with the Memphis Blues Again" played in the background on a record player, repeatedly getting stuck on the words "Memphis blues again." The design writer Barbara Radice, who was present at this rather drunken gathering, recalled that after much discussion about the name of this new furniture collection, "Sottsass said: 'Okay, let's call it Memphis,' and everyone thought it was a great name: Blues, Tennessee, rock'n'roll, American suburbs, and then Egypt, the Pharaohs' capital, the holy city of the god Ptah."[1]

Memphis certainly had the layered meanings Sottsass intended, being both the name of the ancient Egyptian capital of culture and of Elvis Presley's birthplace. It was the perfect moniker for a design collective that relished drawing eclectic inspiration from cultures near and far, high and low. Although no prescriptive directions were given about form, function, materials, style, and so on—that approach being too much like modernism, with all its rigid rules—the designs created had a distinct aesthetic that reflected this taste for sampling and mixing styles from the past and the present in order to create something completely new. This intentionally mischievous practice reflected a more energetic and international outlook. Designers were now also far more self-aware, on the whole, being by this stage well and truly versed in semiotics, the study of language and symbols. Roland Barthes's *Mythologies* (1957) had brought an understanding of the subject to the field, deepened by Umberto Eco's more recent publication, *A Theory of Semiotics* (1976). While Studio Alchimia had sought (and was still seeking) to intellectualize design by introducing semantics, Memphis was far more playful in its use of coded meanings and mixed messages. Above all else, this design collective celebrated the cultural pluralism of postmodernism, and to that end created designs that used eye-catching color combinations, bold totemic forms, and plastic laminates with New Wave style geometric and biomorphic patterning.

This was postmodern design at its loudest and most attention-seeking. Memphis made a startling impact with its provocative debut at the 1981 Salone del Mobile (Milan Furniture Fair). It was a riotous design circus, with the enigmatic Ettore Sottsass taking the role of ringmaster to the youthful band of design renegades. They included not only the designers who had been present at that legendary soirée in December 1980 but also an assortment of foreign practitioners, notably George Sowden, Nathalie Du Pasquier, Javier Mariscal, and Masanori Umeda; over the coming years they would be joined by Hans Hollein, Shiro Kuramata, Peter Shire, Michael Graves, and others. Being extremely media-savvy, Memphis did what no anti-design group had successfully done before: it popularized postmodernist theory by repackaging it, as the design critic Alice Rawsthorn puts it, into "a fun, seductive form that millions understood."[2] The language of postmodern design they introduced was exuberantly playful, capturing the optimism gradually emerging in the early 1980s as the world's economy started to emerge from recession. Memphis designs stood out in a sea of uninspiring furniture at the Salone del Mobile and captivated the international design press, which helped

the group disseminate their message around the world. The diverse nationalities of Memphis members also ushered in a new internationalism that would become a marked feature of design's evolution in the coming years. Memphis's multicultural picking and mixing of references also anticipated the increasing globalization that occurred in the 1980s, the decade in which not just mass travel but also mass emigration created cultures of ethnic diversity worldwide, as so famously celebrated by the art director Oliviero Toscani's United Colors of Benetton campaign during this period. In parallel, the shrinking of the world through the increasingly global reach of the media—catalyzed by the launches of CNN and MTV in 1980 and 1981, respectively—saw design communities in various palces become increasingly aware of one anothers' work. This cross-pollination of ideas contributed to a growing understanding and acceptance of postmodernism throughout the international design community.

↖
Mamounia armchair designed by George Sowden, 1985, upholstered with textile designed by Nathalie Du Pasquier.

→
Secret Springs table designed by Peter Shire, c. 1984, epitomizing "California New Wave" design.

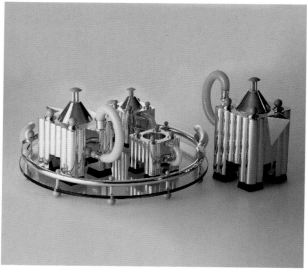

Top: Tea and Coffee Piazza designed by
Charles Jencks for Alessi, 1983.

↑

Tea and Coffee Piazza designed by Michael
Graves for Alessi, 1983.

↗

9093 kettle designed by Michael Graves for
Alessi, 1985.

In America postmodernism found expression in the tongue-in-cheek classicizing designs of Michael Graves, Charles Jencks, and Robert Venturi, the playful "California New Wave" furnishings of Peter Shire, and the quirky buildings and chairs of Frank Gehry. Graves's bird-whistle kettle for Alessi became an icon of the brash new style. Alessi also helped the style coalesce into an international design movement with its Tea and Coffee Piazza project, for which the leading avant-garde designers and architects of the day—including Italian designers such as Sottsass and Aldo Rossi as well as international names including Graves and Venturi — designed innovative silver tea and coffee services that had a distinctive architectonic, postmodern flavor. The project ran from 1979 until 1983, and like Memphis, Alessi was able to rely on traditionally skilled craftsmen to execute the impressive body of work. These pieces transformed the humble tools of tea- and coffee-making into totemic symbols of the postmodern style; Rossi's contribution was enclosed in a temple-like glass case complete with a classical pediment and jaunty little flag. These designs and those produced by Memphis might have relied on craft skills, but they did not have an overt craft aesthetic, possessing instead the type of precision finish generally associated with machine production. In other words, whereas at the beginning of the industrial revolution the machine was used to mimic handcraft, these designs relied on craftsmanship to create the illusion of machine production, rather like the early designs coming out of the Dessau Bauhaus that speculated on standardized mass production. This type of postmodernism was less concerned with functional considerations than with design as a rhetorical statement. The huge public-relations success of Alessi's Tea and Coffee Piazza made the company more conscious of the nationalities of the designers it commissioned, as well as of the overseas markets that it began to pursue.

Seeing that commissioning work from leading postmodernist designers and architects was an efficient way of attracting publicity and raising one's avant-garde credentials with relatively little outlay, other established companies followed suit. The American furniture manufacturer Knoll International produced a product line designed by Robert Venturi and his wife

and partner Denise Scott Brown. With his famous quip "Less is a bore"—a take on Mies van der Rohe—Venturi was one of the earliest and most important proponents of postmodernism. His seminal book *Learning from Las Vegas: The Forgotten Symbolism of Architectural Form* (1972), cowritten with Scott Brown and Steven Izenour, had become required reading for architects and designers, not least for controversially lauding the garish cultural honesty of the Las Vegas Strip and exploring the idea of architecture as symbol. Putting theory into practice, the Venturi Collection (completed 1984) for Knoll comprised nine chairs, a sofa, and various tables that irreverently referenced American

and European furniture history. These simplifications of clichéd forms caricatured historic decorative styles, and in so doing called into question the intellectualized veneration that surrounded them.

Japan, too, saw a blossoming of postmodernism, or as Ettore Sottsass had termed it, the "New International Style"; it was notable in the work of Shiro Kuramata, Arata Isozaki, and Masanori Umeda—all of whom contributed designs to the Memphis lines—and of Toshiyuki Kita, who created the very postmodern Wink sofa (1980) for Cassina. Kuramata, one of the most influential Japanese designers of the twentieth century, took

postmodernism to a new level of refinement and symbolism. His work suffused a minimalist aesthetic with poetic emotion to create objects of rare and ethereal beauty. The Miss Blanche chair from 1988 might best exemplify his alchemical use of synthetic polymers to create otherworldly designs that bridged Eastern traditions and the emerging postmodern design ethos. To understand Kuramata's work, one must appreciate the spatial tension he created between object and environment, in which his "dematerialized" designs often appeared to float lightly in a space. The Miss Blanche chair was named after Blanche DuBois in Tennessee Williams's *A Streetcar Named Desire*, and the designer's use of falling red roses was inspired by a corsage worn by Vivien Leigh in the play's 1951 film adaptation. Like other creations by Kuramata, this evocative design had extraordinary sensory and spatial qualities, and demonstrated that an object could transcend function altogether. Being produced as exclusive limited editions, rather like artworks, the work also transcended the divide between art and design. Thus Kuramata's work revealed, in a very postmodern way, that the primary function of a specific design might have nothing to do with its physical requirements but might rather fulfill metaphysical ones.

↑
Queen Anne chair designed by Robert Venturi and Denise Scott Brown for Knoll International, 1984.

→
Miss Blanche chair designed by Shiro Kuramata for the Ishimaru Company, 1988.

Memphis and postmodernism

The Creative Salvage movement

Another expression of postmodernism that emerged in London during the early 1980s, and that was far more rough-and-ready than the beautifully crafted work produced by Memphis and Alessi and the ethereal designs of Shiro Kuramata, was the Creative Salvage movement. Like its kindred spirit Punk, Creative Salvage had an anarchic aesthetic and an anti-mainstream agenda. The origins of the movement go back to London's club scene of the early 1980s, when design-renegades Tom Dixon, Mark Brazier-Jones, and Nick Jones would wow audiences with onstage performance welding. This youthful group held their first show of assemblages made from scrap in 1983. For this event they wrote a manifesto, which stated:

> We are convinced the way ahead does not lie in expensive, anonymous, mass-produced high-tech products but in a more decorative, human approach to industrial and interior design. The key to Creative Salvage's success is not in the expensive research and development costs of modern-day products, but in the recycling of scrap to form stylish and functional artifacts for the home and office.[3]

A year later a second sold-out Creative Salvage show was staged that also included the work of the French designer André Dubreuil. Liliane Fawcett, a London-based gallery owner, recalls: "It was completely different. There was nothing that could compare to it, only punk fashion. The first feeling you had was that it was an impulse of energy. Everything else in London was kind of dreary in comparison."[4] Meanwhile, the architect Ron Arad had also begun to experiment with similar "ready-made" designs assembled from "found" objects, and in 1981 he established his own furniture

making company, One Off, with his business partner, Caroline Thorman. Two years later, he opened a gallery-cum-studio in Covent Garden to show his own work and that of other up-and-coming avant-garde creatives, such as the glass designer Danny Lane. One of Arad's earliest designs was his well-known Rover chair (1981), which ingeniously used an old Rover 200 car seat bought from a scrapyard, mounted on the Kee Klamp scaffolding elements that had been such a feature of High-Tech interiors. Meanwhile, his record player cast in concrete (1983) resoundingly expressed, as the Design Museum in London puts it, "London's early 1980s spirit of rugged individualism and post-punk nihilism set against a backdrop of urban blight."[5] As part of the wider postmodern movement, Creative Salvage helped to revolutionize design in much the same way that Punk changed music and fashion. Also, it was significant to the subsequent development of avant-garde design because it helped to break down traditional barriers between art, craft, and design.

←
Concrete Stereo designed by Ron Arad for
One Off, 1983.

→
Lyre chair designed by Mark
Brazier-Jones, 1980.

S chair designed by Tom Dixon, 1988, produced by Cappellini from 1991.

As outsiders to the design establishment, those associated with the Creative Salvage movement championed both a new way of making design and a new raw aesthetic. Traditional textures, materials, and functionality were all rejected in favor of rough metal, salvaged scrap, and sculptural forms. As the 1980s progressed, though, the assemblages of Ron Arad and Tom Dixon became increasingly refined, and by the end of the 1980s and the early 1990s these two prodigiously talented designers were beginning to have their work produced by established manufacturing companies, notably the Well Tempered chair for Vitra Editions (1986) and the S chair (1988) for Cappellini, respectively. Their hands-on approach had given these young designers an understanding of materials and processes that would have a major bearing on their later, more mature work.

A similarly raw, experimental, postmodern approach was found in the work of the graphic designer and typographer Neville Brody, who was art director of *The Face* magazine from 1981 until 1986 and also created various album covers that epitomized New Wave graphics. The art director Terry Jones launched *i-D*

FASHION MAGAZINE Nº1 50p

i-D

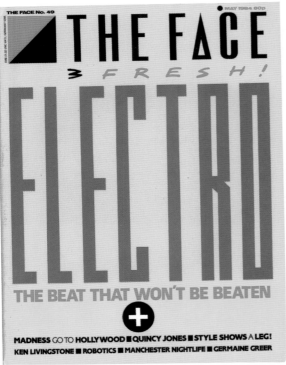

magazine in 1980, and the cover he designed for its first issue, which turned the magazine's name into a pink-on-black emoticon, aligned the publication with a do-it-yourself, postmodern aesthetic that cheekily countered the slick perfection of mainstream graphic design. In America, a similar trashing of modernism's typographic rules was found in the layouts designed by David Carson for *TransWorld SKATEboarding* magazine during the mid-1980s. This brash, liberated graphic style captured contemporary youth culture's creative vibrancy and ran roughshod over the staid aesthetic refinement of modernism.

↑
Cover of the first issue of *i-D* magazine designed by Terry Jones, 1980.

←
Electro issue of *The Face* magazine designed by Neville Brody, 1984.

Philippe Starck and designer hotels

↑
Lobby of the Royalton Hotel, New York
designed by Philippe Starck, 1988.

→
Juicy Salif citrus press designed by
Philippe Starck for Alessi, 1990.

Postmodernism and internationalism

Postmodernism also evolved and mutated into what is best described as the Late Modern style in France during the 1980s, with the work of Philippe Starck, who was not only a prodigious design talent but also a skilled showman. Starck understood the emotional pull of objects with character. His earliest designs, such as the Sarapis bar stool (1985), were in the Matte Black style—a short-lived neo-modernistic mode of the early 1980s that had a hard-edged, masculine sensibility.[6] But his work soon became more playful and colorful in an approach characterized by the skillful reinterpretation of past styles or forms taken out of context. Starck ingeniously used the names of his designs to inject a sense of personality, as, for example, with his Doctor Sonderbar chair (1983) and his Lola Mundo chair (1988). Working with an array of manufacturers, including XO, Driade, and Alessi, he worked his magic on all kinds of objects, from the humble toothbrush to—perhaps most famously—the citrus press (1990). Manufacturers were soon clamoring to collaborate with him, thanks to his commercial track record and high-profile name: the label "Designed by Starck" almost guaranteed success, and even association with him raised a company's profile. Throughout this extraordinarily prolific period, Starck consistently created work that was functionally innovative and that frequently raised its Late Modern qualities to a poetic level.

Starck was also largely responsible for popularizing another manifestation of design, the boutique hotel. These hotels were (and still are) theatrically contrived spaces intended to exude a sense of exclusive, "designed" luxury. The concept was the brainchild of Ian Schrager and Steve Rubell, both of whom had found success and notoriety as the impresarios of New York's infamous Studio 54 nightclub in the late 1970s. Tapping into the emerging "lifestyle" market, the pair first commissioned the French designer Andrée Putman to remodel the Morgans Hotel in Manhattan; this first "design" hotel offered a more intimate and atmospheric experience than the large chains or the stuffy, historic landmark hotels that every city boasts. It was, however, Starck's 1988 redesign of the Royalton Hotel in New York that really popularized the phenomenon. This over-the-top *Gesamtkunstwerk,* skilfully fitted into an awkward long and narrow site, was a thoroughly Late Modern exercise in architectural space as a dramatic stage for experience rather than around functional concerns. Described by the journalist Fred A. Bernstein as "Philippe Starck's Miracle on 44th Street,"[7] the Royalton boasted one of the iconic interior schemes of the period and helped popularize the idea of the designer lifestyle that became a potent theme during the following decade. Although this hip hotel, with all its luxurious accoutrements, might have seemed very different from the previous decades' earnest efforts to promote Good Design, it was responsible for bringing the idea of design as lifestyle into the public consciousness. It also stimulated a feeding frenzy during the 1990s, as people who had enjoyed the stylish delights of designer hotels—or who watched the surfeit of "makeover" interior design programs then popular on television—strove to replicate the "designer hotel look" in their own homes.

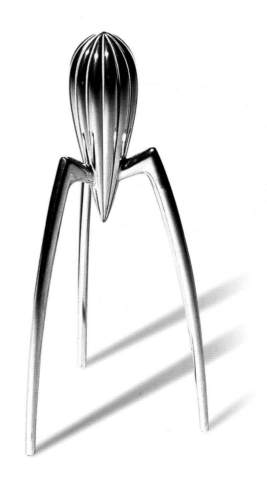

The computer design revolution
and the rise of the brand

↑
Publicity photo for the Apple Macintosh 128k
desktop computer, 1984.

→
Macintosh's revolutionary graphical interface
(including the trash can, the bomb, the smiling
monitor) devised by Susan Kare for Apple,
c. 1983–84.

Despite the opulence of the Royalton Hotel and similar new ventures, all was not well in the financial markets of the late 1980s. The Dow Jones Industrial Average collapsed on October 9, 1987 (Black Monday), and though the economy seemed to rally at first thanks to continuing consumer spending fueled by easy credit, these trends proved insufficient. By 1989 economic growth had stalled. A year later, another spike in oil prices, among other factors, finally turned boom to bust. Although the financial contraction of the early 1990s only lasted about four years, the economic downturn that saw property markets collapse from London to Tokyo was steep. And yet even while the markets crashed, a computer design revolution was taking place that would reinvigorate the economy and—more than that—transform society as it was known. The digital era had truly begun in January 1984 with the release of the original Apple Macintosh desktop computer, conceived by a youthful Steve Jobs as a $500 product. Despite eventually having a price tag about five times that amount, the Apple Mac was a game-changing machine that marked the real breakthrough in personal computing. Launched with the tagline "Insanely great!" and then cleverly marketed as "the computer for the rest of us,"[8] this beige-box design boasted a high-definition screen and easy-to-use mouse, and was the first affordable computer to have a graphical user interface—allowing users to interact with it using images rather than text commands—which made it much easier to operate than previous models. The icons of the Mac's revolutionary graphical interface—the trashcan, the bomb, the smiling monitor, and so on—were devised by one of the great unsung design heroes of the computer revolution, Susan Kare, who, in the words of science reporter Steve Silberman, "gave computing a human face."[9] With these icons Kare created skeuomorphic representations of real-world objects to make the commands familiar and easy to understand—a huge accomplishment given that earlier computers had used off-putting command lines, expecting users to insert text instructions. Kare was also one of the pioneers of digital fonts, notably creating some of the original Macintosh "city" fonts such as Athens, New York, Monaco, San Francisco, Geneva, and Cairo.

The personal computer also began to replace designers' and engineers' centuries-old drafting and modeling with two-dimensional, vector-based drafting systems and three-dimensional solid- and

Snow White +
the Seven Pixels

Seating is limited, so

Reception following the lecture
in the Decker Gallery

Mount Royal Avenue + Cathedral Street
Mount Royal Station Auditorium
College of Art

Visual Presentation
8:00 pm
Thursday, November 6
1986

Designer-In-Residence Program

An evening with April Greiman
presented as part of The Art Litho

surface-modeling software programs. Although computer-aided design (CAD) was first developed at the Massachusetts Institute of Technology (MIT) in the 1950s, its use in that era of colossal mainframe computers was limited to the aerospace and automotive industries. As hardware became less expensive, as well as increasingly powerful in terms of memory and processing speed, CAD began to gain a foothold in the design community. It was not until affordable desktop computers became available during the late 1980s and early 1990s, however, that CAD systems came into serious use in design offices. These early systems helped to revolutionize design practice in that they dramatically reduced the time required from initial concept to working prototype, especially when

combined with computer-aided manufacture (CAM) programs. This made the design process more efficient, and it enabled manufacturers to get new designs to market more quickly and less expensibely. CAD/CAM programs also helped to ensure better standardization of components while permitting greater flexibility in the manufacturing process, enabling lower-volume and customized, batch-type production, too.

↑
Snow White + the Seven Pixels poster designed April Greiman for the Maryland Institute College of Art, 1986.

↗
Cover of the first issue of *Emigre* magazine, designed by Rudy VanderLans and Zuzana Licko, 1984.

As the Berlin Wall was dismantled piece by piece by euphoric crowds of demonstrators in November 1989, a new world order began to take shape. The collapse of this bleak, concrete, barbed-wire-topped structure, which had physically as well as symbolically separated the capitalist West from the Soviet East since 1961, marked a dramatic thawing of the Cold War and its ever-present nuclear threat. In the shadow of this momentous event, other nations across Eastern Europe that had been part of the Soviet Bloc for decades also began to regain their independence, through wave upon wave of public uprisings. As the Soviet Union crumbled state by state, a new feeling of internationalism was born; no longer were vast areas of Europe out of bounds depending on whether you came from the East or the West. In the year the Berlin Wall fell, the British computer scientist Tim Berners-Lee—who was working at the CERN particle-physics lab in Geneva—began a project with his colleague Robert Cailliau that would have a similarly transformative effect, making the world an altogether more interconnected place. He created a new computer language—Hypertext Transfer Protocol (HTTP)—that enabled documents to be communicated over the Internet, which was then just beginning to emerge as a commercial service, having first been developed as a network of supercomputer networks based in government-research and educational organizations. Berners-Lee's hypertext system allowed different operating systems to run across the Internet, which gave rise to the World Wide Web. The full implications of this development would not be felt for several years, but when they were, the impact on society and, indeed, design practice was as great as that of Johannes Gutenberg's printing press in the fifteenth century—or arguably even greater.

← Previous page: Map of all Internet connections on the World Wide Web for a single day (November 3, 2003), generated by The Opte Project, 2003.

← HyperText system using typed links developed by Tim Berners-Lee and Robert Cailliau for use on the World Wide Web, which debuted on August 6, 1991.

Meanwhile, the adoption of free-market economic policies around the world made for an increasingly global economy, in which design played an ever-larger part. Manufacturers in industrialized countries began to recognize and increasingly to implement design as an important part of their business strategies. Even the People's Republic of China had begun to adopt free-market reforms in the late 1970s, under the leadership of Deng Xiaoping, who pragmatically noted, "It doesn't matter whether a cat is white or black, as long as it catches mice."[1] While China geared up industrially, companies in the West came to realize that innovative design could help them capture the attention of international audiences and carve out market share. The designs produced by large international companies—from personal electronics and kitchen equipment to shoes and cars—were at this time beginning to forge a global material culture in which traditional national characteristics were diminished and leading designers were ever more nomadic. The British designer Michael Young, for instance, moved from London to Brussels to Reykjavik to Hong Kong during this period, working for companies all over the world. Similarly, art and design colleges in the United Kingdom and elsewhere began accepting greater numbers of foreign students, which meant that the pool of talent they were selecting from was much more diverse. This accelerated the cross-pollination of ideas and, simultaneously, led to the creation of increasingly specialized centers of excellence. A still greater stimulus for the exchange of ideas, including those pertaining to design, was provided by the Internet, which fulfilled Marshall McLuhan's vision from the 1960s of the world as a "global village." Expanded in 1994 to include more users outside of government and academic networks, the Internet went from having 16 million users in December 1995—the first year of significant uptake—to 361 million users five years later; the number grew to some 2 billion by 2010 to over 3 billion by 2015.[2] As of this writing, in 2016, over 46 percent of the global population is now connected to the Web, and the number continues to grow.

The Internet facilitated the promotion of design on a number of levels: it allowed companies to market their products to a global audience easily, cheaply, and effectively, and it allowed customers to make purchases

↑ GALLERIES
↑ DESIGN MUSEUM SPACE

London, who were benefiting from what is best described as the "Starck Effect." This handful of youthful creatives, who would become the next generation's international design superstars, included Ron Arad, Jasper Morrison, Ross Lovegrove, Marc Newson, and Tom Dixon. Each had a signature approach to problem-solving: Arad and Dixon both came out of the Creative Salvage movement, and so approached their work from a hands-on, craft perspective; Newson worked within a space age aesthetic; Lovegrove developed an essentialist, organic design vocabulary; and Morrison was recognizable for his pared-down, functionalist methodology. These "outliers" in the design world started their careers at exactly the right time and in exactly the right place. They were part of the first generation of designers to benefit from the computer-design revolution, and as the recession of the early 1990s began to lift, they also enjoyed a huge creative revival in London thanks in part to the formation of the London Institute—later the University of the Arts London—in 1986.[3] The institute made London the world center of excellence in design teaching, a position it still holds to this day.

Another important moment in London's development as a major design hub was the opening of the Design Museum—the world's first museum devoted to the promotion and examination of design—in Butler's Wharf in 1989. Arad, Dixon, Lovegrove, Morrison, and Newson soon were winning commissions to create innovative products for companies around the world. Many of these firms had previously collaborated with Philippe Starck and realized the publicity and commercial benefits of working with high-profile practitioners. As the stakes of design for industrial production escalated, and large investment at the front end became more and more necessary, many companies came to value these designers for their boundary-pushing work and their distinctive design vocabularies, which ensured that their work stood out in an ever-expanding array of products that often possessed very similar technical and functional attributes.

designs online rather than having to go to a store or gallery. Most of all, though, it dissolved time and distance: a design launched in Milan, Tokyo, London, or San Francisco, for example, could be viewed around the world in minutes. This democratization of knowledge made developments in the field more accessible to the general public, and contributed to the interconnectedness of the global design community. The Internet also significantly accelerated the convergence of the creative disciplines, and art, music, fashion, and film were soon interwoven in both two-dimensional and three-dimensional design practice, each discipline feeding and being fed by the others.

Just prior to this digital revolution, in the early 1990s, the profile of contemporary design enjoyed a significant boost thanks a new crop of highly accomplished, media-savvy designers based in

↑
Basic thermal carafe designed by Ross
Lovegrove and Julian Brown for Alfi, 1988–90.

←
Design Museum in Butler's Wharf, London,
opened in 1989 as the world's first institution
of its kind.

↑
Bookworm shelving designed by Ron Arad
for Kartell, 1994.

↓
City Storm urban bike designed by Michael Young
for Giant, 2006. Young was a British designer working
in Hong Kong for a Taiwanese manufacturer.

The rise of global design superstardom

Tolemeo task lamp designed by Michele De Lucchi for Artemide, 1986—a universal solution that became a global winner in the 1990s.

Universal solutions versus creative individuality

The Apple factor and Smart Design

The hothouse design scene in London during the early 1990s was formative for many emerging talents, among them Jonathan Ive. Some ten years younger than Tom Dixon, Ross Lovegrove, and Jasper Morrison, Ive belonged to a different generation—Generation X rather than the baby boom—which meant that he was more cognizant of the needs and desires of a cohort weaned on MTV. Recalling his time at Newcastle Polytechnic, Ive noted: "One of the things that was interesting about my time at the school of art and design is that you were in very close proximity to graphic designers, fashion designers, and fine art students. That's one of the things that really characterized my time at college and I think it characterizes a lot of the energy and vitality in London, this density of such creative diversity."[4] After moving to London, Ive worked at the Tangerine agency and began to absorb the city's design mood, which was then defined by a light, transparent aesthetic, thanks to the widespread use of technopolymers and a certain sculptural confidence. Lovegrove was at the forefront of this essentialist movement; his Basic thermal flask for Alfi (1988–90) typified the approach. Meanwhile, Ive was asked to develop a laptop for Apple while still at Tangerine; in 1992 he moved to Palo Alto to join the company's design department. Following Steve Jobs's return to Apple in 1996, Ive and the team began work on the design for a new computer that was a huge gamble for the troubled company. Barely eighteen months later, the revolutionary iMac (1998) was launched. As is now well known, the "i" for "Internet" meant that this machine was intended more as a portal for Web-browsing than as a traditional computing device.

Ken Segall, the Los Angeles–based ad man who came up with the name, recalls that the "i" also stood for "individuality" and "innovation"—both qualities that this design helped to introduce to personal computing. Jobs's introduction at the launch event summed it up: "It looks like it's from another planet, a good planet, a planet with better designers"[5]; for once this was more than mere marketing hype, and Jobs was correct in his assessment that the iMac marked a paradigm shift. Previously, computer housings had been box-like, in either matte beige or pale gray thermoplastic that became grubby after only a few months of use. In contrast, the sleek yet friendly iMac, with its bright color combination of gleaming white and translucent "Bondi Blue" polycarbonate, had a visual freshness that set it apart from all other personal computers. Ive had taken the language of organic essentialism a step further in this landmark design, in which he also achieved a remarkable level of functional clarity: once unboxed, the computer could be set up and used intuitively. The success of the all-in-one iMac and its famous tagline—"Chic. Not geek."—reversed Apple's

← iMac personal computer designed by Jonathan Ive and the Apple Design Team, 1998.

→ Apple publicity photograph showing Steve Jobs with an iMac, c. 1998.

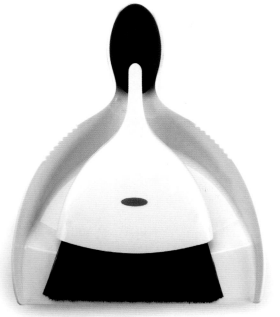

↑↘
Good Grips household brushes and dustpan
made by Smart Design for OXO, 2004.

↗
Photograph showing the development of Good
Grips vegetable peeler made by Smart Design,
1990.

Universal solutions versus creative individuality

decline and expedited the departure of the dull, lifeless box from the computer industry as a whole. Above all, the iMac showed that a little more investment in design and development, and a fraction more in materials and manufacturing, could help manufacturers create premium products with emotive appeal: once the emotional connection had been forged between an iMac and its user, the latter was far more likely to buy other Apple products, which would proliferate in the following decades.

While Apple was revolutionizing the computer market—and, later, the markets for portable media players and smartphones—with Jonathan Ive at the helm of the design team in Palo Alto, over in New York, the Smart Design consultancy was quietly starting it own revolution in the realm of housewares, with its Good Grips range for OXO. This extensive line of kitchen tools, which includes numerous easy-to-use products, from vegetable peelers to dustpans and brushes, was the brainchild of Sam Farber. A veteran of the kitchenware business, Farber was motivated by a paper written by the home economist Mary Reader for the *Journal of the Institute of Home Economics* in which she called for the development of "intergenerational" kitchen products that could be used by people suffering from arthritis. As Farber's wife Betsey suffered from this condition, he knew firsthand how difficult and painful it could be to use a standard peeler with arthritic hands. Farber subsequently tasked Smart Design with creating a range of tools aimed not specifically at disability but at inclusivity—products that could be used by a wide range of users with varying degrees of physical ability. The Good Grips line, featuring ergonomically contoured elastomer handles, was introduced in 1990 and extended over the 1990s and 2000s to comprise hundreds of products. Like Apple's designs, these kitchen items exemplified the criteria of Good Design: both Ive's designs for Apple and Smart Design's work for OXO were guided by the goal of creating the best possible interface between object and user. And while the resulting products were slightly more expensive than others in their market, their enhanced user experience more than made up for the additional cost. Buyers of Good Grips designs, as of iMacs, tended to be so impressed that they went on to buy other products from the company. As a result, both firms grew exponentially in comparison to their competitors, offering conclusive proof that Good Design can make good business sense.

New Dutch Design

While Cool Britannia was enjoying its design pre-eminence and Apple was making waves globally, another strand of avant-garde design began to emerge in the Netherlands. Like Britain, the Netherlands boasted a number of world-class design-teaching institutions that gained particular attention around the turn of the millennium, including the renowned Design Academy Eindhoven (DAE), among the alumni of which were the pioneers of New Dutch Design. Notable members of this group were Maarten Baas, Tord Boontje, Jurgen Bey, Hella Jongerius, Bertjan Pot, and the movement's enfant terrible, Marcel Wanders. Another factor behind this revival in the Netherlands was the 1988 launch of the Fonds BKVB (Foundation for Visual Arts, Design, and Architecture), which provided financial support to students to help them establish themselves as independent design entrepreneurs; the initiative was instrumental in the success of two firms that were key to New Dutch Design: Droog and Moooi. The product designer Gijs Bakker and the design historian Renny Ramakers officially established the former in 1993; the same year Droog showed its first product line—which included Tejo Remy's Chest of Drawers (1991), Rody Graumans's 85 Bulbs chandelier (1993), and Marcel Wanders's Set Up Shades floor light (1989)—at the Milan Furniture Fair. The Dutch word droog means "dry," as in humor, and was chosen by the firm's founders as it perfectly described these sober yet quirky designs made from found objects—old drawers, lightbulbs, and lampshades skillfully reconfigured into eye-catching pieces. Functioning as a curatorial creative agency, Droog pioneered a somber, minimalistic form of late modernism that was utterly at odds with the colorful neo-Pop gaiety of mid-1980s postmodernism à la Memphis. Where Memphis's overblown designs had a strong sense of self-parody, Droog's pieces functioned more as cultural commentary. They were also far more visually restrained and conceptual, the constructions often remarkable for their simplicity and ingenuity. Droog subsequently licensed the manufacture and marketing of its designs to the Voorburg-based company DMD (Development Manufacturing and Distribution), which mainly executed them as exclusive limited editions. These items, created by many different creative individuals, communicated, in the words of Droog itself, "original ideas [and] clear concepts which have been shaped in a wry, no-nonsense manner"[6]—in other words, a typically idiosyncratic Dutch response to late modernism. The archetypal design of Droog's new direction was Marcel Wanders's lightweight Knotted chair (1996), a remarkable seating design formed of a cat's cradle of roped nylon and carbon-fiber, which was hung over a chair-shaped frame and then impregnated with liquid epoxy resin. Once dried, the woven mesh supported itself, appearing to defy the laws of gravity.

But it was Moooi, established by Wanders and Casper Vissers in 2001, that transformed Dutch conceptual design from a thoughtful, experimental movement into an extravagant, theatrical spectacle. The collective took its name from the Dutch word for "beauty," and at first created innovative work very much in the Droog vein, such as Maarten Baas's Smoke furniture line (2002) and Bertjan Pots's Random Light (2001). Bolstered by its successes and the vast amount of publicity generated by its increasingly outré work, Moooi issued work that became ever more detached from functionality; perhaps its greatest folly was the life-size Horse Floor Lamp, designed by the all-female

Chest of drawers designed by Tejo Remy for Droog, 1991.

←

Knotted chair designed by Marcel Wanders for Droog, 1996.

Universal solutions versus creative individuality

Swedish group Front in 2006. This type of design, though playfully subversive, relied heavily on gimmickry, much as Pop design had done in the late 1960s and early 1970s. But where Pop design had been inexpensive and expendable, this new work was exclusive and pricey. Although design based on one-line jokes might have been acceptable during the ecologically naive Pop era, it was a slightly different matter in a period of growing environmental concerns. This sort of work might in many ways be seen as a manifestation of the vacuous celebrity culture of the 1990s and 2000s, which aimed to attract attention with superficial glamour. The buoyancy of the international economy from 1994 to 2007 made such designs viable, and the boutique-hotel phenomenon created a ready market for such work, which could be placed in a relatively plain setting to make a bold designer statement.

←
85 Bulbs chandelier designed by Rody Graumans for Droog, 1993.

→
Horse Floor lamp designed by Front for Moooi, 2006.

↓
Smoke furniture designed by Maarten Baas for Moooi, 2002.

New Dutch Design

Design follows fashion, and Design Art

Universal solutions versus creative individuality

The giddy years of financial growth experienced between 1994 and 2007—fuelled by the dot-com bubble, by ever-growing levels of governmental and personal debt, and by the extraordinary risks taken by investment bankers—were truly glittering ones for design, which became a cultural phenomenon across the developed world. This period of sustained economic growth, interrupted only by the dot-com hiccup of the early 2000s, also coincided, as we have seen, with the dramatic rise of the Internet, which accelerated the transmission of design information and widened its boundaries. As the globe became ever more interconnected, the dominance of designers based in London and Amsterdam decreased somewhat, and talents such as Naoto Fukasawa and Tokujin Yoshioka from Japan, Fernando and Humberto Campana from Brazil, and Ronan and Erwan Bouroullec from France joined the rarefied ranks of international design superstardom. While Fukasawa took a characteristically Japanese essentialist approach, especially with his designs for the no-logo company Muji, Yoshioka built on the poetic legacy of Shiro Kuramata to create works with a Zen-like refinement. In contrast, the Campana brothers took a far more hands-on, *povera* approach, using scraps of material, offcuts of wood, found toys, cheap plastic tubing, and readily available aluminium wire to forge innovative and imaginative designs, which despite their considerable pricetags took inspiration from the make-do-and-mend methods found in Brazil's *favelas*. The Bouroullec brothers similarly made poetic rather than purely functional work, such as their Algue screening system (2004), made of clipped-together plastic branches that resembled seaweed—a creation that shared the lyrical qualities of the exclusive movement that later became known as "Design Art," but that was actually mass-produced on a large scale: the Swiss company Vitra sold more than three million Algue units between 2005 and 2009.[7]

← Algue screening system designed by Ronan and Erwan Bouroullec for Vitra, 2004.

↗ Wall-mounted CD player designed by Naoto Fukasawa for Muji, 1999.

By the early 2000s, avant-garde design was for the most part no longer dictated by function but rather by the whims of fashion. In 2001 a *New York Times* reported, Julie Iovine, interviewed the architect John Pawson at the Milan Furniture Fair; Pawson noted that "designers and architects have a lot to learn from fashion. . . They shouldn't be so blinkered. Haven't they cottoned on that things have changed? It isn't just about making designs to last a thousand years."[8] Some designers and manufacturers had already cottoned on, and, encouraged by a vigorous economy, were beginning to create seasonal collections rather than definitive design solutions (here it is interesting to note that Claudio Luti, the CEO and owner of the Italian manufacturing company, Kartell, who made it the major global brand it is today, was managing director of the Gianni Versace fashion house before he took up the reins at Kartell in 1988). And "design as fashion" was not only a facet of the Milan Furniture Fair, with its avant-garde exhibits; rather, fashionability was increasingly important in mainstream design, especially that of electronic products such as mobile phones, which were constantly being rendered functionally obsolete thanks to the rapidity of technological innovation. Also in the mass market, many products—whether kettles and washing machines or laptops and sofas—

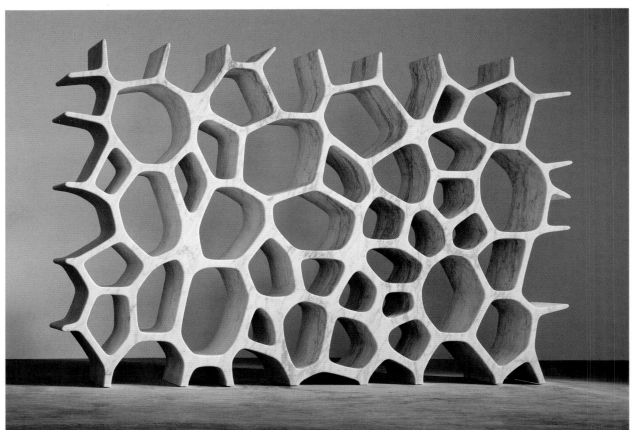

Universal solutions versus creative individuality

were virtually indistinguishable from one another in terms of price and functionality, so appearance was often the only way a manufacturer, and indeed the consumer, could distinguish among products. Being "on trend" came to be increasingly important for sales. And of course those trends were often determined by fashion forecasters, who were now being called upon by manufacturers of goods that had not previously been so influenced by the vagaries of fashion. Given the growing transience of objects, it is perhaps unsurprising that there was also a huge revival of interest in "design classics" during this period, and companies such as Vitra and Fritz Hansen began to reintroduce older, iconic designs. In the late 1980s and early 1990s, for example, the names of Charles and Ray Eames had been virtually unknown to all but a handful of avid design collectors; but in the space of two decades, their work was rediscovered by another generation and grew more popular than ever. It appeared everywhere, from beer advertisements to McDonald's restaurants.

While the classics of the past went mainstream, a sector of contemporary avant-garde design moved decisively upmarket, into the curious netherworld of Design Art. Functioning in much the same way haute couture does in the fashion world, Design Art was unashamedly elitist. Yet it was also where a handful of gifted designers and architects—notably Ron Arad, Marc Newson, Ross Lovegrove, Zaha Hadid, and the Campana Brothers—could pursue a new creative freedom unrestrained by economic concerns; the results would be some of the most beautiful and poetic designs ever made. As markets became more globalized and mainstream design tended toward ever-greater universalism, Design Art countered the trend by creating bespoke, individual designs that were supported by the emerging class of the super-rich—an elite who could afford the luxury of such pieces. The flourishing of limited-edition Design Art was fed during the early 2000s by auction houses, design fairs, and galleries, which introduced these pieces into the feeding frenzy of the contemporary fine art market. The term "Design Art" is, in fact, credited to Alexander Payne, the worldwide director of design at the auctionr and art dealership Phillips de Pury & Company, who organized the sale-room's first of many Design Art sales in 2001. By enabling a small group of practitioners

to explore new forms, materials, and technologies, the movement brought architectural and artistic concepts into the mix, and in so doing provoked discussion about the role of function in design and our interaction with designed objects and environments. Because such designs were produced in very small numbers, they had minimal environmental impact. As collectors' pieces, they also had, like works of fine art and very much unlike most mainstream design of the time, an inherent longevity. While the Campana brothers created Design Art using found objects and traditional production methods, other Design Artists preferred a more high-tech approach; Ron Arad's bronze MT rocking chair (2005), Hadid's Vortexx chandelier (2005), Newson's Voronoi Shelf unit (2007), and Lovegrove's Gingko carbon table (2007) were all developed using state-of-the-art computer-aided design (CAD) software. Being produced using the same CAD software packages, these objects actually shared a similar aesthetic, which sometimes made it difficult to distinguish the work of one designer from another. Nevertheless, the Design Art movement convincingly demonstrated that it was possible to invest limited-edition designs with expressive beauty, and that there was a small but very wealthy coterie of collectors who were prepared to pay a premium price for individuality and saw the investment potential of Design Art. Meanwhile, for all its elitism, Design Art had a trickle-down effect; these exclusive designs influenced mass-produced goods, such that, for instance, a number of Ron Arad's limited-edition pieces were translated into plastic by Vitra and Moroso and sold for a fraction of the price.

↖
Favela armchair designed by Fernando and Humberto Campana, 1999 (produced by Edra starting in 2003).

↖
Vortexx chandelier designed by Zaha Hadid for Sawaya & Moroni, 2005.

←
Voronoi Shelf unit designed by Marc Newson for Gagosian Gallery, 2007.

3D printing, biomimicry, and upcycling

During the mid-2000s laser stereolithography—now better known as 3D printing—was still very much in its infancy, but most of the leading design studios and teaching establishments made the considerable investment to have this new technology at their disposal. These early machines essentially grew prototypes in layers from vats of liquid photopolymer resin that was cured using ultraviolet beams of light. Enabling designers to give substance to their dreams within a matter of hours, they radically reduced the prototyping stage of the design process and allowed greater exploration of first-stage concepts thanks to the ease and low cost of model-making.

Around the time that 3D printing was making inroads into design practice, a new theme was also beginning to gain considerable ground: biomimicry, the late twentieth and early twenty-first centuries' answer to nineteenth-century "design botany," as pioneered by Christopher Dresser. Although the term was coined in the early 1980s, it wasn't in widespread use in the design world until the 1977 publication of *Biomimicry: Innovation Inspired by Nature*, by the biologist Janine Benyus. Biomimicry is a science related to design that takes nature as its model, measure, and mentor. By learning from nature and its evolutionary adaptations, it is argued that we will be able to arrive at design solutions that are better suited to the human condition and also more ecologically sustainable. By translating the laws governing biological systems into a framework that can be applied to the practice of design, we should be able to enhance the natural logic of our products. For instance, at the time of this writing, algorithms based on swarm theory—the actions of ant or bee colonies—are being used to develop artificial-intelligence systems, while studies of insects are being used in the design of miniaturized robotic

drones, known as flybots. The possible ramifications of such developments are disconcerting; as technologies advance, this moral dilemma will doubtless be faced more frequently. Just because something is possible to make doesn't necessarily mean it should be made. On a brighter note, though, biomimicry might offer design solutions to all sorts of ecological problems, from the development of sustainable water schemes to the construction of buildings that store carbon emissions.

Another book that fundamentally altered the design community's approach to the environment was *Cradle to Cradle: Remaking the Way We Make Things* (2002). Its authors, William McDonough and Michael Braungart, highlighted the waste and destruction wrought when consumer products are made, used, and then discarded. They charted the effects at all stages of the process, from the toxic dyes used to the carcinogenic phthalates that leach from degrading plastics, forcing designers to consider in more depth the life cycle of their products. The book also suggested ways in which to lessen an object's net environmental impact, such as sourcing local materials in order to reduce emissions related to transportation or using sustainably harvested woods. Perhaps the most shocking statistic McDonough and Braungart unearthed was that "the product itself contains on average only 5 percent of the raw materials involved in the process of making and delivering it."[9] In 2013, McDonough and Braungart published another book, *The Upcycle: Beyond Sustainability – Designing*

↗
Carbon Tower prototype demonstrating a construction system for an all-carbon and glass fiber high-rise office building, 2005, created using early 3D printer technology.

Universal solutions versus creative individuality

for Abundance, in which they argue that, rather than sustainability, we should design for abundance—that instead of minimizing the ecological footprint of a product, we should instead be trying to maximize the environmental benefits of its design, for example by devising carpets that clean the air or fences that capture solar energy.

Although these books offer intriguing glimpses of better ways to design and make products, the reality is that most manufactured goods are far removed from such ideals. The skies of the city of Shenyang in northeastern China—like so many of that country's industrial hubs—are filled with thick smog as factories belch a toxic cocktail in the process of churning out all manner of ephemeral products, from plastic shoes to gimmicky stocking fillers and poorly made kitchen gadgets. All these products and more can be found piled high in the city's vast Wu'ai Market, the largest international trade center in northern China, which fills a huge complex of linked buildings with floor upon floor of small stalls selling very cheap goods, which are bought and exported to the farthest reaches of the globe with scant regard for the ecological harm caused. This waste can be prevented only by stemming demand, and that will only be achieved through design education, both academic and media-related. In fact, there is little difference between the shoddy goods found in Shenyang and those that were displayed at the Great Exhibition of 1851, except that the scale of production is now infinitely greater and, as a result, the environmental impact infinitely worse.

↖
Gingko carbon table designed by Ross Lovegrove, 2007, its form inspired by nature.

←
Computer model of the Gingko carbon table by Ross Lovegrove, 2007.

↗
Diagram from *Cradle to Cradle: Remaking the Way We Make Things* (2002).

→
Microrobots (also known as flybots) intended for covert surveillance, developed by the Harvard Microrobotic Lab at the Harvard School of Engineering and Applied Sciences.

Universal solutions versus creative individuality

CradletoCradle

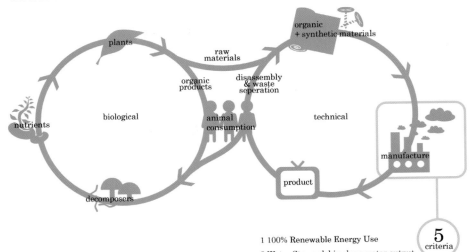

1 100% Renewable Energy Use
2 Water Stewardship clean water output
3 Social Responsibility positive impact on community
4 Material Reutilization recyclability / compostability
5 Material Health impact on human & environmental

3D printing, biomimicry, and upcycling

SOME CONCLUDING THOUGHTS

Although the widespread scientific consensus that climate change is being caused by greenhouse gas emissions has provoked some more enlightened designers and manufacturers to work on developing greener design solutions, there still exists a wanton amount of waste. Resources are squandered and consumers encouraged to update and replace their possessions with startling frequency. Sustainability is about reusing, reducing, and recycling, and can be achieved by making small changes to our buying habits—not replacing the electronic products we rely on until absolutely necessary, furnishing our homes with antiques or secondhand items, and making sure that any new products we do buy are well designed, well made, and so durable. In such an environment, there is a distinct glimmer of hope for design reform, because when people have access to well-designed products they become more discerning in their purchases; and so Good Design effectively breeds Good Design.

Sometimes, though, it is difficult to determine whether a design is really good. Take, for example, the iPhone—a small yet perfectly formed device that is the quintessential design of the present era. Its functional clarity and user-friendly interface are reminiscent of the pioneering work of Dieter Rams for Braun, and its sleek, alluring form is as seductive as any design by Raymond Loewy. Then, Apple's frequent upgrading would have trumped even Harley Earl, tarnishing the existing model by introducing a new look and enhanced capability. More than any other design, the iPhone demonstrates the convergence of technologies, elegantly combining a host of functions that only a few years ago would have been served by a variety of separate products, from music players and cameras to compasses and stopwatches—all of which have now been rendered more or less obsolete. The iPhone also encapsulates the other main themes of contemporary design practice, among them universal solutions that can be subject to mass customization, haptic feedback that engenders emotional response, and, last but by no means least, intuitive interfacing connections. As Charles Eames famously observed, "Eventually everything connects— people, ideas, objects. The quality of the connections is the key to quality per se."[10]

Jonathan Ive's iPhone, like design throughout history, has been guided by connections: forging purposeful and meaningful relationships between form and function, materials and technologies, objects and users in order to make products that enhance everyday life. From our cavemen forebears chipping away flakes of flint to create rudimentary stone tools to today's designers harnessing the power of CAD/CAM to create the latest "smart" products, design is a process driven by the belief that a better solution can be found to any given need. Throughout history, the quality of the connections found in design solutions has determined their success or failure, and they will continue to do so into the future.

→
iPhone 6s designed by Jonathan Ive and the Apple Design Team, introduced 2015.

↗
Drawing of the Utopian Design Antibody by James Irvine, 2008.

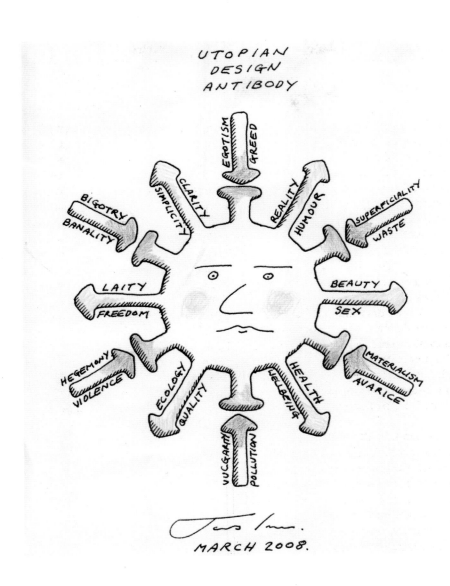

UTOPIAN
DESIGN
ANTIBODY

MARCH 2008.

As for the future of design, new materials and technologies—from superconductive graphene and light-emitting polymeric films to nanotechnology and artificial intelligence—will undoubtedly enable products to become smarter, smaller, and more functionally convergent. "Smart" designs will eventually be implanted into the body to enhance human capabilities. As and when this happens, design's physicality will decrease, but even in the process of dematerialization the discipline will continue to shape society. Design is the means through which the man-made world is molded, for better or worse—and consumers as well as designers and manufacturers have the power and the responsibility to ensure that progress is for the better. Every man-made product has an impact not only on our lives but also on those of future generations—environmentally, and also in showing those generations how different the past was, as well as how familiar it remains. The story of design gives us insight into our own way of life, and provides us with a document of how people have lived through time. What, then, will our own design legacy say about us?

End Notes

INTRODUCTION

1. Herbert Read, Preface to Lancelot L. Whyte, *Aspects of Form: A Symposium on Form in Nature and Art* (London: Lund Humphries, 1951), xxii.

2. Adam Smith, *The Theory of Moral Sentiments, or, An essay towards an analysis of the principles by which men naturally judge concerning the conduct and character, first of their neighbours, and afterwards of themselves: to which is added, A dissertation on the origin of languages* (London: W. Strahan, J. & F. Rivington, W. Johnston, T. Longman, 1874), 263; first published in 1759.

3. Roy Axe, *A Life in Style* (United Kingdom: AR Publishing, 2010), vii.

4. Quoted in Ann Lee Morgan (ed.), *Contemporary Designers* (London and Chicago: St. James Press, 1987), 382.

5. Quoted in Franz Schulze, *Mies van der Rohe: A Critical Biography* (Chicago: University of Chicago Press, 1985), 106.

6. William R. Lethaby, "Art and Workmanship," *The Imprint*, 1914; cited in William S. Pearson, *The Kelmscott Press, A History of William Morris's Typographical Adventure* (Berkeley: University of California Press, 1992), 291. In this quote Lethaby actually uses the term "art," rather than "design," in reference to "art manufactures."

1 – THE EARLY ORIGINS OF DESIGN

1. Hodder M. Westrop, "On the sequence of the phases of civilization," in *Anthropological Review*, Vol. IV (1866), clxxxiii-clxxxiv.

2. Xiaohung Wu, Chi Zang, Paul Goldberg, David Cohen, Yan Pan, Trina Arpin, and Ofer Bar-Yosef, "Early pottery at 20,000 years ago in Xianrendong Cave, China," in *Science* 336, no. 6089 (29 June 2012), 1696-1700.

3. The Bronze Age was the second principal period of the three-age system. Its dates in Europe are 3750-600 BC, in the Near East 3600-1200 BC, and in China 3000-700 BC.

4. Peter James and Nick Thorpe, *Ancient Inventions* (New York and Toronto: Ballantine Books, 1995), 216.

5. Andrew Burnett, *Coinage in the Roman World* (London: Seaby, 1987), 16.

6. John Keegan, *A History of Warfare* (New York: Vintage, 1994), 309.

7. Plutarch quoted in *Maxims of the Wise and Good* (London: James Blackwood & Company, 1876), 282.

2 – DESIGN AND CRAFTSMANSHIP FROM THE MIDDLE AGES TO THE EIGHTEENTH CENTURY

1. John Heskett, *Industrial Design* (London: Thames & Hudson, 1980), 11.

2. Translated by authors from Baldassare Castiglione, *Il Cortegiano*, 1528.

3. Edward Lucie-Smith, *A History of Industrial Design* (Oxford: Phaidon, 1983), 17-18.

4. Hugh Honour, *Neo-classicism: Style and Civilisation* (London: Penguin, 1977), 171; first published in 1968.

5. Horace Walpole, letter to the Countess of Ossory, September 17, 1785, quoted in Ralph Harrington, "Neoclassicism in Britain: The Adam brothers and 'Athenian' Stuart," http://www.artificialhorizon.org/essays/pdf/stuart.pdf.

6. Ibid

7. In speech, "Gothick" is often referred to as "Gothic with a K."

3 – THE AGE OF REASON AND THE INDUSTRIAL REVOLUTION

1. The Factory Act of 1819 eventually limited the hours worked by children to a maximum of twelve per day, and it was not until the Factory Act of 1833 that children under the age of nine were banned from working in the textile industries.

2. Quoted in Henry Dale and Rodney Dale, *The Industrial Revolution* (London: The British Library Publishing Division, 1993), 60.

3. Quoted in John Lienhard, "I sell here, Sir, what all the world desires to have - POWER," in *The Energy Laboratory Newsletter*, no. 31 (1994), 3.

4. Although the term "Industrial Revolution" was actually coined by John Stuart Mill in 1848, it was not employed in its modern context until 1884, when the English economic historian Arnold Toynbee used the phrase in the title of a lecture: "Lectures on the Industrial Revolution in England."

5. Today, nickel (discovered in 1751) and chromium (discovered in 1797) are commonly found in steel alloys; however, it would appear that it was only in the nineteenth century that they were introduced to steel-making.

6. Joseph Whitworth's measuring standard for screws used a constant angle (55°) between threads and a specific numbers of threads per inch for various screw diameters.

7. Adrian Forty, *Objects of Desire: Design and Society since 1750* (London: Thames & Hudson, 1986), 34.

8. Robin Reilly, *Josiah Wedgwood 1730-1795* (London: Macmillan, 1992), 311.

9. By the late 1840s, the era spanning 1815 to 1848 was the subject of a barrage of satirical criticism, which led to the furniture of the period being mocked remorselessly for its bourgeois pretensions. The term Biedermeier is thought to have originated from the publication of two cynical poems entitled "Biedermann's Evening Socialising" and "Bummelmaier's Complaint" in the Munich-based satirical magazine *Fliegende Blätter* (Flying Leaves), written by the painter-poet Joseph Victor von Scheffel in 1848. The German poet and dramatist Ludwig Eichrodt then compounded these two surnames into "Biedermaier" and used them as a fictitious surname for his book *Biedermaiers Liederlust*, published in 1870. The spelling was later slightly changed to Biedermeier.

10. The supplement was published in conjunction with the *Wiener Zeitschrift für Kunst, Literatur, Theater und Mode* (the Viennese Journal of Art, Literature, Theater, and Fashion).

11. Patrick O'Brien and Roland Quinault, *The Industrial Revolution and British Society* (Cambridge: Cambridge University Press, 1993), 55, quoting from Paul Mantoux, *The Industrial Revolution in the Eighteenth Century: An Outline of the Beginnings of the Modern Factory System in England*, published in 1928.

4 – ARMORY PRACTICE AND A NEW SYSTEM OF RATIONALIZED PRODUCTION

1. Eli Whitney, letter to Oliver Wolcott, May 1798, Eli Whitney Museum and Workshop website, www.eliwhitney.org/museum/eli-whitney/arms-production.

2. Quoted in Caroll W. Pursell, *Technology in America: A History of Individuals and Ideas* (Cambridge, MA: MIT Press, 1981), 47.

3. This lack of total interchangeability was borne out by research undertaken in the 1960s, during the course of which one unnamed researcher declared that Whitney's components were "not even approximately interchangeable!" See Pursell, *Technology in America*, 49.

4. The percussion cap replaced the flintlock mechanism previously used on firearms. A far more reliable ignition system, it held a small explosive charge encased in a metal "cap" that was activated when a gun's trigger was pulled.

5. David Hounshell, *From the American System to Mass Production, 1800-1932: The Development of Manufacturing Technology in the United States* (Baltimore: Johns Hopkins University Press, 1985), 47.

6. Colt website, http://www.coltsmfg.com/Company/History.aspx.

7. Colt website, http://www.colt.com/ColtLawEnforcement/History.aspx

8. Alexis de Tocqueville, *Democracy in America*, trans. Arthur Goldhammer (New York: Library of America, 2004), 466; first published in 1835.

9. Quoted in David M. Kennedy and Thomas A. Bailey (eds.), *The American Spirit: United States History as Seen by Contemporaries*, Volume 1, (Belmont: Wadsworth Publishing Co. Inc., 2009), 333.

10. Hounshell, *From the American System*, 194.

11. "A Great American Manufacture," in *Bicycling World*, April 1, 1881, 326.

12. Sigfried Giedion, *Mechanization Takes Command: A Contribution to Anonymous History* (Oxford: Oxford University Press, 1955), 40.

5 – THE NEW INDUSTRIAL AGE AND THE GREAT EXHIBITION
1. *The Graphic*, May 6, 1871, 420.

2. Quoted in John Heskett, *Industrial Design* (London: Thames & Hudson, 1980), 20.

3. Reprinted in *The Illustrated London News*, October 11, 1849.

4. Ibid.

5. Cited by Hermione Hobhouse in *The Crystal Palace and the Great Exhibition: Science, Art and Productive Industry* (London: Continuum International Publishing Group, 2002), 23.

6. Ibid., 34.

7. Owen Jones, "Colour in the Decorative Arts," in *Lectures on the Results of the Great Exhibition of 1851* (London: David Bogue, c. 1853), 257.

8. Ibid., 268.

9. *The Illustrated London News,* May 17, 1851, 424.

6 – THE WINDS OF REFORM
1. Quoted in John Harries, *Pugin: An Illustrated Life of Augustus Welby Northmore Pugin* (Aylesbury: Shire Publications, 1973), 12.

2. J.D. Sedding, *Art and Handicrafts* (London: Kegan Paul, Trench, Trübner & Co., 1893), 144.

3. In this quote Hermann Muthesius was specifically referring to John Dando Sedding, but his comment applies equally to William Morris, Philip Webb, and Norman Shaw. Hermann Muthesius, *The English House* (London: Frances Lincoln, 2007), 75; first published as *Das Englische Haus* in 1904-5.

4. William Burges, *Art Applied to Industry: A Series of Lectures* (Oxford and London: John Henry and James Parker, 1865), 1.

5. Ibid.

6. Ibid.

7. Eugène Emmanuel Viollet-le-Duc, quoted in *The Architectural Theory of Viollet-le-Duc: Readings and Commentaries* (Cambridge, MA: MIT Press, 1990), 6.

8. Quoted in David Watkin, *Morality & Architecture Revisited* (Chicago: University of Chicago Press, 2001), 27; first published in 1977.

9. Ford Madox Brown, "On the Mechanism of a Historical Picture," in *The Germ*, January 1850, 73.

10. Edward Burne-Jones, letter to Cormell Price, May 1853, quoted in Fiona MacCarthy, *William Morris: A Life for Our Time* (London: Faber & Faber, 1994), 67.

11. "An End," *The Germ*, January 1850, 48.

12. "Ad Valorem," in John Ruskin, *Unto This Last* (Minneapolis: Filiquarian Publishing, 2007), 89; first published in 1907.

13. Edward Burne-Jones, quoted in MacCarthy, *William Morris*, 95.

14. First prospectus of Morris, Marshall, Faulkner & Co., April 1861.

15. Reported by Sir Lowthian Bell to Alfred Powell, c. 1877. Cited in W.R. Lethaby and Godfrey Rubens, *Philip Webb and His Work* (Oxford: Oxford University Press, 1979), 94.

16. Morris & Co. did occasionally use machinery in its production of certain items, such as woven carpets, but this was very much the exception rather than the rule.

17. William Morris, *Dream of John Ball* (1886-87), *Collected Works* Vol. XVI (London: Longmans Green & Co., 1912), 230.

18. William Morris, "Address at the Twelfth Annual Meeting of the Society for the Preservation of Ancient Buildings," July 3, 1889, in May Morris (ed.), *William Morris: Artist, Writer, Socialist* (Oxford: Blackwell, 1936), 148.

19. John Goode, "William Morris and the Dream of Revolution," in John Lucas (ed.), *Literature and Politics in the Nineteenth Century* (London: Methuen, 1975), 239.

20. From the title of William Morris, *Useful Work Versus Useless Toil* (London: The Hammersmith Socialist Society, 1883).

21. Gustav Stickley, "William Morris, Some thoughts upon His Life, Work and Influence" article, *The Craftsman* 1, no. 1 (October 1901), (Eastwood, New York: The United Crafts), 32.

22. Ibid., 45.

23. Following Liberty & Co.'s lead, Britain went Japan-mad, and Japanese imports into Britain nearly doubled between 1898 and 1909 from a value of £44,836,000 to £86,227,000. Figures quoted in Oliver Checkland, *Japan and Britain after 1859: Creating Cultural Bridges* (New York and London: Routledge, 2002), 179.

24. G.K. Chesterton, *The Man Who Was Thursday and Related Pieces* (Oxford: Oxford University Press, 1997), 7. *The Man Who Was Thursday: A Nightmare* was originally published in 1908.

25. The term "elementalism" in the context of design history means the use of simple elementary forms.

26. Charles Lock Eastlake, *Hints on Household Taste* (London: Longmans, 1868), 15.

27. Karen Zukowski, "The Artistic Hearth: The Fireplace in the American Aesthetic Movement," in *The Magazine Antiques*, March 2008.

28: Preface to Christopher Dresser, *The Principles of Decorative Design* (London: Cassell, Petter, Galpin & Co., 1873).

29. Christopher Dresser, *Japan: Its Architecture, Art, and Art Manufactures* (London: Longmans, Green & Co., 1882), vi.

7 – THE NEW ART
1. Royal J. Schmidt, "Cultural Nationalism in Herder," in *Journal of the History of Ideas* 17, no. 3 (June 1958), 407.

2. Widar Halén, "The Fairytaleworld of Gerhard Munthe," Réseau Art Nouveau Network, http://www.artnouveau-net.eu/LinkClick.aspx?fileticket=AEZIjzxhVxA%3D&tabid=20, 1.

3. Herbert Percy Home, *The Century Guild Hobby Horse* (London: Chiswick Press, 1886).

4. The Century Guild statues, cited in Stephan Tschudi Madsen, *Sources of Art Nouveau*, translated by Ragnar Christophersen (Oslo: H. Aschehoug, 1956), 146.

5. John Russell Taylor, "Cockneys in Camelot," review of Fiona MacCarthy's *The Simple Life: C.R. Ashbee in the Cotswolds*, in *The Times of London*, April 23, 1981.

6. Charles Robert Ashbee, *Should We Stop Teaching Art?* (London: Batsford, 1911), 4; *Where the Great City Stands* (London: Batsford, 1917), 3.

7. C.F.A. Voysey, *The English Home*, in *British Architect*, January 27, 1911, 60.

8. Muthesius, *The English House*, 161.

9. Nikolaus Pevsner, *Pioneers of Modern Design* (London: Peregrine Books, 1986), 166; first published in 1936.

10. Muthesius, *The English House*, as cited in William Buchanan, *Mackinstosh's Masterwork: The Glasgow School of Art* (Glasgow: Drew, 1989), 4.

11. Muthesius, *The English House*, 178.

12. Natalie Curtis, "The New Log House at the Craftsman Farms: An Architectural Development of the Log Cabin," in *The Craftsman* XXI, no. 2 (November 1911), 196.

13. Charles Sumner Greene, "Bungalows," in *The Western Architect*, July 1908, 3.

8 – ART NOUVEAU
1. Sander Pierron, *L'École de gravure de Liège*, Edition de Savoir et Beauté, 1923.

2. Henry van de Velde, "Was ich will," *Die Zeit*, March 1901, 154-5.

3. Henry van de Velde, *Die Renaissance* (Berlin: Bruno und Paul Cassirer, 1900), 12, 111.

4. Ibid., 110.

5. Translated by authors, French text quoted in Nikolaus Pevsner, *Pioneers of Modern Design, From William Morris to Walter Gropius* (London: Peregrine, 1991), 32; first published as *Pioneers of the Modern Movement, From William Morris to Walter Gropius* (London: Faber & Faber) in 1936.

6. Hector Guimard, "On Nature" (1899), cited in Paul Greenhalgh, ed., *Quotations and Sources on Design and Decorative Arts* (Manchester: Manchester University Press, 1993), 13.

7. Cited in Piya Pal-Lapinski, *The Exotic Woman in Nineteenth-Century British Fiction and Culture: A Reconsideration* (Durham: University of New Hampshire Press, 1994), 98.

8. Pevsner, *Pioneers of Modern Design*, 115.

9. From Ernest Haeckel, *Generelle Morphologie* (1866). Translation as cited in Friedrich Nietzsche, *The Selected Writings of Friedrich Nietzsche* (Radford, VA: Wilder Publications, 2008), 145.

10. Jeremy Howard, *Art Nouveau: International and National Styles in Europe* (Manchester: Manchester University Press, 1996), 44.

11. This enterprise rather confusingly changed its name several times: it was established in 1898 as the "Dresdner Werkstätten für Handwerkskunst Schmidt und Engelbrecht," then renamed the following year the "Dresdner Werkstätten für Handwerkskunst Schmidt und Müller"; in 1905 this was shortened to "Dresdner Werkstätten für Handwerkskunst Karl Schmidt" and in 1907 it became the "Deutsche Werkstätten für Handwerkskunst Karl Schmidt."

12. Thomas Hobbes, *Three Discourses: A Critical Modern Edition of Newly Identified Work of the Young Hobbes*, ed. Noel Reynolds and Arlene Saxonhouse (Chicago: University of Chicago Press, 1997), 94.

13. Otto Wagner, *Moderne Architektur*, 1895. Translation by the authors.

14. projects.ecfs.org/bome/cities/hband2004/Vienna/SKendall/Wagner.html

9 – PUTTING THEORY INTO PRACTICE; FROM ART MANUFACTURES TO INDUSTRIAL PRODUCTS
1. Quoted in Sydney Henry Zebel, *A History of Europe Since 1870* (Philadelphia: J.B. Lippincott Co., 1948), 170.

2. Heinrich Kulka, *Adolf Loos: Das Werk des Architekten* (Wien: Löcker, 1931).

3. Adolf Loos, *Ornament and Crime*, trans. Adolf Opel (Riverside, CA: Ariadne Press, 1998), 169; first published as *Ornament und Verbrechen* in 1908.

4. Ibid., 172.

5. Tim Benton, Stefan Muthesius, and Bridget Wilkins, *Europe 1900-1914: The Reaction to Historicism and Art Nouveau* (Milton Keynes: Open University Press, 1975), 49.

6. Nikolaus Pevsner, *Pioneers of Modern Design*, 34-35.

7. Benton, Muthesius, and Wilkins, *Europe 1900-1914*, 62.

8. Cited by Frederic Schwartz, *The Werkbund: Design Theory and Mass Culture Before the First World War* (New Haven, CT: Yale University Press, 1996), 165.

9. As already seen in Chapter 6, one of the earliest known instances of this type of component interchangeability between products was that used by W.A.S. Benson at his factory in London, but Benson's products were far less "industrial" than those manufactured by AEG.

10. Benton, Muthesius and Wilkins, *Europe 1900-1914*, 59.

11. Ibid., 62.

10 – THE AMERICAN SYSTEM AND FORDISM
1. Ralph Waldo Emerson, "Journal," February 1855, cited in Margaret Miner and Hugh Rawson, *The Oxford Dictionary of American Quotations*, (Oxford: Oxford University Press, 2005), 240.

2. The famed aphorism was attributed to Emerson in 1889 by Sarah Yule in *Borrowings*, an 1894 anthology of quotations compiled by ladies from the First Unitarian Church in Oakland, California. Yule later claimed that the quote was copied from a lecture Emerson delivered in 1871, but it is more likely that it was simply a misquote.

3. Quoted in James D. Newton, *Uncommon Friends: Life with Thomas Edison, Henry Ford, Harvey Firestone, Alexis Carrel & Charles Lindbergh* (San Diego: Harcourt, Brace & Co., 1987), 24.

4. Henry Ford and Samuel Crowther, *My Life and Work* (Minneapolis: Filiquarian Publishing, 2006), 84; first published in 1922.

5. Cited in Robert Lacey, *Ford: The Men and the Machine* (New York: Little, Brown and Company, 1986), 109.

6. Henry Ford and Samuel Crowther, *My Life and Work* (Minneapolis, MN: Filiquarian Publishing, 2006), 83; first published in 1922.

7. Christopher Howe, *The Origins of Japanese Trade Supremacy, Development and Technology in Asia from 1540 to the Pacific War* (Chicago: University of Chicago Press, 1999), 284.

8. Captain A. P. Corcoran, "Wireless in the Trenches," in *Popular Science Monthly*, May 1917, 795-99.

11 – REDUCTIVISM, EXPRESSIONISM AND RATIONALISM

1. This two-volume folio of lithographs of Wright's work included his recently completed Unity Temple (1905–08) in Oak Park, Illinois, the bold geometric massing of which was of particular interest to the founding De Stijl members.

2. Quoted in Ulrich Conrads, *Programs and Manifestoes on 20th-Century Architecture* (Cambridge, MA: MIT Press, 1976), 39.

3. Ibid.

4. Quoted in Hans Ludwig Cohn Jaffé, *De Stijl* (London: Thames and Hudson, 1970), 10.

5. Tim Benton, *The New Objectivity* (Milton Keynes: Open University Press, 1975), 13.

6. Theo van Doesberg later coined the term "elementarism" to explain the group's reductivist approach and wrote an article of the same name in the *De Stijl* journal of January 1932.

7. Quoted in Theodore Brown, *The Work of G. Rietveld, Architect* (Utrecht: A.W. Bruna and Zoon, 1958), 21.

8. Taken from a filmed interview of Truus Schröder-Schräder conducted by Lucien den Arend and Janjelle Stroosma in 1982. See www.denarend.com/encounters/schroder-schrader.

9. Nikolai Punin, "Tour de Tatline," in *Veshch/Gegenstand/Objet* (Berlin: Skythen Verlag, 1922), 22. English translation in Tim Benton, Charlotte Benton, and Dennis Sharp, *Form and Function: A Source Book for the History of Architecture and Design 1890–1939* (London: Crosby Lockwood Staples, 1975), 91.

10. Benton, *The New Objectivity*, 33.

11. Hugh Aldersey-Williams, "Constructivism: the ism that just keeps givin'," *Creative Review 7*, August 2008.

12. Naum Gabo, *Gabo: Constructions, Sculpture, Paintings, Drawings, Engravings, with Introductory Essays* (Cambridge, MA: Harvard University Press, 1957), 157.

13. Quoted in Magdalena Droste, *Bauhaus, 1919-1933* (Cologne: Taschen, 1990), 16.

14. Ibid., 25.

15. From the lecture "Colour in Matter – Painting out of Colour," May 9, 1912, quoted in *Colour: Twelve Lectures by Rudolf Steiner* (Forest Row: Rudolf Steiner Press, 1992), 8.

16. Quoted in Frank Whitford, *Bauhaus* (London: Thames and Hudson, 1984), 143.

17. Weissenhofsiedlung website, www.weissenhof2002.de/english/weissenhof.html.

18. Le Corbusier, *Toward An Architecture,* trans. John Goodman (London: Frances Lincoln, 2008), 151.

12 – ART DECO AND INTERPRETATIONS OF MODERNISM

1. Joanna Banham and Leanda Shrimpton, *Encyclopedia of Interior Design: M-Z* Vol. 2 (Chicago, IL: Fitzroy Dearborn, 1997), 1090.

2. Le Corbusier, *Le Corbusier Oeuvre Complète 1938-1946* (Zurich: Les Éditions d'Architecture, 1966), 104.

3. Le Corbusier, *Toward An Architecture*, 151.

4. Ibid., 9.

5. Ibid.

6. The phrase "Less is More" was adopted by Ludwig Mies van der Rohe but is believed to have been first coined by Robert Browning in his 1855 poem, "Andrea del Sarto (called 'The Faultless Painter)."

7. Although Margaretha Reichardt is often credited with inventing *Eisengarn*, the textile was actually produced much earlier, in the mid 1800s, by the manufacturer Carl Theodor Wuppermann in Wuppertal, Germany. Reichardt should, however, be credited with its adoption at the Bauhaus.

8. While a cantilevered chair might look as though it uses less material in its frame than a traditional four-legged chair, this is not actually the case: it has two uprights, two sled elements, and a joining rear rail on the base, which, in terms of the use of materials, might be seen as a fifth leg. Nevertheless the cantilever form provided a comfortable springiness that meant material could be saved elsewhere, most notably in the seat and back sections.

9. Lucy Creagh and Helena Kaberg, *Modern Swedish Design: Three Founding Texts* (New York: The Museum of Modern Art, 2008), 19.

10. Quoted in Charlotte Fiell and Peter Fiell, *Scandinavian Design* (Cologne: Taschen, 2002), 64.

11. The Svenska Slöjdföreningen, or Swedish Handicraft Association, is also sometimes referred to in English as the "Swedish Society of Industrial Design." It was established in 1845 and renamed Svensk Form in 1976.

12. This vase originally had the curious title "Eskimo woman's leather trousers," but it became known as the Savoy after being used in Aalto's interiors for the Savoy Restaurant in Helsinki. It has also been suggested that Aalto's surname, which means "wave" in Finnish, might have inspired its form.

13. The "Manifesto del futurismo" was first published by the *Giornale dell'Emilia* on February 5, 1909, and days later appeared in French in *Le Figaro*.

14. Filippo Tommaso Marinetti, "Manifesto del futurismo," in *Giornale dell'Emilia,* February 5, 1909 – see: http://www.feedbooks.com/book/6541/manifesto-del-futurismo.

15. Antonio Sant'Elia, *Manifesto of Futurist Architecture* (1914), cited in Caroline Tisdall and Angelo Bozzolla, *Futurism* (Oxford: Oxford University Press, 1978), 130.

13 – THE GREAT DEPRESSION AND THE MODERNE STYLE

1. The term "eye appeal" was coined in America c. 1925-30, to mean attractiveness or beauty, and it was especially used when talking about household products and, of course, young women.

2. The rise in the design of "fancy" homewares was fuelled by Prohibition, as people began to entertain at home rather than going to meet their friends in bars. It is interesting to note that the heyday of the cocktail shaker actually coincided with the ban on alcohol.

3. Henry Ford with Samuel Crowther, *My Life and Work* (Minneapolis, MN: Filiquarian Publishing, 2006), 71; first published in 1922.

4. Quoted in James B. Twitchell, *Lead Us Into Temptation: The Triumph of American Materialism* (New York: Columbia University Press, 2000), 271.

5. Quoted in William Leach, *Land of Desire: Merchants, Power, and the Rise of a New American Culture* (New York: Vintage Books, 1994), 167.

6. Ibid.

7. Foreword to Jeffery Meikle, *Twentieth Century Limited: Industrial Design in America, 1925-1939* (Philadelphia, PA: Temple University Press, 2001).

8. Quoted in Stanley Abercrombie, *George Nelson: The Design of Modern Design* (Cambridge, MA: MIT Press, 2000), 49.

9. "Industrial Designers," *Fortune,* February 1934, 40.

10. Figures cited by New Deal Network: newdeal.feri.org

11. "Industrial Designers," 40.

12. Harold van Doren, *Industrial Design* (New York: McGraw-Hill, 1940), 137.

13. The Belgian-born chemist Leo Baekeland patented Bakelite, a resinous phenolformaldehyde material, in 1907, but it was not put to widespread commercial use until the 1930s.

14. Quoted in *Time* magazine, October 31, 1949, 49. Raymond Loewy was famously featured on the cover of this issue of *Time*, over the memorable strapline, "He streamlines the sales curve."

15. Raymond Loewy, *Never Leave Well Enough Alone* (New York: Simon and Schuster, 1951), 277.

16. Quoted in Véronique Vienne, "Raymond Loewy: Speed Whiskers on Toothbrushes," *Graphis* magazine, February 1998.

17. Harley Earl, "I Dream Automobiles," *Saturday Evening Post*, August 7, 1954, 82.

18. Stephen Bayley, *Design Heroes: Harley Earl* (London: Trefoil, 1990), 41.

19. Christine Frederick, *Selling Mrs. Consumer* (New York: The Business Bourse, 1929), 5.

20. Ibid., 250.

21. Quoted in Roy Sheldon and Egmont Arens, *Consumer Engineering: A New Technique for Prosperity* (London and New York: Harper and Brothers, 1932), 7.

14 – DESIGN FOR WAR
1. The term "monocoque" in this context refers to the aircraft's fuselage being enclosed in a rigid, shell-like outer casing.

2. Quoted in *Jane's Fighting Aircraft of World War II* (London: Random House, 2001), 139.

3. Ironically, the first turbojet engine was invented by British engineer Frank Whittle and patented in 1930, but its development was not kept secret, and the German engineer Dr. Hans von Ohain subsequently refined the technology further by using a centrifugal compressor. His design, patented in 1936, actually constituted the first operational jet engine, used to power the Heinkel He-178 in 1939.

4. General George S. Paton, letter to Chief of Ordnance, January 26, 1945, quoted in Edward Clinton Ezell, *The Great Rifle Controversy: Search for the Ultimate Infantry Weapon from World War II Through Vietnam and Beyond* (Harrisburg: Stackpole Books, 1984), 1.

5. Jon T. Hoffman, ed., *A History of Innovation: US Army Adaptation in War and Peace* (Washington: Government Printing Office, 2010), 10.

6. Gregory Votolato, *American Design in the Twentieth Century* (Manchester: Manchester University Press, 1998), 110.

7. Quoted in Patrick Foster, *The Story of Jeep*, 2nd edition (Iola: Krause Publications, 2004), 63.

15 – THE AMERICAN DREAM AND GOOD DESIGN
1. Quoted in Cherie Fehrman and Kenneth R. Fehrman, *Postwar Interior Design: 1945-1960* (New York: Van Nostrand Reinhold Company, 1987), 18.

2. Edgar Kaufmann, Jr. was the son of the owners of the well-known Kaufmann's department store in Pittsburgh and had studied architecture at Frank Lloyd Wright's school and studio, Taliesin East. It was with his active support that his father commissioned Frank Lloyd Wright to design a mountain retreat for the family that jutted out over Bear Run in south-western Pennsylvania, the extraordinary Fallingwater (1936), which is rightly regarded as one of Wright's great masterworks.

3. Edgar Kaufmann, Jr., "Borax, or the Chromium-Plated Calf," *Architectural Review*, August 1948.

4. Ibid.

5. "Manufacturers Participate in Furthering International Competition for the Design of Low-Cost Furniture," MoMA press release, New York, May 12, 1948.

6. This logo is still used for the annual Good Design awards granted by the Chicago Athenaeum.

7. For more information see: Hugh De Pree, *Business as Unusual: The People and Principles at Herman Miller* (Zeeland, MI: Herman Miller, 1986).

8. IBM at 100, online centennial exhibition: http://www-03.ibm.com/ibm/history/ibm100/us/en/icons/gooddesign/transform/.

9. *American Look*, 1958. Produced by Handy (Jam) Organization; Sponsored by Chevrolet Division, General Motors Corporation.

10. David Halberstam, *The Fifties* (New York: Villard, 1993), preface.

11. Henry Dreyfuss, *Designing for People* (New York: Simon and Schuster, 1955), 27.

12. Eliot Noyes, *Organic Design in Home Furnishings* (New York: Museum of Modern Art, c. 1941), 1.

16 – RECONSTRUCTION AND THE SPIRIT OF OPTIMISM
1. The Mollino historians Fulvio and Napeoleone Ferrari have noted that there is a more exacting and extended version of this well-known quote, which originally appeared in an interview with Mollino in the April 1950 issue of *Domus*: "Everything is allowed as long as the fantasy is preserved, that is a frail beauty, beyond any intellectualized program."

2. Quoted in Rene Spitz, *The Ulm School of Design: A View Behind the Foreground* (Stuttgart: Axel Menges, 2002), 14.

3. Ibid.

4. Eiji Toyoda, *Toyota: Fifty Years in Motion* (Tokyo: Kodansha International, 1987), 119.

5. Sony corporate information, http://www.sony.net/SonyInfo/CorporateInfo/History/SonyHistory/1-05.html.

6. Quoted in Charlotte and Peter Fiell, *Industrial Design A-Z* (Cologne: Taschen, 2000), 485.

7. *Design '46: A Survey of Industrial Design as Displayed in the "Britain Can Make It" Exhibition* catalogue (London: His Majesty's Stationery Office for the Council of Industrial Design, 1946), 5.

8. Charlotte & Peter Fiell, *Masterpieces of British Design* (London: Goodman Fiell, 2012), 15.

9. Quote from a promotional leaflet published by the CoID entitled "Design Fairs," c. 1950.

10. *Design in the Festival: Illustrated Review of British Goods* (London: The Council of Industrial Design), 11.

11. The classic explanation of the concept of "the people's home" is contained in a 1928 speech given by the two-time Swedish prime minister Per Albin Hansson: "The basis of the home is community and togetherness. The good home does not recognize any privileged or neglected members, nor any favorite or stepchildren. In the good home there is equality, consideration, cooperation, and helpfulness. Applied to the great people's and citizens' home this would mean the breaking down of all the social and economic barriers that now separate citizens into the rich and the poor, the propertied and the impoverished, the plunderers and the plundered." Cited in Sheri Berman, *The Primacy of Politics* (Cambridge: Cambridge University Press, 2006), 163.

12. Quoted in Charlotte and Peter Fiell, *Scandinavian Design* (Cologne: Taschen, 2002), 68.

13. Ibid., 40.

17 – POP DESIGN AND THE COUNTERCULTURE

1. *Classic Plastics: A Look at Design 1950–1974* (London: Fischer Fine Art, 1989), 8.

2. Etienne Lullin, ed., *Richard Hamilton: Prints and Multiples 1939–2002: Catalogue Raisonné* (Dusseldorf: Kunstmuseum Winterthur and Richter Verlag, 2003), 188.

3. Fiona MacCarthy, *British Design since 1880: A Visual History* (London: Humphries, 1982), 143.

4. Nigel Whiteley, *Pop Design: Modernism to Mod* (London: The Design Council, 1987), 125.

5. *Architectural Review* 142, October 1967.

6. Peyton Skipworth, "Rebels Against Commercial Ugliness," *Apollo Magazine*, January 2008.

7. John F. Kennedy, speech given September 12, 1962 at Rice University, Houston, Texas. Available to view on NASA's website at http://er.jsc.nasa.gov/she/ricetalk.htm.

8. Ignazia Favata, *Joe Colombo and Italian Design of the Sixties* (London: Thames & Hudson, 1988), 16.

9. Quoted on the Internationale Möbelmesse (IMM)'s website, http://news-imm.koelnmesse.info/en/2010/04/pantons-visiona-ii/.

10. Andrea Branzi, *The Hot House: Italian New Wave Design* (London: Thames and Hudson, 1984), 73–74.

11. Mark Crispin Miller, introduction to Vance Packard, *The Hidden Persuaders* (Brooklyn, NY: Ig Publishing, 2007), 10; first published in 1957.

12. Vance Packard, *The Waste Makers*, 19.

13. Ibid., 21.

14. Ibid., 22.

15. Ralph Nader, "The Safe Car You Can't Buy," *The Nation*, April 1959.

16. www.nader.org/history/bollier_chapter_1.html

17. Ergonomidesign merged with the design company Designgruppen in 1979 and was renamed Ergonomi Design Gruppen.

18 – RATIONALISM VERSUS CRAFT

1. Foster + Partners Press Release, August 12, 2010, http://www.fosterandpartners.com/news/exhibition-bucky-fuller-&-spaceship-earth.

2. United States Department of Labor website, www.osha.gov/about.html.

3. Henry Dreyfuss Asscociates published two further Humanscale manuals in 1981.

4. *Casabella* no. 377, March 1973.

5. Andrea Branzi, *The Hot House: Italian New Wave Design* (London: Thames & Hudson, 1984), 127.

19 – POSTMODERNISM VERSUS CRAFT

1. Barbara Radice, *Memphis: Research, Experiences, Results, Failures, and Successes of New Design* (New York: Rizzoli, 1984), 26.

2. Alice Rawsthorn, "And the Great Furniture Festival Begins," *The New York Times*, April 10, 2011.

3. Quoted in Charlotte and Peter Fiell, *Mark Brazier-Jones* (London: Fiell Publishing, 2012), 10.

4. Ibid.

5. The Design Museum, http://designmuseum.org/design/ron-arad.

6. In the early 1980s, matte black was very much "the new black," and this short-lived design trend was labeled the Matte Black style in homage to the non-color's dominance. Matte Black designs tended to be hard-edged and angular, in a sort of macho neo-rationalist style that suited the period's businesslike ethos.

7. Fred A. Bernstein, "Remembering the Royalton," *Interior Design*, September 2007.

8. Susan Kare website, http://www.kare.com/about/bio.html)

9. Steve Silberman, "The Sketchbook of Susan Kare, the Artist Who Gave Computing a Human Face," November 22, 2011, http://blogs.plos.org/neurotribes/2011/11/22/the-sketchbook-of-susan-kare-the-artist-who-gave-computing-a-human-face/.

10. Confusingly, during the 1980s the term New Wave was used to describe postmodernism in all fields of creative activity—from graphic design, product design and textile design to fashion, music and film. It was, however, postmodern graphic design that was and still is most closely associated with the term "New Wave."

20 – UNIVERSAL SOLUTIONS VERSUS CREATIVE INDIVIDUALITY

1. Quoted in obituary of Deng Xiaoping, *The Daily Telegraph*, February 20, 1997.

2. Internet World Stats: usage and population statistics, http://www.internetworldstats.com/.

3. The London Institute brought together Central Saint Martins College of Art and Design, Camberwell College of Arts, Chelsea College of Art and Design, The London College of Printing (later the London College of Communication), and the London College of Fashion as specialized centers of excellence in the different areas of art and design.

4. Shane Richmond, "Jonathan Ive interview: Apple's design genius is British to the core," *The Daily Telegraph*, May 23, 2012.

5. Steve Jobs, launch of the iMac at Palo Alto, California, 1998. See YouTube: The First iMac Introduction – www.youtube.com/watch?v=0BHPtoTctDY.

6. The Design Museum, http://designmuseum.org/design/droog.

7. *Icon* magazine online, October 2009, http://www.iconeye.com/read-previous-issues/icon-076-%7C-october-2009/ronan-amp-erwan-bouroullec.

8. "Design Notebook: Furniture Fair; In Milan, Form follows Fashion," *The New York Times*, April 12, 2001.

9. William McDonough and Michael Braungart, *Cradle to Cradle: Remaking the Way We Make Things* (New York: North Point Press, 2002), 28.

10. John Neuhart, Marilyn Neuhart, and Ray Eames, *Eames Design: The Work of the Office of Charles and Ray Eames* (New York: Harry N. Abrams, 1989), 266.

Bibliography

Abercrombie, S., *George Nelson: The Design of Modern Design*, MIT Press, Cambridge, Mass. 2000

Anscombe, I. and C. Gere, *Arts and Crafts in Britain and America*, Academy Editions, London 1978

Banham, J., *Theory and Design in the First Machine Age*, Architectural Press, London/New York 1960

Banham, J. and L. Shrimpton, *Encyclopedia of Interior Design:* Volumes 1 and 2, Fitzroy Dearborn, Chicago 1997

Bangert, A., *Italian Furniture Design: Ideas, Styles, Movements*, Bangert Verlag/Bangert Publications, Munich 1988

Barthes, R., *Mythologies* (originally published in French by Editions du Seuil, Paris 1957), Jonathan Cape, London 1972

Baudrillard, J., *The Consumer Society: Myths and Structure* (originally published in French as *La société de consommation*, Editions Denoël 1970), Sage Publications, London 1998

Bayley, S., *The Conran Directory of Design*, Conran Octopus, London 1985

––– *Design Heroes: Harley Earl*, Trefoil Publications, London 1990

––– *In Good Shape: Style in Industrial Products 1900-1960*, Design Council, London 1979

Bayley, S. and T. Conran, *Design: Intelligence Made Visible*, Conran Octopus, London 2007

Benton, T., *The New Objectivity*, Open University Press, Milton Keynes 1975

Benton, T., C. Benton, and D. Sharp, *Form and Function: A Source Book for the History of Architecture and Design 1890-1939*, Open University Press, Milton Keynes 1975

Benton, T. and S. Millikin, *Art Nouveau 1890-1902,* Open University Press, Milton Keynes 1975

Benton, T., S. Muthesius and B. Wilkins, *Europe 1900-1914, The Reaction to Historicism and Art Nouveau*, Open University Press, Milton Keynes 1975

Bertram, A., *Design*, Penguin Books, London 1938

Bosoni, G., *Italian Design*, The Museum of Modern Art, New York 2008

Branzi, A., *The Hot House: Italian New Wave Design*, Thames and Hudson, London 1984

Branzi, A. and M. De Lucchi, *Il Design Italiano Degli Anni'50*, Ricerche Design Editrice, Milan 1985

Brightwell, C.L., *Heroes of the Laboratory and the Workshop*, George Routledge and Sons, London 1859

Brown, T., *The Work of G. Rietveld, Architect*, A. W. Bruna and Zoon, Utrecht 1958

Byars, M., *The Design Encyclopedia*, Museum of Modern Art, New York 2004

Carson, R., Lois Darling, and Louis Darling *Silent Spring*, Houghton Miffin, Boston 1962

Collins, M., *Towards Post-modernism: Design Since 1851*, British Museum Publications, London 1987

Conrads, U., *Programs and Manifestoes on 20th-Century Architecture*, MIT Press, Cambridge, Mass. 1976

Creagh, L. and H. Kaberg, *Modern Swedish Design: Three Founding Texts*, Museum of Modern Art, New York 2008

Dale, H. and R. Dale, *The Industrial Revolution*, The British Library Publishing Division, London 1992

Dormer, P., *Design Since 1945*, Thames and Hudson, London 1993

––– *The Meanings of Modern Design: Towards the Twenty-first Century*, Thames and Hudson, London 1990

Dreyfuss, H., *Designing for People*, Simon and Schuster, New York 1955

Dresser, C., *Japan: Its Architecture, Art, and Art Manufactures*, Longmans, Green, London 1882

––– *The Principles of Decorative Design*, Cassell, Petter, Galpin, London 1873

Droste, M., *Bauhaus, 1919-1933*, Taschen, Cologne 1990

Eastlake, C. L., *Hints on Household Taste in Furniture, Upholstery and Other Details*, Longmans, Green, London 1878

Favata, I., *Joe Colombo and Italian Design of the Sixties*, Thames and Hudson, London 1988

Fiell, C. and P. Fiell, *Charles Rennie Mackintosh*, Taschen, Cologne 1995

––– *Design of the 20th Century*, Taschen, Cologne 1999

––– *Industrial Design A-Z*, Taschen, Cologne 2000

––– *Masterpieces of British Design*, Goodman Fiell, London 2012

––– *Masterpieces of Italian Design*, Goodman Fiell, London 2013

––– *Plastic Dreams: Synthetic Visions in Design*, Fiell Publishing, London 2009

––– *Scandinavian Design*, Taschen, Cologne 2002

––– *William Morris*, Taschen, Cologne 1999

Ford, H. and S. Crowther, *My Life and Work*, first edition, William Heinemann 1922, Filiquarian Publishing, Minneapolis, New Edition 2006

Forty, A., *Objects of Desire: Design and Society since 1750*, Thames and Hudson, London 1986

Frampton, K., *Modern Architecture: A Critical History*, Thames and Hudson, London 1980

Frederick, C., *Selling Mrs. Consumer*, Business Bourse, New York 1929

Friedman, M., *De Stijl, 1917-1931: Visions of Utopia*, Phaidon, Oxford 1982

Gere, C., and M. Whiteway, *Nineteenth-Century Design: From Pugin to Mackintosh*, Weidenfeld and Nicolson, London 1993

Giedion, S., *Mechanization Takes Command: A Contribution to Anonymous History*, Oxford University Press, Oxford 1955

Greenhalgh, P., *Modernism in Design*, Reaktion Books, London 1990

––– *Quotations and Sources: On Design and the Decorative Arts*, Manchester University Press, Manchester 1993

Gunston, B. and F. T. Jane, *Jane's Fighting Aircraft of World War II*, Random House, London 1997

Hamilton, R., *Collected Words*, Thames and Hudson, London 1982

Hearn, M. F., *The Architectural Theory of Viollet-Le-Duc: Readings and Commentary*, MIT Press, Cambridge, Mass. 1990

Heisinger, K. and G. Marcus, *Design Since 1945*, Thames and Hudson, London 1983

Heskett, J., *Industrial Design*, Thames and Hudson, London 1980

Hobhouse, H., *The Crystal Palace and the Great Exhibition: Science, Art and Productive Industry*, Continuum International Publishing Group, London 2002

Hoffman, J. T., *A History of Innovation, US Army Adaptation in War and Peace*, US Army Center of Military History, Military Bookshop, Washington 2011

Honour, H., *Neo-classicism: Style and Civilization*, Penguin 1968

Hounshell, D., *From the American System to Mass Production, 1800-1932: The Development of Manufacturing Technology in the United States*, John Hopkins University Press, Baltimore 1985

Howard, J., *Art Nouveau: International and National Styles in Europe*, Manchester University Press, Manchester 1996

Jaffé, H. L. C., *De Stijl*, Thames and Hudson, London 1970

Jervis, S., *The Penguin Dictionary of Design and Designers*, Penguin Books, London 1984

Juran, J. M., *Quality Control Handbook*, McGraw-Hill, New York 1951

Kries, M. and A. Von Vegesack, *Joe Colombo: Inventing the Future*, Vitra Design Museum, Weil am Rhein 2005

Lacey, R., *Ford: The Men and the Machine*, Little Brown and Company, New York 1986

Leach, W., *Land of Desire: Merchants, Power, and the Rise of a New American Culture*, Vintage Books, New York 1994

Le Corbusier, *Le Corbusier Oeuvre complète 1938-1946*, Les Éditions d'Architecture, Zurich 1966

––– *Towards a New Architecture* (first published in French as *Vers une architecture* in 1923), Frances Lincoln, London, New Translated Edition 2008

Loewy, R., *Industrial Design*, Fourth Estate, London 1979

––– *Never Leave Well Enough Alone*, Simon and Schuster, New York 1951

Loos, A., *Ornament und Verbrechen* ("Ornament and Crime"), first published 1908, translated by Adolf Opel and republished by Ariadne Press, Riverside 1998

Lucie-Smith, E., *A History of Industrial Design*, Phaidon, Oxford 1983

MacCarthy, F., *British Design Since 1880: A Visual History*, Lund Humphries, London 1982

––– *William Morris, A Life of Our Time*, Faber & Faber, London 1994

Margolin, V., *Design Discourse, History, Theory, Criticism*, University of Chicago Press, Chicago 1989

Margolin, V. and R. Buchanan, *Discovering Design, Explorations in Design Studies*, University of Chicago Press, Chicago 1995

––– *The Idea of Design*, MIT Press, Cambridge, Mass. 1995

McDonough, W. and M. Braungart, *Cradle to Cradle: Remaking the Way We Make Things*, North Point Press, New York 2002

––– *The Upcycle: Beyond Sustainability - Designing for Abundance*, North Point Press, New York 2013

Meikle, J., *Twentieth Century Limited - Industrial Design in America, 1925-1939*, Temple University Press, Philadelphia 2001

Muthesius, H., *Das Englische Haus* ("The English House"), 1st edition, Granada Publishing Limited, Frogmore, 1904–5, (English edition), Frances Lincoln, London 2007

Nelson, G., *George Nelson Design*, Whitney Library of Design, New York 1979

Neuhart, J., M. Neuhart and R. Eames, *Eames Design: The Work of the Office of Charles and Ray Eames*, Harry N. Abrams, New York 1989

Newton, J. D., *Uncommon Friends: Life with Thomas Edison, Henry Ford, Harvey Firestone, Alexis Carrel and Charles Lindbergh*, Harcourt, Brace, San Diego 1987

O'Brien, P. and R. Quinault, *The Industrial Revolution and British Society*, Cambridge University Press, Cambridge 1993

Packard, V., *The Hidden Persuaders*, D. McKay, New York 1957

––– *The Waste Makers*, D. McKay, New York 1960

Papanek, V., *Design for the Real World: Human Ecology and Social Change*, Pantheon Books, New York 1971

––– *The Green Imperative: Natural Design for the Real World*, Thames and Hudson, London 1995

Perris, G. H., *The Industrial History of Modern England*, Kegan Paul, London 1914

Pevsner, N., *Pioneers of Modern Design: From William Morris to Walter Gropius*, (originally published as *Pioneers of the Modern Movement* in 1936; 2nd edition, New York: Museum of Modern Art, 1949; revised and partly rewritten, Penguin Books, 1960) Penguin, London, New Edition 1991

––– *The Sources of Modern Architecture and Design*, Thames and Hudson, London 1968

Ponti, L. L., *Gio Ponti: The Complete Work 1923-1978*, Thames and Hudson, London 1990

Pursell, C. W., *Technology in America: A History of Individuals and Ideas*, MIT Press, Cambridge, Mass. 1981

Radice, B., *Memphis - Research, Experiences, Results, Failures and Successes of New Design*, Thames and Hudson, London 1985

Read, H., *Art and Industry: The Principles of Industrial Design*, Faber & Faber, London 1956

Reilly, R., *Josiah Wedgwood 1730-1795*, Macmillan, London 1992

Schwartz, F., *The Werkbund: Design Theory and Mass Culture Before the First World War*, Yale University Press, New Haven 1996

Shanks, M., *The Innovators: The Economics of Technology*, Penguin Books, Harmondsworth 1967

Sheldon, R. and E. Arens, *Consumer Engineering: A New Technique for Prosperity,* Harper and Brothers, London and New York 1932

Sparke, P., *Did Britain Make It?: British Design in Context 1946–86*, The Design Council, London 1986

Sudjic, D., *Design in Britain: Big Ideas (Small Island)*, Conran Octopus, London 2009

––– *The Language of Things*, Allen Lane, London 2008

Thomson, D., *England in the Twentieth Century*, Penguin Books, London 1965

Tisdall, C. and A. Bozzolla, *Futurism*, Oxford University Press, Oxford 1978

Triggs, T., *Communicating Design, Essays in Visual Communication*, B.T. Batsford, London 1995

Twitchell, J. B., *Lead Us Into Temptation: The Triumph of American Materialism*, Columbia University Press, New York 2000

van Doren, H., *Industrial Design*, McGraw-Hill Publishers, New York 1940

Walker, J., *Design History and the History of Design*, Pluto Press, London 1989

Watkin, D., *Morality and Architecture Revisited*, University of Chicago Press, Chicago 1977

Whiteley, N., *Design for Society*, Reaktion Books, London 1993

––– *Pop Design: modernism to Mod*, Design Council, London 1987

Whitford, F., *Bauhaus*, Thames and Hudson, London 1984

Woodham, J., *Twentieth Century Design*, Oxford University Press, Oxford 1997

EXHIBITION CATALOGUES

American Modern, 1925-1940: Design for a New Age, Metropolitan Museum of Art and the American Federation of Arts/Harry N. Abrams, New York 2000

Art and Design in Europe and America, 1800-1900, Victoria and Albert Museum/Herbert Press, London 1987

Art Deco: 1910 –1939, Victoria and Albert Museum/V&A Publishing, London 2003

Bent Wood and Metal Furniture: 1850-1946, American Federation of Arts/University of Washington Press, Seattle 1987

Brani di storia dell'arredo (1880–1980), Museo dell'arredo contemporaneo/Edizioni Essegi, Ravenna 1988

British Art and Design, 1900-1960, Victoria and Albert Museum, London 1983

British Design from 1948: Innovation in the Modern Age, Victoria and Albert Museum/V&A Publishing, London 2012

Design 1935-1960: What Modern Was, Le Musée des Arts Décoratifs de Montreal/Harry N. Abrams, New York 1991

Design in America: The Cranbrook Vision, 1925-1950, Detroit Institute of Arts and Metropolitan Museum of Art, New York 1983

High Styles: Twentieth-Century American Design, Whitney Museum of American ARt/Summit Books, New York 1985

Il Modo Italiano: Italian Design and Avant-garde in the 20th Century, Le Musée des Arts Décoratifs de Montreal/Skira 2006

Industrial Design: Reflection of a Century (published in conjunction with the exhibition *Design, Miroir du Siècle*) The Grand Palais/Flammarion, Paris 1993

Italy: The New Domestic Landscape, Museum of Modern Art, New York 1972

The Machine Age in America, 1918-1941, Brooklyn Museum of Art/Harry N. Abrams, New York 1986

Modernism, 1914-1939: Designing a New World, Victoria and Albert Museum/V&A Publishing, London 2006

Pugin: A Gothic Passion, Victoria and Albert Museum/Yale University Press, London 1994

Index

Illustration Credits

The publishers would like to thank the following sources for their kind permission to reproduce the pictures in this book. Key: t=Top, b=Bottom, c=Center, l=Left and r=Right

Abet: 413; © ADAGP - RMN (Musée d'Orsay)/Hervé Lewandowski: 205bl; Alamy: 8 (Glyn Thomas), 98 (jvphoto), 103 (Geoffrey Kidd), 138 (The National Trust Photolibrary), 164 (d78photograhy), 173 (Robert Harding Picture Library), 186t (Tim Street-Porter/EWA Stock), 190 (Thomas A. Heinz), 200 (B.O'Kane), 210t (Bildarchiv Monheim GmbH), 211, 258 (©LOOK Die Bildagentur der Fotografen GmbH), 263t (©frans lemmens), 289t (Arcaid Images), 289b (©YAY Media AS), 326 (©Photos 12), 328b (©Rick Pisio\RWP Photography), 332b (©on-white.de), 333t (©INTERFOTO), 336l (©INTERFOTO), 337t (©Military Images), 360 (©redsnapper), 364 (©VIEW Pictures Ltd), 365 (© Randy Duchaine), 386 (© INTERFOTO), 417b (©simon clay), 420 (© Motoring Picture Library), 438 (© VIEW Pictures Ltd), 451r (© INTERFOTO), 451r (© INTERFOTO), 474 (© graficart.net), 476 (© mark Phillips), 496 (© Anatolii Babii); Alessi: 452, 458t, 458b, 459, 467; Akg-images/Erich Lessing: 49t; Apple.com: 468, 480, 481; Arcaid/Richard Bryant: 194, 466; Archivio Superstudio: 427t; B&B Italia: 410; Barrett-Kacson Auction Co.: 417t; Bauhaus Archiv, Berlin: 271t, 272b; Bialetti Industrie SpA: 300; Bob Comlay- images@comlay.net: 73t; Bonhams: 37, 52, 316 388; Bröhan Design Foundation, Berlin: 237, 238, 279; Bukowskis: 400b; Casabellaweb.eu: 444; Cassina: 366, 416; Connecticut State Library: 96, 97t, 97b, 99t; Corbis: 16r (Nathan Benn), 60t (Burney Burstein), 76b (Gianni Dagli Orti), 166t (Mario Cipriani), 172t (Yadid Levy/Robert Harding World Imagery), 172b + 174t (Mark Fiennes/Arcaid), 179b (Peter Harholdt),197 (Ludovic Maisant), 201 (PoodlesRock), 202 (Sylvain Sonnet), 204 (Jean-Pierre Lescourret), 219 (Pascal Deloche/Godong), 274-275 (Jens Wolf/dpa), 425 (KIM KYUNG-HOON/Reuters); © Country Life: 53,54; Darin Schnabel/RM Auctions: 370; David Mellor: 390b; Domus: 445; Droog - photo: Tejo Remy: 485, 486; Eames Office LLC, Photo: Grant Taylor, Courtesy of JF Chen: 341bl; Edra: 490tl; Fiell Archive: 21t, 24, 26, 35b, 38-39, 55, 68t, 70, 71, 75t, 76t, 78, 79t, 83, 91, 92, 99b, 101, 113b, 122, 124, 128, 130, 132t, 133b, 134, 134b, 139, 142, 143, 149, 150, 152t, 159, 160, 166b, 170, 174b, 178, 179t, 181, 199r, 209, 210b, 216b, 218b, 220, 222, 227, 229, 230t, 230b, 231, 232, 233t, 236b, 240, 262, 277, 278, 285b, 288b, 290, 292, 293t, 294, 295, 296, 298, 299, 304, 310, 313, 315, 321, 322, 323, 339, 341t, 341br, 345b, 348, 349b, 352, 357tr, 374, 389, 391, 393b, 396, 401, 409b, 415t, 420, 429, 430, 431, 432, 436, 437t, 439t, 442, 447t, 449, 461 (courtesy of Philippe Decelle/Plasticarium), 464t, 465b; Fiat: 371; Flickr: 45, 382 (Ryann Quintano); Fritz Hansen: 398, 399t; Gagosian Gallery: 490b; Getty Images - Arnold Newman: 355; Getty Images/Business Wire: 493; Getty Images/De Agostini: 12, 18, 21b, 23, 25t, 27t, 34, 192, 214, 261, 301; Getty Images/ Fox photos/Stringer: 107; Getty Images/ Hulton Archive: 31, 119, 215, 216t, 218t, 224, 225, 245r, 272t; Getty Images/IWM: 331t; Getty Images/ National Geographic: 15; Getty Images/New York Daily News: 359, 361; Getty Images/Redferns: 419t, 447b; Getty Images/Roger Viollet: 283; Getty Images/SSPL: 16l, 22l, 35t, 41t, 46, 104t; Getty Images/Steven Allen: 134t; Getty Images/Time & Life Pictures: 345t, 351; Getty Images/ Universal Images Group: 20, 25b, 27b, 110, 157, 266; Getty Images/ Werner Forman: 22r; Giant-bicycles.com: 477b; Gordon Russell Museum: 297; Gufram: 402; Harris Lindsay/Kunstindustimuseet, Copenhagen: 59; Hemmings.com: 393t; Herman Miller: 418t; Hille: 443r; Imperial War Museums, London: 334b; iStockphoto: 328t (©mikvivi), 330t (©GNeesam), 331b (©Nobilior), 332t (©fotofritz16), 337b (©Blade_kostas); © J. Paul Getty Trust/Julius Shulman Photography Archive, Research Library at the Getty Research Institute: 346; Henry Dreyfuss Associates: 362; Joe Colombo: 423, 424; John Makepeace: 440; Junghans: 373; Kartell: 477tr; Knoll International: 357bl; Lassco: 75b; MAK, Vienna: 82; Marcel Wanders: 484; Marialaura Rossiello - James Irvine S.r.l: 497; Mark Brazier Jones: 463; Mary Evans Picture Library: 36t (British Museum), 88; Matt Damora: 357tl; Memphis Milano: 455; Michael Furman: 319t; Michele De Lucchi: 478-479; Mick Jayet for the Velvet Galerie: 415b; Montreal Museum of Fine Arts: 369t, 412b; Moooi: 487; Muji – Photo: Hidetoyo Sasaki: 489; NASA: 422; Paul Tahon/Bouroullec: 288; Phillips: 303,446b; Porsche: 372; Private Collection: 260; Quittenbaum Kunstauktoinen: 305; Rago Arts and Auction Center, Lambertville: 183; Loewy Design LLC, licensed by CMG Worldwide: 312; RIBA Library: 117t; Ross Lovegrove: 477tl (photo: John Ross), 494; Robert Bosch GmbH: 233b, 234-235; Science & Society Picture Library/National Railway Museum: 66; Science & Society Picture Library/ Science Museum: 73l, 108, 118, 120-121, 123, 125, 357br; Scala/The Metropolitan Museum of Art, NYC: 81, 198b; Scala/The Museum of Modern Art, NYC: 271b, 291l, 291r, 368, 376, 377, 418b, 428, 443l, 470, 471; Sciencemag.org: 495b; Shutterstock: 17, 309 (Stuart Monk), 330b; Smart Design: 482-483; Sony.com: 384, 385, 387, 448; Sotheby's London: 212, 311t, 456; Studio Andrea Branzi/Centre Pompidou Archive: 414, 426, 427b; Studio Tord Boontje: 469; Susan Kare: 469; Terry Jones/i-D Magazine: 465t; The Bridgeman Art Library/Badisches Landesmuseum, Karlsruhe: 267t; The Bridgeman Art Library/Calmann & King Ltd: 268; The Bridgeman Art Library/Christie's Images: 74, 153, 155, 162, 184; The Bridgeman Art Library/Hunterian Art Gallery, University of Glasgow: 176; The Bridgeman Art Library/Minneapolis Institute of Arts (Gift of Cowtan & Tout, Inc): 419b; The Bridgeman Art Library/Richard Brumbaugh Trust: 273; The Bridgeman Art Library/© The Fine Art Society: 171t, 171b; The Bridgeman Art Library/The Israel Museum, Jerusalem: 434; The Bridgeman Art Library/The Stapleton Collection: 147, 158; The Bridgeman Art Library: 32, 41b (Museo Leonardiano), 47t (The French Hospital), 62 (Universal History Archive), 64-65 (Ken Welsh), 67 (Science Museum, London), 132b (Dreweatt Neate Fine Art Auctioneers), 177, 191b, 263b (The Sherwin Collection, Leeds); The Library of Congress Prints & Drawings Division, Washington DC: 56, 68bl, 68br, 86, 90, 94, 102t, 102b, 104b, 182, 185b, 186b, 187, 188, 189, 306, 342, 354; The Morse Museum, Florida: 185t; The National Gallery of Art, Washington: 129; The Old Flying Machine Company (photo: John Dibbs): 324; The Opte Project: 472; Thinkstock: 73br; Thonet: 84; Tom Baptist: 390t; Topfoto: 140, 334t (©Ullstein Bild); Vasekino.net: 77; ©Victoria & Albert Museum: 44, 47b, 49b, 50b, 79b, 112, 113t, 114-115, 127t, 127b, 133t, 145, 151, 165, 168, 169, 199l, 276, 293b, 338, 462; View: 286 (©Collection Artedia), 302t (©KLAUS FRAHM/ARTUR); Vitra: 363, 399b; Volkswagen: 379; Volvo: 394; Von Zeschwitz Kunst und Design: 213; Walters Art Museum, Baltimore: 205br; Wikimedia Commons: 14, 28, 29, 30, 36b, 40, 42t, 42b, 43, 48, 50t, 51, 60b, 61, 80, 93t, 93b, 105, 106t, 106b, 117b, 131, 144, 146, 152b, 154, 167, 191t, 195, 196, 198t, 203, 205t, 206, 207, 208t, 208b, 217, 226, 236t, 239, 242, 244, 245l, 247t, 247b, 264, 265, 269, 280, 282, 285t, 288t, 317, 319b, 333b, 353b, 357cr, 375, 381, 383t, 383b, 433, 437b, 450, 457, 460, 464r, 495t; Wired.com: 451l; Wright: 267b, 311b, 314, 335, 336r, 340, 344, 349t, 353t, 356l, 356r, 369b, 378, 395t, 395b, 397, 400t, 400c, 406t, 412t, 441, 446t, 454; Zaha Hadid: 490tr; Zanotta: 302b, 404

This project has been a colossal undertaking and we would like to thank all the people that have helped to make it happen, with extra special thanks to: Isabel Wilkinson for her wonderful project management skills; Ellie Robins for her painstaking copyediting and insightful suggestions; Abbi Wilkinson for her careful proofreading of the UK edition and Phil Freshman for his meticulous efforts on the US edition; Stuart Smith of Smith Design for his beautiful graphic design work; Mabel Chan, Billy Waqar, and Katie Baxendale for all their additional design input; Steve Behan, Ben White, Emma Copestake, and Jenny Meredith for their skillful picture sourcing; Maria Petalidou for overseeing the book's exacting production; and lastly but no means least, Jonathan Goodman for his belief in this project from its very outset.

Additional and heartfelt thanks must also go to our daughters, Emelia and Clementine who have put up with two very distracted parents working all hours to make "the deadline," and our own parents for their unfailing support as ever.

We would also like to thank all the many designers, design studios, museums, manufacturers, picture libraries, and auction houses that have allowed us to use their images in this book.

With special thanks to: Stephen Bayley, Andrea Branzi, Sir Terence Conran,Michele De Lucchi, Ross & Miska Lovegrove Richard Paice, ennifer Pietereit, and Phil Whatmough of the Gordon Russell Museum, Broadway, Marialaura Rossiello of James Irvine S.r.l., Milan, and Richard Wright of Wright, Chicago

Originally published in the United Kingdom by Goodman Fiell

First published in the United States by The Monacelli Press

The image credits on page 512 constitute a continuation of the copyright page. All reasonable efforts have been made in identifying the copyright holders for the images in this book. Any oversights or omissions will be corrected upon reprint, provided notice is given to the authors or publisher.

Library of Congress Cataloging-in-Publication Data

Names: Fiell, Charlotte, 1965- author. | Fiell, Peter, author.
Title: The story of design : from the paleolithic to the present / Charlotte Fiell and Peter Fiell.
Description: First American edition. | New York : The Monacelli Press, 2016.
Identifiers: LCCN 2016017894 | ISBN 9781580934701 (paperback)
Subjects: LCSH: Design--History. | Art and design--History. | Industrial design--History. | BISAC: DESIGN / History & Criticism. | DESIGN / Industrial. | DESIGN / Reference.
Classification: LCC NK1175 .F54 2016 | DDC 745.409--dc23
LC record available at https://lccn.loc.gov/2016017894

ISBN 978-1-58093-470-1

Page 2: Ball chair designed by Eero Arnio for Asko, 1963
Book design by Stuart Smith/Cover Design by Shawn Hazen
Printed in China

www.monacellipress.com